The Social Psychology of Communication

The Social Psychology of Communication

Edited by

Derek Hook
London School of Economics and Political Science, UK

Bradley Franks
London School of Economics and Political Science, UK

Martin W. Bauer
London School of Economics and Political Science, UK

Hm
1206
S65425
2011

UAN

palgrave
macmillan

ßlv

First published 2011 by
PALGRAVE MACMILLAN

Palgrave Macmillan in the UK is an imprint of Macmillan Publishers Limited,
registered in England, company number 785998, of Houndmills, Basingstoke,
Hampshire RG21 6XS.

Palgrave Macmillan in the US is a division of St Martin's Press LLC,
175 Fifth Avenue, New York, NY 10010.

Palgrave Macmillan is the global academic imprint of the above companies and
has companies and representatives throughout the world.

Palgrave® and Macmillan® are registered trademarks in the United States, the
United Kingdom, Europe and other countries.

ISBN 978–0–230–24735–2   hardback
ISBN 978–0–230–24736–9   paperback

This book is printed on paper suitable for recycling and made from fully managed
and sustained forest sources. Logging, pulping and manufacturing processes are
expected to conform to the environmental regulations of the country of origin.

A catalogue record for this book is available from the British Library.

Library of Congress Cataloging-in-Publication Data

The social psychology of communication / edited by Derek Hook, Bradley
    Franks, Martin Bauer.
       p. cm.
    Includes index.
    ISBN 978–0–230–24736–9 (pbk.)
    1. Communication—Social aspects   2. Communication—Psychological
    aspects. I. Hook, Derek.   II. Franks, Bradley.   III. Bauer, Martin W.
    HM1206.S65425 2011
       302.2—dc22   2011001645

10   9   8   7   6   5   4   3   2   1
20 19 18 17 16 15 14 13 12 11

Printed and bound in Great Britain by
CPI Antony Rowe, Chippenham and Eastbourne

For Elliott, Dominic and Ana

Contents

List of Figures, Tables and Boxes

Figures

Tables

Boxes

List of Extracts

List of Contributors

Edmund Arens is Professor of Fundamental Theology at the University of Lucerne, Switzerland. He has published 14 books on critical theory, communication theory, political theology, and communicative theology.

Sharon Attia is a doctoral candidate at the Institute of Social Psychology at LSE, UK. Her research concerns the spread or contagion of cultural representations, and focuses on the spread of concepts of 'religious sacrifice' in Israel, using an evolutionarily based, online research technique.

Martin Bauer is Professor of Social Psychology at LSE, UK, and Editor of *Public Understanding of Science*. His research is concerned with issues aiming at the interface of science, technology and society.

Catherine Campbell is Professor of Social Psychology at LSE, UK, and the Director of the MSc in Health, Community and Development. She has a particular interest in health inequalities in less affluent countries.

Ama de-Graft Aikins is a research fellow in social psychology at Cambridge University (Department of Social and Developmental Psychology) and a visiting fellow of LSE Health, LSE, UK. Her primary research interest focuses on social representations and experiences of chronic physical and mental illness in African communities.

Japinder Dhesi is a doctoral candidate at the Institute of Social Psychology at LSE, UK. Her doctoral thesis brings together social psychological, evolutionary and anthropological ideas as a means of generating new insights into the cognitive foundations of social group stereotyping.

Lauren Feldman is Assistant Professor in the School of Communication at American University, Washington, DC, US. Her research on the effects of political communication has been supported by grants from the Carnegie-Knight Task Force on Journalism and published in several journals, including *Political Communication* and *Communication Research*.

Bradley Franks is a Senior Lecturer in Psychology at LSE, UK. His research interests concern the relations between culture, mind and evolution. He is the author of, inter alia, *Cognition and Culture: Evolutionary Perspectives* (Palgrave Macmillan, 2010).

Vlad Petre Glăveanu is a doctoral candidate at the Institute of Social Psychology at LSE, UK. His main interests are in creativity, the psychology of art and crafts, social representations and qualitative methodologies. His doctoral research, funded by the ESRC, is focused on proposing a cultural psychological understanding of creativity.

Helen Amelia Green is a PhD student at the Institute of Social Psychology at LSE, UK. Her research focuses on embodiment and embodied cognition in the use of metaphorical expressions in everyday language.

Jane Gregory is a Senior Lecturer in Science and Technology Studies at University College, London, UK. Her research focuses on public understandings of science and the history of science.

Joanne Hardman is a Senior Lecturer in Educational Psychology at the University of Cape Town, South Africa. Her research is currently focused on conceptual development in primary school children; the use of socio-cultural and activity theory in understanding development as contextually embedded; and on investigating the mediation of conceptual tools as a foundation phase in development.

Derek Hook is a research fellow in Psychology at the University of the Witwatersrand, South Africa, and a lecturer in Social Psychology at LSE, UK, where he co-convenes the Social and Public Communications MSc Programme.

Caroline Howarth is Lecturer in Social Psychology at LSE, UK. Through her writing, teaching and research she seeks to push social psychology in general and social representations theory in particular in a more critical direction by addressing questions of racism, power, identity, exclusion and resistance.

Michel Meyer is Professor of Philosophy at the Université Libre de Bruxelles, Belgium; Director of the Center for the Study of Argumentation, and Editor of the *International Journal of Philosophy*.

Matthew C. Nisbet is Associate Professor in the School of Communication at American University, Washington, DC, US. As a social scientist, he studies strategic communication in policymaking and public affairs, with a focus on controversies over science, the environment, and public health. His current work on climate change communication is funded by the Robert Wood Johnson Foundation, where he serves as a Health Policy Investigator.

Gordon Sammut is Associate Lecturer in Social Psychology at the University of Malta. He is editorial assistant for *Papers on Social Representations*. His work aims at developing a social psychological understanding of points of view.

Kerry Scott is a health and social development specialist who recently completed the MSc in Health, Community and Development at the LSE, UK. She is currently working on health projects in India.

Cathy Vaughan is a public health practitioner who, since 1996, has worked in South East Asia and the Pacific in the areas of HIV and AIDS, youth health and the evaluation of health care programmes.

Introduction: Towards an 'Interfield' Approach

Derek Hook, Bradley Franks, and Helen Amelia Green

The perspectives on the social psychology of communication gathered in this book provide a distinctive vocabulary for conceptualising how and why communication takes place, ways in which it may succeed or fail, and how instances of communicative exchange relate to potential for change. The following chapters offer a series of interlinked concepts or tools for thinking about communication; and while they each propose a specific point of scrutiny onto varied aspects of the vast phenomenon of communication, they are all informed by three fundamental emphases in their approach.

Social psychological relations and intersubjectivity

We emphasise the importance of the intersubjective factor that makes effective communication possible and that necessarily underlies any prospect of meaningful communicative change. Much communication takes place via a social relationship between communicators; indeed communication may itself indicate and characterise this relationship. Communication may involve the exchange of meanings or information, but it always does so within a social relationship that has its own qualities and constraints that intertwine with those of communication. Our focus in this book differs from the prevailing orthodoxy of the public relations, cultural studies, and mass media-centred approaches to communication by virtue of its attention to the *social psychological* underpinnings of communication. Rather than prioritising new technology and novel mass media formats of communication, we focus on the psychology of communication itself.

Communication in social psychological context

In attempting to understand communication, we forego a primarily strategic approach that focuses on the isolated techniques and procedures of communicative control. Viewing communication as intertwined with the relations between communicators, and as seeking to establish forms of understanding, leads to seeing communication as flexible and variable, and fundamentally related to the context in which the social relations function. The changes that communication can foster in both the sender and receiver of messages are modulated through their prior and unfolding relations which themselves depend on the cultural and practical context. Communication is as much a means of mutuality, joint understanding and dialogicality as it is medium of influence and control. A social psychological perspective emphasises that communication serves ends that are as multifarious as the diverse social relationships with which they are intertwined.

Communication as social psychological process

We avoid fixating on the semantic *contents* of what is communicated, on discursive or representational material alone, and consider the psychological dimensions or processes regarding how this material is *integrated*, made sense of, or, indeed, potentially resisted. This work is committed to the view that to cut off the study of mass communication from its social psychological dimensions will leave us with an instrumental rather than an adequately *social psychological* understanding of communication, one which loses sight both of how this material is processed and integrated, and of the agency that characterises individual social actors and the social groupings and communities of which they are a part.

An interfield theory approach

While these three principles hold fast throughout the chapters of this book, a distinctive quality of this collection is the premise that there is no over-arching 'meta-narrative' or theoretical framework that underlies this undertaking. Readers will not emerge from this book with a single story about communication. Instead, we have proposed a number of routes of exploration that share the same object of study, each foregrounding differing points of scrutiny within the complex and varied phenomenon of communicative interaction. Such a multiplicity of viewpoints allows us to remain aware of the benefits and difficulties of different explanatory routes, and the potential contradictions between them. While there is a coalescence of themes, a set of recurring tensions – a 'family resemblance' of concerns – that unites the differing perspectives in this book, our aim has been to remain open to such divergences, to facilitate an eclectic and original variety of engagements with the social psychology of communication.

With this aim, we have not sought to impose a single explanatory structure between concepts and phenomena, which the area of research cannot support. Rather, we would conceive of this enterprise as part of the beginnings of something like an 'interfield theory' of the social psychology of communication (on interfield theories in the natural and cognitive sciences, see e.g. Bechtel, 1986, 1988; Bechtel and Hamilton, 2007; Darden and Maull, 1977; Grantham, 2004). Darden and Maull (1977, p. 50) suggest that, 'an interfield theory is likely to be generated when background knowledge indicates that relations already exist between the fields, when the fields share an interest in explaining different aspects of the same phenomenon, and when questions arise about that phenomenon within a field which cannot be answered with the techniques and concepts of that field'. In such an interfield theory, each field or approach offers its own contribution, but does not aim to address the substance of the contributions of other approaches. Fields are characterised by a central problem, domain, technique, or method, and can be more or less inclusive in their range. At its most general, a field might be a discipline or subdiscipline; but more specific fields also indicate divisions within disciplines, and other fields still cross traditional disciplinary boundaries.

Within fields, there are likely to be competing explanations and theories. But in general, different fields do not compete with each other, and explanations from different fields do not usually compete, except when the fields overlap at their margins. Questions arise in one field, which cannot be addressed by the tools and techniques of that field. The gaps left by one, ideally, are filled by the contributions of another, and so on. As the contributions develop, the possible contradictions at the margins of the different fields can be debated so as to form the basis for mutual change on a case-by-case basis. Following Darden and Maull, we do not assume a single explanatory relation between fields, nor that one approach will simply 'ground' another. In this light, we do not consider that it is obvious that, when contradictions arise, one approach should concede to another.

The fields covered by the chapters in this book reflect the interfield nature of social psychology itself, concerning evolutionary, developmental, intra-psychological, interactional, intragroup, intergroup, societal and cultural phenomena, among others. It may be too early to list the essential constituents of an interfield theory of the social psychology of communication, as this would require an account of the explanatory coverage and gaps of each field, and their relations. Current practice can be likened to the localist, anthropologically inspired 'trading zone' concept of intertheoretic relations proposed by Galison (1998). Galison notes that two groups can establish rules of exchange or trade of an object, even if they disagree on the significance of that object or the exchange. Such exchanges are viewed as cultures in interaction, which can generate 'contact languages, systems of discourse that can vary from the most function-specific jargons, through semi-specific pidgins, to full-fledged creoles rich enough to support activities as complex as poetry and metalinguistic reflection' (Galison, 1998, p. 783). Galison cites the development of the radar to exemplify the emergence of a specialised theoretical vocabulary during interactions among physicists and engineers.

This vocabulary expressed a shared understanding of radar that crucially depended on different representations, with physicists drawing on field theory and engineers viewing radar as special variants on radio technology.

Such local coordinations of practical and symbolic activities in understanding the social psychology of communication mirror the overlaps and relations between the contributions in our chapters, suggesting a variety of trading zones at play. Candidates for concepts used in the contact languages for the trading zones in the social psychology of communication are compiled in the *Glossary of Keywords and Definitions* provided at the end of the book. We have explicitly not attempted to arrive at a single, overarching definition for concepts that are shared between fields, with differing degrees of significance for those fields. In this way, their status as coordinated, partly shared trading zone concepts – but not strict, agreed definitions – is preserved.

If it is too early to seek a single overarching interfield theory for the social psychology of communication, we can nonetheless take the important step of proposing a set of key trading zone concepts and an initial set of theoretical tensions that arise across the 15 chapters of this book. The contributions to the volume are organised into three parts. Part I introduces some of the key foundational theories in the study of communication from social psychological perspectives. Part II explores a series of special topics of particular contemporary relevance in the social psychology of communication. Part III presents a series of applied areas of practice, in which the theories and special topics discussed in Parts I and II are exemplified and developed in the context of pressing real-world concerns of religion, health, politics, and science.

Contributions to this volume

The first part opens with a discussion of developmental psychology and engages with Lev Vygotsky's approach to cognition, which emphasises an interpsychological to intrapsychological trajectory in learning. Communicative interchange is proposed as a 'basis for thinking' as higher cognitive functions – memory, reasoning, symbolic tool use – begin as communicative relations between people before being effectively internalised. Dialogical interaction is thus posited as a crucial means of cognitive and educational change. Dialogical communicative exchange, as developed in the Brazilian pedagogue Paolo Freire, is the focus of Chapter 2. Extension', a top-down imposition of technical knowledge, is contrasted with the cultivation of equal forms of dialogue, where all participants in communication, regardless of apparent technical knowledge or contextual cultural knowledge, can co-constitute a dialogue that transforms all participants. Freire thus leaves us with a challenge to everyday conceptions of communication and learning, prompting us to think about how the process of communication involves more than the transmission of knowledge by one subject to another, but instead their coparticipation in the act of comprehending a mutual object.

Interplay among communicative actors is considered in a different light when we come to notions of impression management, highlighted in Chapter 3. The distinction between consciously controlled message-sending (typically symbolic or linguistic expressions) and the realm of expressivity (bodily signs we 'give off' that are less controlled and less controllable) sets up a view of communication as a constant tussle among communicators to project favourable, influential images of themselves and to 'see behind' others' projected images. One area that offers great scope for exploring this is non-verbal communication. Bodily signalling mechanisms are vast, ranging from facial expressions to eye contact and gazing, from voice tonality to gestures and demeanour, from the use of space and touch, to non-verbal customs of respect and reverence. The breadth of the possible interpretations of a person's multiple signals – verbal and non-verbal alike – always exceeds what the person had consciously intended to say.

Issues of intention, context, and how meanings beyond those conveyed via conventional words are interpreted are addressed by pragmatic theories, the focus of Chapter 5. Many pragmatic theories take it that interpretation is a process guided by the speaker offering evidence of their communicative intentions, which the hearer then infers, based on 'theory of mind' – the awareness of and capacity to infer others' states of mind. However, this process might be complicated by feelings, emotions, or egocentrism. Evidence suggests that current theories of pragmatics may not fully reflect the role of affect and emotion in interaction, and may overstate the extent to which people try to entertain others' mental states and intentions in communication, and overstate their success in doing so even when they try. These arguments suggest some significant challenges to pragmatic theories in light of broader understandings of social relations and interaction.

Communication, social relations, and interaction as they serve consensus-building processes and the negotiation of common understanding are the focus of Chapters 4 and 6. Social influence – the processes by which attitudes and beliefs of an individual or group can be affected or changed – is inherent to all communicative interaction, and is particularly important in the context of conflict between divergent perspectives on social issues. Chapter 4 describes the processes and modalities by which interlocutors seek to influence one another and to settle the emergent conflict by convincing the other to adopt one's own perspective. Ultimately, the manifestation of social influence occurs in the negotiation of common understandings in the public sphere; here innovations are proposed and jostle for ascendancy in their striving towards legitimation and normalisation.

Notions of dialogical communication (Chapter 2) and the performative dimension of speech-acts (Chapter 5) are developed further in Chapter 6's discussion of Habermas's influential theory of communicative action, which distinguishes communicative action – whereby joint understandings are attained and through which consensus can be achieved – from the realm of strategic gain. This theory opposes the instrumental aims of any form of strategic action that seeks to influence others to act in accordance with the wishes of an individual or group, and is introduced via an account of the important philosophical concepts of the lifeworld, language games, the ideal speech situation, and the public sphere. Of considerable importance in Habermas's theory is the specification of validity conditions – truthfulness, rightness and sincerity – through which we may assess speech acts, a necessary process if the power of rational and non-strategic arguments is to prevail within the public sphere.

The second part of the book, *Special topics in communication*, begins with a focus on identity and representation. Notwithstanding the progressive properties of communication as a means of dialogue, cementing social bonds, and advancing mutual forms of understanding, we should not lose sight of the fact that communication can also function as a means of violence. In Chapter 7, the discussion of identity and resistance in communication draws attention to the symbolic violence of communicative exchanges that marginalise and stigmatise others – as in the case of cultural stereotypes and racism. Utilising concepts from both social representations theory and Stuart Hall's influential encoding-decoding model, communication is considered in terms of 'the ideological battle of representations'. Representations here are viewed both as potentially violent, as instruments of racism, and as a means of resistance, a valuable resource for threatened identities and communities alike. So, although communication is always ideological, potentially damaging, it is also collaborative, agentic and potentially transformative.

Rumour and gossip, key phenomena in informal communication and cultural transmission, are presented in Chapter 8. Gossip is understood as a specific genre of informal communication, governed by its own implicit conventions on bullshit – the lack of direct concern with the truth of the utterances – affective or moral judgement of a third party, and the resultant cementing of social identity. Gossip may form one link in a chain of rumour, which involves a group communicating in chains of transmission in order to make sense of some situation, event or issue, so as to help cope with anxieties. Rumours have been investigated both 'in the wild' (with a focus on their anxiety-reduction and other affective qualities), and in the laboratory (using, for example, serial reproduction techniques, where change or retention of important contents of beliefs is studied) to understand the factors of content, affect, and culture that make some rumours more prone to be spread than others.

Everyday communicative exchange can lead to stalemates and conflict in which the demands of recognition outweigh the prospect of hearing or saying anything new. Chapter 9 focuses on an ever-present tendency within intersubjective communication – a defensive egocentrism that compromises the possibility for reaching truth or attaining subjective change. The chapter draws on psychoanalysis as a means of conceptualising two interlinked registers of communication. The first is the imaginary register; the domain of one-to-one intersubjectivity and behaviour that serves the ego and functions to consolidate the images subjects use to substantiate themselves. The second, symbolic register links the subject to a *trans-subjective* order of truth, provides a set of socio-symbolic coordinates, and ties the subject into a variety of roles and social contracts. This distinction is useful in pointing to the difference between 'empty' speech – idle chatter predominantly concerned with shoring up an ego, affirming images a subject has of themselves – and 'full' speech – the truth-potential of a form of speech that can challenge given forms of knowledge, upset subjective illusions, and induce change within the subject.

Rhetoric, for some, is an art of deception used to manipulate the public. For others it represents a form of public reasoning, a heuristic for finding the best means of persuasion in a given situation; for others still, it is simply the art of speaking well, a discipline of eloquence, a literary concern of cultivating expression. Chapter 10 provides a novel perspective on rhetoric, the negotiation of difference between individuals on a given question. Of course the centuries-old debate rages on as to whether rhetoric represents a valid means of persuasion or merely a strategic means of forwarding unsubstantiated claims in the garb of truth. Nonetheless, the vocabulary of rhetoric provides us with a valuable set of tools to analyse and critique the persuasive means of communication, particularly in terms of the 'three musketeers' of logos (the soundness of the argument presented), ethos (the credibility of the speaker) and pathos (the emotive dimension of the argument).

Chapter 11 discusses evolutionary aspects of communication and how they contribute to understanding the role of communication in cultural transmission. An evolutionary approach suggests that much every day communication is strategic, in that it is geared towards persuading others to act in specific ways and towards achieving adaptive goals, even when it does not appear so to the parties to that communication. A close link between affect, emotion, and mind is advocated by views of evolved, 'embodied' cognition. On this view, cognition is simultaneously 'extended' beyond the skin into the environment, and 'grounded' by intrinsic connections to action, emotion, and bodily experience. The argument is that much interaction and communication involves coordinated intentions and beliefs, rather than shared intentions and beliefs. The appearance that we share intentions and beliefs is partly a function of culture and, in particular, what is referred to as an External Theory of Mind.

The chapters in Part III seek to apply the communication theories and topics presented in Parts I and II, in effect 'putting them to work' in the real world context of pressing societal, political and community challenges. Extending the insights of the discussion of communicative action in Chapter 6 into the realm of religion, Chapter 12 reminds us that the success of communication is not always about forms of cognitive gain or consensus established through deliberation. The importance of religious communication is thus not to be measured in terms of new learning or gains by way of rational argument; but in its ability to disclose and name a shared reality, thus consolidating a community. Such communities exist outside of the hierarchically arranged system of fixed positions apparent in a given social structure; they provide a communion of equals – an egalitarian community. Communicative-religious speech and action have creative, innovative, and anamnestic potential to substantiate and potentially extend the community via: collective forms of memory; capacity to bring about change; or ongoing joint work of interpreting, understanding, and engaging everyday reality.

Chapter 13 on media health campaigns confronts a longstanding dilemma in the social psychology of communication, the fact that information is a necessary but insufficient condition for behaviour change. For instance, awareness of the detrimental health effects of smoking in no way guarantees that a person will stop smoking or never start. This chapter sees beyond the simple dissemination of information to explore and explain the importance of community strengthening and social participation approaches to health. Communication is seen not merely as a means of extending information, but as a means of establishing a wider set of ties and associations (family, neighbourhood. and community networks) that encourage participation of such individuals and that empower them to resist unhealthy influences. 'Transformative social spaces' are those domains in which people are able to engage in just such dialogue, critical reflection, and social capital construction. Communication in these forms of dialogue and networking enable people to make actionable insights into the links between social inequalities and ill-health, develop an increased sense of agency, and build strong networks to facilitate action at the individual, community, and even macro-social levels.

Political communication can be defined as the exchange of information, messages, and symbols between institutions, elected officials, social groups, the media, and citizens with implications for the balance of power in society. As discussed in Chapter 14, the social psychology of political communication is informed by contributions from a variety of intellectual traditions. An important sociological tradition concerns how interpersonal conversations and community contexts shape individual news choices, opinions, political decisions, and participation. A more philosophical tradition questions how such processes of influence might be evaluated in the context of an idealised vision of public deliberation and participation, while nonetheless drawing attention to important power imbalances. A third influential tradition focuses on how political language and symbols lead to the selective definition and interpretation of policy issues and social problems. Yet another major strand of research derives from the cognitive revolution in social psychology, with general theories of information processing and persuasion applied to the study of political communication. This chapter reviews and integrates strands from each of these scholarly traditions to present a tentative set of guidelines for communicating complex problems and issues; structuring media presentations; strategically designing messages; and effectively reaching and empowering citizens.

The book's closing chapter is an overview of science communication. For many years the prevailing conceptualisation of science communication was a vertical and linear schema that viewed scientists as 'gods on high' sending information to the public either directly or via mediators such as journalists. Although this model remains deeply entrenched in scientific culture, the last decade has seen the emergence of more lateral and dialogical forms. Scientists have begun to enter into discussion with the public, especially on policy issues of economic significance, often using corporate-style communications strategies. Science communication has thus diversified: it is not only about the transfer of the facts of science from scientist to laypeople; it is also about direct approaches to the social relations of science via the affective content of messages about the value, promises, and uses of science. Science communication serves not only the traditional interests of science, but now crosses once clear boundaries to incorporate the interests of governments, businesses and media institutions. Importantly, it also now serves the interest of a public who, as subjects, customers, and citizens of a scientific society, continue to defy, exploit, and enjoy the scientists' epistemological and ideological hegemony over the natural world.

Key tensions in the social psychology of communication

In viewing the possibility of an interfield account of communication, the three key social psychological concerns flagged earlier – *the intersubjectivity of social psychological relations, communication in a social psychological context, and communication as a social psychological process* – underpin a range of *key tensions* in how aspects of communication are conceptualised. These tensions (see Figure I.1) are reflected in the chapters, in different fields. Thus, they reveal the possibility of different conceptual trading zones between those fields, regarding the aspect of communication in which the tension arises.

Communication is hypothesised to create change – incidentally or necessarily in the communicated content, in the speaker, the hearer, in their actions, and in the wider cultural context. The key tensions that emerge in this work revolve around this question of change. Some, but not all, of these tensions are between an ideal type or normative model on the one hand, and actual instances of practice on the other. The extent to which the contributions to this book prioritise, assume, or develop a position that reflects either side a particular tension differentiates the ways in which these tensions can be interpreted and exploited in developing trading zones.

Unavoidability-improbability

Perhaps the nearest to an overarching tension that is shared by all contributions, is a tension of the *perfectibility of communication*. All contributions directly or indirectly subscribe to the view that communication is, in some sense, unavoidable as a practical and social necessity. In a sense, it is impossible for social beings *not* to communicate, whether intentionally or not. But this unavoidability of communication is opposed by the apparent improbability of successful communication; 'perfect' communication – the uncorrupted, felicitous transmission of information from sender to receiver – is at best an ideal type that regulates aspects of interaction, but which in every instance of application is always marked to some degree by failure, error, and compromise.

In exploring the perfectability of communication in these terms, we may consider the ambitious notion of communicative action discussed in Chapters 6 and 12, Vygotsky's conceptualisation of notions of mediation and the zone of proximal development (Chapter 1), and Freire's hopes for truly dialogical interaction (Chapter 2). The participatory goals of dialogue, critical reflection, and the construction of social capital discussed in Chapter 13 clearly pivot on ideals of what improved models of communicability can achieve. Here the progressive refinement of communicative efficacy and hopes for social change go hand in hand. Discussions of this perfectibility tension lead directly into the question of how exactly to frame and assess *successful* communication.

Controlled-unintended

A related tension – indeed, perhaps a specific instantiation of the first tension – concerns *controllability*. This starts with an ideal of deliberate, intentional communicative design or control, where not only is communication successful but it is also controlled and intentionally circumscribed in its content and effects. This is in direct contrast with the practical sense that instances of communication are fraught with unintended and uncontrollable meanings. The latter involves both aspects of communication that seem intrinsic to linguistic channels of communication (such as ambiguity, vagueness, mis-hearing, entropy, noise), as well as aspects that relate more generally to social interaction and relations (such as attempts at social and political influence, Chapters 4 and 14; deception, Chapter 11; or the generation of rumour and gossip, Chapter 8).

The potential controllability of communication can be explored in Goffman's impression management (Chapter 3), pragmatic theories' emphasis on the perlocutionary dimension of speech-acts (Chapter 5), and the psychoanalytic interest in unintended meanings (Chapter 9). These perspectives

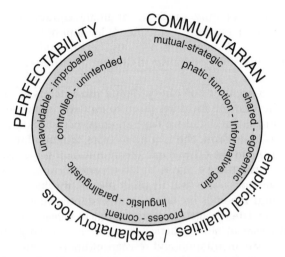

Figure I.1 Key tensions in the social psychology of communication

share the view that the breadth of possible interpretations for a given utterance necessarily exceeds the more delimited range of its underlying intention. Communication is necessarily ambiguous and error-prone; and for some, indeed, the degree to which communication cannot be entirely controlled and the fact that one cannot but say more than one means, are what make communication work to any degree at all. Discussions of this controllability tension lead into the question of how to frame and explain intended communication and how to differentiate it from the unintended.

Mutual-strategic

The *communitarian* tension is also often expressed as another ideal-versus-actual polarisation. This starts from the ideal of a true dialogue between communicators in which the aim and the outcome are concerned with advancing joint understanding, mutual transformation, and consensus through rational argumentation. On such a view, communication is a vehicle for enabling community-building and delivering democratic forms of agreement. Its antipode is communication that necessarily involves strategy or instrumental action, in which one party seeks to gain some advantage over the other via communication, perhaps by deception or persuasion. Communication here is taken to be a vehicle for asserting and maintaining power relations between communicators. One variation on the mutual-strategic tension is thus the distinction between shared, participatory, or 'bottom-up' forms of communication and more hierarchical 'top-down' or vertical structures. This will be an oft-revisited theme in what follows, a crucial tension not only in understanding community development (Chapter 2) and social influence (Chapter 4) but also in grappling with the practical challenges underwriting religious, health, political, and science communication (e.g. civic journalism in Chapter 13, citizen empowerment in Chapter 14).

The mutual-strategic tension can be viewed also in terms of an opposition between conflict and the measures taken to establish workable parameters of sociality. On the one hand we have an emphasis on modes of partnership, dialogical interaction, the forging of types of mutuality (Chapters 2, 6, 9, 12, and 13). On the other hand, communication is viewed as a mode of contestation and struggle that is far less concerned with establishing collaborative forms than it is a 'war by other means', a vehicle for advancing multiple instrumental ends including those of aggressive gain (Chapters 3, 4, 7, 8, 10, 11, and 14). If aggressive strategic gain appears to be an irreducible aspect of communicative practice, we must also recognise the utility of certain forms of argumentation and resistance that communication makes possible. *Argumentative* rationality for a theorist like Habermas (Chapters 6 and 11) is not simply about a surrendering to social consensus; rather it entails an awareness that debate and dialogical contestation are necessary in the attainment of a deliberated consensus. Thus, despite the apparently clear opposition of the mutual-strategic tension, an important question arises: to what extent is either extreme of this tension achievable without involving at least some aspect of the other?

Shared-egocentric

A fourth, *egocentrism* tension relates to the communitarian tension, though it is concerned less with posing an ideal-versus-actual contrast and more with an empirical question of the range of qualities of communication. On the one hand, an egocentric approach suggests that communication is governed by principles and processes that make the sharing of meaning between communicators rare, difficult, or even impossible; this might be the case either as a result of the basic 'design' of the faculties of communicators (see Chapter 11 on evolutionary theory), or of intent on the part of the communicators (Chapter 5 on pragmatics). These principles would suggest that the idea of sharing information about one's mental states, for example, is one that informs or regulates our behaviour but does not determine it. By contrast, a non-egocentric approach would take communication as governed by principles and processes that are derived from the intention to share one's mental states, and success in doing so. Such an approach – epitomised in Habermas's theory of communicative action (Chapter 6) – would suggest that the idea of sharing meanings drives the process of communication.

If it is the case then that much communication is continually conditioned by the tendency (on the part of speaker and listener alike) to affirm images they have of themselves, to protect and insulate given 'presentations of self' (Chapter 3) – and indeed, to mobilise defences against hearing anything too disruptive (Chapter 9) – then such defences would seem necessarily to involve an epistemological dimension. On this basis, we could consider the shared-egocentric tension in terms of the potential for communication to enable learning something new. This opposition – a theme evoked in the discussion of developmental cognitive processes in Chapter 1 – takes us to a crucial distinction in assessing communicative change, namely the distinction between assimilation and accommodation. These longstanding concepts – typically used to distinguish between the cognitive operations of fitting of new experiences into existing schemas (assimilation) and the construction of altogether new structures of understanding (accommodation) – might be recast as a means of separating instances of communication that result in no effective change from those that do. In this respect, assimilation would refer to a mode of reception in which new information is simply coopted into existing structures and strategies of understanding. No significant advance is made is made in this way; the receiver of the communication is not changed by what has been assumed. In accommodation, by contrast, the subject *is* necessarily changed: the failure to adequately grasp what they receive within their existing structures of comprehension means that the development of new cognitive schemas is necessary if adequate understanding is to occur at all (Chapter 13 on health communication, and Chapter 11 on social influence).

Phatic-informative

A fifth tension of *gain* thus revolves around the question of what, if anything, is gained via a communicative exchange. This is another tension concerning the degree to which all or most of everyday communication possesses a given range of qualities. One extreme considers that for an exchange to qualify as communicative it must involve some form of change or gain – perhaps in the form of acquiring new information or knowledge, or increased understanding of a topic. A presupposition here is that the *content* exchanged is essential to that exchange. At the opposite extreme, communication may be broadly seen as 'phatic', involving no ostensible gain in information itself, beyond the apparent indication that a social bond is being maintained, that channels of communication are being kept open, or that community is being consolidated. Here, any specific content exchanged is largely redundant.

Important then as the above-mentioned assimilation/accommodation distinction might be in assessing communicative change, it would be an error to view successful communications as necessarily entailing cognitive gain. As crucial as learning and behavioural change are as indications of the impact of public communications strategies, it is nonetheless true that some of the most important forms of communication lead to no new information being absorbed, nothing new being learned. Aside then from any question of strategic or information gain, one might opt to analyse communicative exchanges simply on the basis that they support and strengthen relationships, communal ties, reiterating – even in seemingly inessential moments of exchange – that further communicative support is possible. The relationship-substantiating role of communication can in some instances outweigh the aim of establishing truth or accuracy, as is evidenced in the functioning of rumour and gossip (Chapter 8). The phatic dimension of communication concerns the strengthening of roles, identities (Chapter 7), community belonging and understanding (Chapters 2, 6, 12) and a reinstantiation of a society (Chapter 9). Even empty gestures (making an offer that one clearly expects will be denied) like meaningless everyday greetings play their part in installing a rudimentary social bond, a 'kinship of communication' that ties both participants into their shared socio-symbolic world. Communication is thus involved in the constant renewal – the reinstantiation – of the social contract itself.

Process-content

A *process-content* tension concerns the explanatory focus of theoretical accounts in their attempt to pinpoint the key functional dimension of communicative behaviour. Some models are primarily concerned with explicating the nature and patterns of meaning of the contents of communicated material. These views take it that the process of communication in itself has little to add to the understanding of what is communicated. A case in point would be the code models discussed in Chapters 3 and 7, a focus on representations above and beyond what is *done with* representations, and, historically, the tradition of semiotics that places considerable emphasis on a culturally located reading of the various significations and associations (denotation and connotations) of texts and images.

By contrast, other models place greater emphasis on the processes of communication, in the terms both of the activities and components that underpin the exchange of meanings, and, second, via the performative dimension of communicative acts. In terms of activity and components of the communicative process, attention has been focused on the sequence of communicative mechanisms, and has generated an analytical language that compartmentalises the trajectory of message-sending (information source, transmitter, signal, channel, receiver) and its potential impediments (probability of error, noise, information destination, channel capacity) (Weaver and Shannon, 1963). In a different vein, an awareness of communicative processes can also prioritise communication as an act, a 'form of doing', as action comparable with other actions. In this line of thinking – discussed in Chapters 5 and 6 – communication is best understood not simply in terms of its representational or descriptive capacities, but rather by means of how it effects changes in the world (e.g. the declarative act of a police officer reading someone their rights changes the legal status of the person arrested). Both such prioritisations of process take it that the content of an exchange is highly dependent on, and intertwined with, these kinds of process.

Linguistic-paralinguistic

A final, *format* tension, concerns the formats or channels that command attention in theoretical treatment. Some contributions focus solely on uniquely human verbal or linguistic channels – this is especially the case in those approaches that are much indebted to language, discourse or representation-based models of communication (e.g. Chapters 5, 6, 7, and 9) – and do so at the cost of other channels of communication (non-verbal, paralinguistic, and so on). These views contrast with those that locate linguistic communication in the context of a broader array of aspects of human and non-human communication, such as evolutionary adaptations (Chapter 11), deception, and bodily expressions and signals (Chapter 3). Once again there are theories that link both sides of this tension: Vygotsky's attempt to connect elementary and higher cognitive functions via distinct forms of mediation is one way of connecting paralinguistic and linguistic operations. Likewise important here is the affective dimension of communications – a factor pinpointed by models of rhetoric, by evolutionary theory and the analysis of science communication (Chapters 10, 11, and 15) – which while interestingly combined with linguistic performance, are not always reducible to it.

Pathways through the text

Our aim is to provide a series of conceptual and practical tools for understanding the social psychology of communication. In order to achieve this understanding, readers can take various pathways through the text. The most straightforward pathway through the text is a *Theory-to-Applications* approach, reading from the foundational theories of Part I, through the special topics in Part II, and culminating in the applications of Part III. However, there are also other ways of exploring the text that readers may prefer.

Applications-to-theory

This pathway through the text begins by focusing on a specific area of application (i.e. religious, health, political, or science communication). Each application chapter deploys a range of theoretical ideas, and these ideas can be further articulated and developed by tracing their introduction and description in different ways in Parts I and II. Here is one example of such a pathway: Chapter 12 on religious communicative action shares Chapter 7's topical focus on identities. Indeed, it also involves the importance of consolidating communal forms of identity through communication, a foundational

theory presented in Chapter 5's introduction to the theory of communicative action, and its theoretical precursor, Chapter 2's discussion of community development and the ideal of dialogical communication. Likewise,
Chapter 14 on political communication can be linked to the foundation
theory of social influence (Chapter 4), via an engagement with the special
topic chapters on gossip and rumour (Chapter 8) and notions of argument
and rhetoric (Chapter 10), on the basis that all share the topic of influence.

Key concepts and trading zones

This pathway begins by focusing on a set of keywords introduced at the
beginning of each chapter (see Table I.1 for a listing of all the keywords
listed by chapter), and explores a series of interconnected themes by plot-
ting the differing articulations of these keywords in other sections of the
book. This may prove to be an interesting way of highlighting resonances
between chapters whose theoretical and empirical concerns may seem otherwise mutually exclusive. For example, the first and last chapters of the
book both perhaps unexpectedly prioritise the question of how scientific
concepts might be communicated. Similarly, Chapters 5, 9, and 11, on pragmatics, psychoanalysis, and evolutionary theory respectively – intellectual
traditions not typically brought together – all engage with the issue of
egocentrism in communication, a topic also broached by Chapter 1, albeit
in differing ways. Two further examples: the topics of affect (see Chapters 8,
11, and 15) and of cultural transmission (Chapters 3, 8, and 11) are present
in chapters with otherwise differing conceptual and practical concerns.

This means of exploring connections can be further developed by making
use of the book's extensive glossary. Not only do nodal concepts clearly
represent points of overlap between otherwise distinct traditions; it is also
the case that the definitions offered here break ideas down into component parts, which may likewise be compared, contrasted, plotted across the
various chapters of the book. Such key-concepts and ideas can also be cross-
referenced, compared in different applied contexts, via the book's index.
Reading through the glossary – even treating it as a chapter in itself – offers
a means of highlighting potential synergies and innovative conjunctions
between theories, and between theoretical and applied concerns. We have
then a series of strategies by means of which the trading zones between
the different fields exemplified by the chapters can be brought into clearer
relief.

Key tensions

This pathway begins by focusing on one of the key tensions outlined above,
and traces the way in which it is developed, debated, and revisited in different fields as outlined in the different chapters. Table I.2 provides an indication of which chapters evoke specific tensions, and can therefore be used as
a guide through the text oriented around this theme.

Table I.1 Keywords for each chapter

Chapter 1: The developmental impact of communicative interaction	Egocentrism; elementary/higher cognitive functions; mediation; metacognition; optimal learning; scientific (schooled) concepts; zone of proximal development
Chapter 2: Dialogue, critical consciousness, and praxis	Conscientisation; dialogue; doxa; education; extension; praxis; problematisation; problem-solving
Chapter 3: Non-verbal communication and culture	Culture; decoding; display rules; encoding, impression management; nonverbal behaviour; nonverbal communication; self-presentation
Chapter 4: Social influence: Modes and modalities	Accommodation; assimilation; attitude; belief; compliance; conformity; conversion; deviance; imitation; informational influence; leadership; majority; minority; normalisation; normative influence; norms; obedience; persuasion; social influence; public sphere; soft power
Chapter 5: Pragmatic theory and social relations	Affect-laden interpretation; code model; collective intention; conversational implicature theory; egocentric communication; illocution; inferential model; locution; perlocution; pragmatics; relevance theory; schema; speech act theory; theory of mind
Chapter 6: Communicative action and the dialogical imagination	Communicative action; intersubjectivity; language games; lifeworld; perspective-taking; public sphere; speech acts; strategic action; validity claims
Chapter 7: Identity and resistance in communication	Cultural difference; culture; encoding-decoding; identity; ideology; resistance; social representation
Chapter 8: Rumours and gossip as genres of communication	Bullshit; cultural epidemiology; gossip; genre; minimal counter-intuitiveness; rumour; social reproduction method
Chapter 9: Empty and full speech	Empty speech; founding speech; full speech; the Imaginary; *méconnaissance*; phatic communication; the Other; speech-acts; the Symbolic
Chapter 10: Argument and rhetoric	Argument; audience; celebratory speech; composition; deliberative argumentation; delivery (eloquence); ethos; invention; juridical argumentation; logos; metaphor; metonymy; orator; pathos; question; rhetorical situation; style; the 'three musketeers of rhetoric'; tropes
Chapter 11: Evolution and communication	Adaptation; cues, signals and signs; culture; deception; ego-centrism; theory of mind; cultural niche construction
Chapter 12: Religion as communication	Communicative action; community; memory; narrative; religious-communicative practice; ritual; strategic action; transcendent reality

(continued)

Table I.1 Continued

Chapter 13: Media health campaigns: From information to social change	Civic journalism; collective action; edutainment; dialogical critical thinking; health communication; health communication strategies; journalism of conversation; journalism of information; KAB (Knowledge + Attitudes = Behaviour) approach; mediated health campaigns; networked journalism; social capital; transformative social spaces; social identity; networked journalism
Chapter 14: The social psychology of political communication	Agenda-setting; deliberation; framing; hostile media effect; knowledge gap effect; miserly public; polarisation; political trust; priming; public opinion; social trust
Chapter 15: Science communication	Boundary work; deficit model; dominant model; popular science; public engagement; public understanding of science

Table I.2 Key tensions and dimensions of communication

Key tension	Key dimension	Relevant chapters
Unavoidability-improbability	Perfectibility	Chapters 1, 2, 3, 6, 12, 13
Controlled-unintended	Controllability	Chapters 3, 4, 5, 8, 9, 10, 11, 14
Mutual-strategic	Communitarian	Chapters 2, 3, 4, 6, 7, 8, 10, 12–15
Shared-egocentric	Egocentrism	Chapters 1, 2, 3, 5, 6, 9, 11, 13
Phatic-informative	Gain	Chapters 2, 6, 7, 8, 9, 12, 13, 14
Process-content	Functionality	Chapters 1, 3, 5, 6, 7, 10
Linguistic-paralinguistic	Format	Chapters 1, 3, 5, 6, 7, 9, 10, 11, 15

Communicative change

One of the cornerstone arguments underlying our approach in this book concerns the need to grasp the psychological dimension of communication, to appreciate how communications are processed, integrated, responded to by agentic subjects and communities. It is thus fitting that we end this Introduction by designating a pathway that explores modalities of communicative change. Our aim is not to offer an exhaustive catalogue of all aspects of communicative change but rather to present a cross-section of perspectives, and to thus prompt further exploration in this regard. Clearly the way such change is understood and explained varies greatly according to the field under consideration. Table I.3 provides an indication of which chapters address the various modalities of communicative change, and can therefore be used as a guide through the text oriented around this theme.

In conclusion, we have stressed the intersubjectivity of communication, the nature of communicative processes in varying social psychological

Table I.3 Modalities of communicative change

	Goal of change	Attained by means of	Impediments
Chapter 1: The developmental impact of communicative interaction	Learning; acquisition of new symbolic tools, skills or 'higher cognitive functions'; accommodation of cognitive structures	Mediation; internalisation of symbolic skills; pedagogical input occurring within the zone of proximal development; scaffolding	Forms of instruction occurring outside of the zone of proximal development; pedagogies that pay no attention to effective forms of mediation
Chapter 2: Dialogue, critical consciousness, and praxis	Conscientisation (i.e. critical consciousness); praxis	Problematisation; equal, reciprocal forms of dialogue; horizontal relationships that entail empathy and mutual recognition	Extension; imposed, top-down communiqués; vertical relations of power; 'anti-dialogue'; doxa
Chapter 3: Non-verbal communication and culture	Cross-cultural understanding; improved socio-cultural mediation	Awareness of the communicative importance of various non-verbal bodily signals and expressions (many of which are non-conscious and/or culturally specific)	Different cultural codes; ambiguity of emotional expressions and bodily signals; deceptive use of such signals
Chapter 4: Social influence: Modes and modalities	Innovation; accommodation and legitimisation of a minority perspective	Modalities of social influence (leadership, imitation, normalisation, conformity pressure, obedience and compliance to authority, persuasion, viral replication of beliefs, conversion)	Conformity; social influence that preserves consensus and stability by eliminating dissent
Chapter 5: Pragmatic theory and social relations	Sharing with others one's mental states and intentions for action so as to coordinate action	Pragmatic principles relating to the linguistic expression and interpretation of mental states (e.g., relevance or Gricean inferential principles, relations between component acts of a speech act)	Egocentric and affective factors that limit the extent to which one intends to and succeeds in communicating mental states
Chapter 6: Communicative action and the dialogical imagination	Reaching mutual understanding; enabling joint action; establishing and renewing social representations and background assumptions; building and challenging consensus	Dialogue, perspective-taking, argumentation through the exchange of validity claims about self (sincerity/authenticity), self–other relations (normative rightness), world (truth of propositions)	Exclusion and/or denial of the Other; individualism; breakdown of social cohesion and solidarity

(Continued)

Table 1.3 Continued

Chapter 7: Identity and resistance in communication	Agentic development of identities and representations; social change	Social representation, decoding dominant discourses and imaginative/communicative exchange	Hegemonic representations, ideologies, and institutionalised cultures of prejudice and exclusion
Chapter 8: Rumours and gossip as genres of communication	Anxiety management (rumour); enhancing social identity and bonding (gossip)	Shared inferential interpretation based on cultural conservation and constructiveness (rumour); inferential interpretation/bullshit and emotional rapport using normative judgements of others or issues (gossip)	'Uncontrolled' contagion of anxiety-evoking ideas based on specific kinds of content, context and affect (rumour); failure to take up the implicit invitation to gossip, lack of recognition of other's right to judge the target (gossip)
Chapter 9: Empty and full speech	Subjective change, attaining subjective truth	Symbolic means, particularly full speech, i.e. speech that maintains an element of the Other in its ability to surprise the subject, to say more than they mean, in its declarative and founding (or naming) functions capable of bringing about change	Empty-speech, ego-centred talk that operates to affirm the ego, to protect and insulate it against what it finds unpalatable, and to mobilise defences against hearing anything too disruptive
Chapter 10: Rhetoric and Argumentation	Negotiation of difference between individuals on a given issue	Persuasive speech typically aided by factors of logos, pathos, ethos, enabled via deliberative, celebratory, and juridical engagements and assisted by formal means of invention, style, composition, delivery, and memory.	Breakdowns between projected and effective ethos, between projected and effective pathos, and effective and projected logos
Chapter 11: Evolution and communication	Overcoming miscommunication between interlocutors	External theory of mind acting as an offline resource for cognition which can ameliorate egocentricism in communication	Egocentricism is a cognitive default and as such provides an economical use of cognitive resources

Chapter 12: Religion as communication Chapter 13: Media health campaigns: From information to social change	Understanding and agreement; community and solidarity Increases in: health-enhancing behaviour, ability to access services and support, health-enabling social capital, collective action to tackle obstacles to health, health-related social policy (at the local, national, and/or global levels of influence)	Communicative action; religious-communicative practice The promotion of 'transformative social spaces' which provide opportunities for subjective and objective empowerment through dialogue, critical thinking, and networking – through communication strategies that facilitate community participation, partnerships, and bonding/bridging social capital	Strategic action; Indoctrination Power inequalities; lack of political will to support the empowerment of health vulnerable communities
Chapter 14: The social psychology of political communication	Perceptions of importance or causes and solutions to problems; promote knowledge and participation; promote dialogue and avoid polarisation, build trust in others, government, and the media.	Changing journalistic and news media norms; educating and training campaign professionals and advocates in the applications of theory and research; applying research to the design of media; offering special curricula and skills training for students and citizens	Cognitive biases of the public and disparities in SES status; economic pressures on the media; journalists' dependence on élite sources; advantages to élites and resource-rich interest groups in influencing news coverage and in sponsoring expensive campaign initiatives
Chapter 15: Science communication	Develop a social mandate for science as a profession; to validate scientific authority; to license scientific processes and products; to frame an innovation-ready society.	Communication of the facts and ideologies of science; negotiation of the values, policies and uses of science.	Co-constructions of the clever scientist and ignorant or stupid laypeople; tensions between hierarchies and networks; differing mass media capacities for conveying cognitive and affective content; pursuit of competing interests (e.g. between politics, business, and civil society)

contexts, and the prospective goal of enabling forms of mutuality and dialogue. Additionally, we have emphasised the important and perhaps necessarily diverse topic of the modalities of communicative change. By moving across a range of theoretical perspectives, applied areas, and contexts, we have attempted to avoid the closure of a single theoretical frame.

As we stated at the outset, it is the goal of the authors to enrich and inform an exploration of the social psychology of communication, and not to compose what would necessarily be a restrictive and limited 'unified' account of communication. We would have failed if the subject of communication was too easily assimilated into one homogeneous entity or too readily reconciled into a recognisable set of assumptions. The lack of *prima facie* convergence, of easy recognisability, is part of our objective: this book will have succeeded if the set of perspectives advanced here inspires the reader to think differently about the nature, the goals, and mechanisms of communication, if it brings about even a partial defamiliarisation of the everyday phenomenon of human communicative interaction. We hope to have provided the rudiments of an interfield approach and to have supplied a heterogeneous set of conceptual and practical tools, which readers can combine and interweave in a variety of different ways as a means of understanding the hybrid and rapidly changing nature of communication in today's world.

Part I

Introducing the Social Psychology of Communication

1
The Developmental Impact of Communicative Interaction

Joanne Hardman

Keywords: Egocentric/egocentrism; elementary/higher cognitive functions; mediation; metacognition; optimal learning; scientific (schooled) concepts; zone of proximal development.

Introduction

> The distinctive characteristic of human learning is that it is a process of meaning making – a semiotic process: and the prototypical form of human semiotic is language. Hence the ontogenesis of language is at the same time the ontogenesis of learning.

> (Halliday, 1993, p. 93)

This bold claim made by the sociolinguist Michael Halliday points to the developmental importance of language. This quotation resonated with a piece of research I was doing in an extremely disadvantaged kindergarten in the Western Cape region of South Africa. The research focused on Sipho and Nandi's verbal interaction as they were trying to build a train out of a variety of blocks. Of particular interest was how these two three-year-old children used language (in this case their mother tongue is isiXhosa, the first language of the majority of people in the Western Cape, South Africa) to solve a problem that they encountered building this train. This use of language as a problem-solving tool soon became of major interest in the research because it resonated so well with the psychological theory of learning postulated by the Soviet psychologist Lev Vygotsky (1978). Of particular interest in this context is trying to understand how humans learn together through communicative interaction. Figure 1.1 below illustrates these children as they solved their problem together.

In Figure 1.1 Sipho and Nandi are building a train using blocks of various shapes. The children are both three years old and are speaking while they work on the problem to be solved. The problem they are battling with is how to build the train that is hidden in front of Nandi in the absence of

Figure 1.1   Learning to build a train through communicative interaction

any more yellow round wheels. All the children have to use are green square and rectangle blocks.

At this developmental level where children's thinking is characterised as **'egocentric'**, what one sees is a form of speech that serves as a tool to assist in problem-solving. Speech here is a type of instrument that helps the children to solve the problem they are engaged with. We do not yet see the level of collaboration we expect to see in fully developed communicative interaction, but we have the buds of that development. Here language is a tool that is *externalised* to assist these two children to build a train (see Extract 1.1). Watching these children solve a problem with the use of language to guide their actions highlights the fact that language is an essential tool for learning in school.

Other chapters in this part of the book discuss theories of *how* we communicate (sometimes nonverbally, for example, see Chapter 3, or pragmatically, see Chapter 5), and have emphasised the importance of the *contexts* in which communication occurs. While Chapter 2 provides a critical engagement with communication theories that focus solely on the impact of cultural transmission in the development of human thinking, the current chapter introduces a *socio-cultural* approach to mind that views human thinking as socially mediated while still recognising the biological basis and evolutionary aetiology of this thought. To this end, this chapter will draw on the work of the Russian teacher and psychologist Lev Vygotsky,

Extract 1.1 Speaking in problem-solving: first steps towards communicative interaction

What follows is translated from the original isiXhosa.

Nandi: You take this block. Green block. Uh. Green block for here and tyres. *[Nandi tries to dislodge a green block which she then attempts to use as a tyre for the train hidden in front of her.]*

Sipho: *[Talking to Nandi, but also to himself.]* The wheels is round silly! *[He giggles, and tries to dislodge the yellow round wheels from the truck he has in front of him.]* Not green. *[He seems to be referring to the square shape rather than the colour green.]* Did you ever see wheels like this? *[He points to the green blocks.]* I *[inaudible]* wheels. Round. I take him off and then I put him. I put him here. Round wheels. *[Sipho is talking out loud while he takes the round wheels off the truck and puts them onto the train. Nandi continues for a while to fit the green square blocks to the undercarriage of the train but then emulates Sipho and takes round wheels off the truck she has and fits them onto the train.]*

to understand how language serves as a cognitive tool and, consequently, how communicative interaction develops our uniquely human cognitive capacity. Throughout the chapter empirical examples of communicative interaction will be drawn on in order to illustrate the concepts covered. The empirical work is drawn from my research in disadvantaged urban, rural, and farm schools in the Western Cape Province of South Africa, and utilises the body of work that has come out of the Vygotskian tradition (Hardman, 2004, 2005b, 2007, 2008).

Central to a Vygotskian perspective of development is the understanding that learning (and hence teaching) is a culturally based social endeavour (Lektorsky, 1990). This approach foregrounds the communicative aspects of teaching and learning in which knowledge is shared and co-constructed primarily through semiotic (meaningful signs) **mediation** (especially language) (Mercer and Fisher, 1997a; Palincsar, 1986; Wertsch, 1991; Mercer, 2005). For Vygotsky, mediation, understood as the guidance of a more expert peer or teacher, is the key to understanding how children learn through communicative interaction. This is a central Vygotskian concept and it is explored in some depth in this chapter.

Mind in society

It is not the consciousness of men that determines their being but, on the contrary, their social being that determines their consciousness.

(Marx, 1859, pp. 328–9)

Since Descartes's exposition of the cogito as a rational principle, psychologists and philosophers have debated the nature of knowledge: How does one come to know something and what can one know with certainty? An answer to this question is contained in the quotation from Marx above: one comes to know through the determinants of social being, which are necessarily linked to interaction with others. The very act of consciousness, so often thought to be a part of the individual's biological make-up, is, following this line of thinking, socially derived. While this stance might not sound so remarkable in the twenty-first century, it is useful to contextualise this thinking. At the time that Vygotsky was writing, Behaviourism and, to a lesser degree, Psychoanalysis, were the dominant psychological paradigms. Behaviourism, at that time, held that one cannot study anything that one could not actually see; hence the focus on external behaviour as an object of study and the use of observation as a method for studying psychological questions. Psychoanalysts, however, postulated that most of our psychic life is driven by dynamic unconscious forces, of which we are generally unaware. The notion, then, that one's mind is socially derived is in contrast to both dominant paradigms.

In a bid to address the question of how knowledge develops within a Marxist psychology, Vygotsky (1978) postulated that mind is socially constructed during communicative interaction between culturally knowledgeable adults and children. While Marx analysed a 'cell' of capitalist society, for Vygotsky, the 'cell' of psychology is the interaction between the infant and the mother (the culturally more competent guide). For Vygotsky *the path from the object to child and from child to object passes through another person*. After the onset of higher cognitive functions, we never approach the world directly, in a 'non-mediated' manner; it is rather the case that our interaction with the world is from this point always *mediated* by someone or something else. Meaning is not something that resides in objects but is rather derived through interaction with others. This leads to the pedagogical appreciation of *guided assistance* within a space where this learning can most fruitfully occur. Vygotsky called this space the **zone of proximal development** and this concept is developed in more detail below. This picture of the development of mind led to Vygotsky's theorisation of learning as *requiring mediation through communicative interaction* within the zone of proximal development.

Mediation

A fundamental premise of Vygotskian theory is that basic biological (or '**elementary**') processes are transformed into **higher cognitive functions** through the use of culturally meaningful tools (such as language) during social interaction (Vygotsky, 1978). That is, children are born with certain basic, biological processes, such as, for example, perception (Diaz, Neal and Amaya-Williams, 1993). As the child develops within the social world, these elementary processes are transformed by the child's interaction with the social world. Higher cognitive functions develop first as interpsychological functions, with m/other initially guiding the child's activity, and later 'turn inward' becoming intrapsychological functions. Higher cognitive functions, then, have *social* origins. This conceptualisation of development claims to overcome the prior dualist stance to development, which holds that mind is either naturally 'given' or socially derived. In the terms of Vygotsky's general genetic law:

> Every function in the child's cultural development appears twice: first, on the social level, and later on the individual level; first, between people (interpsychological), and then inside the child (intrapsychological). This applies equally to voluntary attention, to logical memory, and to the formulation of concepts. All the higher functions originate as actual relations between human individuals.
>
> (Vygotsky, 1978, p. 57)

What emerges from this law is a clear understanding that the nature and the quality of *mediation* are crucial in the development of higher cognitive functioning and self-regulation. Thus it is the m/other who originally *mediates* the child's activity and externally regulates the child's interaction with the environment (Moll and Greenberg, 1993). Mediation thus occurs when a 'culturally more competent' person instructs a learner about a concept (say a number) in a very structured manner. If the mediation is successful, the concept will be *internalised* through use and practice, and will begin to serve as a psychological tool with which to order new experiences. So, a number, for example, becomes a category that can be used to classify objects in the world. Similarly, language becomes a tool that helps you to go beyond the here and now – to develop intentional thinking. This aspect of Vygotsky's developmental theory is graphically represented in Figure 1.2.

Figure 1.2 represents how a human interacts with the world by means of cultural artefacts or tools; the world is never approached directly in the

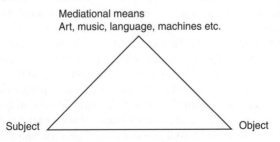

Figure 1.2   Higher cognitive functioning as mediated

course of the development of higher cognitive functions but is always mediated (Bateson, 1972; Wertsch, 1991, 1998). That is, the natural relationships represented at the base of the triangle become subsumed under cultural relationships represented at the apex of the triangle (Davydov, 1975, 1982). The elementary cognitive functions represented at the base of the triangle are inborn and shared with animals. Perception is an example of such an elementary cognitive function. However, advanced symbolic tool use – implicated in higher cognitive functions – such as numerical systems and mathematics, or the grammar and syntax of language, need to be learnt by and therefore taught to the growing child. Logical memory, for example, is not innate – it is something that children learn in their cultural setting. The following quotation illustrates the difference between innate, elementary inborn cognitive functions and learned higher cognitive functions:

> In the elementary form something is remembered: in the higher form humans remember something. In the first case a temporary link is formed owing to the simultaneous occurrence of two stimuli that affect the organism; in the second case humans personally create a temporary link through an artificial combination of stimuli ... the very essence of human memory consists in the fact that human beings actively remember with the help of signs.
>
> (Vygotsky, 1978, p. 51)

Have you ever tied a knot into a handkerchief in order to remember something? Perhaps drawn a symbol on your hand indicating that you need to remember to pick up dinner? Well this is what Vygotsky is referring to here when he says that humans actively remember; we use things to help us to do so. If we look at Figure 1.2, the knot we tie into our handkerchief would be viewed as a symbol for something else, our need to buy dinner on the way home, for example. This tool then, helps us to remember in a way that an animal cannot. The handkerchief knot has become a mediational means for helping us to remember something. Higher cognitive functions, then, have a social origin and are social in nature. Language is the most important tool in the development of higher cognitive functions. In this chapter communicative interaction is representative of the process through which higher cognitive functioning comes about. So, in Figure 1.2, the subject, an individual or group uses mediational means or tools in order to act on the object of the activity (Newman and Holzman, 1993). For Vygotsky (1978) human activity is mediated by tools. Tools are created and transformed during the development of the activity itself and carry with them particular culture-historical traces from their development. The use of tools therefore represents an accumulation and transmission of social knowledge. Tool use influences the nature of external behaviour and also the mental functioning of the individual. Think back to the knot in the handkerchief. The tool (the handkerchief) has altered your external behaviour (it now has a knot in it) but simultaneously has also altered your internal behaviour: you now have more space in your working memory for other more pressing things.

For Vygotsky (1978) our psychology, our 'humanness' and consciousness, is mediated by tools *as well as* by signs/symbols (such as language or other symbolic systems such as mathematical notations). Both tools and signs mediate activity. However, they differ in that tools alter external behaviour while signs alter internal behaviour. It is problematic, though, to think of these mediational means as separate because they are intimately linked through coordination in action and mutual transformation. Internalisation refers to the psychological reconstruction of an external action or operation. Once this cognitive operation has occurred, internal processes can be externalised in action and thus objectified for study. Consider language – the primary symbolic tool for Vygotsky. Once a child is able to use language they have a means of representing their environment and, importantly, of *reflecting* upon aspects of it. In this sense the child is freed from the contingency and immediacy of their environment. They are also provided with a rudimentary problem-solving device; to be able to speak one's self through a task is often an important aid in exploring different options, in guiding one's actions. Speech initially accompanies action; during development an aspect of speech could be said to 'turn inward', beginning thus to function intrapsychologically as a planning function.

We can thus, following Vygotsky, identify a series of transformations that make up the process of internalisation. As he puts it:

1. An operation that initially represents an external activity is reconstructed and begins to occur internally.
2. An interpersonal process is transformed into an intrapersonal one.
3. The transformation of an interpersonal process into an intrapersonal one is the result of a long series of developmental events.

(Vygotsky, 1978, p. 57)

In Figure 1.3 below, grade 3 students are learning to write using their fingers to create signs in the sand. Their finger is a tool that both alters the external world while simultaneously altering the students' cognitive functioning.

As Figure 1.3 indicates, the object is *what is acted upon* using mediational means. The object can be material (e.g. the sand), or an idea (a concept), but crucially, it is acted upon so as to advance a cognitive function (to remember, learning how to use symbols, etc.). The triangle in Figure 1.2, then, is a graphic representation of Vygotksy's central principle of mediation; in the course of developing higher cognitive functions a person never approaches the object of his/her action directly but is always led to understand that

Figure 1.3   Learning to write using fingers as a tool

object meaningfully through the guidance of another person or mediating artefact. As Vygotsky suggests:

> Just as a mould gives shape to the substance, words can shape an activity into a structure. However, that structure may be changed or reshaped when children learn to use language in ways that allow them to go beyond previous experiences when planning future actions ... once children learn how to use the planning function of their language effectively, their psychological field changes radically. A view of the future is now an integral part of their approaches to their surroundings.
>
> (Vygotsky, 1978, p. 28)

How does mediation work?

A central premise of mediation is that a student can accomplish more with assistance than on their own. This notion of guided assistance is articulated in Vygotsky's work as mediation within the zone of proximal development (ZPD) (Hedegaard, 1998; Daniels, 2001).

> To implant [something] in the child ... is impossible ... it is only possible to train him for some external activity like, for example, writing on a typewriter. To create the zone of proximal development, that is to

engender a series of processes of internal development we need the correctly constructed processes of school teaching.

(Vygotsky, 1987, p.134)

For Vygotsky (1978, 1986) the ZPD represents the gap between what a student can accomplish with assistance and what that student can accomplish on his/her own:

> [It] ... is the distance between the actual developmental level as determined by independent problem solving and the level of potential development as determined through problem solving under adult guidance or in collaboration with more capable peers ... the actual developmental level characterises mental development retrospectively, while the zone of proximal development characterises mental development prospectively.
>
> (Vygotsky, 1978, pp. 86–7)

Mediation within the ZPD, then, is simply a matter of how much an individual student can benefit from assistance. Where a student benefits greatly from assistance, we can say that he/she has an expansive ZPD; where a student does not benefit much from assistance, we can say that he/she has a more constricted ZPD. The ZPD is opened in dialogue between the more knowledgeable peer or teacher and the student. Asking a question in a lecture, for example, potentially opens up a student's ZPD because it shows the lecturer what the student knows and what he/she needs to know. When the lecturer begins to answer the student and provides the requisite assistance that interaction opens up the student's ZPD, effecting cognitive change through communicative interaction. Hence the ZPD helps the lecturer in the design of future communicative strategies by indicating the existent skills of a given audience and by focusing attention on the particular level at which the future communicative attempt should be directed and avoiding redundancy arising through repetition of work already known. The notion of mediation within the ZPD, then, becomes a powerful tool for understanding the importance of dialogical interaction in developing the person cognitively. One should note that the ZPD is necessarily a social concept. It refers very specifically to social interaction as a developmental principle and it cannot, as such, be individually determined. For the ZPD to 'open' a learner must be interacting with someone (or in some instances, something, like a book) that represents a higher order of knowledge, one that the learner has not yet attained.

In Extract 1.2 below we get a sense of how mediation, in the form of communicative interaction, plays out in a primary school classroom in the Western Cape area of South Africa. This is a disadvantaged school and the class consists of 44 students (average age of 11-and-a-half years) and one teacher. They are beginning to learn about fractions.

Extract 1.2   Mediation in the zone of proximal development

1. **Teacher:** Question? *[Begins to hand out worksheets.]*
2. **Wayne:** Explain the denominator again sir. *[Puts up his hand.]*
3. **Teacher:** Right, explain the denominator again.
4. Come let's go further. *[Gets another apple.]*
5. Now, what is this? *[Holds up an apple.]*
6. **Students:** Whole.
7. **Teacher:** Whole.
8. And I cut it exactly, exactly, in how many parts?
9. How many parts are there?
10. **Students:** Two.
11. **Teacher:** Now, my denominator tells me how many parts I have divided my whole into. *[Holds up parts.]*
12. In this case, it's two. *[Holds up parts.]*
13. So my denominator in this case will be?
14. **Students:** Two
15. **Teacher:** Two.
16. And now I'm going to cut him further. *[Puts apple back together and begins to cut it again.]*
17. Again, exactly, exactly. *[Cutting apple.]*
18. Let's pretend it's exactly. *[Smiling.]*
19. **Walter:** Into a quarter.
20. **Teacher:** *[Nods.]* Must [cut] him exactly, exactly. *[Cuts apple.]*
21. And I cut him up. *[Cuts apple.]*
22. In how many parts? *[Cuts apple – holds up pieces.]*
23. **Students:** Four.
24. **Teacher:** And if you look carefully, how many pieces? *[Holds up pieces.]*
25. **Students:** Four.
26. **Teacher:** Four pieces.
27. This piece, he is my? *[Holding up a piece.]*
28. **Students:** Quarter.
29. Quarter.
30. **Teacher:** You are clever.
31. You are clever! *[Smiling.]*
32. But these four pieces show me, if I put them together, they are my whole. *[Puts pieces together again.]*
33. But I want to know, what is my denominator?
34. And my denominator is going to tell me into how many parts?
35. **Students:** Parts.
36. **Teacher:** Parts I have cut him into and it is?
37. **Students:** Four.

38. **Teacher:** Four.
39. And Bokaas told us very nicely that denominator stands ['staan']?
40. **Students:** Under.
41. **Teacher:** Under.
42. Denominator tells us how many parts we have. *[Goes up to the boy – Wayne – who asked the question and shows him the four pieces of apple.]*
43. OK now Wayne? *[Wayne nods.]*
44. I could cut him further, but that would be difficult.
45. I give Wayne. *[Gives him a quarter.]*
46. **Students:** A one.
47. **Teacher:** One of what?
48. **Students:** The whole.
49. **Teacher:** I give him one of the four parts.
50. So he sits with one of the four pieces. *[Writes on the board a 4 and then 1 over it – ¼.]*
51. And I sit with? *[Holds up his pieces.]*
52. **Students:** Three.
53. **Teacher:** Three of the pieces. *[Writes ¾ on the board.]*
54. And if I take my three and I put the other piece with it ... *[Puts the pieces together.]*
55. Then I have?
56. **Harvey:** Your whole
57. **Teacher:** My whole. *[On board: ¼ ¾ =]*
58. Come let me put in a plus. *[¼ + ¾]*
59. Then I have $\frac{4}{4}$.
60. And then my numerator and denominator are the ...
61. **Students:** The same.
62. **Teacher:** Good.

Before analysing this text for mediation and evidence of the ZPD, we need to know something about how classrooms tend to function in rural areas of South Africa. Generally teachers completely occupy talk time. Often I have been in lessons where children never speak, not even when questions are asked because the questions posed are rhetorical and are answered by the teacher themselves. Where teachers do give students access to talk time, this tends to happen in a particular format, identified as an Initiate, Respond and Evaluate (IRE) discourse structure (Nystrand, Wu, Gamoran, Zeiser and Long, 2003; Wells, 1999). This is a discourse structure in which a teacher will initiate an interaction (usually through asking a question) and students will respond; the teacher will then evaluate the response before moving on. Such an IRE structure is common across classrooms around the world. Much has been debated (see Dillon, 1986, 1988; Hardman, 2000) in relation to this pervasive discourse structure and the general consensus is that it is potentially limiting in terms of developing authentic communicative interaction because the teacher asks closed questions that close rather than open discussion. When used to bring discussion to an end, closed questions do not develop higher cognitive functions as they deal only with what the child already knows, that is, what is within the child's actual developmental level rather than extending the child's knowledge and opening up the zone of proximal development (Vygotsky, 1978; Hardman, 2000). However, this conclusion is somewhat problematic in many South African classrooms, which are characterised by extreme asymmetrical power relations between teachers and taught which seriously prohibit students' gaining talk time in a period. (The effect of such asymmetries on communication is a key concern of Chapter 2.) For a student to ask a question they must negotiate talk time; they must in effect seize the opportunity to dominate talk time (Cazden, 1986; Corno and Snow, 1986; Carlson, 1991). This takes a lot of initiative, requiring activity, energy, self-esteem and independence on the learners' behalf (Dillon, 1988). Most learners are unwilling, or even unable, to make this move. It takes more than merely wanting to know an answer to ask a question, it requires real courage, requiring that one 'puts oneself in question' (Shotter and Gergen, 1992; Miller, 1994). Hence in disadvantaged schools in South Africa (and I would argue in most schooling contexts) closed questions, that require only single answers, can serve as tools to at least give students access to talk time (Hardman, 2000, 2008). Whether a question is used as a tool to mediate learning or as a low-level drill and practice tool depends very much on the context of that questioning (Hardman, 2000). If we look at the way the teacher uses closed questions in Extract 1.2, we get a picture of questioning as a developmental tool, rather than as a drill and practice one.

In line 14, the teacher draws students' attention to the real apple, using a question to focus their attention on what it is that he is going to explain to them, namely, the relationship between parts and a whole. While cutting the apple, the teacher engages students in a question and answer session (lines 17–25). Note how he incorporates definitions (line 20) with the physical act of cutting the apple. He repeats the same process of cutting the apple and asking leading, closed questions (lines 25–51) until he is satisfied that Wayne (the student who asked him to repeat his explanation) understands the work (line 52). Five things are happening, then, when the teacher asks a closed question: he uses questions to focus students' attention; the questions serve to lead students to the answer he is looking for; the simplicity of the questions makes it relatively easy for all students to engage in the interaction by providing a form of scaffolded (see Box 1.2 for more on this) or structured engagement with the task; the simple questions lead from a concrete representation of fractions to an abstract representation of them; finally, the questions provide students with the opportunity to engage in communicative interaction. The use of questions as scaffolds coupled with feedback and mathematical definitions, serve to *mediate* or guide students' engagement with the abstract fractions the teacher ultimately draws on the board. What is important to note here is that mediation leads to the acquisition of higher cognitive functions, hence not every instructional action can be said to mediate students' engagement with a problem (see Box 1.1). And while it is clear that the teacher dominates talk time (of the 63 coded units of speech in the episode, children use only 16 units or 25 per cent of the talk time), the fact that children occupy as much as 25 per cent of the overall talk time is extraordinary in this type of primary school. Of the 24 hours of data I transcribed from lessons in four rural, disadvantaged schools only three hours of lessons recorded student talk time in excess of 25 per cent and those lessons were exceptional. This is extremely problematic if we take seriously the Vygotskian notion that higher cognitive functions develop through communicative interaction, where we understand communicative interaction as mediating students' access to the world of meaning. However, extract 1.2 illustrates how even when only 25 per cent of talk time is occupied by students, students' ZPD can be opened and a level of communicative interaction can begin. Wayne's question, in fact, opens his ZPD by showing the teacher what he knows and what he needs to know. The teacher then provides a bridge, through communicative interaction (the use of questions and answers), between the known and the unknown. That is, he provides assistance in Wayne's ZPD.

A final question we might want to ask of Extract 1.2: What is it that mediation actually achieves here? What information is transmitted, and by contrast, what problem-solving abilities are effectively integrated by the learner? Of interest here is the fact that mediation in the ZPD happens in this extract not only because of how the teacher guides students' engagement with the problem, but, more importantly, because the teacher is concerned *with the development of conceptual knowledge*. This is crucial because for Vygotsky, the *object* of mediated action in the ZPD is ultimately conceptual, not technical, a matter of mere rote-learning. The following quotation highlights this:

> Instruction is only useful when it moves ahead of development. When it does, it impels or awakens a whole series of functions that are in a stage of maturation lying in the zone of proximal development. This is the major role of instruction in development. This is what distinguishes the instruction of the child from the training of animals. *This is also what distinguishes instruction of the child which is directed toward his full development from instruction in specialised, technical skills such as typing or riding a bicycle.* The formal aspect of each school subject is that in which the influence of instruction on development is realized. Instruction would be

Box 1.1 How to analyse communicative interaction

Mediation post-Vygotsky: Scaffolding as a pedagogical strategy

In the above text we get a sense of mediation as a concept that can enable us to investigate how people learn through communicative interaction. However, 'mediation' is a very high-level concept. How can we actually use this concept to analyse communicative interaction? What does 'mediation in the ZPD' look like in actual classrooms? Since the seminal paper published by Wood, Bruner and Ross (1976) on 'scaffolding' as a means of mediating students' access to knowledge, much work has been carried out that utilises the scaffolding metaphor to operationalise mediation in the ZPD. In their study with pre-schoolers, Wood et al. showed how a teacher could offer structured assistance at appropriate points in a problem-solving activity, guiding the child's actions to accomplish with assistance what the child was unable to achieve alone. They outline the following processes that are involved in scaffolding:

- *recruitment*: gain the student's attention
- *reduction in degrees of freedom*: simplifying complex task into smaller tasks
- *direction maintenance*: verbal prodding to keep student's focus on the goal
- *marking critical features*: pick out critical issues, interpret discrepancies
- *frustration control*: respond to student's emotional state
- *demonstration*: show/model solution.

In their discussion of how these scaffolds work in a teaching/learning situation, Wood et al. point to the complex nature of scaffolding as an interaction between teacher and taught.

While not utilising the scaffolding metaphor explicitly, Tharp and Gallimore (1993) have elaborated Vygotsky's notion of mediation in the ZPD as *guided assistance*. They suggest six means of teaching by assisting progress through the ZPD. These highlight how instruction can usefully provoke learning in the ZPD.

- *modelling*: The teacher should model appropriate learning actions for students to imitate.
- *contingency management*: A reward (e.g. praise, or for a schoolchild a gold star) or punishment (e.g. reprimanding students for not doing their work) should directly follow behaviour.
- *feedback*: Verbal and written feedback to the tasks provide a model for the students, both in terms of demonstrating what a 'good' answer

should look like as well as modelling the cognitive moves required to reach the answer. This should attempt to scaffold for students how to approach tasks.

- *instruction*: Effective instruction is embedded in a context with other effective assistance means, such as encouragement and feedback.
- *cognitive structuring*: Especially where a student is unfamiliar with the task, the mediator must provide the structure for thinking and acting, scaffolding/organising the student's experience. Such assistance may be providing for grand theories for the student to approach his/her work, or simply naming and defining concepts. Essentially this assists the student to process 'raw' data, all the facts, helping him/her to sift through them, providing a framework for interacting with the text.
- *questioning*: Here the teacher uses questions to develop an understanding of what the child knows and what he/she needs to know. In this sense, a question provides the teacher with access to the person's actual developmental level, pointing also to the ZPD.

The reader will recognise similarities across the work of Wood et al. and Tharp and Gallimore's (1988) classification of adult interactions with children in a teaching context. Modelling, for example, resonates with 'demonstrating'; questioning is a technique one could use to 'recruit attention'; cognitive structuring involves both 'marking critical features' and a 'reduction in degrees of freedom'; feedback serves potentially to 'maintain direction', and, finally, contingency management (in the form of praise) helps manage 'frustration'. These two important and widely cited studies, then, point to certain key strategies that teachers can use to guide students' actions in the ZPD. These pointers should enable you to: (a) design an analytical framework that you can use to analyse dialogical interaction as a developmental tool; and (b) even design your own developmental task. Extract 1.3 below shows how you can use these principles to approach the analysis of communicative interactions.

Extract 1.3   Is Kim doing the correct thing?

1. **Mrs De Wet:** So Kim says her group is finish[ed].
2. Come up Kim,
3. Stick it here. *[Gives Kim some glue and indicates that she should stick her sheet of paper on the board for all to see.]*
4. **Kim:** $\left(\frac{4}{9} \times \frac{5}{3}\right)$ OK, so I divided nine by three … *[Kim has a large sheet of work paper in her hand on which the answer is worked out. She sticks this to the board and begins to explain her group's solution.]*
5. And three by three.

6. **Mrs De Wet:** OK, must we stop Kim there?
7. Hmm? Must we stop Kim there?
8. Is Kim doing the correct thing?
9. **Students:** Uhuhhmm.
10. **Mrs De Wet:** Why not?
11. What has she done? *[There are seven hands up bidding for a chance to answer – Ishmael very eager.]*
12. What has her group done?
13. Anybody?
14. Ishmael? *[Teacher calls on Ishmael.]*
15. **Ishmael:** Miss, miss, um, the reason why she's wrong miss is because *[Ishmael stands at his desk and begins to provide an answer regarding why Kim's response is incorrect.]*
16. You can't have the, the denominator must divide the numerator.
17. But she done the denominator and the denominator.
18. **Mrs De Wet:** OK, there must be a numerator with a denominator.
19. OK, let's turn it around. *[Teacher turns the cardboard over and writes the sum on it: spends the rest of the episode illustrating how to arrive at an appropriate answer.]*

In Extract 1.3 Mrs De Wet uses *questions* (6–8; 10) to *encourage* students to provide *reasons* for why Kim's answer is incorrect as well as to *recruit student attention*. Note that the teacher does not give students the correct answer immediately, but rather, draws the answer from the students. Her question illustrates to the students that Kim's answer is wrong but by probing further she gets a sense of what the other students know and need to know: that is, gets a sense of individual students' ZPDs. The teacher goes on in lines 18–19 to model an appropriate response by creating cognitive structures, in the form of steps in the problem-solving task, to assist students. Of particular interest in this extract is the fact that *students* are in a position to reflect on why their peers are incorrect and to provide the evaluative criteria required to develop a correct answer. In lines 16–18 Ishmael provides an elaborated reason for why Kim's answer is wrong: the denominator must divide the numerator. This is evidence that illustrates that some students in this class have managed to acquire the criteria for producing a legitimate mathematical text and have the ability to draw on a repertoire of mathematical tools to assist them in problem solving. This extract exemplifies various aspects of a mediator role:

- The teacher uses questions that encourage students to reflect on their problem-solving actions, developing students' **metacognitive** understanding of mathematical knowledge. The object, then, is the development of students' metacognitive understanding of the content.

- Linguistic tools serve to explicate mathematical content.
- Material tools (such as cardboard sheets) are used to serve a generative purpose encouraging students to develop new ways of thinking.

completely unnecessary if it merely utilized what had already matured in the developmental process, if it were not itself a source of development.

(Vygotsky, 1987, p. 212, emphasis added)

This quotation is important because it clearly indicates that mediation in the ZPD is directed towards the development of abstract (what Vygotsky calls '**scientific**') **concepts**, not 'technical skills'. Scientific concepts are a result of instruction, of schooling. Of course, one does, on the basis of everyday experience, possess basic concepts, what Vygotsky calls spontaneous or everyday concepts. However, when one enters a formal educational context, these spontaneous concepts prove insufficient in moving beyond a rudimentary level of understanding. For example: one knows on the basis of empirical observation that getting into a bathtub causes the water-level rise. This general 'know-how' knowledge falls short, however, of the precise notions of displacement and buoyancy as explained in Archimedes' Law, a proper scientific concept.

The central conceptual relationship being worked on in Extract 1.2 is that between parts and a whole. The teacher elaborates this relation with reference to the students' everyday lived experience and to the more abstract school-based concepts. The teacher makes use of everyday objects (in this instance an apple) to develop students' understanding of fractions, specifically of the relationship between parts and the whole. He begins his explanation, in fact, by using this object before moving onto more abstract representations of fractions (line 59). Children in this classroom are familiar with apples as the school is located in an apple farming district of the Western Cape and most of the students' parents are employed work on these farms. By connecting subject matter knowledge (school or 'scientific' concepts) to the children's lived experience (everyday concepts) the teacher makes these concepts more meaningful and personal, and creates the motivation for subject matter learning (Hedegaard, 1998). That children are indeed motivated to learn in this instance is born out by Wayne's question as well as the students' choral responses to the teacher's questions. There is a clear linking between the students' everyday understanding of sharing pieces of an apple and the more sophisticated understanding of what a fraction actually is and how it can be represented. By working from the empirical to the theoretical and back again, the potential exists here for the teacher to make the scientific concept meaningful while still maintaining the distinction between the different types of knowledge.

For Vygotsky, the school is that 'space' in which children learn to manipulate scientific concepts. For him, these concepts are introduced by the teacher as distinct from everyday concepts which can be learnt through everyday personal experience in the absence of systematic instruction (Vygotsky, 1986; Daniels, 2001; Karpov, 2003). Scientific concepts form a coherent, logical, hierarchical system and are characterised by a high degree of generality and abstraction (Vygotsky, 1986; Hedegaard, 1998, Daniels, 2001; Karpov, 2003). Scientific concepts are those concepts that children are consciously aware of and can reflect on.

> The development of the scientific ... concept, a phenomenon that occurs as part of the educational process, constitutes a unique form of systematic co-operation between the teacher and the child. ... In a problem involving scientific concepts, he must be able to do in collaboration with the teacher something that he has never done spontaneously ... we know that the child can do more in collaboration than he can do independently.
>
> (Vygotsky, 1987, pp. 168–9)

In the quotation, it is clear that the development of understanding of a scientific concept arises in the relationship between the teacher and student in the zone of proximal development *through communicative interaction*. Explicit guided instruction, then, is central to the development of scientific concepts. Vygotsky's differentiation between scientific and everyday concepts provides us with a mechanism for describing the object of school teaching: that is, scientific concepts. This understanding of scientific and everyday concepts enables us to view teaching in the ZPD as a double move between the students' everyday concepts and their exposure to scientific concepts, and facilitates an understanding of scientific concepts (or subject content concepts) as the object of schooling (Hedegaard, 1998). This double move plays out as a finely tuned movement between the teacher's model of subject-matter (scientific) concepts and the student's everyday concepts. By linking abstract knowledge to students' lived experience, students are able to own the concept in a meaningful way. Figure 1.4 provides a graphic representation of the dialectical relationship between scientific and everyday concepts.

In summary, Vygotsky's theory of learning provides us with a view of pedagogy as involving the mediation of scientific/subject-content concepts within the ZPD by a culturally more competent other. This is a profoundly different view of pedagogy to the more traditional notion of it in which views students as empty vessels waiting to be filled by the expert pedagogue. In Vygotsky's theory the expert pedagogue is absolutely essential to learning but this happens in a dialogical space where the active student participates in his/her developmental trajectory. The primary vehicle through which development happens in this pedagogical theory is language. This theory,

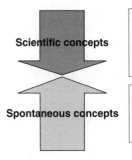

	• Imposed
Scientific concepts	• Scientific concepts move from abstract to concrete
	• Developed in structured environment of the classroom
Spontaneous concepts	• These concepts emerge from everyday experience
	• Move from concrete to abstract
	• Develop from everyday, empirical experience

Figure 1.4   A graphic description of scientific and everyday concepts

Source: Daniels, 2001, p. 7

however, leads to a potentially problematic issue: variation in semiotic mediation leads to differential cognitive development (Hasan, 1992).

Variation in communicative interaction and its cognitive consequences

The importance of semiotic mediation in the development of higher cognitive functions must lead us to ask about the cognitive outcomes of variation in semiotic mediation. What happens when children are not uniformly given access to the requisite semiotic mediation to help develop, for example, syllogistic reasoning or categorical thinking? In his famous studies in Uzbekistan, Luria (1976) found that

> [c]ategorical classification involves complex verbal and logical thinking that exploits language's capacity for formulating abstractions and generalizations for picking out attributes, and subsuming objects within a given category ... 'categorical' thinking is usually quite flexible. ... The ability to move freely, to shift from one category to another, is one of the chief characteristics of 'abstract' thinking' or the 'categorical behaviour' essential to it.
>
> (Luria, 1976, p. 77)

Rather controversially, Luria found that categorical, abstract ways of thinking were intricately linked with formal education, in particular with schooling. Those participants in his study who had little or no access to formal schooling were simply unable to think in the categorical ways outlined by Luria. For example, farmers who had never attended school were unable to categorise objects according to superordinate categories. Rather than categorising objects into such abstract categories, such as 'tool' (in the case of hoe and spade), the farmers categorised objects in terms of use: therefore a hoe and a potato would be in one category because you use a hoe to plant a potato. Chapter 11 makes a similar point regarding the intersection of culture and evolutionary tendencies in the development of 'essentialist' and 'cold' cognition.

Much has been written about Luria's work and there is a pervasive misunderstanding of his finding. Some attacks on his work indicate that Luria's findings suggest educated people are in some way better, or more conscious of their humanness, than non-educated people. This is not in fact what his work points to at all. Whether one thinks in categorical ways or uses concrete situational thinking, one is still developing the unique higher cognitive functions characteristic of humans. However, what his work does suggest is that access to different semiotic mediation during development will lead you to think in very different ways. Note however, that 'different' does not mean 'better'. The point to be made is that variation in semiotic mediation has a developmental impact on cognition. Perhaps an example will illustrate the point. Ongoing campaigns in many countries to educate people about the risks of HIV provide, in the best cases, an example of how semiotic mediation can deliver not merely a message regarding behaviour change, but also a new way of understanding in relation to healthy lifestyles as well. Of course, the success of such campaigns depends very much on how the advert mediates its message and how the recipient of this message is positioned in relation to the advert. (For another example of how semiotic mediation is developmentally formative, see Chapter 2's discussion of how the use of photographs as mediational means can shift young people's identities in relation to their elders and, indeed, in relation to their bodies.)

Vygotsky, Freire and critical pedagogy: Opening the debate

Chapter 2 develops an account of Freire's work. Hence, I shall not delve into its finer details here, although I do want to briefly call into question the often-held assumption that Vygotsky and Freire's theories are absolutely congruent. Like Vygotsky, Freire was interested in transformative pedagogy, and both develop their foundational ideas from readings of Marx. Nonetheless, how their respective ideas play out in relation to pedagogy differs quite considerably. Vygotsky and Freire alike are opposed to the traditional behaviourist notion that views schoolchildren as empty vessels that need to be filled with the teacher's expert knowledge. However, in their theorisation of **optimal learning** in school, the theorists diverge. Freire is opposed to top-down instruction characteristic of traditional schools and espouses a view of learning that relies on true dialogue, where partners construct knowledge together and learn from each other. Vygotsky, by contrast, is very specifically a school theorist who views the teacher as central to mediating scientific or schooled concepts in the zone of proximal development. In this scenario, there is very definitely a knower (the more culturally advanced teacher or peer) and a novice (the learner). Vygotsky is quite clear here that explicit guided instruction in the ZPD leads to the development of scientific concepts. This is not simply then, an open dialogue where both parties construct knowledge together in a horizontal manner. Rather than the co-construction of knowledge in horizontal dialogues (Freire's ideal), Vygotsky's view of learning emphasises a mediational model where novices appropriate symbolic tools through processes of mediation facilitated by those with different symbolic skills. These points are worth bearing in mind when approaching Chapter 2 and, indeed, when thinking about how communicative interaction is theorised in this book by different theorists. The difference in Freire and Vygotsky's respective approaches alerts us to the importance of the specific pedagogical conditions and contexts under which learning and the transmission of knowledge happens. Clearly the situation of children's classroom learning is very different to that of the communication of scientific/technological information in cross-cultural community contexts; we obviously need to heed these differences in considering which theoretical framework could best be applied.

Conclusion

This chapter has offered an introduction to a socio-cultural approach to communicative interaction. While focusing predominantly on how the social world (and most crucially our dialogical interactions within this world) develops our unique human mental functions, the arguments presented here resonate with both the dialogical approach presented in Chapter 2 and various of the evolutionary ideas (as in the case of the biological basis and evolutionary aetiology of the ZPD) presented in Chapter 12. Vygotsky's work is of importance in understanding communicative interaction because he illustrated how specific kinds of dialogical interaction – which he called semiotic mediation – led to the development of unique human higher cognitive functions, such as language, categorical thinking, and even art and music. However, what Vygotsky's work points to is how to set up effective (in the developmental sense) dialogical spaces in social interaction, which can lead to learning and, consequently, cognitive change. The following chapter looks more closely at the challenges to setting up such a dialogue from a Freirian theoretical base. Its focus on asymmetrical power-relations and their consequent impact on communicative interaction provides a very useful lens through which to reassess some of the concepts covered in this chapter.

2
Dialogue, Critical Consciousness, and Praxis

Cathy Vaughan

Keywords: Conscientisation; dialogue; doxa; education; extension; praxis; problematisation; problem-solving.

Introduction

Social psychological analyses of communication inevitably encounter the debate between those social theorists convinced of the possibility of genuine communicative exchange, and those who doubt that effective and properly equal forms of communicative exchange are practically achievable at all. However, what is often overlooked in this debate is the role of *interaction* between self and other in the development of persons in the first place:

> The psychology of self–other relations shows that while communication between self and other is indeed a difficult process, fraught with contradictory and destructive energies, it also contains a positivity without which there would be no person at all.
>
> (Jovchelovitch, 2007, p. 131)

As highlighted in the previous chapter, Vygotsky posits that interactions between self and other are the basis for the development of higher cognitive functions in humans. This chapter will explore the role of self–other interaction in the construction of social worlds, and outline the foundational role of communication between self and other in efforts towards transforming those social worlds (social change).

For social psychologists drawing upon the work of Brazilian educator Paulo Freire, the ontogenetic nature of communication moves the focus of analysis from whether or not communication occurs between self and other, towards *how* self and other relate and whether their relations achieve the ideal of genuine communication. This chapter will draw upon pedagogical theory, particularly the influential work of Freire, to explore the notion that genuine communication changes both how a person understands *and acts upon* the world. Concepts at the heart of Freire's pedagogy – **dialogue**, critical consciousness, and **praxis** – will be introduced and explored through the lenses of critical theory and empirical examples drawn from the author's research in the area of community health. Challenges to the establishment of dialogical relations and the achievement of genuine communication will be discussed in relation to social change efforts.

Communication and social worlds: The example of education

[T]he social, human world would not exist if it were not a world able to communicate. Without communication human knowledge could not be propagated.

(Freire, 1974/2005, p. 123)

Freire notes that 'the thinking Subject cannot think alone' (Freire, 1974/2005, p. 124), claiming that *communication is central* to the human world. For Freire the achievement of genuine communication is made visible in change – changes in the way 'thinking Subjects' understand their world and act in relation to it. He notes that all humans are subject to **doxa** (governing stereotypes or beliefs) which shape their relations with the world, but that doxa can be challenged, tested and shifted through genuine forms of communication, resulting in new understandings that are based on critical reflection. As Freire puts it: 'Knowledge is built up in the relations between human beings and the world, relations of transformation, and perfects itself in the critical **problematisation** of these relations' (1974/2005, p. 99). Freire thus highlights the transformative potential of communication, describing the process as 'humanising' and emphasising that 'knowing is the task of Subjects, not objects' (1974/2005, p. 93). The transformative power of genuine communication is a key theme in the theorisation of effective communications, and it is a preoccupation both of Habermasian notions of communicative action (see Chapter 6) and of psychoanalytic approaches to 'full speech' (see Chapter 9); it is also debated by theories of pragmatics (Chapter 5), and evolutionary approaches to communication (Chapter 11).

Freire's analysis of communication draws upon the rich field of **education** – he was heavily influenced by Vygotsky (see Chapter 1) – and he emphasises that education *is* communication (Freire, 1974/2005). There is no one definition of education that is universally agreed upon, even by professional educators. The Oxford English Dictionary defines education as being the 'systematic instruction, schooling or training given to the young in preparation for the work of life', and common sense understandings of education describe a process whereby one develops knowledge and skills. Inherent in these understandings is the idea that for education to occur, information needs to be passed from one person to another – that in order to be 'prepared for the work of life', the less-educated need access to the knowledge and skills of the well-educated. These understandings have influenced approaches to education both in and out of the classroom.

Freire was highly critical of the notion that education should be *extended*, 'given' or graciously bestowed from one (expert) person to another (ignorant) person and of how this idea had influenced the formal education system in his native Brazil, throughout Latin America and elsewhere (see also Chapter 1 for description of the one-way interactions between teacher and students typical of South African classrooms).

> Education thus becomes an act of depositing, in which the students are the depositories and the teacher is the depositor. Instead of communicating, the teacher issues communiqués and 'makes deposits' which the students patiently receive, memorize, and repeat.
>
> (Freire, 1970, pp. 45–6)

Freire noted that this 'banking concept' of education serves to encourage passivity and acceptance of the status quo among students. Students preoccupied with 'storing deposits', with trying to recognise the content that has been chosen for them, and memorising the information presented, are less likely to think critically about the relevance of this information to their lives but rather are consumed by the task of absorbing their teacher's worldview. Indeed passivity, malleability, and receptiveness are qualities often encouraged and rewarded in classroom settings. In Freire's Marxist conceptualisation the (even if well-intentioned) banking clerk/teacher preparing the young for the 'work of life' is part of a system which serves to maintain social inequity and the oppression of the majority.

Instead of education being a monological task of extending information or content from an expert to another person, Freire proposes that education should rather be a *dialogical act of communication* where knowledge is jointly constructed by two parties, and through which both teachers and students come to new understanding (as teacher-learners and learner-teachers). For Freire, *genuine* communication could only be said to have occurred when both interlocutors were able to learn from each other – and learn so as to be able to transform the world. Freire's social psychological view of knowledge informs this approach, as he notes that knowledge is not an object that can be extended from one person to another but is rather built in human interrelations and between human beings and the world (Freire, 1974/2005).

In order to foster communication rather than **extension**, Freire's work outlines a problem-posing approach to education, as an alternative to the banking model (see Box 2.1 for more on Freire's critique of extension). Two of Freire's key essays – 'Education as the Practice of Freedom' and 'Extension or Communication' – have been published together in English translation as *Education for Critical Consciousness* (1974/2005). *Education for Critical Consciousness* outlines the process of Freire's problem-posing method, as initially used in adult literacy education in poor north-east Brazil. Rather than the programme's content being preordained by outside experts in literacy and then 'extended' to students, the problem-posing method generates content for exploration from issues arising in the local 'thematic universe'. (For more on the rhetorical uses of questioning and **problem-solving** see Chapter 10). In doing so the approach tries to acknowledge the historically and structurally grounded nature of all participants in a communication process (recognising

Box 2.1   Roots of a theory: Challenging rural extension

Freire's pedagogy was substantially shaped by his exposure to the agricultural reform programmes conducted in Brazil in the 1950s and 1960s. These programmes had the objective of rural development through the education of farmers in agricultural technology and were known as rural 'extension'. Education of farmers in the latest scientific knowledge was the responsibility of extension agents (usually agronomists).

Freire criticised the notion that *extension* of information or skills from the 'expert' agronomist to the 'ignorant' farmer would lead to an increase in agricultural production, insisting that what instead was required was *communication* – dialogue between the agronomist and farmer, based on a recognition of each other's knowledge. This would enable the co-construction of new knowledge relevant to the specific local environment and the situation that the interlocutors were seeking to change. However, Freire (1974/2005, p. 106) often encountered the critique that dialogue with farmers was not possible ('How can we dialogue with peasants about a technical method they are not familiar with?') or feasible within the short time frames of extension programmes ('How can we waste so much time on dialogue with them?'). In response Freire would argue that a focus on short-term programmatic outputs (number of community members sitting in extension trainings; number of villages reached by experts; technical guidelines produced, etc.) did not lead either to the production of knowledge relevant to a local context, or save time in achieving behavioural or cultural change. This resonates with my experience of HIV prevention programmes, and is one that has been repeatedly described in community development programmes from a range of sectors throughout the world. Rather than dialogue being a waste of time, time is clearly lost when the superficial 'busy-ness' of development projects (the launches, the workshops, the demonstration activities – what Freire would describe as the blah blah blah) is ineffective in supporting long-term social change. Extension is counter-productive when it creates the resistance commonly seen if local knowledge and priorities are dismissed, and can erode community confidence or the belief that any kind of change is in fact possible.

that both teacher-learners and learner-teachers are subject to doxa). This acknowledgement is necessary for fostering the process of *dialogue* central to Freire's pedagogy.

Characteristics of dialogue and anti-dialogue: Examples from health education

> Since dialogue is the encounter in which the united reflection and action of the dialoguers are addressed to the world which is to be transformed and humanised, this dialogue cannot be reduced to the act of one person's 'depositing' ideas in another, nor can it become a simple exchange of ideas to be 'consumed' by the participants in the discussion.
>
> (Freire, 1970, p. 61)

Freire based his pedagogy on the possibility for and necessity of dialogue (see Box 2.2 for discussion of contrasting notions of dialogue). Freire frames dialogue as a *horizontal* relationship between persons A and B, based on genuine two-way communication, empathy, and mutual recognition (Freire, 1974/2005). In contrast, anti-dialogue is presented as a vertical relationship of person A over B, based on person A 'issuing communiqués' to person B, without empathy or recognition. The monological information dissemination associated with traditional didactic education could be characterised as anti-dialogue. Though extensively criticised by Freire and others, a one-way anti-dialogical approach has significantly influenced efforts at social change through education in a range of fields.

Health education, for example, has been a major tool in initiatives aimed at promoting health since at least the 1960s. The majority of these initiatives have been based upon social cognition frameworks underpinned by the notion that people will make rational decisions about their health-related behaviour if they have access to sufficient information about a particular health issue (Nutbeam and Harris, 1998; Fishbein et al., 1994 and see Chapter 13). Therefore, health education has focused on providing people with accurate, accessible and appropriate information.

Health professionals have historically been positioned, and have seen themselves, as 'knowing best' – as the actors holding the most accurate and appropriate knowledge about health (Campbell and Jovchelovitch, 2000). Health professionals also have access to enormous symbolic power and their knowledge is recognised as 'expertise' (Frank, 2005; Foucault, 1973; Farmer, 2003). In dominant public discourses the knowledge held by well-educated health professionals is described in any number of positive ways: 'evidence-based', 'best practice', 'best available', 'cutting-edge'. In contrast, the knowledge of the (assumed to be) uneducated public tends to be described in ways that indicate its lesser value: 'lay-theories', 'folk beliefs', 'old wives' tales', 'home remedies'. Health education has therefore been based on strategies for *extending* the valued expertise of well-educated health professionals – the knowledge and skills necessary to be 'prepared for the work' of living a healthy life – to the uneducated public (or patient) through the mass media, awareness-raising campaigns, school curricula, and clinical interactions. That is, health education has been based on *monologue*. Evidence for the efficacy of this approach to health education is patchy, with research demonstrating that information about health risks is often a very weak

Box 2.2   Contrasting notions of dialogue

Some theorists understand dialogue as joint *'I intentions'*, where both intentions exist prior to the communicative interchange, and emphasise the speakers' logos, rationality, and effectiveness in communicative interaction with the other. Here communicative effectiveness is evident when, through strategic action, a speaker is able to exert authority and render the other's intention subordinate. Strategic action, as discussed more fully in Chapter 6, may involve appearing to accommodate the other's perspective, but this, importantly, is not for the purpose of developing new knowledge and a mutually derived communicative goal. Rather the purpose is effective achievement of the speaker's 'I intention'.

In contrast, Freire's concept of dialogue emphasises the process of developing *'we-intentions'*, in which both actors in a communicative exchange mutually determine the communicative goal. That is, Freire and other 'dialogists' (such as Vygotsky, Gadamer, and Bakhtin) suggest that genuine communication is evident when the intention of the communicative interaction is changed through the process of communication itself. The process of developing joint communicative goals and 'we-intentions' is seen as true dialogicality – an ideal type of communication – and is understood as being at the basis of collective action.

The horizontal communicative relationship between persons that Freire suggests is necessary for dialogue depends on whether interlocutors are able to recognise each other's knowledge as legitimate, and have the ability to take the perspective of the other (Jovchelovitch, 2007). These characteristics of dialogue shape its radical potential. Perspective-taking and recognition of the other are at the basis of many social psychological theories of self (Mead, 1962), but in the practice of dialogue are fraught processes easily derailed in contexts of unequal power relations, democratic inexperience, different (and differently valued) identities and communication styles (see Chapter 5 on pragmatics, Chapter 9 on psychoanalysis, and Chapter 11 on evolutionary theory for other reasons why attempts at dialogue might fail). The circumstances in which efforts at dialogue occur may lead interlocutors to dismiss the other's knowledge, or not recognise it as such. The conditions in which dialogue, perspective-taking, and recognition of the other are supported warrant further exploration.

determinant of health-relevant behaviours (Campbell, 2004). However, approaches to health promotion based on 'campaigns' of unidirectional information-provision remain dominant within the field.

In contrast, *dialogue* – reciprocal conversation between two or more actors – implies two-way and ongoing communication. Dialogue can support the understanding of multiple perspectives, and the development of new knowledge constructed by actors from these understandings. However, the achievement of dialogical relations is no easy task, and cannot be assumed to occur whenever two actors meet (Freire, 1970). For example, when a health worker, however well intentioned, encounters a young person considered 'at risk' of HIV infection, and then presents that young person with pamphlets about HIV transmission, strongly encourages them to seek HIV testing, and extols the benefits of young people 'knowing their status', there is no dialogue. The health worker has assumed that what they know (that, for example, being aware whether or not one has HIV enables a person to access early treatment) is more valuable knowledge than what the young person knows (that, for example, being aware whether or not one has HIV comes with considerable costs and does not necessarily mean treatment will be available in their poorly serviced community). In this case recognition by the health worker and the young person that they both know about this issue, but that what they know is different, would be a first step towards them engaging in dialogue. Dialogue may enable the co-construction of new knowledge about young people and HIV-testing grounded in the interlocutors' experience of historical and political context. New knowledge – achieved through the act of communication – can more effectively contribute to change. This new knowledge about young people and HIV-testing may be made visible through behaviour change on the part of the young person, but also on the part of the (usually) more agentic health worker. The new knowledge dialogically achieved may also potentially support the joint action of the interlocutors to change the environment to make it more supportive for young people seeking HIV-testing.

Dialogue in context

In order to communicate effectively, educator and politician must understand the structural conditions in which the thought and language of the people are dialectically framed.

(Freire, 1970, p. 69)

Jovchelovitch (2007, p. 133) emphasises that social psychological theories of how self is able to take the perspective of the other give 'primacy to the space of the "between", which is precisely where recognition and the intersubjective lie'. Though often unexplored, the *context* (the historical, sociological, cultural, and structural conditions) of this space is crucial. Actors bring to the 'space between' beliefs, assumptions, experiences, fears, and hopes shaped by their histories and social situations. Interlocutors may have differing communicative power and bring different skills (or otherwise) in listening, probing, presenting ideas, and in articulating or shutting down arguments. They may recognise and interpret verbal and non-verbal communicative acts quite differently. Interlocutors may also be unequally motivated to engage in the hard work of dialogue. Given the contexts of structural violence and inequality in which programmes striving for social change operate, it is unsurprising that their achievement of dialogue is rare. This is not to say that dialogue between persons with different skills, experiences, and access to power cannot occur – in fact for Freire's pedagogy, it is in encounters with difference that the potential to interrupt and reflect upon the taken-for-granted lies, and the encounter between change agents (outsider-activists) and communities is crucial. However, it is important to recognise that the achievement of dialogue should never be assumed, or the barriers to it underestimated.

Dialogue can, and does, occur in difficult contexts. Strategies to support this happening can be identified by reviewing communication-focused projects from different settings. Actors can be supported to develop a range of communicative skills, for example, in deliberate listening or articulating ideas (Faubert et al., 1996). Participants with access to the 'rich language' of visual and multimedia technologies (Humphreys and Brezillon, 2002) may have a more extensive 'vocabulary' with which to initiate and sustain dialogue. The novelty and impact of the rich language produced by the combination of images and text may also influence actors' motivation to engage in dialogue. Specific examples of health communication projects where dialogue has been supported are also described in Chapter 13.

The possibility of engaging in dialogue is influenced by the freedom individuals and groups have in shaping what that dialogue will be about – by their freedom to bring issues 'to the table', to express their values and priorities, and to share their lived experience. This freedom is mediated by identity. The differential way that people are viewed, and view themselves, structures the content of the representations that they hold as well as their communicative power. The ability to speak and be heard, and the recognition and legitimacy that is given to the knowledge thus expressed, is shaped by the position and status of interlocutors in a social field – that is, in a particular context. In the field described in Box 2.3 following, the social identities of young Papua New Guineans living in rural areas, community leaders, and an outside researcher, mean these actors can access and construct very different knowledge, and that they bring differing and contextually dependent communicative power to the intersubjective 'space between'. Freire notes that people with marginalised social identities

Box 2.3   Researching dialogically: Space for stories as a precondition for dialogue

In recent research with young people in Papua New Guinea, I was substantially influenced by sociologist Arthur Frank's (2005) challenge to undertake dialogical research. The intention of this research was to see whether, through dialogue, we could jointly construct new knowledge about youth health in the Highlands and develop the critical thinking necessary to identify strategies for action for improving health and specifically preventing the transmission of HIV.

In a social field shaped by structural inequalities and a difficult recent history of 'development', it was clear that all the participants in this research project – the young villagers, urban health workers, community leaders, and an Australian researcher – had access to very different knowledge. I recognised the existence of substantial barriers to the young Highlanders and I being able to communicate about health at all. In addition to language and logistical barriers, our relationships were based on my previous work in the aid and development sector, and therefore underpinned by unequal power relations. Our differing life experiences had shaped our respective communicative power, and despite my 'commitment' and 'empathy' I realised that it was going to be very difficult for me to take the perspective of the young research participants.

The research approach needed to create a *social space* where dialogue (between the youths and me, among the youths themselves, and between the young people and their community leaders) could potentially be fostered. Photovoice proved to be an excellent tool for initially engaging young people, building trust, and creating a safe space where dialogical relations could be established. As developed by Caroline Wang, Mary Ann Burris, and colleagues, Photovoice draws upon Freire's approach to education for critical consciousness and is a 'method by which people can identify, represent, and enhance their community' (Wang and Burris, 1997, p. 369). Young people were given cameras and basic photography training, and working together over a period of ten months, shared their stories about health with each other and with me through photographs and accompanying text, and in group discussions about these photostories. The topics of our discussions were driven by what the young people chose to take photographs of and which images they chose to discuss – they determined which issues were 'brought to the table', and selected what the priority health issues were from their perspective of the local situation (or, in Freirian terms, their thematic universe).

The artefacts of the project (the printed photo-stories) were not the 'end result' of this dialogical process but rather acted as a further *mediator of communication* (Freire, 1974/2005 p. 124; see also Chapter 1), with local photography exhibitions fostering a safe social space in which young people and their community leaders could meet to communicate about health (Examples of such photographs are given in Figures 2.1–2.3). The 'rich language' of the photo-stories effectively motivated the community leaders to engage in a communicative process with the youth. This tangibly increased the young people's confidence, with their photographs acting as 'evidence' of their expertise in what it was like being a young person growing up in Papua New Guinea today. The Photovoice process worked to create a space where trust was developed, and perspectives could be presented, explored, encouraged, and supported, as well as disagreed with, fought over, resisted, and resented. The dialogical space enabled some, but not all, of the youths to rework their identities, with observations and interviews confirming that some participants moved from seeing themselves as naïve young villagers to identifying themselves as community members with valuable knowledge to share. The dialogical space supported young people to negotiate new critical perspectives on some issues, but not others – for example, there was little evidence that the youths developed new understandings of gender and gender-based violence, with pre-existing positions seemingly particularly entrenched.

The work of dialogue is not easy – particularly in an environment of democratic inexperience and structured inequality. However, in this case the research data revealed that it was a valued struggle – over time we were able to jointly construct new knowledge about young people's health in the Papua New Guinean context, and in the process many of the participants felt genuinely listened to, often for the first time. While this did not lead to an epidemic of actionable health-promoting strategies being successfully implemented across the Highlands, a number of the young people involved have subsequently reported 'small wins' in working together to change some of the health compromising issues they identified.

There were considerable differences in how the Photovoice process unfolded in the three different community settings in which this research project took place. The young people's ability to engage in dialogue with each other, with me, and with their local leaders (and vice versa) was significantly affected by the *specific contextual preconditions* supporting or hindering dialogical relations in each community. Factors such as the strength of local-level leadership, pre-existing community cohesiveness and group identity all influenced the degree to which dialogue was possible, and whether it then contributed to collective action for social change. At times Freire's writings, particularly his early essays such as *Extension or Communication* (written in 1968), suggest a linear pathway from dialogue to critical consciousness to critical action, inadequately discussing the impact of context and emotion on the *practice* of dialogue and any subsequent *process* of collective action. The experience of this research project highlighted the complex, non-linear nature of participation in dialogue and its relationship with subsequent social change.

Figure 2.1   Julie taking photographs in her community at Bunum-Wo village, Western Highlands Province

Figure 2.2   Youths from Banz, Western Highlands Province, discussing how they will use a 'problem tree' to present their perspectives on the lack of government services in their community to the leaders invited to their photography exhibition. This was a theme these young men had identified as a priority in their photographs

Figure 2.3 Regina discussing her photo-stories with women's leaders at the exhibition in Kainantu, Eastern Highlands Province

'with no experience of dialogue, with no experience of participation ... are influenced by the myth of their own ignorance' (1974/2005, pp. 108–9). The construction and reconstruction of social identities can both constrain and open spaces for people to be able to represent their knowledge, priorities, and aspirations in dialogue.

Where dialogue happens: Safe spaces for dialogue

The value of safe communicative settings is increasingly recognised, but the *qualities* of those spaces that might support dialogue and the development of critical thinking are less often described. Freire's work recognises the contextually embedded nature of communication on a theoretical level, but does not provide clear guidance as to the characteristics of safe social spaces that might support it. In theorising conditions that may enable dialogue, researchers most often draw on Habermas's (1987) notion of the public sphere as a conceptual resource for thinking through the qualities of a safe communicative space (Westhues et al., 2008; Campbell et al., 2007; Parfitt, 2004; Ramella and De la Cruz, 2000; Greenhalgh et al., 2006). Habermas describes the public sphere as an inclusive space in which participants freely assemble to discuss issues of common concern, in conditions of equality, and where ideas are evaluated through rational argument (see Chapter 6). Researchers and activists have been able to draw upon these qualities of the idealised public sphere to guide reflection upon those contexts that may potentially support dialogue and critical thinking.

However, in her critique of Habermas's concept of the public sphere, feminist writer Nancy Fraser's call to recognise the limitations to genuine participation in the public sphere 'as if' interlocutors are equal, when they are in fact not, poses problems for thinking about a space where dialogue may be fostered in a broader setting of structured inequality. (It should be noted that in stating that interlocutors in the public sphere are not equal, Fraser is not referring to the dignity and worth of individual persons, but rather emphasising that the knowledge, identity, and communicative abilities that interlocutors bring to a public space will have been shaped by unequal life experiences.) Fraser (1990) questions the possibility of equal participation in the public sphere given that communities' 'discursive arenas are situated in a larger societal context that is pervaded by structural relations of dominance and subordination' (p. 65).

Fraser highlights that in response to the constraint of their speech, marginalised groups have repeatedly found it to their advantage to constitute alternative publics. In discussing the 'subaltern counterpublics' established by women, workers, people of colour, and gays and lesbians, she emphasises that these spaces play the dual role of allowing for safe withdrawal and regrouping while simultaneously providing a 'training ground' for overcoming democratic inexperience and developing 'agitational' projects aimed at transforming the wider public sphere (1990, p. 68). Fraser highlights that it is 'precisely in the dialectic between these two functions that their emancipatory potential resides' (1990, p. 68). Few development interventions seeking to effect cultural or behavioural change consciously build on the notion of supporting alternative publics for marginalised groups – safe spaces where people can regroup, reflect, and collectively build skills for articulating their views and engaging in wider public spheres in order to change them. However, building safe social spaces is an important starting point for fostering the dialogue on which the critical thinking and action necessary for change are based. Realistic assessment of the contextual preconditions may point to ways in which the social environment supports or hinders dialogue, and help change agents working with communities to identify where there may be opportunities or entry-points for potentially viable collective projects (Schugurensky, 2002).

What dialogue does: Conscientisation and critical thinking

Where interlocutors are able to meet in communicative interaction, recognise each other's knowledge as legitimate, and take the perspective of the other, a process of dialogue can begin. In supporting the understanding of multiple perspectives, dialogue can lead to critical reflection upon one's own knowledge and the development of new knowledge co-constructed with others. The process of dialogue creates space for critical thinking and the consideration of a new, broadened perspective. Recognising the value of this new co-constructed knowledge – what this jointly achieved critical perspective can *do* – provides the rationale for dialogical approaches to communication for social change, including in health and development work.

Some social psychologists suggest that participation in dialogue can impact positively on individual and community life by increasing people's critical consciousness of their own situation, leading to collective action aimed at social change (Campbell and Jovchelovitch, 2000). Communication between self and other is seen as being the basis for action aimed at transforming social worlds. Freire's theorisation of critical consciousness is central to understanding the potential of dialogue to facilitate the participation of people in the social change necessary to create environments that enable political engagement, economic development, health promotion, and environmental protection, to give just a few examples.

Freire's theory of how marginalised communities can act collectively to produce social change, detailed as the *Pedagogy of the Oppressed*, is based on the notion of *conscientização* (Freire, 1970). *Conscientização*, most often translated as '**conscientisation**' or the development of critical consciousness, is a process which emerges in dialogical relations. Conscientisation is fostered through dialogue about the contexts in which people live, where interlocutors co-construct a reflective and critical understanding of the broad range of (social, economic, cultural, psychological) factors shaping local circumstance. Freire's problem-posing approach stimulates the dialogue fundamental to conscientisation, encouraging reflection upon, and critique of, the inherent relationship between the construction of knowledge and power (Freire, 1974/2005, 1998). This is in stark contrast to the problem-solving techniques often 'taught' to community members in traditional educative interventions. Problem-posing instead has the potential to interrupt assumptions (of both professionals and community members) and redefine the nature of 'problems'. The problem-posing method has been used in a diverse range of settings by educators, psychologists, development workers, health practitioners, and others to promote conscientisation in work with marginalised communities (Campbell, 2003; Ramella and De la Cruz, 2000; Guareschi and Jovchelovitch, 2004; McCaffery, 2005; Wallerstein and Sanchez-Merki, 1994; Wang and Burris, 1997; Cornish, 2004b). (Given that problem-posing is based on classic Socratic methods of posing questions and facilitating dialogue, it is not surprising that this tradition has much in common with the different approaches to rhetoric discussed in Chapter 10.)

The process of developing critical consciousness

Freire's pedagogy, based on bringing the knowledge of different actors into dialogue, argues that knowledge is an expression of historically, socially, and psychologically situated lived experience. When one actor's knowledge is brought into dialogue with that of another, the process illuminates the 'diversity, expressiveness and limitations' inherent in all knowledge (Jovchelovitch, 2007). When actors recognise the partial nature of knowledge, the social order can be seen as arbitrary and possible alternatives can emerge. As such 'the world becomes one which is open to change' (Cornish, 2004a). Or, turning to Freire:

> A deepened consciousness of their situation leads men to apprehend that situation as a historical reality susceptible of transformation. Resignation gives way to the drive for transformation and inquiry, over which men feel themselves in control. ... The world becomes the object of that transforming action.
>
> (1970, p. 58)

Recognition of the contextual nature of knowledge enables interlocutors to critically reflect upon their lived experience – how and why they each know what they know – and co-construct a new understanding of the world from which to *act* upon this context. In Freire's words: 'Integration results from the capacity to adapt oneself to reality *plus* the critical capacity to make choices and to transform that reality' (Freire, 1974/2005, p. 4). For Freire, the development of critical consciousness through *reflection* is inextricably linked with critical *action*. This action-reflection dynamic, which both emerges from and gives support to conscientisation, Freire calls *praxis*.

Freire's psychological theorisation of the process of conscientisation describes dialogue as supporting people to move through different stages of consciousness (Freire, 1974/2005, pp. 13–15), from the 'semi-intransitive' where actors are focused on survival; to a 'naïve' consciousness characterised by an oversimplification of problems and an inability to identify realistic strategies for change; to the final stage of 'critical transitivity' where actors can critically reflect upon problems, analyse explanations, and be receptive to new ideas. The critically transitive thinker can work with others to develop a reflective understanding of their lived conditions, and act to change them. For Freire, transition through these stages requires 'an active, dialogical educational program concerned with social and political responsibility' (1974/2005, p. 15) in which both outsider-activists and local people participate.

Problematising conscientisation

Freire's psychological theorisation of the process of conscientisation, with its division of consciousness into linear 'stages', is prone to overemphasis and simplification (Roberts, 1996; Cornish, 2004a). It also reveals a potential contradiction within Freire's work: that for dialogue to occur, interlocutors must recognise each other's knowledge as legitimate, and yet stages of consciousness are presented in a hierarchy along which a person can 'progress' (that is, advance), suggesting that some states of knowledge could be considered 'more legitimate' than others. The individualising of consciousness and its hierarchical ordering have been criticised on philosophical grounds (Berger, 1974; Cornish, 2004a) and for the rationalist assumptions on which the model is based (Ellsworth, 1989; Blackburn, 2000). In outlining such an individualistic, psychological model of critical consciousness, Freire appears to step away from the engagement with power and the broader social field so explicit in his overall body of writing (see Box 2.3 for more on critiques of Freire's work).

However, in her critique of the psychological emphasis inherent in a 'stages' model of the conscientisation process, Cornish (2004a) finds a 'pragmatist angle from which 'critical consciousness' can be a productive concept' (p. 65). She notes that different interlocutors may bring to an interaction knowledge that is more or less useful for resolving a particular issue in a given context. Rather than viewing these different knowledges as being positioned in an absolute hierarchy, she notes the *context-dependent nature* of their productive use in achieving social change. It is the reflective co-construction of knowledge inherent in the conscientisation process that supports actors to identify, test, and implement strategies for transformative action in the social world.

Grappling with power and empowerment

The complex and dual-edged nature of a social change agenda gives rise to a major challenge within Freire's work. Freire's pedagogy emerged from, and at the same time sustained, a lifetime of committed political activism. His theorisation of social change merges with the practice of engaged politics in working towards liberatory goals: 'I reject categorically realpolitik, which simply anesthetise the oppressed and postpone indefinitely the necessary transformations in society' (Freire, 1998, p. 75). Freire contends that all education is ideological, and is transparent concerning the ideological presuppositions of his own position. ('Even before I ever read Marx I had made his words my own', Freire [1998, p. 115]). This challenges all those working within a Freirian framework to be equally as transparent in naming their own agenda for social change.

However, Ellsworth (1989) notes that in the writings of those inspired by Freire there is 'widespread use of code words such as "critical" which hide the actual political agendas' (p. 300) that the authors are working towards. While this may in part result from the pragmatism (or realpolitik?) required of those working within repressive social structures, it can also result from the non-reflexive (mis)use of Freire's methods on the part of the outsider-change agent. Where outsider-change agents obscure their political agenda they prevent this position being problematised, interrogated, and evaluated by the other, and rather assume the superiority of their world-view, a consciousness to which others need to be 'raised'. In this situation, rather than dialogue, there is the risk of manipulation, domination, and 'the inappropriate imposition of a certain vision of power on people who may not want to be empowered in the way that is being prescribed' (Blackburn, 2000, p. 11). While outsider-change agents may write about the unequal power relations present in the contexts within which they work (classrooms, communities, cooperatives etc.), the challenges that these inequalities present to dialogue are often glossed over to be dealt with through 'commit-ment', 'empathy', 'creativity', and 'love' on the part of the activist. The need for *all* participants in dialogue to grapple with power, including their own, is often downplayed in presumption of the justness of an empowerment agenda.

Even noting that his use of terminology is grounded in time and place, Freire's description of communities as 'the oppressed' can give the impres-sion of a group of people without power. Anthropologists suggest, however, that the notion of a 'powerless population' is highly questionable (Blackburn, 2000), with groups who have been marginalised by powerful others none-theless exhibiting resistance through various demonstrations of power including sabotage and defiance, subtle strategies of non-cooperation and non-participation (including non-participation in dialogue), and by means of different forms of talking back and silence.

As Foucault (1981) asserts, power is not a static structure but is a rela-tional, productive force (in this respect, see also Hook, 2007). It is within the relations between outsider-change agent and the groups with whom they work, and between those groups and privileged others in the social field, that power is productive. Understandings of power must recognise the con-struction of constraint, but also allow for the possibility of empowerment (Campbell, 2003).

Exposing the power relations between marginal groups and privileged others is at the heart of the Freirian problem-posing method, with possi-bilities for disrupting these relations emerging through dialogue. However, the unequal and contingent power *within* marginal groups is less explored in Freire's work. The multiple and contradictory positions within groups, indeed within individual participants, defy idealistic notions of 'commu-nity' working as one to disrupt power relations with privileged others. In addition, the power relations between outsider-change agents themselves and communities are often unexamined. Concurring with Blackburn's statement above, Rappaport emphasises the need for change agents to resist using their power to determine the social change agenda, but rather to listen to communities to 'allow them to tell us what it means to be empowered in their particular context' (Rappaport, 1995).

The imperative to listen to communities, however, raises the difficult issue of their often divided and conflicted nature (Campbell, 2003). In settings where harmony is prioritised (or indeed necessary for survival), conflict is often 'silent', and may be unnoticed by outsiders in their participatory and dialogical endeavours (Tam, 2006). When conflict is unacknowledged there is the risk that outsiders will reinforce local inequalities in unquestioning acceptance of the position of participating (privileged) representatives as the authentic 'voice of the people'.

The real-world contexts of interventions intending to effect social change are complex and do not readily lend themselves to a dialogical approach. As Ellsworth notes, 'Acting as if our classroom were a safe space in which democratic dialogue was possible and happening did not make it so' (1989, p. 315). Working within a Freirian framework poses inherent challenges and involves putting 'praxis' into 'practice' – that is, the critical and intentional reflection upon, and enaction of, strategies to foster a communicative space where dialogue and critical thinking are possible and where domination can be recognised and resisted. That the achievement of dialogue is a fraught and complex process does not mean that Freire's notion of dialogue is not useful in practice in real-world settings, but it does suggest that the Freirian notion of genuine dialogicality is a Weberian ideal type of communication

Box 2.4   Critiquing Freire

Critiques of Paulo Freire's work – and of the way he has been idolised, romanticised and at times misunderstood – are plentiful. Authors have criticised his writing style, which is often abstract and convoluted. His writings can seem far removed from the reality of his experience of literacy programmes with poor men and women, living in concretely difficult circumstances, and with – presumably – very real barriers to praxis and transformation. Critics argue that his writing is at times so ambiguous that activities with a polarised range of agendas have claimed to have 'Freirian roots'. In response, Freire claims that 'My language *has* to be contradictory in order to grasp a contradictory reality' (Freire 1981, cited in Facundo, 1984).

Freire's pedagogy has also been criticised as being hopelessly idealistic: 'Utopianism is a problem in Freire's thought. It is evident in an uncritical tendency to regard his notion of literacy as the key to liberation' (Stanley, 1972, pp. 392–3). Stanley goes on to note that Freire does not take much note of the complexities, and the dark side, of what liberation might actually entail. Freire's work gives the impression that people are either the oppressed or oppressors, with little acknowledgement of the inherently contradictory and contextual nature of human relations in all societies. Elias and Merriam (1980) put it this way: 'His theory of conscientisation depends on some sort of transcendent view of reality through which individuals come to see what is real and authentic. There appears to be little room in his view for the painful struggling with different views and opposing viewpoints' (Elias and Merriam, 1980).

Freire argues that 'the dialogical man' has faith in other men but that 'his faith, however, is not naïve. The "dialogical man" is critical and knows that although it is within the power of men to create and transform, in a concrete situation of alienation men may be impaired in the use of that power' (1970, p. 63). Freire goes on to acknowledge that this impairment in the use of power strikes the dialogical man as a 'challenge to which he must respond'. However, beyond his emphasis on dialogue, literacy, and conscientisation, Freire rarely engages with the complexities of *how* actors can actually respond to this challenge in real-world contexts of oppression.

While Freire's work strongly engages with the structural conditions of the oppressed in *theory*, it has been criticised for insufficiently acknowledging the impact of context on the way his pedagogy may unfold in *practice*. This includes his neglect of the gendered nature of oppression (hooks, 1993; Weiler, 1994) and of the acutely historical and situated nature of any successful revolutionary social change (Darcy de Oliveira and Dominice, 1974; Woock, 1972). In analysing Freire's literacy work in Guinea-Bissau, Blanca Facundo (1984) emphasises the social, structural, and political complexities of Guinean society, noting that these do not appear to have been considered by Freire in his work with the government to implement literacy programmes across the country. Facundo suggests that in his conceptualisation of problems as fundamentally a political struggle between the oppressed and oppressors, Freire does not address the practical material conditions of working with marginalised communities or provide guidance on actionable strategies for doing so. In emphasising the struggle of the oppressed, and urging the middle and upper classes to commit 'class suicide' in order to side with the masses, Freire's work has also been criticised as leaving the role of top-down direction and policy change unexplored.

However, in his later work in particular, Freire recognises the role of catalysts working within institutions in providing support to social movements advocating for social change from the grassroots: 'I have been trying to think and teach by keeping one foot inside the system and the other foot outside ... to have an effect, I cannot live on the margins of the system. I have to be in it' (Freire, 1985, p. 178). Critiques that Freire is 'too theoretical' and does not provide sufficient 'concrete guidance' are perhaps based in the limited view that Freire's work simply outlines a series of techniques or a method – rather than an *approach* to promoting social transformation (Mayo, 1999). In warning against 'cultural invasion', Freire emphasises that techniques he has used in different settings cannot and should not be 'transplanted' from one context to another, but that his approach to the development of (political) literacy, dialogue, and praxis should rather be 'reinvented' to fit with local context (Freire, 1978). Freire's emphasis on two-way learning and questioning suggests that he would welcome practitioners engaging in dialogue with and about his work – and that through the critical interrogation and problematising of his approach, and how it might unfold in different settings, new knowledge could emerge.

to strive towards and against which communicative encounters can be assessed.

It is worth noting that many of the problems noted here in respect of the alleged idealism of equal dialogical communications are not faced by Freire alone. Most of these dilemmas will in fact be revisited by Habermas, whose theory of communicative action – as discussed in detail in Chapter 6 – responds to these problems with a very different set of theoretical tools. The current chapter is thus best read in conjunction with Chapter 6, which extends the debate apropos the possibility of equal non-strategic forms of communicative engagement.

Conclusion: Research and practice for social change

This chapter has drawn upon Paulo Freire's pedagogical theory to explore the notion that genuine communication between two actors will change how *both* participants understand and act upon the world. If communication has in fact taken place, the *communicative goal will have changed* and become mutually determined through dialogue. This has direct implications for research and practice with a social change agenda.

Researchers and practitioners often acknowledge the foundational role of communication between self and other in efforts towards transforming social worlds. Communication is acknowledged as being at the basis of initiatives aimed at changing behaviour – how people act upon the world – in a range of sectors. However, the fact that *all* participants in a communicative interaction (be they experts or laypeople, teachers or students, agentic or marginalised) are subject to doxa, and that for communication to actually occur there is a need for all participants in the communicative process to change and come to new understandings, is far less often acknowledged by those working towards social change. Engaging in dialogical research and practice necessitates that practitioners are open to *themselves* changing and coming to new understandings, achieved through communication in safe social spaces, and to the 'reinvention' of approaches appropriate to that particular context. While not naïve to the structural barriers and struggles involved, this open stance is inevitability linked to practitioners working from a position of hope and possibility, perceiving the 'reality of oppression not as a closed world from which there is no exit, but as a limiting situation which they can transform' (Freire, 1970, p. 26). It is in this possibility that the radical potential of communication lies.

3
Nonverbal Communication in Everyday Multicultural Life

Ama de-Graft Aikins

Keywords: Culture; decoding; display rules; encoding; impression management; nonverbal behaviour; nonverbal communication; self-presentation.

In February 1995 Judge Lance Ito publicly reprimanded all persons attending the trial of O.J Simpson for displaying their emotions and reactions to courtroom events. Judge Ito said, 'Let me remind you that any reactions, gestures ... facial expressions ... made during these court sessions, especially when the jury is here, those activities are inappropriate and will result in your expulsion'.

(Aronson, Wilson and Akert, 1999, p. 106)

One of our leading artists had just made an enormous wooden figure of a god for a public square in Bori. I had not seen it yet but had read a lot about it. In fact it had attracted so much attention that it soon became fashionable to say it was bad or un-African. The Englishman was now saying that it lacked something or other.

'I was pleased the other day,' he said, 'as I drove past it to see one very old woman in uncontrollable rage shaking her fists at the sculpture ...'

'Now that's very interesting,' said someone.

'Well, it's more than that,' said the other. 'You see this old woman, quite an illiterate pagan, who most probably worshipped this very god herself; unlike our friend trained in European art schools; this old lady is in a position to know ...'

'Quite.'

It was then that I had my flash of insight.

'Did you say she was shaking her fist?' I asked. 'In that case you got her meaning wrong. Shaking the fist in our society is a sign of great honour and respect; it means you attribute power to the person or object.'

(Achebe, 1966, pp. 49–50)

If I am playing a real character, I'll watch endless footage and try to reach an understanding of what that person looked like – and behaved like – in a neutral state of being. And that involves delving into his physicality. Capote's voice, for example, was the strangest voice I'll ever have to do, so we looked at the anatomical basis of the voice, we looked at how his jaw was formed, we explored whether he'd been tongue-tied, and then we noticed that actually he had a very long tongue. We could also see that he's been ashamed of his teeth. And then you move from observing the specifics of his behaviour to exploring how they might have come about. So in relation to the fact that he always spoke very loudly, we knew, for example, that he had been brought up by four old women, so he probably had to raise his voice to be heard. But it's also possible that they formed a willing audience for him from a very young age, and so he was used to people listening to him. And when I've begun to get a feel for that, then I can work upwards.

(Jones, 2009)

Nonverbal communication has been described as 'the silent but eloquent language' (Baron and Byrne, 1994, p. 42). This is an apt description, because nonverbal communication constitutes 'bodily communication' (Argyle, 1975) that expresses our inner feelings, reactions, and personality and facilitates our understanding of the inner feelings, reactions, and personalities of others in a variety of potent ways that do not only support spoken language but also often transcend spoken language. Nonverbal communication is crucial to everyday communication in many human societies. It constitutes a 'body language' that is expressed through a number of basic embodied (biological) channels that encompass facial expression, use of the eyes, of the voice, of the whole body and of (bodily) space (see Table 3.1). Nonverbal communication serves a number of important functions including emotional expression, **self-presentation**, conveying attitudes and behavioural intentions, regulating interpersonal interactions (including intimate relations), and – as the first opening quotation suggests – facilitating or undermining verbal communication (Argyle, 1975; Patterson, 2001; Richmond et al., 2008). Aronson, Wilson and Akert (1999) argue that Judge Ito was forced to outlaw **nonverbal communication** in his American courtroom because of its powerful and potentially disruptive nature, especially for a case as controversial, and 'racially' charged, as the African

Table 3.1 Six types of nonverbal behaviours at different levels of analysis

	Cultural	Gender	Personality and individual differences
Physical appearance	Different cultures have different dress codes (e.g. Islamic dress and western dress). Different cultures establish different codes around body shapes, height, weight and skin colour or shade. For example, in some non-western societies (such as African), plumpness or fat, especially among women, is equated to health, wealth, and beauty (Prentice, 2006). In European countries, thinness is preferred (ibid.).	Women are reported as typically weight conscious in western societies, e.g. US and UK. But the gender gap is closing with more men taking up diets in these societies. Similar arguments are made for gender differences in managing physical attractiveness.	There is a consensus that one's body shape and size can communicate nonverbal messages. Sheldon (1940, 1942, 1954, cited by Richmond et al., 2008) pioneered the idea of three different body shapes: endomorph (rounded, oval shaped, and heavy), mesomorph (triangular body shape, firm and muscular), ectomorph (bony, thin, tall, and fragile-looking). Each body shape is hypothesised to determine a specific set of psychological characteristics that shape nonverbal communication. An individual's height, weight, and skin colour ('race') or skin shade ('caste' in Indian cultures; 'shadism' in African cultures) also determine their nonverbal behaviours and others' interpretation of these behaviours.
Kinesics *The study of gesture and the movements of the body and their communicative functions; e.g. emblems, affect displays (which include posture and gait).*	Emblems are culturally specific. Even when a physical gesture embodied by an emblem is identical across two or more cultures, the meaning it evokes differs in these countries (e.g. the 'OK' sign is shared by many countries, but the emblem means OK in the US, money in Japan, 'zero' in France, and sex in Mexico). Different cultures often impose rules on affect displays such as posture.	Studies suggest that women tend to use compliant and acquiescent gestures (e.g. pull in their bodies, play with their hair, lower their eyes, cross legs, and keep legs and feet together). Men tend to use dominant or commanding gestures (e.g. take up more space, stare more, stand with legs apart, sit with legs stretched out).	Individual physical appearance (see above) will often shape gestures and movements. Height, for example, can shape limb movements and stride. Age and membership to subcultures can also shape gestures and movements. For example, older people may walk with a shuffling gait.

(continued)

Table 3.1 Continued

Face and eye behaviour	In some cultures, such as in the US and Japan, display rules forbid men from expressing extreme sadness or joy. This is in direct contrast to the display rules for men in some Arabic cultures. Some cultures (Latin American, southern European, Arab) focus their gaze on the eyes or face when talking and listening. Others (northern European, Indian-Pakistani, Asian, some African countries) avert the gaze.	Women express their emotions more accurately than men. Women also tend to look more on all measures of the gaze compared to men. These gender differences are often attributed to cultural display rules and societal norms around gendered behaviour.	Personality characteristics affect eye behaviour. Dominant and extrovert individuals gaze more steadily. Shy individuals establish less eye contact.
Paralinguistics *The study of aspects of communication that are not purely linguistic, i.e. not morphophonemic, syntactic or semantic; e.g. meanings conveyed by tone of voice, pacing, pausing, emphasis, hems and haws, snorting etc.*	Languages across cultures differ in tonal quality, e.g. soft, harsh or nasal. Within cultures, different regions often produce different dialects and accents that shape voice quality. Other paralinguistic practices are specific to certain regional cultures. For example 'kissing teeth' (Figueroa and Patrick) is a common practice in the Caribbean and some African societies. Silence can be used to increase or decrease psychological distance. Some cultures, such as Japanese, have mastered the use of silence in conversation (Braithwaite, 1999)	Addington (1986) identifies nine qualities of the voice: breathiness, thinness, flatness, nasality, tenseness, throatiness, orotundity, increased rate, increased pitch variety. These qualities of the voice are often assigned male and female characters. For example, people like a breathy or high-pitched quality more in a woman's voice than in a man's; they also like throatiness more in a man's voice than in a woman's.	Addington's (1986) nine qualities of the voice are also applicable in terms of individual differences. Each quality shapes the impression people have of speakers; see e.g. Jones (2009) on Truman Capote's voice quality.

Proxemics *The study of space and its use in different social and cultural situations.*	High-contact cultures (e.g. Latin American, southern European, Arab) interact at closer distances. Low-contact cultures (e.g. North American, northern European, Asian, Pakistani, Indian) interact at greater distances.	Studies suggest that women interact at closer distances compared to men. However, there are a number of caveats. For example, male-to-female dyads interact more closely than either male-to-male and female-to-female; women approach their best friends very closely whereas men do not discriminate between close or 'just' friends.	Extroverts, low authoritarians and people with high self-concepts require and use less space when interacting, compared to introverts and people with general anxiety dispositions (Richmond and McCroskey, 1998; Hickson, Stacks and Moore 2004). People maintain greater social distances with individuals with physical and social stigmas (Hickson, Stacks and Moore 2004).
Haptics (Touch) Touch	Low-contact cultures (North Americans, Europeans, Japanese) exhibit less frequent body contact compared to high-contact cultures (e.g. Latin Americans). Studies show complexities in this area. For example, in Latin America subcultural differences in touch have been identified (Shuter, 1976).	Women appear to touch more than men. However, US studies show that women discriminate more about acceptable body parts to touch compared to men. Women associate the type of touch and the body part being touched in terms of friendship or sexual desire (Richmond et al., 2008).	The concept of touch apprehension divides people into two categories: *high touchers* (who constantly touch friends and acquaintances) and *touch avoiders* (who rarely touch). Extroverts are more likely to be touchers, introverts are likely to be touch avoiders.

American O.J Simpson's alleged double murder of his White American ex-wife Nicole Brown Simpson and her friend Ronald Goldman.

There is a vast multidisciplinary body of work on nonverbal communication and behaviour with antecedents in Darwin's (1872) *The Expression of Emotion in Man and Animals*. Research traditions span anthropology, architecture, communication, and psychology. In psychology, Patterson (2001) identifies two main groups which have worked in this area. The first group comprises social psychologists and communication scholars who have focused on how nonverbal communication is produced, expressed, sent or, to use the technical term, 'encoded'. The second group comprises social cognition researchers who have focused on how nonverbal communication is perceived, received, interpreted or 'decoded'. Traditionally these groups have worked in isolation from one another (Patterson, 2001). However, there has been a recent collaborative shift in focus to how both expression and interpretation of nonverbal communication occur simultaneously. This is because in everyday communicative encounters we engage in both processes. As we express ourselves verbally and nonverbally to friends or strangers, we listen to, observe, and even anticipate their verbal and nonverbal responses to us (see also Vaughan, Chapter 2; and Franks and Dhesi, Chapter 12 on embodied representations).

This chapter offers a social psychological reading of nonverbal communication in everyday multicultural life. It is presented in three parts. In the first part I examine the extent to which **culture** influences the expression and interpretation of nonverbal communication. Research suggests that there are pan-cultural (biological, universal) and intracultural (group, individual) dimensions to nonverbal communication (see Table 3.1). I review research evidence on nonverbal communication at these levels of analysis. This provides the relevant context for deconstructing the complex role of culture, society, and self in nonverbal communication in multicultural contexts.

The second part explores the nature of nonverbal communication within multicultural settings. While biology, culture, and personality in combination determine the way we behave and communicate nonverbally, communication occurs in specific contexts, between specific people. Barker (1968, cited by Patterson, 2001) refers to the 'behavioural settings' that host (communicative) encounters between people who often have some type of relationship with one another. Researchers identify three mediators of behavioural settings: the social environment, the cognitive-affective state of the communicators, and social cognition and behavioural processes. The 'behavioural settings' and mediators of nonverbal communication offer complex permutations of successful and unsuccessful communication goals (see Tables 3.1 and 3.2). Multicultural nonverbal communication is examined through these three mediators.

I draw on eclectic sources of everyday multicultural interaction in the UK and the US to present key ideas: available research (within and outside the

Table 3.2 Types of cross-cultural contact

Contact variables	Between members of the same society (usually interracial, interethnic and subcultural)		Between members of different societies (usually intercultural/cross-cultural/transcultural or international)	
	Type	Example	Type	Example
On whose territory	Usually joint	White Americans or British and second-third generation minority groups (e.g. African-Americans/Black British; Asian-Americans/British Asian)	Home or foreign territory	Tourists; overseas students; immigrants and their respective hosts
Time-span	Long-term	White Americans or British and second-third generation minority groups	Short-term Medium-term Long-term	Tourists; Overseas students; Immigrants
Purpose	Make a life in	White Americans or British and second-third generation minority groups	Make a life in Study in Make a profit Recreation	Immigrants Overseas students Workers (e.g. transnational) Tourists
Type of involvement	Participate in society	White Americans or British and second-third generation minority groups	Participate Exploit Contribute Observe	Immigrants Workers Experts (e.g. development) Tourists
Frequency of high contact	High to low (variable)	White Americans or British and second-third generation minority groups	High Medium Low	Immigrants (variable) Overseas students Tourists

(continued)

Table 3.2 Continued

Degree of intimacy between participants	High to low social distance (variable)	White Americans or British and second-third generation minority groups	High to low social distance (variable)	Immigrants Overseas students Tourists
Relative status of power	Equal to unequal (variable)	White Americans or British and second-third generation minority groups	Equal to unequal (variable)	Immigrants Overseas students Tourists
Numerical balance	Majority-minority	White Americans or British and second-third generation minority groups	Majority-minority	Host and students Immigrants Tourists
Visible distinguishing characteristics	Race	White Americans/British vs African-Americans/Black British Asian (e.g. Hindu, Sikh) Muslims	Race	Immigrants (black vs white; Christian vs Muslim; national languages)
	Religion		Religion	
	Language	Original languages of second-third generation minority groups	Language	Overseas students (as above) Tourists (as above)

Source: Adapted from Bochner (1982) and Richmond et al. (2008).

field of nonverbal communication), autobiographies, television, film, and the mass media. The literature on multicultural or intercultural nonverbal communication deals with communicative encounters between social groups or individuals marked by the difference of culture, ethnicity or 'race'. Thus difference, unfamiliarity, misunderstandings, and emotional tensions lie at the core of these communicative processes.

Conceptually, my reading of the literature is informed by concepts and theories in social psychology, and in particular the social representations theoretical (SRT) tradition (Moscovici and Duveen, 2001), which coalesce around three themes. The first theme focuses on the importance of understanding different levels of social organisation in the production of practical social knowledge (Bochner, 1982; Doise, 1986, Moscovici and Duveen, 2001). Doise (1986), for instance, identifies four interrelated levels of analyses: the intrapersonal or intrasubjective, the interpersonal or intersubjective, the social group, and ideological.[1] Within the SRT tradition a similar argument is made. Moscovici (1998) places emphasis on the shifting nature of social representations at different levels of social organisation:

> There is a world of difference between representations envisaged at the person-to person level and at the level of the relations between individuals and group, or at the level of a society's common consciousness. At each level, representations have a completely different meaning. The phenomena are related but different.
>
> (p. 228)

The second theme focuses on the importance of everyday experience, and attitudes to the familiar and unfamiliar, in the construction of practical social knowledge (Bartlett, 1932; Flick, 1998; Moscovici and Duveen, 2001). SRT (Flick, 1998; Mosocvici and Duveen, 2001) takes 'everyday life' as its unit of analysis and focuses on the production of practical social knowledge within this context. A central aspect of SRT is the emphasis placed on the production of social knowledge through encounters with the unfamiliar. Anthropological studies identify different types of cultures on the basis of their 'preferred persistent tendency' towards the unfamiliar: cultures can be 'closed', 'adversarial', 'accommodative' or 'open'. As Bartlett observes, it is important to study how the 'preferred persistent tendencies' of different cultures are 'organised and arranged' in order to understand both how the group directly constrains the individual and how the group itself may be best controlled, if rearrangements of the basic tendencies are desired in response to a changing environment' (Bartlett, 1932: 255, 258). This necessitates nuanced attention to social group and individual differences in relation to the novel and strange, and especially the familiar stranger (e.g. in the multicultural context, the publicly known but privately misunderstood ethnic minority or majority group/member). Finally, I consider the role of dialogicality in producing effective communication at different levels of social organisation (Markova, 2003). Dialogicality has been defined as knowledge (including self-knowledge) constructed through Ego (self), Alter (other) and Object, or the 'capacity of the human mind to conceive, create, and communicate about social realities in terms of, or in opposition to, otherness (Markova, 2003, p. 231). I explore the possibility that social groups or individuals who possess the ability to take the perspective of the other (Mead, 1962) are more effective intercultural nonverbal communicators. In the final part of the chapter I draw on these concepts to examine the implications of the discussed research for positive nonverbal communication in multicultural settings.

Nonverbal communication: Multilevel dimensions

Three basic or primary determinants of nonverbal communication are recognised: biology, culture, and personality.

Universal (biological) dimensions of nonverbal communication

Evolutionary theories have been posited for the role of biology in shaping adaptive patterns of communication, especially in the area of facial expression (Eibl-Eibesfeldt, 1970; Fridlund, 1994; Box 3.1; see also Franks and Dhesi, Chapter 12, on a comprehensive discussion of the evolutionary basis for communication). For example, research on the *encoding* and *decoding* of facial expression demonstrates that six emotions are universal: anger, fear, happiness, surprise, sadness, and disgust (Ekman and Friesen, 1986; Russell, 1991). This evidence was first produced by a series of cross-cultural field experiments, conducted by Ekman and colleagues in the 1970s, in which New Guinean and American research participants were able to decode six emotions expressed in photographs by American and New Guinean individuals, respectively. While these studies and follow-up studies have been criticised on conceptual and methodological grounds, their fundamental insights, of a restricted set of universal emotions, remain true (Ekman, 2003; Markus and Kitayama, 1991; Sweder and Haidt, 2003).

For instance, in a cultural analysis of emotions in third-century Sanskrit, Shweder and Haidt (2003) note that Hindu philosophers of poetics and drama posited the existence of eight or nine basic emotions: (a) sexual passion, love or delight; (b) amusement, laughter, humour or mirth; (c) sorrow; (d) anger; (e) fear or terror; (f) perseverance, energy, dynamic energy or heroism; (g) disgust or disillusion; (h) amusement, wonder, astonishment or amazement; (i) serenity or calm (pp. 139–40). The authors compare the Sanskrit emotions with Ekman's list of basic emotions and observe that the 'two lists are not closely coordinated, although they are not totally disjoint either' (p. 144).

The evidence of a universal set of basic emotions suggests that in the area of decoding, at least, an 'innate emotion perceptual ability' (Altarriba et al., 2003) is the primary mediating factor.

Cultural dimensions of nonverbal communication

While some aspects of nonverbal communication – such as basic emotions – are mediated by universal, biologically rooted processes, culture plays a key role in expression, interpretation, and functions (Gudykunst, Ting-Toomey and Nishida, 1996; Hall, 1966; Shweder and Haidt, 2003). In the second opening quotation, the novelist Chinua Achebe's fictional account of European misunderstandings of (Nigerian) Igbo nonverbal behaviour describes the way one gesture – shaking the fist – embodies anger in the former culture and respect in the latter.

Research on emotion expression provides insights on the role of culture in nonverbal communication. The sociologist Arlie Russell Hochschild (2003) discusses the concept of 'the collectively shared emotional dictionary'. This concept essentially describes the lexicon of emotions prevalent and sanctioned in a society. Hoschschild notes that 'like other dictionaries, the emotional dictionary reflects agreement among the authorities of a given time and place. It expresses the idea that within an emotional "language group" there are given emotional experiences, each with its own ontology'. The literature suggests that within each collectively shared emotional dictionary there will be at least three categories of emotions. The first category constitutes primary emotions: 'natural emotion responses' that are biologically given and exist independently of sociocultural influences and learning. These encompass the six aforementioned emotions that are shared across cultures. The second category constitutes 'secondary' emotions which are acquired through socialising agents: these include guilt, shame, pride, gratitude, love, and nostalgia (Kemper, 1987). Guilt, for example has been described as socialized fear (of punishment for inappropriate behaviour); shame as socialized anger (with self); and pride as socialized satisfaction. Socio-culturally mediated emotional phenomena which straddle the universal and particular, such as 'saving face', can be placed under this category. Emotions that are clearly labelled in one culture but not others, but which can be expressed in these foreign cultures, can also be placed under this category. Two examples are the much discussed German emotion word *schadenfreude*, defined as 'the malicious enjoyment of another's misfortune' and the English emotion word 'depression'.[2] Altarriba and colleagues (2003) observe: '[A]lthough there may not be a one word equivalent across cultures it is possible that languages can express emotions and ideas other than those that are coded in single words.' The final category constitutes emotions that are culture-bound. Researchers often highlight highly culturally specific emotions that have no lexical equivalents in other cultures. For example, the contemporary Hindu conception of *lajja* (Shweder and Haidt, 2003) is an emotion, a moral state that applies to both men and women but is 'a virtue [more] associated with a certain feminine ideal'. Women display *lajja* the way that western cultures 'might show gratitude, loyalty or respect' – e.g. acting shyly, modestly, covering one's face, remaining silent, lowering one's eyes. Therefore it has been described in western linguistic terms as 'shame', 'embarrassment' 'shyness' or 'modesty'. However, the roots and functions of *lajja* are more complex than Western equivalents; *lajja* helps 'women swallow their rage' at the way patriarchal systems exploit female power, strength, and perseverance, and by so doing maintains the social order in less emotionally destructive ways (Shweder and Haidt, 2003, p. 160).

Alongside emotional lexicons, cultures have display rules regarding emotional expression. Often these rules are gendered. For example, American cultural norms discourage emotional displays in men – 'big boys don't cry' – but encourage emotional displays in women (Ramsey, 1981). Japanese cultural norms discourage the excessive display of facial expression compared to the West and encourage the masking of negative emotions with smiles and laughter. Furthermore, while women are discouraged from exhibiting wide uninhibited smiles, women are allowed to be more facially expressive compared to men (Ramsay, 1981). Some South Asian cultures prohibit women from expressing anger through the use of *lajja* (Shweder and Haidt, 2003).

Fundamentally, culture is important but has limits. Culture is important because it circumscribes the **nonverbal behaviours** (emotional expression, affect displays, language and voice quality) and influences the ability to express and interpret nonverbal communication and behaviours through display rules. But culture has limits, because individual and gendered level nonverbal behaviours often bypass or transcend cultural codes during communication.

Individual dimensions of nonverbal communication

While culture exerts significant influence on the way individuals express themselves nonverbally, unique individual characteristics such as physical appearance, voice quality, mood, level of engagement or disengagement with a situation also shape individual expression (see Table 3.1). In the third opening quotation, a technical study by British actor Toby Jones of the physicality of Truman Capote in preparation for the 2006 film *Infamous* demonstrates how a complex interplay of physiology (the anatomy and quality of voice), personality (image fixation and high self-monitoring), and personal history (dynamics of upbringing) mediate an individual's system of nonverbal expression. If we turn attention to personality types, distinctions have been made between extroverts and introverts, high-anxiety individuals and low-anxiety individuals, individuals with high self-concepts and those with low self-concept, between high self-monitors and low self-monitors, and a vast range of other opposing personality types. These personality types have been identified across different cultures and especially through the clinical work of psychiatrists, psychologists, and other therapists, as well as through employment-oriented personality tests. For example, extroverts exhibit a collection of traits including being 'talkative, outgoing, cheerful, social and less bound by societal norms' (Richmond et al., 2008, p. 149); introverts are characterised by being 'less talkative, more shy, emotionally fragile and socially withdrawn' (ibid). Studies consistently show that extroverts tend to project confidence in an interpersonal or group encounter and use closer distances, gaze more and for longer periods, touch more and use encouraging facial expressions such as a smile. The opposite is true for introverts. High self-monitors are 'social chameleons' – they are able to adapt their behaviour to different social situations. Low self-monitors show a high degree of behavioural consistency across social situations. High self-monitors are more successful at self-presentation and **impression management**, such as in masking inappropriate emotions in public, projecting the correct affect displays, and flattering when the situation demands it. Low self-monitors struggle with these social tasks. Because communication occurs in specific settings between specific people, individuals who are able to manage the different demands of different 'behavioural settings' will have greater success with communication and social interaction.

Secondary determinants of nonverbal communication: Gender and 'race'

These basic determinants of nonverbal communication often combine to produce secondary determinants. Gender and 'race', for example, are secondary determinants. They are viewed as a combination of 'biology (the hardwired patterns) and culture (societal norms)' (Patterson 2001, p. 163) or as 'primitive' categories (femaleness, maleness, skin colour) that are immediately processed perceptually and are thus prioritised over all other possible categories (Brewer, 1988).

Research on gender differences has focused primarily on facial expression, the use of space and touch, and voice quality. Major findings suggest that women tend to gaze more during interpersonal interactions, use less distance, and touch more compared to men (Gamble and Gamble, 2003). Put together, these social skills make women more successful at self-presentation and at decoding self-presentation. Differences have been attributed to biology: women and men inherit different bone structures and body types that determine nonverbal behaviours such as posture, gestures and walk (Richmond et al., 2008; see Table 3.1). Gendered social roles and stereotypes in many cultures are also implicated. For example, women are socialised to be responsive and nurturing, while men have to be assertive and emotionally aloof. However, there is counter-evidence that bridges the gender gap. For example, while women are excellent in decoding nonverbal behaviours, they lose this superior skill when confronted with deceptive individuals.

A recent global study on deception which focused on 2230 individuals from 58 countries, demonstrated that both men and women were generally poor at detecting lies from behaviour being expressed as the lie is told; most tended to engage in retrospective decoding (GDT, 2006).

Laboratory-based studies have examined the decoding of non-verbal communication in intercultural and 'interracial' encounters. Research has focused on facial recognition (e.g. Teitelbaum and Geiselman, 1997), the ability to decode intensity of facial expression (e.g. Matsumoto et al., 2002), the ability to decode affect displays (e.g. Bailey et al., 1998; Weathers et al., 2002) and the implicit associations ('preconscious automaticity') individuals make of different groups (e.g. Payne, 2001). This body of work provides important psychological and sociological insights including: (a) some 'race' groups (African American, White American) are better adapted to recognising same-group faces than faces from other groups; (b) some cultural/ethnic groups (Latino, Asian) can recognise faces from other races (White American) with relatively high accuracy; (c) there is greater accuracy for recognising faces for other races when one is in an unpleasant mood; (d) some 'races' (White American) are better at identifying emotion in the tone of voices and posture of their in-group and of different races and ethnic groups; and (e) there is a tendency for different racial groups (including black) to automatically associate black skin colour with negative attributes. Most studies conclude that there are racial differences in the ability to decode nonverbal communication. Some suggest that the differences disappear when the effects of acculturation are removed (Bailey et al., 1998) or when interracial experience and familiarity is factored into experiments.

As noted earlier, while biology, culture, and personality in combination shape nonverbal behaviours and communication, the specific context within which communication unfolds is a critical determinant of the quality and outcome of nonverbal communication. Context underscores the importance of examining nonverbal communication at different levels of social organisation, of focusing on the 'related but different' representational phenomena (Moscovici, 1998). In the next section of the chapter I focus on how behavioural settings and mediators of these settings shape multicultural nonverbal communication.

Nonverbal communication in everyday multicultural contexts: Behavioural settings and mediators

The social environment and multicultural nonverbal communication

The social environment and the primary determinants provide the context for communicative interaction: for instance, is the communicative encounter occurring in a familiar or unfamiliar location with a stranger, acquaintance, friend or romantic partner?

Two areas of research on intercultural communication provide useful insights. The first has focused on intercultural encounters: (mis)communication when westerners travel (e.g. US businessmen in Japan or US teachers in Nigeria or China) or when westerners are confronted by immigrants on home turf (e.g. US teachers and immigrant students, US students and immigrant teachers, or co-workers) (Richmond et al., 2008). These are often short encounters between strangers or acquaintances (see Table 3.2). Miscommunication centres on differences in nonverbal forms of greeting (the Japanese bow vs the American handshake), of showing attentiveness or respect (the Nigerian student's refusal to make eye contact as a sign of respect vs the American teacher's desire for eye contact as a sign of respect), of decoding vocal behaviour (the American teacher and the immigrant child with poor English skills and a foreign accent). There is an emerging body of reflexive accounts from 'westerners' with 'hyphenated identities' (Modood, 2004) – Japanese-American, British-Jamaican, British-Ghanaian, etc. – who return to their countries of origin and experience verbal and nonverbal intercultural miscommunication (Eshun, 2005; Kondo, 1990). This group of individuals have been acculturated into American or British culture and find they no longer share the cultural attributes of their home countries. Their affect displays and vocal behaviour (e.g. accent) set them apart even though they might share fundamental aspects of physical appearance.

The second area has focused on nonverbal communication within subcultures in urban western cities and predominantly on 'interracial' encounters. Like the afore-discussed laboratory studies, naturalistic studies highlight several instances of poor nonverbal communication in these encounters. In public spaces, such as streets and shops, the affect displays (posture, walk) of (usually young) black men are imputed with aggression and criminality by white and sometimes black people (Sewell, 1997). In schools, physical appearance (skin colour), vocal behaviour (dialect, accent), and affect displays (use of eye contact) are implicated in conscious and unconscious prejudiced communication between teachers and pupils (Connolly, 1998; see also Howarth, Chapter 7). Within law enforcement, frequent instances of racial bias have led to the term 'racial profiling', the process whereby some police officers impute black or brown skin with criminality. This has led to black, Asian, and Latino men being stopped, searched, and arrested disproportionately more often than young white men. In the UK, black men are six times as likely as white men to get stopped and searched by the police. Racial profiling has increased considerably for American Muslim men since 9/11 (AIUSA, 2004). A similar process is implicated in courtroom prejudice where poor cross-cultural readings of non-verbal behaviours leads to harsh sentencing of minority ethnic youth, especially Latinos and Blacks (Mustard, 2001). Finally, the transcultural psychiatry literature highlights the way in which experts impute meaning into 'national culture' and racial differences in nonverbal behaviours such as affect displays ('the physically imposing aggressive black male') and voice quality ('the loud Nigerian'). These misattributions can lead to misdiagnoses and the use of harsher pharmacological treatment and physical restraint (Ahmad, 1993).

The outcome of these interracial misunderstandings and miscommunication is usually negative, as in when it causes psychosocial stress for minority ethnic groups (Ahmad, 1993; Nazroo, 1997). Sometimes the outcome can be fatal, as in when miscommunication in the law enforcement, legal, and clinical settings leads to serious injury or death (the most famous examples being the brutal police beating of African American Rodney King in Los Angeles in 1991 and the police shooting of Jean Charles de Menezez in London in 2005).

The role of familiarity

The available evidence suggests that preconscious automaticity can shape (usually negative) communication in some settings. This happens both when the encounters are between strangers (e.g. racial profiling on the street and in the courtroom) and between individuals with some level of familiarity (e.g. school, therapy situation). However, intercultural communication is not always negative. Familiarity pays an important role, both in literal and representational terms. Ethnographic work on multicultural friendship groups suggests that everyday familiarity between different cultural and 'racial' groups fosters more positive communicative behaviours (Alexander, 1996, 2000; Baumann, 1996; Harris, 2006). Research shows that 'cosmopolitan' non-westerners and westerners actively adopt the nonverbal and verbal behaviours of the other, and thus become the bridge for successful intercultural communication (Appiah, 2006). This active learning and representational process, which involves taking the perspective of the other (Mead, 1962) is evident in multicultural friendship groups and offers a bridge for successful nonverbal communication within the contemporary multicultural setting.

Cognitive-affective states and multicultural nonverbal communication

Cognitive-affective mediators combine the cognitive resources we draw on to manage our everyday lives and the affective states that derive from our momentary dispositions (or mood), goals, relationship to the one(s) we are communicating with, and the constraints of the communicative setting (Patterson, 2001). Studies and clinical work on affective states demonstrate how positive emotional states such as happiness, interest, and relaxation determine fluid open body movements which in turn determine successful communication. In contrast, negative emotional states such as sadness, anger, and disgust determine tense and closed body postures and movements which can undermine the quality of communication. Laboratory studies on interracial nonverbal communication show that some 'races' (White American) are better at identifying emotion in the tone of voices and posture of their in-group and of different races and ethnic groups and there is greater accuracy for recognising faces for other races when one is in an unpleasant mood (see previous section).

This suggests that the nature of the nonverbal encounter will be shaped by the cognitive-affective states of the communicators (positive pairs of emotions, negative pairs of emotions or a pair of mismatched emotions) and the ability of both communicators to decode the other's cognitive-affective state. These processes will be shaped to some extent by the social environment (familiar or unfamiliar), cultural display rules (how to express cognitive-affective states), and the social identities of the communicators (in particular, ability to take perspective of the other or not).

Social cognition and behavioural factors in multicultural nonverbal communication

Social cognition and behavioural processes facilitate the regulation and monitoring of a communicative goal. Patterson (2001) observes that while social judgement may sometimes require reflection and behaviour may require monitoring and management, both processes for the most part operate automatically. With respect to social judgement, for example, 'preconscious automaticity' (Bargh, 1989, cited in Patterson, 2001) often operates. Preconscious automaticity occurs when the mere registration of a stimulus event (such as noticing an out-group person) in a person's sensory system sets off a judgement process that runs to completion without conscious awareness (a stereotype judgement). This process was demonstrated in the case studies of interracial encounters in schools, with the police and in courtrooms. With respect to behavioural processes, a cognitive representation of a goal (for example, impression management) is sufficient to trigger an automatic behavioural sequence (flattery, an ingratiating smile).

In the UK, 'coconut' and 'banana' are derogatory terms used by Black and Asian communities, respectively, to describe in-group members 'acting white'. Coconut denotes 'black on the outside, white on the inside', banana denotes 'yellow on the outside, white on the inside'. These terms reveal intra-group, and sometimes out-group, rules and processes around race-specific impression management.

Acting white – a simplistic stereotype itself that ignores a broad range of interethnic nonverbal behaviours in white majority groups – denotes specific sets of verbal and nonverbal middle-class white behaviours including vocabulary (extensive, devoid of street slang), vocal behaviours ('posh' or 'plummy' accent, measured tone, articulate), physical appearance ('preppy' dress style), and body movements (restricted, fewer illustrators). Black or Asian individuals who express themselves through these 'middle-class white' multi-level communication channels are believed (by their in-group members) to be successful at self-presentation and impression management during interracial encounters and thus – consciously or unconsciously – escape poor communication and its negative effects.[3] The most recent and famous example would be the charge by US Senator Harry Reid in his book *Game Change* (about the 2008 US presidential campaign) that US President Barack Obama had a good chance of being elected as America's first black president because he was 'light-skinned' and did not speak with a 'negro dialect, unless he wanted to have one'. While Harry Reid's views caused national controversy, some social commentators, including African American journalists and academics, conceded that the views were bad politics, but good sociology (The Week, 2010): Barack Obama was a successful interracial communicator because he possessed the ability to turn his 'blaccent' (black accent) on and off, depending on the social circumstances.

Future research directions

The nature and speed of globalisation in the late twentieth century has transformed the nature of migration and cross-cultural relations. Globalisation may be seen to be exerting its force in many spheres including economic, political, technological, cultural, and ecological. Its cultural impact is most relevant to our discussion. Theorists note that globalisation shrinks territorial space and creates new forms of consciousness and identities for many cultures (Cowen, 2002).

London accommodates at least 50 non-indigenous communities, each with populations of 10,000 or more, and more than 300 spoken languages (Benedictus, 2005).[4] Other major western cities like New York and Toronto boast similar globalised and multicultural status. If facial expressions, gestures, posture, and other nonverbal behaviours mean widely different things to different cultural groups then, many researchers argue, the potential for intercultural miscommunication in these multicultural cities is great. Crucially, the potential for miscommunication is further deepened by cultural and religious clashes in a 'post-terror world'. In many globalised cosmopolitan western cities, where different cultures and religions mingle, appearances have become deceptive. Minority ethnic groups who share the 'national culture' identity of the majority culture and simultaneously express Muslim identities are scrutinised and stigmatised on the basis of physical appearance, posture, vocal behaviour, and other embodied markers. Multiculturalism, with its key pillars of race, culture, and religion, has become a highly contested issue (Gilroy, 2004). The current consensus, in the UK at least, is that multiculturalism has failed (CRE/Ethnos, 2005; Gilroy, 2004). Instead of creating an 'assimilationist' convivial Britishness, multiculturalism has produced atomised separatist communities of majority and minority ethnic groups who do not know, or care to know, each other. Within this context, as Smith and Bond (1996) observe, research on culture and nonverbal communication goes beyond 'the academic' into the realm of practical everyday life: research provides a way of understanding the 'practical concerns when people from different cultures meet' even when these cultures coexist within nations sharing a broader single culture (p. 163).

Research challenges

Researchers recognise limitations in current approaches on intercultural communication. Some observe the problem of imposed etic with the examination of decoding in laboratory experiments. Others criticise the use of force-choice questions in the examination of emotional labels. The lack of work on nonverbal expression and decoding in real-life contexts, especially of multi-channel communication, is a third area of limitation (Altarriba et al., 2003; Smith and Bond, 1994). It is in this third area that a social psychology of socio-cultural change can contribute significantly.

There are at least four points worth noting about the body of work on intercultural nonverbal communication that open up avenues for transformational research. First, the negative interracial interactions and communication described usually occur between strangers. Encounters between strangers (the unfamiliar) – even those from the same cultural, racial, and ethnic group – are psychologically different from encounters between friends (the familiar) (Simmel, 1950; Gudykunst and Hammer, 1988; Moscovici and Duveen, 2001). Research suggests that race-based bias occurs with in-groups as well as out-groups. This adds a layer of complexity to the psychological determinants of encoding and decoding, which at the same time opens up new ways of conceptualising experimental and naturalistic experiments. Second, closer examination of the dynamics of interracial encounters suggests that gender, class, and personality mediate the negative effects of miscommunication. For example, young black men from low socio-economic backgrounds are most likely to be at the receiving end of the negative impact of nonverbal miscommunication, even within the black community.[5] Third, it is likely that a focus on interracial encounters between friends and partners might yield more nuanced insights for effective interventions. As the laboratory studies and the concept of behavioural settings suggest, the context, communicative partner, and socio-cognitive mediators are important in any nonverbal encounter. In laboratory studies familiarity undercuts the dominant finding of racially biased preconscious automaticity. Ethnographic research on multicultural friendship groups shows active intercultural borrowing of verbal and nonverbal behaviours (Alexander, 1996, 2000; Baumann, 1996; Harris, 2006). These borrowings are products of strong social identities forged through group membership: hip hop culture, for instance. Finally, specific subgroups – cosmopolitan groups, groups with hyphenated identities (see also Howarth, Chapter 7, on multicultural identities) – which are able to take the perspectives of the other may be better at intercultural communication. Fundamentally, successful intercultural communication, whether verbal or nonverbal, is rooted in dialogicality (Markova, 2003), it requires recognition and understanding of the (ethnic, cultural, racial) other.

Is positive multicultural nonverbal communication possible? In the practical everyday sense, current research suggests that 'it depends'. It depends on whether the focus is on encounters between strangers, acquaintances, friends or partners. It depends on whether these strangers, acquaintances, friends or partners belong to the same culture or ethnicity. It depends on where these encounters take place. It depends on the personalities and social status of the individuals engaged in the encounter, their affective states, the knowledge and (positive or negative) stereotypes or social representations they hold about both out-group and in-group members, and their skill at expressing and interpreting self-presentation and impression management. If all these factors are positively and naturally aligned, then the prognosis for intercultural and interracial communication between either strangers or friends will be good. If not, as often is the case in the messiness of everyday life, the prognosis can range from satisfactory to catastrophic.

Notes

1. The 'intrapersonal' or the intrasubjective level (shapes the 'mechanisms by which the individual organises her/his experience' (p. 11)); the 'interpersonal' or the intersubjective level ('the dynamics of the relations established at a given moment by given individuals in a given situation' (p. 12); the social (group) level ('the social experiences and social positions of subjects' (p. 14)); the 'ideological' or the structural level (constitutes societal 'ideologies, systems of beliefs and representations, values and norms, which validate and maintain the established social order' (p.15)).
2. While other cultures may have no lexical equivalent to *schadenfreude*, many have the propensity to feel and elaborate on this emotion (Spears and Leach, 2004). Similarly, while there is a claim that there is no word for 'depression' among many non-western cultural groups, a study conducted by Brandt and Boucher (1986) suggests that depression-type words were a part of both western and non-western cultures. Much of the research concerned with cross-cultural similarities and differences in emotion lexicons focuses on single words, such as 'love' and 'sadness' when it is more useful to examine more comprehensive feeling states (Altarriba et al., 2003; see also Shweder and Haidt (2003)).
3. The extent to which this strategy actually works is debatable. See the recent 'racial profiling' case of African American Harvard Professor Henry Louis Gates and ensuing discussions about the way 'uppity blacks' receive as much censure as low-class blacks in Obama's America (www.hufingtonpost.com; www.nytimes.com).
4. These include Americans, Australians, Brazilians, Canadians, Chinese, French, Ghanaians, Indians, Jamaicans, Nigerians, Pakistanis, Poles, Portuguese, Somalis, and Turks. Each community congregates in specific parts of the city. 'According to the last census, in 2001, 30% of London residents had been born outside England – that's 2.2 million people, to which we can add the unknown tens of thousands who didn't complete a census form' (Benedictus, 2005).
5. In terms of intraracial stereotyping, research shows how children across different cultures in the UK learn, by the age of five, to stigmatise black skin colour and the social attributes of black people. The classic Bobo doll experiments in the US yielded similar findings.

4
Social Influence: Modes and Modalities

Gordon Sammut and Martin W. Bauer

Keywords: Accommodation; assimilation; attitude; belief; compliance; conformity; conversion; deviance; imitation; informational influence; leadership; majority; minority; normalisation; normative influence; norms; obedience; persuasion; public sphere; social influence; soft power.

Introduction

Increased travelling and migration within and between regions of the world, and the multiplication of mass media of circulation in print and the digital space, have brought about radical changes and reshaped the nature of the modern **public sphere**. Contemporary public spheres are characterised by a plurality of views that seek expression and legitimacy in public approval. Individuals in modern societies, protected by freedom of speech, are entitled to hold views and opinions outside the dominant viewpoint, and to express them freely in the public domain. The modern public sphere is thus characterised by tensions of conflicting views and disagreements. Few places in the world, if any, remain Durkheimian in the sense that a dominant world view rules supreme as 'collective representation'. Modern individuals are routinely confronted by others whose views differ radically from their own (Benhabib, 2002; Jovchelovitch, 2007). Conflicting views expressed in public create tension as they undermine consensus and imply that some ideas, possibly one's own, may be incorrect. Communication is at the heart of this tension, that arises whenever individuals project and expose their ideas and opinions and others disagree, and the greater their distance, the greater the potential for conflict.

There are several universal ways of resolving conflict: by brute force or the threat of it; by appeal to an external authority; and by **social influence**. People may coerce others to adopt a perspective or behaviour by brute force and violence. Such 'hard power' (Nye, 1990, 2004) tactics eliminate deviants, physically or psychologically, and protect consensus by force or fear. Within the rule of law, 'civilised' modern states secure a monopoly of force vested in the police and the military, such that violence is no longer the default form of conflict resolution. Within such arrangements, the default method for conflict resolution arises from appeal to the law through the authority of courts. Conflicts over these rules make appeal to public discussion, where differences between interlocutors are displayed in conversation in an effort to bring people together in communication without redress either to the authority of the law, or to violence or the threat of it. The appeal is to recognise the authority of informal **norms** and the relevance of information provided. Truth claims can be tested as to their objective truth, expressive authenticity, and moral rightness, which thus have the power to convince and reconcile opposition (see Chapter 6 on communicative action). In this way conflict resolution is negotiated through the exercise of social influence within the public sphere. **Soft power** tactics aim at resolving conflict through communication, by convincing the other party that one's perspective is right. Social influence is the communication strategy that underlies soft power. The intended outcome is for the recipient of communication to shift their position in line with the source of the communicative act. Aside from coercion and appeal to authority, social influence is a conflict-resolution strategy resulting in consensus. Consensus is achieved by the elimination of discrepant views without the need for coercion. Social influence is a communicative genre that is 'rooted in conflict and strives for consensus' (Moscovici, 1985a, p. 352).

From a functionalist point of view, social influence is a generalised communication medium that constrains the interlocutors to make the improbable more likely, i.e. making communication successful. Like power and money it replaces the vagueness of language. In politics everything is settled by power, in the economy by money, in the public sphere by influence and prestige (see Parsons, 1963; Luhmann, 1990). However, this functional analogy of substituting complex language by a simpler medium does not fully extend to social influence. Contrary to money and power, social influence remains tied to the pragmatics of lifeworld conversations and cannot thus replace, but only complement, speech acts (Habermas, 1981, p. 408ff). Social influence cannot be reduced to one dimension, e.g. ethos, trust or prestige, but remains tied to the triplet of what is true (logos), right (ethos) and sincere (for more on this triplet see Chapter 5 on pragmatics, Chapter 6 on communicative action, and Chapter 10 on rhetoric).

Licit and illicit social influence: A grey area of morality

The distance between interlocutors defines the rhetorical situation (as discussed in Chapter 10 on rhetoric). In this situation, people reserve the right to influence each other, but without recourse to power. Consequently, one of the issues that arise is the fuzzy boundary between licit and illicit social influence. Figure 4.1 schematises an intuitive moral continuum between

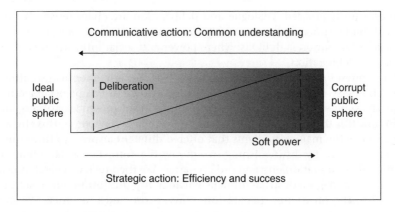

Figure 4.1   The intuitive continuum of social influence

extreme types. Any real-life context seems a mix of deliberation (towards the left) and soft power (towards the right), depicted in the graphic as a vertical cut through the rectangle. Social influence covers the hybrid space in the middle of this continuum, being neither power-free deliberation nor deliberation-free violence power, thus always dubious. Deliberation establishes a common understanding between interlocutors; soft power biases the understanding in one or the other direction. In practice, interlocutors often join a discussion with pre-established **beliefs** as to what might be true and right, i.e. their own position, and will seek ways to persuade others of the 'facts' through various means. Persuasive communication seems the 'magic bullet' that brings about a desired adjustment in others. Thus, communication is often strategic while the tactics to achieve this are flexible. Yet herein lies a productive attraction towards 'true deliberation' (see Chapter 2 on dialogical communication and Chapter 6 on communicative action) which, through understanding of the perspective of the other, brings about a change in one's own views and establishes a new basis from which both

Table 4.1   Modes and modalities of social influence

	Social order	Social change
Subrational	Obedience	Leadership
		Imitation
		Persuasion (peripheral)
Rational	Norm-setting	Conversion
	Conformity	Persuasion (central)
		Resistance to change

interlocutors proceed. Dialogue and deliberation are characteristics of the ideal public sphere, where not only the guns are silenced, but all strategic social intervention is dubious: where power and social influence was, there shall be deliberation.

The quest for the laws of social influence has concerned social and cultural psychologists since the nineteenth century. Two questions preoccupied this quest: (a) how individuals change their minds in the presence of others; and (b) how this this change of mind determines their behaviour. In this chapter we review the major paradigms that offered different answers to these questions. We start by distinguishing two modes (i.e. forms) of social influence: rationality/sub-rationality and order/change. We then review several modalities (i.e. strategies) of social influence: **leadership**, **imitation**, norm-setting, **conformity**, **obedience**, **persuasion**, **conversion**, and **resistance**. We conclude by exploring a cycle of influence that involves a dynamic interplay of modes and modalities in the formation of collective action. These modalities of influence are classified in Table 4.1.

Modes of influence

Two modes of influence are at work anytime a group attempts to change another group's perspective in line with its own. First, a dominant group might be concerned with the maintenance of order and the smooth coordination of social life, just as much as a **minority** group seeks recognition and hopes to bring the social order around towards its own perspective. Second, both rational and subrational social influence may serve to achieve social coordination and social change.

Creating and maintaining or changing the social order

Individual behaviour in society is regulated by social norms that permit certain acts and prohibit others; thus we coordinate collective activity. Social norms establish what is normal in a group and in society and what is deviant, in terms of behaviours, **attitudes**, perceptions and beliefs. **Deviance** is branded abnormal and antisocial by a dominant group, usually a **majority**, which seeks the preservation of a normative order that bestows it with legitimacy and rightness (Paicheler, 1988). Once conflict breaks out because of a minority challenge that arises from divergent perspectives, the dominant group seeks to preserve the status quo. Social conflict is thus characterised by mutual attempts at mobilising social influence with the quest for order on the one side and a quest for change of this order on the other (Moscovici, 1985a).

A conflict between a dominant group and a subordinate deviant group is a situation of asymmetrical relations. Importantly, however, although the power of A over B might be stronger than that of B over A, power nonetheless resides on either side and this imbalance can change in certain circumstances. Dominant groups use social influence to put pressure on dissenting members in an effort to preserve the existing consensus and achieve conformity. Conformity results in overall stability as the local change it brings about aligns the deviant's perspective with the dominant group's perspective. In this way, the dominant group perpetuates the order by securing its own version of reality as the legitimate version. Dominant groups seek to impose their views on deviants unilaterally, achieving uniformity through conformity (Deutsch and Gerrard, 1955). Conformity with rules and expectations is necessary for the coordination of collective action; there is no game to be played without sticking to the rules.

The power of a minority, however, arises from the ability to violate uniformity, challenge the established consensus, and resist conformity pressure. Minorities are not only a target, but also a source of influence (Moscovici, 1985a). Asch (1948) noted that 'a little rebellion, now and then, is a good thing, and as necessary in the political world as storms are in the physical'. Deviants are a source of social influence through persistence and conversion that leads to *innovation*. Deviants unsettle existing norms, perturb social uniformity, turn the certain into the uncertain, and make the previously familiar appear unfamiliar. When, in the face of conformity pressure, a subordinate group persists in projections, it has a chance to succeed in making its own perspective familiar. This dynamic favours the smaller subordinate group (Moscovici, 1985a). The resolution of the conflict is resolved in the direction of overall innovation, and the minority position can also achieve its objective for recognition. Its perspective is accommodated in a social field that has changed by virtue of the arising conflict. An innovative minority sets in motion a process that cannot base itself on established norms – its perspective is labelled deviant de facto by the dominant group. Nevertheless, the negotiation of innovation centres on a conflict that is provoked and necessary. Consequently, innovative individuals or groups are able to bring about overall shifts in the social field in contrast to the quest for order and uniformity of the dominant group. This duality of maintaining order and changing order tied with majority and minority positions in society, defines the first mode of social influence.

Rationality and subrationality: The doctrine of suggestion

For any overview of ideas of social influence it is important to recall what Asch (1952) criticised as the 'doctrine of suggestion' which pandered to a mythical paradox: individual humans are capable of rational reasoning, but in collectives they become irrational. This idea of increased suggestibility, somnambulance, reduced faculties as a consequence of sociability, or in other words, the social as a deteriorating influence on the individual, has dominated much speculation in social and cultural psychology. Under this presumption, social life makes us irrational humans. This one-sided view of social influence persists in social theory and has undergone a revival in recent years with a renewed focus on subliminal influence processes (see below). It is useful in this respect to make a qualified distinction between rational and subrational modes of social influence.

Whenever individuals are exposed to symbols, that is, the basic means of communication, they will necessarily engage in an individual process of evaluation to decide whether or how to act on them. There is a longstanding idea that this evaluation and enactment take a rational or irrational form. This distinction has often been aligned with other distinctions, such as cognitive versus emotional, conscious versus unconscious, explicit versus implicit processing, and a normative expectation that the one side is generally superior to the other, otherwise known as 'civilised'. In the light of recent psychological research, it is no longer so clear that emotional, unconscious, and implicit processes are irrational; similarly it is not necessarily the case that conscious, explicit, ..., cognitive operations are more rational and more civilised. Increasingly, it is clear that emotions have a rational core; so have automatic, unconscious, and implicit meaning processes. These all have functionality in supporting efficient and effective forms of activity. Rationality of action is embodied both in explicit reasoning and in 'gut feelings' (see Gigerenzer, 2007).

Despite this new uncertainty as to what constitutes 'irrationality', we want to maintain a contrast to rationality in speaking about social influence. Of all semantic opposites of 'rationality', we have opted for 'subrational'. This avoids the term 'irrationality' whose negative connotations are not helpful analytically.

Modalities of social influence

Studies of social influence have demonstrated that the exercise of influence takes place in different ways. The origins of the study of this phenomenon lie in the analysis of human behaviour in crowds. In pursuing these lines of investigation, scholars have demonstrated various modalities by which social influence is exercised. We distinguish eight such modalities, namely leadership, imitation, norm-setting, conformity, obedience, persuasion, conversion, and resistance. Modalities of influence can serve in the establishment of conformity as in the case of innovation. The exercise of social influence through these modalities can be both rational and non-rational, and can serve an innovation just as much as it can serve the perpetuation of social norms.

Leadership of masses

Le Bon's (1896) widely read work on crowd psychology set a key agenda for the study of social influence. Le Bon's study outlines how in collectives, individuals are subject to *'the law of mental unity of crowds'*, by which a collective mind is forged into clearly defined, lesser characteristics, namely the disappearance of conscious personhood and the dominance of feelings and thoughts with fixed direction. Instincts, passions and feelings are the common denominator that binds individuals together. Consequently, in a crowd, individuals, along with their intellectual aptitudes, are weakened. According to Le Bon, by the mere fact of being in a crowd, 'man descends several rungs in the ladder of civilization. Isolated he may be a cultivated individual; in a crowd, he is a barbarian' (p. 10).

Crowds are disqualified by Le Bon and can never accomplish intelligent acts, because it is the primitive emotions that bind humans together in a crowd. The educated and the ignorant are equalised in a crowd. An archaic anxiety to which the speculations of Le Bon and others give expression to (see van Ginneken, 1992) is the notion of crowds as a 'social mass'. The mass is a root metaphor arising from pottery; masses are inert and need an external agent to put them into shape, to give them a design, and this design is provided by the leader. Le Bon attributes this 'materiality' of crowds to three features of social influence: the sentiment of *invincibility* that arises from *numerosity*; *contagion*, by which sentiments spread among crowd members; and *suggestibility*, by which individuals deprived of personhood follow the suggestions of operators in a hypnotic way.

Le Bon's theory of leadership is the natural complement of the notion of crowd. Crowds need and call for leadership. This stream of investigation has been extended to the study of leaders and leadership styles, to identify the features effective leadership possesses that allure the masses. Moscovici (1985b) distinguishes between totemic leaders and mosaic leaders. The charisma of the former resides in their personality, that of the latter in the doctrines they advocate. The interest in the study of leadership (Chemers, 2001; Lord, Brown and Harvey, 2001; Lord and Hall, 2003; Hogg, 2007) is sustained by the fact that some directing function is basic for all groups, even in presumably leaderless ones (Cranach, 1986; Counselman, 1991), and by the fact that leadership has been identified as a significant factor of collective performance (Barrick et al., 1991; Joyce, Nohria and Roberson, 2003). Moreover, bad leadership, as Le Bon argued, remains today a worrying concern (Kellerman, 2004). This concern for leadership as a form of non-rational influence in the service of social transformation and innovation competes with the concern for rational design in managerial thinking.

Imitation and contagion

According to Gabriel Tarde (1890/1962), in any crowd there is a class of individuals that draw others through their power of suggestion. What these few do, others will imitate. The few, whose actions and beliefs are imitated by others, rule the many. This process creates similarity and difference, as well as progress in society. Similarity arises from either genetic inheritance or social influence, and the latter from imitation through contact. The many imitate the few because they are susceptible to contagion, and this arises from a lowered level of awareness. Imitation makes people similar to each other; but imitation also propagates innovation and different traditions.

Imitation is a factor of progress. Novelties, invented by the few, diffuse among the many by contagion at the point of contact. While the invention of novelty is unpredictable, its imitation is lawful and amenable to a quest for 'the laws of imitation'.

Tarde speculated on the reasons why not all conduct diffuses equally through society and only a limited number of ideals, attitudes, or behavioural innovations are adopted by others. For example, innovations that are 'logically parallel' to a culture spread more readily than ones that are not. Inventions that are too daring or too traditional do not spread well.

Box 4.1   Evolutionary accounts of cultural transmission

Evolutionary reasoning has spawned three accounts of cultural transmission in recent years: memetics, epidemiology, and gene-culture coevolution. The first two contradict each other, and the third one is a combination of both. **Memetics** constructs a strong analogy between 'genes' and 'memes', the cultural units of ideas, fashions, art etc. (Dawkins, 1976). Memetic evolution compares with genetic evolution on the basis of replication, variability, selection of one idea at the expense of others (Aunger, 2000). However, in memetic evolution it is less a case of copying than of making inferences (Wilson and Sperber, 1981). So, while the replicator model competes with models of contagion, the 'dual inheritance theory' is a hybrid model (Feldman and Cavalli-Sforza, 1976). It seeks to account for cultural change via processes of interdependent evolution of genes and culture.

The epidemiological perspective

Epidemiology is the study of the distribution of agents such as disease viruses as a function of virulence, host susceptibility, and ecological milieu. Similarly, cultural epidemiology studies patterns of culture items within a human population. Cultures are distributions of linked mental (e.g. beliefs, attitudes) and public representations (e.g. pots, tools) that are stabilised through chains of communication. This process of stabilisation depends on psychological factors rather than blind selection: mental modularity (e.g. Atran, 1990, 2002; Boyer, 1994a, 2001; Sperber, 1990, 1996) and social psychological biases such as in-group favouring, prestige and conformity make some items 'easier to think' (Nisbett and Norenzayan, 2002). For more on evolutionary accounts of cultural transmission and gene-culture coevolution in particular, see Chapter 11.

(For a critical assessment of the assumption of the epidemiological model of thought contagion, see Kitcher (2003)).

The *law of close contact* explains how people have a greater tendency to copy those immediately around them. The *law of imitation of superiors* describes how imitation follows the hierarchy of social prestige, the poor and the young imitate the affluent and the experienced. The *law of insertion* observes how newly adopted behaviours are superimposed and that they reinforce or displace existing behaviours. Tarde also observed that changing the 'inner person' precedes changing the 'outer person', in other words private attitudinal change anticipates behaviour change in public.

For Tarde, and here agreeing with Le Bon, 'society is imitation and imitation is a kind of somnambulism' (1962, p. 87). But Tarde made a far-reaching observation on the difference between the crowd and public opinion. Crowds are face-to-face with their leadership in a defined location, in a public place or on a street. Public opinion arise from conversations and the distribution of mass media (at that time newspapers), which create a common focus of attention without any co-presence among people. People read the news at different places and pay attention to the same topics, and this constitutes a new form of pressure on authorities which cannot be ignored but may be dreaded (Tarde, 1901/2006). The influence from a news source to a reader is also a process of imitation, a mental contact of interspirituality. Importantly, the doctrine of suggestion applies to opinion formation just as it does to crowd behaviour. What distinguishes public opinion from crowds is their psychology. Public opinion, on the basis of attention to news, is characterised by conversation and distributed opinion. Like the numerosity of crowds, what matters is not the merit of opinion, but its numbers, that is, quantity before quality. From here the modern enthusiasm for the study of public opinion, mass communication, and diffusion research take their inspiration, whether recognised by protagonists or not (see Valente and Rogers, 1995).

Public opinion is normative not by merit of content, but through critical mass. This basic notion has recently been repopularised by what Gladwell (2000) calls the 'tipping point'. Such an account is rooted in biological analogies of cultural diffusion (see Box 4.1). As in the notion of social contagion, one gains a sense here of how ideas, beliefs, attitudes and behaviours seem to spread like microorganisms through infection. In analogy to 'biological warfare', some opinions could be brought about rapidly and with great effect depending on factors like virulence, host susceptibility, and milieu. The bacteriologist reminds us that the milieu is crucial. The tipping point marks the moment when a minority enthusiasm becomes majority and thus normative with little prospect of containment. We regard contagion and imitation as a subrational modality of social influence in the service of social change.

Normalising and framing for future reference

One of the defining characteristics of groups is that they develop norms by which their members abide and by which newcomers are judged. On their part, individuals gain guidance from a frame of reference that establishes confidence and certainty in conduct. How group norms are established in the first place and come to guide future behaviour of individuals have been demonstrated in experimental studies. Sherif (1935) demonstrated how individuals come to base their judgments on norms established in the presence of others. The effect of these norms, even if counterfactual, guided respondents' future judgement, these judgements typically remained stable, even when others were not present, provided the norms were properly recognised and established in the first place. **Normalisation** results from reciprocal influence among social partners who are looking for a reasonable solution to their disagreements as a basis for future action (Moscovici, 1985a). Sherif's experiments (see Box 4.2) demonstrated that norms persist through internalisation: individuals continue to judge things according to a standard, once established, even in the absence of others. What Deutsch and Gerard (1955) termed **normative influence** was demonstrated to be a more powerful social influence than new information per se. The importance of normalising is highlighted by theories of group formation. Tuckman (1965) argues that goal-directed groups go through stages of formation: (a) forming – when the people come together; (b) storming – when the people conflict, struggle, and debate to iron out differences; (c) norming – establishing the group parameters for future behaviour, and (d) performing – where the group starts functioning as a unit to achieve its goals. In organisational settings, group norms that orient members towards performance lead to increased productivity and job satisfaction (Weldon and Weingart, 1993). A key point of studies of normalisation is the demonstration that group formation and sociability are not a process of decadence, as expounded in crowd psychology and its doctrine of suggestion, but a precondition of collective action. Norm-setting is therefore a rational modality of social influence that constitutes order.

Conformity

The need to belong to a social group is part of an embodied psychology of dependency. Being left out is experienced as painful (Eisenberger et al., 2003) and makes people feel cold and crave for warm food (Zhong and Leonardelli, 2008). This logic of social dependency is also the basic cultural dimension along which a society can be organised, offering an entire language of self, virtues, anxieties, and pathologies (see Doi, 1971 for a discussion of these issues in respect of Japanese culture).

Conformity pressure was the topic of landmark studies conducted by Solomon Asch (1952/1987). He set out to study the behaviour of individuals in groups when faced with a dilemma between objective truth and normative rightness and belonging. Asch's intention was to refute the prevailing dogma of a 'doctrine of suggestion', which assumes the paramount irrationality of individuals in groups. His experiment aimed at demonstrating that when presented with an unequivocal situation, individuals will resist conformity pressure. Asch hoped to explain conformity by way of ambiguity of perception rather than as a form of irrationality. But Asch's significance lies in his failure to achieve his stated aims (Moscovici, 1985a). Asch explained his findings with a 'pull towards the group'. He noted how errors in estimation were biased towards the majority view, and this led him to conclude: 'as soon as a person is in the midst of a group he is no longer indifferent to it' and that 'if conditions permit, individuals move toward the group' (1987, p. 483). Conformity is the adaptation of individuals to group norms, by which they maintain a positive self-esteem and a sense of orientation. Conformity demonstrates the priority of social and self-oriented rationality over objective rationality.

The risks of conformity, however, have also been documented. Collective actions organised under conformity pressure can end in failure. Janis's work on 'groupthink' describes constraints in thinking processes in highly cohesive groups, using the example of foreign policy decisions in the American invasion of Cuba in 1961 and in the defence of Pearl Harbor in 1941 (Janis, 1972; Janis and Mann, 1977). Conformity pressure leads individual members to adopt group goals and frames of reference unquestioningly and uncritically. Legitimate concerns and alternative options are often not considered, in favour of maintaining an illusion of consensus. Maybe the ancient role of a 'devil's advocate' considers this functional need for contradiction. With regards to public opinion, a similar risk of conformity is described in the 'Spiral of Silence' phenomenon (Noelle-Neumann, 1990). People express their opinion in public by considering what others are saying. If the mass media give clues, which puts an individual into a minority position, these individuals will no longer express themselves; conform in public, while in private continue to dissent. In such conditions, modern opinion polls will report a biased opinion that leads to failures to anticipate election results correctly, and to the misjudgement of public moods on the basis of easily available indicators. We consider conformity as a rational modality of social influence in the service of social order, rational in so far as the individual makes a trade-off between objective facts and social obligation in favour of the latter.

Obedience to authority

The question of whether and to what extent individuals yield to morally dubious social demands was the subject of a famous psychological study. Stanley Milgram (1974), influenced by Asch's experiments and the events that took place in the concentration camps of the Second World War, sought to study social influence in the form of *obedience*. When and how will people obey or defy authority? His studies have become perhaps the best known modality of social influence. Milgram tested how common people behave when instructed by a legitimate authority to inflict harm on another.

He concluded that the 'banality of evil' comes closer to truth than one might dare imagine. Arendt (1963) famously claimed that the great evils of the Nazi regime were not executed by exceptional sociopaths, but by ordinary people who believed their actions were simply normal in the circumstances. Milgram (see Box 4.2) demonstrated that with an appeal

Box 4.2   Classical experiments of social influence

Sherif (1935) studied participants' perceptual judgements in estimating the movement of a projected light point. To viewers in the dark a stationary light appears to move erratically, which is known as the autokinetic effect. Sherif demonstrated how in discussion with others, subjects' previously established judgements of the light movement regressed towards a central tendency establishing a group norm, the frame of reference for future purposes.

Lewin (1947) studied how group involvement affected whether people would be buying and cooking offal meat. In an effort to promote the consumption of underused meats during the Second World War in the US, Lewin studied social influence under variable conditions. Participants were taking part either in a lecture situation or in a discussion group. The identical talk, outlining the nutritional value and recipes for cooking offal, was delivered in both conditions. The study demonstrated the advantage of *normative influence* compared to **informational influence** (Deutsch and Gerard, 1955). Subjects who were only informed were much less likely to follow the cooking advice than those who elaborated the information in group discussions. Mobilising community and reference groups is part of an American tradition of social engineering (Graebner, 1986; see also Chapters 13 and 15 on media health campaigns and science communication).

Asch (1952) devised an ingenious experiment in which groups of seven to nine people were shown lines of different length. The task was to match a single line to one of three presented together. All participant subjects were 'confederates' of the experimenter except one, the critical subject. In the first two rounds each subject called out the matching lines. On the third and subsequent trials, the confederates declared 'matching' a line that was visibly incorrect. In 33 per cent of cases, the critical subjects followed the instructed majority into a false judgement. Less than half remained independent and gave correct answers against the majority. During debriefing, the subjects reported how puzzled and confused they were when the majority made errors. They struggled with the dilemma of their own judgement and longing to agree with the others. Some, but not all, yielded to the conformity pressure and succumbed to *majority influence*.

Milgram (1974) invited participants for a learning experiment that involved a 'teacher' who punishes the errors of a 'learner' with increasing electric shocks. Subjects always played the teacher who applied shocks of between 15 and 450 volts. In reality, unbeknown to the subjects, no such shocks were given. The switches ranged from 'Slight Shock' to 'Danger-Severe Shock' and 'XXX'. Subjects could also hear the learner acting out the pain of increasing shocks and pleading for mercy. Whenever the 'teachers' demonstrated apprehension at going on with the experiment, the experimenter reminded them to continue in the interest of the science of learning. Milgram wanted to know whether obedience had any limits in this situation. All of the participants in his study went on to 'administer' 'Very Strong' shocks (195–240 volts), and nearly two-thirds went on to the very end. These findings of obedience rates of 60 per cent and above were surprising and shocking. Milgram observed that 'many subjects will obey the experimenter no matter how vehement the pleading of the person being shocked, no matter how painful the shocks seem to be, and no matter how much the victim pleads to be let out' (p. 5).

Facheaux and Moscovici (1967) demonstrated the logic of minority influence. In their experiments, subjects were shown geometrical designs varying on various dimensions. They had to decide which one dimension they preferred to describe the object. Participants shifted towards those subjects who were briefed by the experimenters to give consistently one particular response. Another experiment (Moscovici, Lage and Naffrechoux 1969) further demonstrated this minority effect. The authors showed slides and subjects had to identify the colour of these slides. Reversing Asch, only one or a few of the subjects were briefed to consistently identify blue slides as green (green is the after-image of blue, which makes blue-green perceptually ambiguous). The experiment showed that subjects swayed the responses of the majority. The more consistent the few were in their 'green' response, the stronger was the shift of the majority. Moreover, in a test of blue-green discrimination after the experiment, participants identified green faster than control subjects; they were primed on green despite having seen the blue slides. Even more strikingly, subjects tested for green even faster when they had not succumbed to influence during the experiment. This suggested that minority influence might have a *response latency*. People may still disagree in public when privately they already have changed their minds. This dynamic manifests itself in public as a delayed response.

to obedience to (scientific) authority, ordinary people went on to deliver potentially life-threatening electric shocks to fellow citizens after abdicating responsibility and claiming, just like war criminals, that they were simply doing their expected duty. After all, the instructor wearing a white garment (a symbol of authority) had instructed them to continue the experiment and thus to contribute to the progress of science.

Milgram's striking demonstrations have been replicated many times (e.g. Mantell, 1971; Kilham and Mann, 1974; Meeus and Raaijmakers, 1986), and have reported obedience rates between 28 per cent and 91 per cent, on average around 60 per cent (Blass, 2004, p. 301ff). Recently, situational rather than dispositional explanations of **compliance** have been advanced (Benjamin Jr and Simpson, 2009; Blass, 2009). Subjects obey authority even when asked to do things that violate their own moral standards. Burger (2009) reports how this tendency to submit to authority persists, and that Milgram's situational factors remain operative in spite of a societal trend towards nonconformity (Twenge, 2009). Obedience and compliance should be considered a subrational modality of social influence serving to maintain the social order and to coordinate social action.

Persuasion: Convincing by elaboration or simple cues

The experiments by Sherif, Lewin, Asch, and Milgram supported Tarde and Le Bon in showing that social influence was difficult for individuals to avoid. However, they disagree in showing that conformity, compliance, and normalisation are not entirely irrational processes. This conception of rational behaviour also guided research that sought to discover what occurs when people are the target of persuasive communication.

The Yale group (Hovland, Janis and Kelley, 1953) sought to discover the characteristics of the communicator, the message features, and the types of audience that increase the likelihood of attitude change. These studies were part of a renewed interest in propaganda and rhetoric at the time (see Chapter 10 for more on rhetoric). Their findings have provided an extensive list of variables that can enhance the success of targeted influence and that are widely applied in advertising, promotion, and marketing communications (see Belch and Belch, 2004). As an experimental rhetoric and a quest for the 'magic bullet', it produced disappointing results. More recently, scholars have turned their attention to psychological processes to explain why communication changes attitudes.

Dual-process theories posit two routes by which recipients of a message may be influenced. Petty and Cacioppo (1981, 1986a, 1986b) suggested that cognitive elaboration moderates persuasion, for which they proposed a central and a peripheral route. Their Elaboration-Likelihood Model (ELM) posits that the mental effort invested defines the route that is taken. When depth of processing and elaboration is high, the slower *central route* to persuasion is involved. In this case, persuasion is achieved as a function of argument content and quality. Conversely, when the elaboration is low – that is, the cognitive effort invested in processing the information is low – persuasion is achieved through the fast *peripheral route*, and as a function of factors other than the argument. Peripheral processes select only cues and mobilise heuristics, attribution biases, affective reactions, conditioned responses, and social identities, leading to in-group bias. The ELM expects that persuasion via the central route resists further changes once it is achieved, while persuasion via the peripheral route is more open to further changes. The two routes support an understanding of both the slow and lasting, and the fast and fickle changes of attitudes. Importantly, for any particular message, the type of persuasion afforded is determined by the individual's elaboration likelihood, a personal disposition. ELM assumes that messages are processed either centrally or peripherally. Whether the central or peripheral route is engaged depends on the individual's motivations and abilities. Message elaboration might thus be a wasted effort. Therefore many uses of ELM assume humans to be 'cognitive misers' mostly engaging the peripheral route most of the time.

Eagly and Chaiken (1984, 1993) propose the heuristic-systematic model (HSM) to overcome some limitations of ELM. The *systematic* route, like ELM's central route, is based on deep processing of information. The *heuristic* route, like ELM's peripheral route, involves only shallow processing using shortcuts for quick processing. Examples of mental heuristics include 'consent implies correctness', or 'experts can be trusted'. The former heuristic seems to recognise conformity pressure as in Asch's experiments, whereas the latter seems to refer to prestige or obedience to authority, as in Milgram's study. Again HSM suggests that persuasion resulting from deep processing is more resistant to further change. However, in contrast to ELM, HSM allows for parallel processing, that is, both routes are engaged simultaneously. Persuasion takes place through rational and subrational routes at the same time. This seems to be in line with insights of traditional rhetoric which argued for a balance between logos, ethos, and pathos to convince an audience (as in Chapter 10 on rhetoric).

ELM and HSM conceive persuasion as individual responses to some fixed message; little attention is paid to actual conversation and social interaction involved in persuasion. The interlocutor figures as an external parameter setting the prestige or conformity heuristic. Models of persuasion are mostly concerned with attitude change and involve rational as well as subrational processes.

Conversion

Moscovici (2001) reminds us that the key issue in social influence is the psychology of minorities, as minorities have the mental and emotional capacity to bring about innovation through the power of ideas. The theory of *minority influence* (Moscovici, 1976) took inspiration from a critique of the dominant concern of social influence studies with conformity and deviance. In the light of the minority paradigm (Mugny, 1982), deviance loses its negative connotations and is considered innovative and functional for collective development (Paicheler, 1988).

When a minority challenges the majority, the *behavioural style* of the minority is the key factor of success (Faucheux and Moscovici, 1967). A consistent minority appears as credible and independent and is thus more likely to influence others in terms of a new definition of the social situation, with itself as a social actor. Minorities seek both recognition and influence. By being consistent a minority can establish a different perspective, creating instability and challenging established norms. Consistent minorities break the social contract to negotiate a new one. The model of minority influence assumes that the impact is informational; it highlights the power of ideas. People align with minorities because they are convinced by the ideas and the information provided, not because of some normative pressure. The individual process is one of *conversion*, a deep reorientation, private and public, and lasting. This is in contrast to conformity pressure, which leads to changes that are superficial, public but not necessarily private, and only temporary.

There are a number of factors that moderate the success of minorities. Not every minority is equally likely to be successful with their ideas and attitudes simply on the basis of their minority status. The consistency of behaviour displayed implies that the minority is organised, which excludes any anomic deviance or any non-conformity from exerting immediate social influence. This also means that successful minorities need conformity and discipline for themselves. Rather than being in contradiction, conformity is a necessary condition of minority success. Furthermore, minorities that remain part of the moral community, that is, they hold to the majority in part and challenge only some social norms, are more likely to exert influence than actors who are total outsiders and challenge the entire norm system (Moscovici, 1985a).

Another irony of minority influence arises from latency of impact and the *'sleeper effect'* (Hovland and Weiss, 1951). Attitude change might set in with a delay. Information might initially be dismissed because it is put forward by a non-prestige and thus non-credible source, that is, the social minority. Later, people remember the information and change their minds, but do not readily remember the source. Ironically, minorities might be the agent of change, but might not get the credit for it. Once a new idea has become common sense, it becomes obvious and nobody in particular will deserve any credit for it.

Resistance to change

One of the paradoxes of social influence is that resistance is a reaction to past change and also a factor of future change. Resistance features large as a concern of change agents who try to alter social attitudes and social structures with a strategic plan to do so.

Research on attitude change defines resistance as attitude strength that works against further change. And this is achieved by previous inoculation, that is, through forewarning (McGuire and Papageorgis, 1962), by selective attention to new information, by existing knowledge on the topic and cognitive elaboration, and by 'reactance', that is, the arousal arising from any 'feeling of being pushed' (Eagly and Chaiken, 1993; Struck et al., 2001; Sagarin and Wood, 2007). Resistance renders attitudes permanent and allows us to stabilise behaviour across variable situations. Resistance of dispositions is necessary for social influence to persist once it has been achieved.

Resistance to change features prominently in the management of organisational or social change projects. In change projects, resistance is often treated as a nuisance, a barrier to overcome, a culprit that allows one to blame others for failure, to treat them as the main problem on the road to success. In this analysis resistance is the dependent variable, and the purpose of intervention is to reduce resistance in order to make change less costly (Coch and French, 1947; Lewin, 1947; Knowles and Riner, 2007).

An alternative take on the issue suggests that resistance functions analogously to pain in relation to goal-directed activity, that is, it is an alarm signal (Bauer, 1991). Considered a signal, the action consequences come into focus urging a change of tack. This functional analysis suggests that resistance is the 'reality principle' of any strategic intervention. The first victim of strategic action is the plan because 'stuff happens' and things turn out differently than expected. Resistance directs the attention to where the problems are; it stimulates a re-evaluation of the course of action, and urges alterations towards a sustainable project (see Bauer, 1997). The pain analogy suggests that inadequate responses to resistance can make things worse. But they can also stabilise as avoidance learning ('never again this way!'), or lead to novel insights on how to do things better (see Leavitt and March, 1988). Resistance adds value to projects of change by correcting unrealistic assumptions. Resistance to change increases the difference between imagination, planning, and reality; it is a rational modality of social influence, paradoxically leading to change.

The cycle of common sense: Towards an integrative model

So far, we have briefly introduced eight different modalities of social influence. These are focused on maintaining social order or bringing about social change. They achieve this in a manner that could be characterised as rational or subrational. We now ask whether we can say more about how these modalities might work together, and thus go beyond a mere classification.

One of the key starting points of social influence research is the majority or minority status of the source of influence. What seems to be a choice of paradigms is in reality two interlocked processes. The two modes of social influence are locked in a dynamic governed by the principle of social impact (Latané and Wolfe, 1981). For example, in the tradition of diffusion research, the assumption is that the early stages are governed by the minority logic of conversion and persuasion and the logic of obedience to authority, while beyond the 'tipping point' the normative influence of conformity kicks in. Similarly, ambitious minorities need the conformity of members to exhibit the behavioural consistency that makes all the difference. Influence needs discipline. Social influence is characterised by a dynamic interplay between establishing norms, maintaining norms in the face of challenge, and changing them through conflict.

Figure 4.2 is an attempt to visualise the cycle of development of collective activity oriented in common sense, where many modalities of social influence may be said to interact. The constitution of collective action and common sense starts with the **normalisation** of what can be expected from every member. The entry point is the endorsement of a frame for future reference that later will be taken for granted. What is normalised or unproblematic for founding members will need to be accepted by new members of the group, including those of a younger generation; thus, the problem of conformity arises. In a first cycle, conformity pressure is brought to bear to maintain common sense. However, resistance also manifests itself in the mode of an alarm: we cannot continue like this. This first cycle we might call **assimilation**, because the influence is dominated by the majority trying to assimilate the minority in terms of the majority. This cycle might also involve the mobilisation of authority to secure obedience and compliance to existing norms, as well as persuasion and imitation, that is, the fast

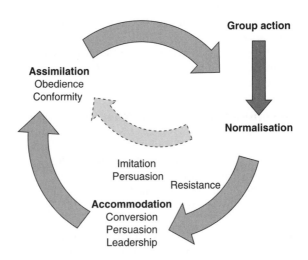

Figure 4.2 The cycle of normalisation, assimilation, and accommodation

processing of symbolic cues and the contagion with 'sticky' ideas on subrational pathways and restricted deliberation.

From the beginning, or with time, it is likely that some members will widen their horizon and no longer agree with the terms of reference. Once the challenge by the nonconforming minority is posed, a conflict builds up and the consensus is doubtful and made labile. Slowly but steadily the subordinate minority manages to attract sufficient attention and exert its influence potential. The means to achieve this include leadership and communication to persuade others that the new position is sincere, correct, and right. Under favourable conditions the process of conversion can take its course, and **accommodation** will occur. The majority accommodates the minority by making concessions and by resetting the consensus on a new position. The terms of reference have changed and can go into a new cycle of assimilation of newcomers and deviance. The guiding ideal of a 'public sphere' requires that no perspective is privileged and excluded from deliberation.

This tentative integration of modalities of social influence postulates a recurring cycle of three processes: the normalisation of terms of references, the assimilation of newcomers and deviants, and the accommodation of disciplined minorities. It would appear that collective projects for the future develop an identity through several of these cycles and thus increase performance capability and sustainability (see Cranach, 1996). This quest for integration opens further theoretical work on social influence. We have not even started to talk about how humans influence each other by ways of objects and technology, designed to afford lock-in, lock-outs, and interlocking of behaviours. Technical artefacts structure what we will do and not do; for example, we tend to leave the house through the door and not through the wall. Social influence has both subjective and objective avenues, and here we have considered only the subjective side. We need to recognise again that normalisation produces both subjective norms and material results, and both sides can constitute opportunity and scandal (see Asch, 1952; Bauer, 2008).

Conclusion

This chapter considers social influence as a process of conflict resolution occurring through non-violent and non-coercive means. Normative notions of social influence study how the many accept direction from leaders and how they conform to group pressure. Studies of minority influence provide insights into the power of ideas, the processes of resistance, counter-influence, and innovation, how the few can convert the many against all odds. Social influence studies the imitation of behaviour and the contagion of powerful ideas. Biological analogies inform much model-building: ideas spread like viruses; more or less virulent, they need a host and strive in certain milieus more than others.

Because social influence models explore non-violent means of conflict, they assume an historical context of modernity, the differentiation of private and public spheres of life, and a public sphere where conversations can take place before casting judgement and making decisions on issues of common concern in the absence of violence (see Taylor, 2007, p. 185ff). However, this public sphere and its events straddle the tensions between communication oriented towards common understanding and the strategic efforts of interested parties to move others towards a particular position. Soft power musters the means of unilateral influence – despite being instrumentally rational from the point of view of a powerful actor, it still violates the assumptions which inspire real dialogue. The notion of social influence thus remains in a productive tension with a communicative rationality (see Chapter 2 on dialogue and critical consciousness, and Chapter 6 on communicative action).

5
Pragmatic Theory and Social Relations

Bradley Franks and Helen Amelia Green

Keywords: Affect-laden interpretation; code model; collective intention; conversational implicature theory; egocentric communication; illocution; inferential model; locution; perlocution; pragmatics; relevance theory; schema; speech act theory; theory of mind.

Introduction

The cops are here! (1)

Imagine a situation in which two people are engaged in attempting to blow up the safe of a bank. One says (1) to the other. The literal meaning of (1) is something like, *There are members of the police force in the vicinity.* But the meaning that the speaker intends to communicate, and indeed that the hearer is likely to grasp, is something like *Drop everything and run!*

This simple case exemplifies an essential quality of human communication – it involves **pragmatics**. The message communicated can in some sense 'go beyond' the literal meaning of the utterance, as the hearer generates inferences about the implicit or intended meaning of the speaker. Moreover, the use of language does more than simply describe the way the world is; it prompts or constitutes actions on the part of the speaker and hearer. These two aspects are taken up in this chapter, in discussing **inferential** theories of pragmatics on the one hand, and speech act theory on the other; ideas from the former are important in rumour and gossip (Chapter 8), and in Habermas's theory of communicative action (Chapters 6 and 12).

The issues addressed by pragmatic theories concern the nature of the interaction between speakers and hearers and how meaning is conveyed between them. How do speakers make meaningful utterances, and how is meaning recovered by hearers? To what extent does this depend on the speaker taking the hearer's perspective into account and vice versa? Different answers to this question are offered by Chapter 2, which takes it that dialogue involves shared perspectives, and Chapters 9 and 11, which argue that such shared perspectives are not a recurrent feature of communication. How do conventions of language–meaning relations intersect with the intentions of speakers as they use language? Such issues touch on fundamental questions concerning the nature of social interaction, and in particular how cognitive, emotional, and motivational processes interact with our attempts to understand others via language; some of these issues are taken up regarding nonverbal communication in Chapter 3, and regarding evolutionary factors in Chapter 11.

We begin by reviewing some background to the study of pragmatics, followed by sketching some major pragmatics theories. We then examine ways in which those theories might relate the roles of cognition, affect, and the role of understanding other peoples' intentions in social interaction and communication.

Codes, literal meaning and pragmatics

The force of pragmatic considerations is best understood by contrast with a widely held metaphor of how communication works, the 'conduit' metaphor (Reddy, 1993). If language were a conduit along which we send meanings, it would operate broadly as follows: a speaker would form a clear, intended message in mind, which would then be encoded into words that would capture all of the intended meaning; the words would then be uttered; and the hearer, on hearing them, would decode their meanings so as to arrive at a representation with identical meaning to that intended by the speaker. Communication would then be a matter of the speaker and hearer both knowing the code, and the conduit of language telling the hearer which codes to access and when.

The basic principles of a **code model** are apparent in perhaps the most widely employed theory of meaning in the social sciences – semiotic theory (e.g. de Saussure, 1959; Barthes, 1968; Eco, 1976). Semiotics assumes that meanings involve associations between 'signifiers' and 'signifieds'. A word is a signifier, which is associated with two aspects of a signified – its denotation (the referent or thing in the world to which it refers), and its connotation (the characteristic thoughts which the word elicits). Such associations can themselves be signifiers that are associated with higher-level signifiers, and so on. The broad claim of semiotics is that understanding language or engaging with other forms of symbolic culture operate via tracing out the complex associations of these signifiers and signifieds. Examples such as (1) would involve tracing out lengthier chains of associations (of codes associated with other codes) to arrive at a more nuanced decoding than a literal reading. This process of making meaningful connections would be more or less automatic; and those connections are known in advance by the speaker and the hearer.

There are reasons to take issue with code models. One concerns the implausibility of such a code, as a full account of the shared knowledge of associations between words and meanings. No evidence from psychology supports language understanding as an extensive use of a code – for example, for automatically accessing a code from its associated word. A code model might envisage knowledge as a mental lexicon, similar to a large dictionary, where each word is associated with a 'file' of information which constitutes all of its meaning. Accessing that meaning would simply involve retrieving the appropriate meaning 'file' using the word as the access 'key"'. But evidence from cognitive psychology (e.g. Barsalou, 1982; Clark, 1996; Franks and Braisby, 1990; Murphy, 2002) suggests that accessing the meaning of a word is constructive, so that what is retrieved from memory is already altered to fit the context and interlocutors.

However, even cases of meaning that are not highly idiosyncratic – for example, *he, she, here, now* – nonetheless depend on context to determine their literal meaning.

The executive fired the secretary because *she* had discovered *her* guilty secret (2)

This is ambiguous between two readings, one where *guilty secret* is held by the secretary, and another where it is held by the executive. The meaning of (2) – to whom the indexical expressions refer – appears to depend on context. But it is hard to see how a process that accesses meanings for words in a way that is automatic and mandatory could be appropriately context-sensitive. An automatic code does not require additional input to access the meaning; the word is the only access 'key' needed.

If it is difficult to account for context-sensitive literal meanings like those in (2) with the use of codes, it seems even more difficult to explain the kinds of implicit meanings regarding (1) with a code model. It seems highly unlikely that such meanings could be expressed by additional associations between more-or-less conventional words plus meanings, since they are very often generated 'ad hoc' for a specific context – they would and could not be encoded prior to the act of communication. Finally, if implicit meanings cannot be reflected by codes, nor, it seems, can the use of language to perform actions.

An alternative view of the psychological processes in pragmatics would take them as primarily *inferential*. An inferential process involves arriving at a conclusion that is supported by, warranted, or justified by a set of premises or assumptions. In pragmatic interpretation, some of the premises would be the meanings of the constituent words, and others would arise from contextual information; the resultant interpretation would be an inference that is not completely determined by those premises, but is the 'best bet' based on using the premises as evidence for that interpretation. Even if interlocutors share a common knowledge of the meanings of the constituent words of an utterance, they may arrive at different pragmatic interpretations of the overall utterance by drawing on different additional premises in their inferences.

The upshot is that communication, on an inferential view, is a risky business – it can fail or only succeed by degrees, even if all the constituents are in place. By contrast, if communication only involves the use of codes and relevant associations, and if interlocutors know the codes, successful communication is guaranteed. It seems likely that everyday communication accords more closely with an inferential model rather than a code model.

A final – and major – limitation of the code model concerns its presumption regarding the nature of communication. A conduit is a channel for a speaker to tell a hearer precisely what is in their mind; a code is the way this is achieved. But this raises the question: Is all or even most communication so collaborative or is it highly strategic? Do I really want to tell you what is in my mind (even if I were able to do so)? Or do I only want to manipulate what is in yours?

Pragmatic theories

Speech act theory

In contrast to a concept of communication as instances of coding and decoding, speech act theory conceives of communication as performing acts. Language use goes beyond making descriptions or statements: 'to say something is to do something ... by saying or in saying something, we are doing something' (Austin, 1962).

Types of speech acts

Acts performed in speaking – speech acts – were initially divided into two categories: constatives – utterances that described some state of affairs in the world; and performatives – utterances that, simply by virtue of being uttered, 'do' something or effect some change in the world (e.g. 'I object,' or 'I second the motion') (Austin, 1962). Moving beyond this dichotomy, Austin proposed that virtually every utterance is simultaneously both constative and performative. Further analysis differentiated three aspects of acts performed in language use. **Locution** is the act of saying something (i.e. making an utterance); **illocution** is the act performed in saying something (e.g. making a statement, an observation, a bet, a promise, etc.); and **perlocution** is what is accomplished by saying something – the result or consequence of the utterance on the beliefs, emotions, and actions of the hearers or the speaker (e.g. surprising, convincing, annoying, amusing someone) (Austin, 1962). Illocution and perlocution are the speech acts that are of particular interest in the study of communication from a social psychology perspective.

Many illocutionary acts are 'conventional' – they can be made explicit by a conventional performative statement where conventions determine the nature of the act performed. For instance, there are semantic conventions about what the word 'command' refers to, and social conventions about how commanding is done – by whom, to whom, when and where. Perlocutionary acts are less conventional in this sense, and are heavily (if not entirely) context-dependent. Perlocutions are 'based on the totality of the context in which the utterance occurs' (Austin, 1962). The perlocutionary consequences of someone's uttering a command, the effects on the beliefs, feelings, and actions of hearers, are far less conventional or predictable than its illocutionary aspects. Determining perlocutions requires taking into account who the interlocutors are, the social structures or premises of power or influence that exist between them and around them, and their shared knowledge, with respect to each other and the subject of the communicative exchange.

Direct and indirect speech acts

Another important distinction among speech acts concerns whether an illocutionary act is performed directly via the speaker's utterance, or is performed via another illocutionary act. In an indirect speech act, a speaker performs an illocutionary act indirectly, by performing another one. In a classic example, 'Can you reach the salt?' is not only a yes/no question, but also a request to pass the salt. Likewise, in the exchange:

> A: Let's go to the cinema tonight. (3)
> B: I have to study for an exam.

In (3), B performs the 'primary' illocution, rejecting A's proposal, by performing the 'secondary' illocution of stating that she must prepare for an exam (Searle, 1979). How a hearer interprets the primary illocution depends crucially on the context in which the utterance is being made, and A and B's mutual awareness of this context. Because A is likely to understand the time commitment involved in both studying for an exam and an evening at the cinema (and because A has proposed something and can reasonably expect a response to the proposal, see below), A can infer that B is declining his proposal. So an utterance can be either a direct or an indirect speech act, depending solely on its context. For indirect speech acts, utterance comprehension necessarily goes beyond literal meanings and conventional uses of words, and relies on the context – social, psychological, physical – in which communicative exchanges take place.

Felicitous acts

Speech act theory also characterises the conditions under which speech acts should be performed (felicity conditions), and the ways in which acts might fail if these conditions are not met (infelicities). There are four such felicity conditions: preparatory conditions, executive conditions, sincerity conditions, and fulfilment conditions (Austin, 1962). Preparatory conditions govern whether the circumstances and participants are appropriate for the speech act; executive conditions concern whether the act has been properly executed; sincerity conditions require the sincerity of the speaker executing the act; and fulfilment conditions are met if the intended perlocution is achieved. Where these conditions are not met, infelicities arise. Misinvocations involve violations of preparatory conditions (e.g. a bartender officiating a wedding ceremony). Misexecutions arise when executive conditions are not met (e.g. words of a solemn oath of office uttered in the wrong order, a marriage official using names that do not actually belong to the two people being married). Abuses occur when participants do not possess the thoughts or sentiments normally associated with the utterances they generate, breaching sincerity conditions (e.g. insincere apologies or condolences).

Speech act theory formalises an understanding that using language goes beyond simply saying things, and involves *doing* things. As such, it opens an interesting perspective on other dimensions of communication. First, how are speech acts typically performed? Or more generally, what is the nature of the interaction between speakers and hearers? Second, if meaning is created and transmitted not simply by virtue of saying particular words, but in the process of performing speech acts, how is meaning conveyed between interlocutors? How do speakers make meaningful utterances, and how is meaning recovered by hearers? The next section describes Grice's theory of implicature, which offers an important entry point into discussion of these questions.

Implicature

Grice's theory of implicature is based on 'basic rational assumptions' of how people communicate (Levinson, 1983). Conversations are not typically series of unconnected, unrelated remarks: they would not be rational if they were (Grice, 1975). Rather, in communication, 'each participant recognises in [their utterances], to some extent, a common purpose or set of purposes, or at least a mutually accepted direction' (Grice, 1989). This 'mutually accepted direction' is the basis of the Cooperative Principle, by which interlocutors are expected to 'make [their] contribution such as is required, at the stage at which it occurs, by the accepted purpose or direction of the talk exchange in which [they] are engaged' (Grice, 1975, p. 45). The Cooperative Principle characterises a 'default mode' in which typical communication occurs. Because this principle is an important part of the foundation of pragmatic theories, it is worthwhile to note that 'cooperative' in this sense is descriptive rather than prescriptive, and does not entail cooperation in a general sense – where people are mutually helpful and consciously act in ways to reach a common goal. The Cooperative Principle refers more generally to a tendency towards rationality in behaviour and communication, rather than cooperation in a conscious, helpful sense (Davies, 2007).

Maxims

A set of maxims describes in detail how this cooperation plays out. Speakers should be sufficiently, but not excessively, informative (maxim of Quantity); they should make true statements, for which they can provide proof (maxim of Quality); they should be relevant (maxim of Relation); and they should be clear (maxim of Manner) (Grice, 1975). This framework describes what a hearer can generally expect of a speaker. Again, these maxims are not prescriptive. Indeed, how and if the maxims are followed vary depending on the context of communication. For instance, the appropriate quantity of information for the purposes of a legal disclaimer would likely be inappropriate for a casual chat. In some cases, maxims are violated. A person can opt out of a maxim, by refusing to speak, for example. There can be a clash of maxims; one might not be able to provide sufficient information while making a statement for which proof can and normally should be given. A speaker can also flout a maxim intentionally, by saying something that seems superficially uncooperative.

This theoretical principle of cooperation, and the maxims of how interlocutors rationally engage in communication, are crucial to how people understand one another. Consider:

> A: We're running out of petrol. (4)
> B: There's a garage around the corner.

Within this framework, A can presume that the Cooperative Principle is being fulfilled, i.e. that B is saying something that generally fits with the common goals of their conversation, and that B is being informative, truthful, relevant, and clear. As such, presuming that B is communicating cooperatively: B is presumably replying in a way that is relevant to A's announcement of low fuel, and it is true that there is a garage around the corner. Thus, A can infer 'petrol can and should be procured from the garage' from B's utterance, even if B does not indicate it explicitly. This implicit meaning that fills the gap between what speakers say explicitly and what they might mean is a **conversational implicature**. Implicatures are the meanings inferred by the hearer that link the actual words uttered to the direction and goals of the conversation, preserving the assumption that the speaker is being cooperative (Grice, 1975). An implicature arises in cases where a speaker flouts a maxim; the hearer will infer that the speaker is behaving intentionally and rationally and intends to communicate something implicitly, something other than the simple literal meaning of her utterance. Furthermore, the hearer also infers that the speaker intends the intended, implicit meaning to be recognised (Levinson, 1983).

Such an account is important inasmuch as exchanges like (4) and non-literal utterances are not at all atypical. Certain figures of speech, like metaphor ('Their partnership is on a rocky road') and irony ('All I needed was another parking ticket') are based on implicit rather than explicit meanings. Grice's model describes how interlocutors interact, in rational cooperation, to reveal and recognise intentions and meanings as completely and accurately as possible, given the goals, constraints, and other circumstances of any given context.

Next we describe another inferential pragmatic theory, **Relevance Theory**, which argues that communication is based on the fundamental nature of the evolved human mind.

Relevance theory

Like implicature, relevance theory assumes that communication happens primarily through the expression and recognition of intentions (Sperber and Wilson, 1995). It does not, however, include a theoretical principle of cooperation nor the flouting of maxims. Rather it claims that communication is made possible by fundamental characteristics of human cognition within the framework of two principles.

The Cognitive Principle

The First (or Cognitive) Principle: Human cognition tends to be geared to the maximisation of relevance. Relevance can be considered a feature of any input into cognitive processes and how this input is processed. Input can be external stimuli, like feeling a cold wind, seeing someone run, hearing a spoken utterance; or internal representations, knowledge or experiences that are acquired, stored, and can be recalled. When one can combine inputs in a context to generate a new inference, they are said to be relevant (Sperber and Wilson, 1995).

If a commuter sees a clock on the station platform, recalls the scheduled arrival time of her train, and then infers that her train is late, the time displayed on the clock (an external stimulus) and the knowledge of the train timetable (an internal representation) are relevant in this context. Either input alone (seeing the clock time, or knowing the schedule) would not suffice to infer the train is late. Inputs are thus relevant when they can be combined to yield positive cognitive effects – inferences that can answer a question, confirm a hunch, or dissolve a doubt. The degree of relevance is a matter of the positive cognitive effects generated by inputs and the processing effort that is required to achieve them. Maximisation of relevance follows basic rules of economy, detecting the most relevant inputs using the least effort in recalling, observing, calculating or inferring. Generally, the greater the positive cognitive effects achieved by processing an input, the greater its relevance; the greater the processing effort expended, the less its relevance (Sperber and Wilson, 1995).

The Communicative Principle

The Second (or Communicative) Principle: Every act of overt or ostensive communication communicates a presumption of its own optimal relevance. Any overt utterance carries with it a 'tacit guarantee of relevance'; by virtue of making a statement, a speaker not only conveys some content, but also generates a presumption of optimal relevance, whereby a hearer can expect that the utterance is relevant enough to warrant attention.

According to relevance theory, there are two types of intention whenever language is used. These are the informative intention, or the intention to inform an audience of something, and the communicative intention, the intention to inform the audience of one's informative intention (Wilson and Sperber, 2004). In other terms, an utterance can be considered in two parts: the first part is the message (e.g. words, gestures, symbols, etc.). The second part of the utterance conveys that the first part was communicated overtly, or ostensively. In this view, communication succeeds or understanding is reached when the communicative intention is fulfilled, i.e. when the audience recognises the informative intention. Meanings are recovered following a 'relevance-theoretic comprehension heuristic': the hearer seeks an interpretation of the speaker's utterance that satisfies the presumption of optimal relevance, and aims to do so using the least effort possible. In (4), B's overt statement explicitly conveys the fact that there is a garage nearby (B's informative intention) and B's intention for A to know that there is a garage nearby (B's communicative intention). A works out the explicit meaning of B's utterance, and then makes further inferences, given their shared circumstances, that complement the explicit meaning, until A reaches a reasonable conclusion that makes B's utterance relevant in the expected way. Hence, A follows a path of least effort to compute that B is suggesting they go to that garage to fill the tank, presuming that B's utterance is not only relevant, but the most relevant utterance that B can make in context. Satisfied with this inference, A does not expend further effort on generating other interpretations.

Relevance and modularity

The processes of expecting and detecting relevance and building and testing hypotheses about a speaker's intentions based on her utterances are part and parcel of human cognition. As such, relevance theory describes not only cognitive processes, but also the structural nature of a mind that enables these processes; relevance-oriented cognition is enabled by a specific type of autonomous computational 'module' (Sperber and Wilson, 2002). A modular view of cognition argues that the mind comprises a complex suite of interconnected modules (e.g. Fodor, 2000; Sperber, 1996; Tooby and Cosmides, 1992). Modules are special-purpose devices that process a single kind of information according to procedures that are specific to that information, and do so by reference to that kind of information only. For example, if one were to hypothesise a module for processing visual perceptual information, the module would be characterised in terms of the kinds of information it takes in (e.g. from the retina), and the kinds of processes it uses to process this information (e.g. to construct geometrically structured visual representations). The module would not have available to it any 'top down' or contextual information about the kinds of objects in the environment, and it would not be used to process other kinds of information (e.g. auditory information). Additionally, relevance theory argues that such modules were shaped by evolutionary pressures to contribute to solutions of specific adaptive problems presented by humans' evolutionary past (see also Chapter 11).[1] Relevance theory hypothesises a module for 'meta-representation' for understanding others' and one's own representations *qua* representations, and a pragmatic interpretation device as a dedicated submodule of this 'mind-reading' module (Sperber, 2000). (See Box 5.1 for applications of pragmatic theories).

Pragmatic theory, cognition and social relations

Pragmatic theories of speech acts, implicature, and relevance differ from code and semiotics models in that they bring to bear important cognitive and social psychological factors in explanations of communication

Box 5.1   Persuasion, mass communication, and politeness – some applications for pragmatic theories

Persuasion

The study of persuasive communication is one area where pragmatic theories come to the analytical fore. Understanding 'the ways in which words and symbols influence people' and 'the way in which opinions and beliefs are affected by communication symbols' (Hovland, Janis, and Kelly, 1953) delves into perlocutionary acts, moving beyond the content and form of a message to consider the communicative context: individual and group goals and motivations, interpersonal and group relations, structures and dynamics of power and influence, common knowledge and shared references and conventions.

Dual-process models of persuasion, the Heuristic Systematic Model (Chaiken, Wood, and Eagly, 1996), and the Elaboration Likelihood Model, (Petty and Cacioppo, 1986a, 1986b) for instance, build on pragmatic concepts of relevance-oriented inferential processes. They propose distinct modes of processing a persuasive message: *systematic* or *central* – effortful and analytical processing that focuses on the informational content of a message – and *heuristic* or *peripheral* – processing that uses simple inferential rules or cognitive 'shortcuts' about the context of the message (e.g. 'experts know best' or 'the more people who believe something, the more likely it is to be true'). The extent to which someone formulates judgements based on a message's content or on contextual information is determined by factors including their motivation, availability of relevant heuristics, and availability of cognitive resources. In dual-process models, assessments of relevance and economy of information processing underpin the formulation of judgements and the degree to which persuasion is achieved. However, they also find a role for affective and motivational factors in influencing the persuasiveness of a communication. Such factors have a role in determining whether a message is processed according to central or peripheral route principles, and also in determining whether a message is persuasive.

'Loaded' and covert communication

Pragmatics can be instrumental in the analysis of forms of mass communication. Leech (1966) considers political journalism, religious oratory, and advertising to be 'loaded' language, as it 'aims to change the will, opinions, or attitudes of its audience' (Leech, 1966, p. 25). Investigation into these types of communication explores perlocutionary or persuasive effects, but also usefully analyses intentions. To what extent is communication ostensive, where both the informative intention and the communicative intention are made manifest to the hearer? To what extent is it covert, where the speaker intends to make the hearer know, think, or believe something (the informative intention) but seeks to conceal this intention (the communicative intention)? Tanaka (1998) has argued that many advertisements seek to conceal their communicative intentions, since to make them manifest may breach social conventions (e.g. where the advertisement uses appeals to sexual arousal or status to try to persuade someone to buy a product). This claim is a matter of debate, but it seems clear that, in relevance theoretic terms, the relevance in covert communication is not optimal, yet in many cases the informative intention is conveyed and recovered nonetheless (Taillard, 2000).

Pragmatic considerations emerge clearly in these applied questions. How do the audience's feelings, opinions, beliefs, or actions change as a consequence of the message? Do the changes occur in the expected or intended way? Are the intentions of the speaker overt or concealed? How are these intentions interpreted and how does this affect the outcomes of the communication? How does the communication indicate or influence the relations that exist between the interlocutors – trust, mistrust, respect, admiration, fear, authority, desire to emulate?

processes and outcomes. For example, performative and perlocutionary aspects of communication begin to address the social structures that link speakers and hearers, the premises of power or influence that exist between them, and their knowledge and attitudes about each other. Speech acts' felicity conditions are in part defined by notions of sharing beliefs and intentions, and these are related to the conventions regarding communication. Preparatory conditions, the conventions that govern appropriateness, are perhaps most clearly understood as cultural beliefs regarding the social psychological relations between interlocutors and settings – institutional, collective agreements, similar to other social institutions (e.g. Searle, 1996). Regarding cognition, theories of implicature and relevance view meaning in terms of communicators' capacities to detect and interpret others' intentions and motivations, and their tendency to use this to drive inferential processes. More explicitly still, relevance theory integrates its account of pragmatic interpretation with a modular view of cognition. Its postulation of a pragmatic interpretation submodule of a general mind-reading/theory of mind module, would be verified if, for example, utilising theory of mind during communication was automatic (not context-sensitive), and if the only influences on interpretation were the semantic and effort-related.

Opening up these complexities also generates further questions about the interface between pragmatics and broader issues of cognition and social interaction – a particularly salient issue is context. Pragmatic theories appear to agree on the importance of context in arriving at a reasonable interpretation of an utterance. Two types of context in language understanding have been differentiated (Bach, 1994). Limited or restricted context relates to specific types of information that combine with linguistic information to fix limited kinds of content: for example, indexical meanings (*you, me, this, here, now, today*) are fixed by limited contextual information types (time, place, identity of speaker/hearer, etc.). By contrast, broad context relates to anything that the hearer is to take into account to ascertain the speaker's communicative intention, including idiosyncrasies of belief and details of social interactions. This kind of context is potentially unlimited. Pragmatic inference appears to depend on broad context. Relevance theory offers an important development of the idea of context, in terms of the 'mutual cognitive environment'. This is understood as the range of information that is either directly available through perception, or shared by speakers, or inferable from either of these two sources. It suggests a dynamically changing subpart of broad context, limited by what is known or directly knowable.

Important questions about context remain, however. How do pragmatic theories account for contextual factors like emotion or mood and their influence on communication? What role does mood play in utterance interpretation? Other issues arise in the inferential processes described by pragmatic models. Such processes seem to require 'reading the mind' of one's interlocutor – interpreting a speaker's utterance based in part on conventional meanings of her words, and in part on what she must be intending by saying them. How does this mind-reading work? Does it work all the time? Is there always 'access' to others' intentions? Or might there be times when a speaker's intention is less 'readable'? In order for pragmatic theories to explain their chosen phenomena, they need to take into account findings concerning the nature of cognition, in particular as implicated in social relations. Two issues will be considered: the role of emotion and mood in the formulation and interpretation of utterances, and understanding the intentions of others and 'theory of mind' in communication.

Pragmatics and affect

An increasing body of evidence suggests that affect and cognition are closely related, which gives rise to the possibility of **affect-laden interpretation**. Surprisingly, however, pragmatic theories do not systematically address the role of emotion and mood in the design and interpretation of utterances. There are several ways in which emotion and mood relate to cognition, with differing implications.

Mood and recall

An important link between mood and utterance interpretation may emerge from the finding that recall from memory depends on mood. Utterance interpretation may be subject to mood-congruency effects – people are better able to recall items with positive valency when in a positive mood, and the opposite for items with negative valency (e.g. Bower, 1981). This has implications for relevance – if items congruent with a person's current mood are easier to access from memory, this reduces the associated cognitive effort and thereby increases the associated relevance of those items. Interpreting an utterance in mood-congruent terms appears to sit well with the spirit of relevance. Mood might be integrated as a specific kind of (psychological) context, which impacts on processing effort. Similarly, illocutions and perlocutions may depend on affective context, so that, for example, whether a hearer interprets a statement as a request or not, and whether they act on that interpretation, may relate to their mood.

Mood and interpretation

The tendency to engage in elaborative, constructive processing also varies according to mood. Positive mood makes people more flexible in interpretation, whereas negative mood makes people more constrained in interpretations. In particular, the tendency to use **schemas**, stereotypes, and other kinds of default information to make inferences increases with positive mood; but the tendency to focus more analytically on detailed information about specifics increases with negative mood (Clore and Huntsinger, 2007). Again, this has implications for implicature and relevance theory's notion of explicature – pragmatic interpretation in filling out explicit meaning. Making expansive inferences in implicit and explicit interpretation requires less effort and will therefore be more relevant if the mood is positive. If the mood is negative, then such inference is less likely and more effortful. A relevance framework might incorporate such mood effects as aspects of the psychological context informing utterance generation and interpretation – related largely to processing effort. In this case, mood is not associated with specific contents of interpretations, but with whether the possible interpretations are schematic and generative, or more literal and constrained. A parallel may arise for speech acts in that the flexibility of interpretation required to derive an indirect speech act from a direct speech act may be more likely if a hearer is in a positive rather than a negative mood.

Affect and embodied information processing

A final way mood appears to influence interpretation relates to processing effects. It has traditionally been assumed in psychology that cognition involves a form of more or less rational information processing, and that mood and emotion may alter input to that processing or filter its outputs, but that they do not form part of the processing itself. Indeed, emotion and mood have often been viewed as noise or distortion in erstwhile rational thought. A growing body of evidence suggests that this may not be the case. Damasio (1995) has argued that we should conceive of both emotion and cognition as information processing, and of them as interpenetrating each other. Clore and Storebeck (2006) have argued that in many cases of social and inferential uncertainty, emotion and mood may be treated as evidence regarding the possible inferential outcomes. This 'affect as information' hypothesis suggests that where there is empirical uncertainty, affect is used to fill in the interpretive gaps and to act as information to support a preferred inferential outcome (or to contradict a dispreferred outcome). Pragmatic interpretation is subject to precisely this kind of inferential uncertainty.

This matter may be exacerbated by recent findings suggesting that concepts – the mental representations associated with lexical items, hypothesised to form the basic contents for pragmatic interpretation – may incorporate not only descriptive information about the object of representation (e.g. features of the object), but also affective information regarding those objects. This relates to broader debates concerning the 'embodiment' of cognition (see Chapter 11), and the possibility that mental representations are not amodal symbols, but are rather intrinsically connected to bodily sensations, including tactile, sensory, kinaesthetic, and emotional sensations (e.g. Barsalou, 2008; Meteyard and Vigliocco, 2008). If representations are embodied in this way, this suggests that the understanding of mind in pragmatics theories may be rather impoverished. Processing effort might then relate not only to mood congruence as above, but also to other kinds of embodied congruence (see Pecher, Zeelenberg, and Barsalou, 2003 who argue that following verbal instructions to switch from one perceptual modality to another in thinking about an entity incurs processing costs).

So recent evidence of the interconnections of mood, other embodied states and cognition may raise significant challenges for pragmatic theories. A framework integrating such phenomena into pragmatic interpretation has yet to be fully developed.

Pragmatics and theory of mind

Pragmatic theories' relation to broader issues of cognition and social interaction also raises matters concerning the role of 'theory of mind'. A key role in pragmatic theories is played by the hearer aiming to and succeeding in working out the communicative intentions of the speaker; this happens with such regularity that speakers design their utterances with it in mind, and hearers are entitled to process utterances with this design principle in mind. It entails an ability and a tendency to understand in a very fine-grained way the contents of others' mental representations. The ability to grasp a speaker's mental state is central to relevance and Gricean accounts of pragmatics, and is also important both to the felicity conditions of illocutionary acts, and the way that locutionary, illocutionary and perlocutionary acts are related in **speech act theory**. However, pragmatic theories may not sufficiently reflect the finer points of people's 'mind-reading' in social interaction and in communication. Box 5.2 addresses the topic of understanding the intentions of others in more detail.

Mind-reading

A growing body of evidence suggests that people are not hugely successful at entertaining the mental representations of others when such representations are needed for use in online processing.[2] Keysar, Lin and Barr (2003) provide evidence of a dissociation between, on the one hand, being reflectively aware that one's own belief about something differs from someone else's belief about it and, on the other hand, actually using this awareness in routine interactions with that other person. Although one may know that one's own beliefs are different from someone else's, this knowledge may simply not be employed when one communicates and interacts with that other person. Apperley, Riggs, Simpson, Samson and Chiavarino (2006) also found that, although adults were able to make clear distinctions between reality and someone else's false belief, they had difficulty in holding this information in mind then using that information in reasoning. This also interacts with mood and emotions. Conversely, Lin, Keysar and Epley (2008) found that being in a negative mood makes people more likely to try to adopt the perspective of others; being in a positive mood makes one less likely to try do so. They connect this to the finding that being in a positive mood decreases the likelihood that one will engage in deliberate process- ing, (Bless and Igou, 2005), since this has been found to inhibit executive control (Oaksford, Morris, Grainger and Williams, 1996) – that is, to inhibit complex planning and monitoring of extended patterns of action and thought.

Egocentric communication

Evidence related to comprehension in interaction also suggests that prag- matic theories overestimate the use **theory of mind** in everyday commu- nication. Keysar and colleagues claim (e.g. Keysar, 2007; Epley, Morewedge and Keysar, 2004; Keysar and Barr, 2002) that speakers typically do not take into account what they think their hearers have in mind in framing their utterances; and hearers do not typically take into account what they know of speakers' beliefs in interpreting their utterances. Rather, speakers and hearers behave 'egocentrically', adjusting utterances or interpretations based on what they think their interlocutor knows or intends only if there is reason to do so. Typical 'reasons' to do so might involve indications that the communication exchange is failing for some reason – so entertaining the other's mental states is a means to repair a failure.

Keysar suggests two reasons for **egocentric** interpretation. The first is that one's own perspective is dominant in one's understanding, and so constrains interpretation of what a speaker says (see also Birch and Bloom, 2004). The second builds on the general point above, that consideration of others' mental states is not automatic, but a deliberate and effortful affair. Regarding speaking egocentrically, Keysar suggests that in cases where speak- ers superficially appear to be acting cooperatively, their reasons are, in fact, egocentric. For example, when speakers disambiguate their speech, which appears to help the hearer, it is often effected with no real consideration for how ambiguous it is to the hearer. Other cases include speakers being insensitive to what the hearer knows when providing atypical and typical information regarding a topic of conversation. Moreover, Keysar and Henly (2002) found that speakers systematically overestimate the extent to which they are understood by hearers – even where it could be clear that they are not understood. Keysar offers an explanation of these effects partly in terms of 'construal' (Ross, 1990) – the speaker already knows what they are trying to convey, and their communications seem to them to convey that inten- tion uniquely and to only have that one meaning. This is allied, again, to one's own perspective being more 'visible' to oneself (see also Chapters 9 and 11).

In sum, there is evidence that the general capacity to entertain the mental states of others, and the specific tendency to do so while communicating, are less systematic and widespread than pragmatic theories suggest.

Box 5.2   Understanding the intentions of others in communication: principle or paradox?

Pragmatic theories (and commonsense thinking) presume that people regularly entertain the beliefs and mind states of others during communication. Yet evidence suggests that is not the case most of the time, and that when we try to do so, we are not especially successful.

Why, then, do we think we think of others' thoughts when we communicate? One argument is that communication is influenced by 'paranoid optimism' – an evolved heuristic for social information processing that combines excess optimism about one's own ability to control events and generate positive outcomes for oneself, with hypersensitivity to possible harm originating from other people or external sources (Haselton and Nettle, 2006). The belief that one is understood in communication may be a form of self-deception that both enhances optimism about oneself and diminishes pessimism about others. As Trivers (2000) has argued, the propensity to engage in self-deception bolsters our capacity to deceive others. If we consciously represent true information about being in competition with someone, for example, it is more likely for this to 'leak' to others via communication. The belief that we regularly and successfully share intentions and beliefs in communication – when we in fact, do not or cannot – may originate in such a bias.

Evolutionary considerations also suggest that much communication is strategic – geared towards achieving adaptive purposes, which may be enhanced by self-serving biases; for example, communication between males and females in finding and retaining a mate, or communication between people seeking to establish and retain their positions in a hierarchy of status or power. Such communication is characterised by intense affective states, and there no priority on communicating one's true intention to the hearer, or indeed in wanting to know the speaker's true intention. They may involve deception and context-dependent asymmetries in communication related to its strategic goals or functions. For example, it is less vital for males to be aware of the long-term intentions of a potential partner than it is for females; and high and low-status communicators have different reasons for wanting to conceal or communicate different kinds of information. Such asymmetries are predictable if egocentrism is the default mode of communication (see Chapters 9 and 11).

So what role does the belief that we can and do share intentions actually play in communication? Consider Searle's (1969) distinction between types of rules. Regulative rules govern forms of behaviour that pre-existed the rule – rules of polite dining regulate eating, where eating pre-existed those rules. Constitutive rules not only govern the activity, but also in some sense constitute it – football, chess or marriage; following such a rule allows an action to 'count as' an instance of the appropriate type.

How does the intention to share intentions have a role in communication? One option is that it is constitutive of communication, as relevance theory appears to suggest. So such rules involve a description or definition – e.g. 'communication involves the intention to share intentions'. Another option is that it is a regulative rule that governs how we communicate, but that failure to do so would not entail not communicating. Such rules involve a hypothetical imperative – e.g. 'if you are communicating, try to share your intentions with your hearer', or even, 'if you are communicating, give the impression that you are trying to share your intentions with your hearer'. The latter accords more directly with an egocentric view.

Box 5.3   Intentions in communication: individual or collective, or both?

The discussion of the role of the recognition of intentions in communication raises questions about the very nature of those intentions. Individual intentions are those in which an individual represents him or herself as the subject or agent of a projected activity or belief. These intentions are describable by phrases such as 'I intend'. By contrast, joint or collective intentions place more than one individual as the subject or agent of an activity or belief. They can be described by phrases like 'we intend'.

How are the two types of intention related? A joint intention might comprise a combination of individual intentions together with a belief that each and the other holds those intentions. Thus, a joint intention to have dinner together would involve two people each thinking 'I intend to have dinner with my friend', plus the shared belief that the other person is thinking the same thing.

Another possibility is that joint intentions are not reducible this way – that they comprise an unanalysed 'primitive' mental state relating to sharing and engaging in a joint project or activity (e.g. Searle, 1996). While there is debate over the formulation of **collective intentionality** (Gilbert, 1989; Tuomela, 2003), there appears little doubt that some aspects of collective intentions are not reducible to a combination of individual intentions plus shared beliefs about those intentions. Because collective intentions involve commitments to future action or belief on the part of those who enter into them, they generate a normative or deontic constraint regarding what the participants should do, think, or feel.

Pragmatic theories differ concerning the nature of the intentions involved in communication. Relevance theory assumes that the hearer attempts to recover the speaker's communicative intention and informative intention. Both of these intentions are individual intentions. If there is a sense in which the speaker and hearer engage a joint intention to produce and interpret utterances according to relevance, such a joint intention would comprise a conjunction of the individual intentions of each to act according to relevance and a belief that the other possesses the appropriate intention.

By contrast, some versions of speech act theory (e.g. Searle, 1990) utilise a notion of collective or joint intention that does not reduce to individual intentions. Moreover, individual intentions may be derived from the collective intention (as opposed to creating that collective intention). Searle cites the difference between a bar-room brawl (governed by individual intentions), versus a boxing match (governed by a joint intention that determines individual intentions). In communication, speaker and hearer are guided in their generation and interpretation of utterances by 'we' intentions. Individual communicative intentions are generated via the collaborative interaction of the speaker and hearer, since they possess the 'we' intention to achieve the joint communicative goal by fulfilling their roles in the exchange. This does not imply that each has awareness of the individual intentions of the other – there is no contradiction between an egocentric approach to communication and a role for collective intentions as reflective beliefs. Carassa and Colombetti (2009) go further to suggest that collective intentions not only have a role in how meanings are arrived at, but may partly constitute such meanings.

Conclusion

The pragmatic theories examined in this chapter allow for a study of communication that enriches analyses of codes and language conventions by integrating the actions and interactions of interlocutors and the context in which they communicate. At the same time, pragmatic theories, considered in conjunction with a range of emerging empirical phenomena in cognitive and social psychology – the influence of mood and emotion on communication, and the role of theory of mind – spark challenging questions.

It may be that pragmatic theories offer explanations of core processes, to be supplemented by variations to deal with mood, intentions, and so on. Or perhaps pragmatic theories need to be overhauled, placing social-motivational and emotional factors at the core, so that the current explanations offered by the theories would be special cases in which those factors are for some reason not present. A third option is to view the pragmatic theories as providing useful ideal type models of communication, relative to which everyday communications will vary considerably according to, for example, social and affective factors.

Notes

1. Or more specifically, the 'environment of evolutionary adaptedness' or EEA, often characterised as the composite of selection pressures most evident in the Pleistocene era (see also Chapter 12).
2. 'Online' processing refers here to the use of mental processes while engaged in and influencing the process of communication or interaction with others. It is intended to contrast with reflective or offline processing, which relates to processes that take place when such communication or interaction is not present. In terms of theory of mind, online processing relates to making inferences and assumptions about the beliefs and intentions of another person while in the process of interacting or communicating with them, so that those inferences guide the process of the exchange, and where the inferences made have the potential to alter the trajectory of the exchange. Offline use of theory of mind involves, by contrast, inferences about another's mental states in planning prior to interaction, or in reflection subsequent to interaction.

6
Communicative Action and the Dialogical Imagination

Sandra Jovchelovitch

Keywords: Communicative action; intersubjectivity; language games; lifeworld; perspective-taking; public sphere; speech acts; strategic action; validity claims.

Introduction

For over 50 years Jürgen Habermas has pursued and developed a project which is rooted in the idea of communication. This concern, which as Habermas himself declared, expresses deeper biographical themes, has been addressed directly in *The Theory of Communicative Action* (TCA from now on), a two-volume book published in 1981 (English translations appeared in 1989–92). At the core of Habermas's contribution is the idea of communication as mutual understanding, a universal human ability embedded in the structures and rules we all learn when we learn how to speak a language. As we learn to speak we learn more than language: we also learn how to communicate for reaching mutual understanding.

In this chapter I will identify central elements of TCA, discussing in particular (a) the relations between communication and language and the tripartite model of the communicative act offered by Habermas: subjective, intersubjective and objective; (b) how communication is intertwined with claims to validity and the contexts in which these claims are rendered meaningful; and (c) the concepts of the **public sphere** and the **lifeworld** as grounds for the development and exercise of **communicative action**. I will then examine TCA in light of current developments in sociocultural psychology and the psychology of self–other relations, in particular processes of **perspective-taking**. Box 6.1 contextualizes Habermas's broader intellectual project.

Central to this chapter is the aim of counteracting the alleged 'idealism' of the Habermasian view, and the objective of demonstrating that communication for mutual understanding is necessary for producing practical solutions and indeed for the very production of the human mind and the survival of the human species.

Box 6.1   Habermas's project

The theory of communicative action is linked to a wider and ambitious project that seeks to place the very act of communication at the centre of a theory of rationality, a theory of society, and an assessment of the present. Commentators (Honeth and Joas, 1991) have pointed out that in TCA Habermas had four main objectives: first, he wanted to sketch a meaningful concept of what human reason is; second, to delineate a theory of action that could differentiate between communicative and strategic action; third, to produce a theory of societal order that offered a connection between the concepts of lifeworld and systems, or between human actions, representations, and cultures and formal systemic arrangements; and last but not least, to offer a diagnosis of contemporary societies that could operate as a warning that our social orders today typically overlook the human dimension, being as they are dominated by systems and based on strategic action.

It is here, perhaps, that we can better appreciate what is truly innovative about Habermas: his theory of communication is not only about unpacking the phenomenon of communication per se, but using it to understand the making – and unmaking – of persons, societies, and cultures. We cannot understand what we are without a clear assessment of communicative action and it is through an understanding of its distortions and failures that we can understand our troubles and the dangers embedded in current societal orders. Habermas dedicated himself to this very ambitious project with impressive scholarship and a radical imagination that relates back to the influence of the early Frankfurt School on his intellectual development and to the personal, social, and political experience of growing up in Nazi Germany. This is reflected in the breadth and vast scope of the book: it offers a theory of communication and much more. With great erudition, Habermas revisits major intellectual sources in philosophy and the social sciences and sets out to reassess and rescue the concept of rationality that was proposed by the European Enlightenment and the project of modernity. In doing so he takes us through the shortcomings and distortions of this project as well as its historical achievements to try and convince us that there is hope ahead if we manage to redefine human rationality as a communicative act.

Communication and language

Habermas argues that our ability to communicate is universal and is to be found in the basic structures and rules that all human subjects master in learning how to speak a language. In becoming speakers of a language we learn not only how to vocalise words and master grammatical sentences but also, and perhaps more importantly, we acquire a competency to communicate that is in-built in language (Habermas, 1976/1998). Speaking a language is not just a matter of being able to produce grammatical sentences; when we speak we also relate to the world around us, to other people and to our own intentions, feelings, and desires. Communication is action because language is a human practice for doing and relating rather than a formal set of signs that conveys messages and is held together by formal rules. The fundamental communicative competence of *Homo sapiens* is embedded in the structure of language and **speech acts** that need to be understood beyond the syntax and grammar of one language or another. It is in the ways in which ordinary people use language in everyday settings to co-construct, sustain or challenge social relationships that we find the universal core of communicative action.

As human subjects we are born to engage and seek understanding with our conspecifics, and the very ways in which we speak to one another can demonstrate this. The binding and bonding functions of language as it is spoken by social actors have a central role: language connects us to each other, to the world, and to ourselves. The understanding of language in terms of a social theory of everyday interactions can reveal what is at work when language is used. This, however, requires a theory of language that moves away from the monological view which separates language rules and structures from language use and everyday interaction. To this end, Habermas turns to a detailed examination of the Anglo-American traditions of analytical philosophy and the theories of language and speech acts it developed (Habermas, 1988/1988). Wittgeinstein's (1953) insight about **language games** and their connection with forms of life and the theory of speech acts of Austin and Searle (see Chapter 5) are particularly important.

Wittgenstein offers a break from the idea that truth is to be found in descriptive statements and formal propositions by suggesting it has a social context: it depends on language games that are always bound to 'forms of life'. Wittgenstein (1969) writes: 'when language games change, then there is a change in concepts, and with the concepts the meaning of words change'. The notion of language game is central to elucidate the context-dependent nature of words and meaning. So, when we speak, what we say does not travel unmodified, and concepts and words that make sense or are funny in the UK may become unintelligible or very weird in the middle of the Amazon (even if we translate it into Portuguese or Yanomami) where different social interactions and rules lead to a different language game. As with all games, language games obey rules and regulations that pertain to the terrain in which they are played. The statement 'The Bororo are Arara' makes perfect sense in the language game of the Bororo Indians of central Brazil, connected as it is to a culture and form of life that links the identity of the Bororo Indians to the being of the Arara bird (see Box 6.2). Alternatively, a statement proposing that human beings are birds can be problematic in most Western contexts, where other language games are at work. Wittgenstein's insight about language games and the context-dependent nature of the truth of propositions is central for emphasising the social context of actions and interactions.

In the theory of speech acts of Austin (1962) and Searle (1969, 1979), Habermas identifies the first step to unfold the inherent communicative character of language and its connection to action. Austin's original claim that 'speaking is doing' (Austin, 1970; see also Chapter 5) is central to Habermas's efforts and becomes a major foundation for the theoretical development of TCA. The idea that we can do things with words appeals to Habermas because it focuses on utterances rather than sentences – on what is spoken, said, uttered by concrete people in concrete settings and relations – and highlights what speech acts do. They clearly do more than just describe states of affairs in the world and convey messages from senders to receivers and back. Through speech acts social actors coordinate action and engage in a variety of intersubjective relations.

The idea that we can do things with words was not only important for Habermas. It marked what some consider a general paradigmatic shift in the social sciences as a whole, consolidating a linguistic turn that moves away from a monological to a dialogical paradigm (Marková, 2003). Habermas's TCA itself became an important contribution to this change, offering as it does a theory of rationality and language based on dialogue and **intersubjectivity** rather than on the monologue of a solitary individual detached from others and social context. This emphasis echoes many sociocultural traditions in psychology, such as Vygotsky's approach to cognitive development (discussed in Chapter 1) and the reiteration of the importance of the symbolic realm in psychoanalysis (Chapter 9).

Communication based on an ideal speech situation that facilitates action oriented towards reaching understanding fundamentally depends on the concept and practice of intersubjectivity. Communicative competence inheres in language because when learning and speaking a language actors do much more than engaging and mastering formal syntaxes and grammars. We do things with words – we relate, we perform, we disclose and so forth. What we do in what we say, as we will see in the next pages, always involves action at three levels: towards world, others, and our own selves. And this crucially depends on the language game of the context we are in. Words make sense or not depending on the language game that establishes their meaning and how they are used.

Contexts of use, in which speech acts are enacted, are central for how meaning and therefore understanding is produced. What is said and what is understood depends on the language games of specific intersubjective contexts and on how the actions and interactions of interlocutors define the meaning of a sentence. Speech act theory is able to make a distinction between what speakers say about the world and the kinds of intersubjective relations that they establish in doing so. This distinction is crucial for TCA because it places intersubjectivity – or self–other relations in the language of social psychology – at the heart of a theory of language and communication. Intersubjectivity (self–other relations) becomes central for any analysis of what goes on when people communicate and offers the blueprint for Habermas's assertion that communication is action oriented towards reaching understanding.

Communication for mutual understanding

In the first volume of TCA, Habermas writes:

> I shall speak of communicative action whenever the actions of the agents involved are coordinated not through egocentric calculations of success but through acts of reaching understanding. ... In communicative action participants are not primarily oriented to their own individual successes; they pursue their individual goals under the condition that they can harmonize their plans of action on the basis of common situation definitions. In this respect the negotiation of definitions of the situation is an essential element of the interpretative accomplishments required for communicative action.
>
> (1989b, pp. 285–6)

In defining communicative action through acts of reaching understanding, Habermas emphasises that understanding is the medium for coordinating action, which necessitates common definitions for situations and the erasure if egocentric calculations of success. Two key issues emerge here, both recurrent themes in this book. The first is how egocentric calculations relate to communication, a problem emphasised by both evolutionary and psychoanalytic approaches to communication (see Chapters 11 and 9 respectively). The second is the role of common definitions for situations, a major problem the social sciences deal with, expressed in constructs such as background (Searle, 1995), habitus (Bordieu, 1994), collective and social representations (Durkheim, 1898; Moscovici, 2000) and of course, the lifeworld, which I shall be discussing later. In TCA both issues come together. Dialogue that seeks mutual understanding is the focal point that displaces egotistic preoccupations while allowing the coordination of action through the consolidation of a shared view on how to define the situation. It is out of this dialogue that common definitions and the coordination of actions are eventually habitualised and institute historically the basis of shared representations and meanings that form the lifeworld, or the background (Searle, 1995; Berger and Luckman, 1966). Incidentally, both requirements – erasing egotistic calculations and establishing a shared view of situations – open TCA to a great deal of criticism, and it is here that we find the origins of the alleged idealism of Habermas's view. I shall consider the criticisms towards the end of the chapter, but for the time being let us try to understand what substantiates his proposal. Intersubjectivity again is the key to understand Habermas.

Habermas is after a model that can take the analysis of action beyond its purposive functions to consider the ways in which its coordination is intertwined with interpersonal relations and necessitates mutual understanding if it is to succeed. Previous theories of action may have been helpful for clarifying the structures of purposive activity, but have remained limited by an atomistic conception that takes the isolated actor operating in the objective world as its point of departure. Habermas wants to leave behind this isolated actor and the idea that action is only about goals. He turns to acts of reaching understanding to unpack the intersubjective processes that constitute action in the world and analyse the cooperation between persons who meet each other in the world as co-constituted addressees. The process at stake here is the making of joint intentions: it is not the isolated, discrete 'I' or the unidirectional, discrete 'I + I' view of action but the very constitution of the 'we' actor of joint intentionality (Tomasello, 2005). Habermas's overall project becomes once again visible as he moves away from a model centred on the individual subject as sender and/or receiver of information to a model of co-constructed interaction that in intersubjective encounters seeks to build a shared view and an understanding of what speakers raise with their utterances. Note here the strong parallel with Freire's overall view of communication (as discussed in Chapter 2) in which speakers involved in dialogue co-construct a given object of knowledge.

To appreciate this theoretical move, let us imagine social action as an empirical fact: any two or more individuals want to pitch a tent. One way of conceiving what happens is to look at the problem 'pitching a tent' as an existing and objective state of affairs in which each one of the individuals confronts the environment and each other from a self-contained perceptual/cognitive base. Individual actors are independently constituted and holders of previously acquired individual knowledge; the focus is on the goal of 'pitching a tent'. Alternatively we can consider that 'pitching a tent' is an activity jointly produced. Whereas persons arrive at the field with previous ideas, knowledge, and even traditions about how to pitch a tent, as they meet with others and engage in the pitching of the tent they will seek/need to establish a mutual understanding about what is to be done and how to define the situation. To arrive at some kind of consensus about the situation and what needs to be done, actors per force engage in a dialogical process of mutually recognising one another and the claims that they make as to what, how, and why things should be done. In doing so they end up with a pitched tent but also more: they have interacted, renewed relationships, and expressed themselves as psychological beings.

This kind of situation illustrates what is necessary if social actions oriented to goals are to succeed: there must be communication between actors that puts the coordination of action and the requirement of mutual understanding at the centre of the interaction. Egocentric calculations of success are not allowed here, not least because they would be detrimental to the goal. When A communicates with B to pitch a tent, the focus is not on the previously held views, opinions, and desired course of action of A and B. The focus of the communicative act is on how these partners in interaction can find a joint course of action as they seek to understand each other and construct a shared understanding that enable the pitching of a tent. There may be asymmetries or symmetries in the knowledge, status, and role of the partners, but if communication is to be present, they will bracket out these issues and focus on understanding each other to coordinate action. In this process they integrate their individual actions into a plan that emerges as *a shared plan of action* from the communicative act. In communication for mutual understanding, calculations of success are erased from the equation and we find action, definitions of reality, and individual goals intrinsically bound to the dialogical processes embedded in the communicative act.

This dimension of intersubjective dialogue, that is inherent in the structure of language/speech acts and fundamental in Habermas's theory of social action, leads him to consider action oriented towards reaching understanding, or *communicative action*, the most basic and fundamental type of action, upon which all other forms depend. Action that does not prioritise mutual understanding is action of another kind: communication it is not. It is also important to note that communication is placed in an ideal speech situation where interlocutors disregard issues of status and positioning so as to concentrate on mutual understanding, something that crucially links TCA to Habermas's theory of the public sphere. One final aspect to keep in mind here is that the search for mutual understanding is always grounded in a language game and a form of life, which for Habermas is expressed in the concept of the lifeworld. In this way communicative action is always already connected to a public sphere and to a lifeworld.

Communicative action, language and validity

In his analysis of communicative action, Habermas presents the thesis that everyday language has an in-built connection with validity. Linguistic utterances, as they are used in everyday processes of communication, can be construed as claims to validity. When people talk and engage in everyday linguistic interaction what they do is to raise and respond to **validity claims**, and communication is primarily a matter of raising and responding to validity claims. This thesis again combines the insights of Searle's theory of speech acts (see Chapter 5) and Austin's important distinction between locutionary and illocutionary speech acts. However, Habermas goes one step further in his analysis of acts of mutual understanding by bringing to his framework a third expressive dimension. The expressive dimension is taken from Karl Bühler, a German psychologist who proposed that sentences employed communicatively serve at the same time to express intentions, represent a state of affairs and establish an interrelation.

So Habermas reworks Austin's twofold distinction into a tripartite model to argue that claims for validity operate at three different levels: the propositional level of content; the intersubjective level of interactions; and the expressive level of the individual subject. For Habermas, previous theories of meaning had failed to take into account all three dimensions, until Searle tried to address this problem with his theory of speech acts. With Bühler's theory of language functions and Austin's paradigm change in the philosophy of language, he constructs the theoretical edifice of his own thesis that everyday communication has an inbuilt connection to validity.

The model Habermas advances involves thus a twofold and then threefold distinction between the locutionary or constative dimension; the illocutionary or performative dimension, and finally the expressive dimension. When we speak, we make validity claims in these three dimensions at once: our linguistic utterances contain validity claims about a state of affairs in the world, about the rightness of our interactions with others, and about our own sincerity as speakers. It becomes very clear then that as we interact with other people, we say and claim more than what is there in the propositional content of our utterances. Embedded in our spoken sentences are claims about the validity of our ways of cognitively stating a situation in the world, its rightness in a given context and our own positioning and behaviour as speakers. Understanding that validity claims operate at all these three levels is very important to the definition of communication as mutual understanding. The propositional content of speech acts, or its constative dimension, usually seen as purely 'objective' and detached, is carried through energies that are also social and subjective, that is, fuelled by the desire of interlocutors to connect and to understand each other as they disclose themselves and claim their sincerity and authenticity.

Let us try to examine how this tripartite model of claims to validity unfolds in a set of simple examples. When I say 'It is raining today' I am referring to something in the external world. I am describing a situation using language to produce a statement that has propositional content, that is, it proposes cognitive content about a situation or thing in the external world: rain rather than blue skies. 'Marion is telling Rob about last night's party' or 'This table is red' are examples of similar types of statements. In these three sentences there is a claim to the validity of what I propose; in claiming that the table is red I affirm that this is valid to the table that I am pointing to. This is the dimension that most theories of language have addressed, and according to Habermas been limited by, when constructing theories of meaning and language. But criticising this limitation does not mean that we should dismiss this important dimension. The propositional content of utterances matters a great deal because these are ultimately representations we deploy to narrate states of affairs in the world. The cognitive dimension of our speech links our talk to something that is outside ourselves in the world and expresses our efforts to understand and communicate with accuracy what we see and perceive in our objective world. In everyday communication, speakers claim that what they say and propose in representing the objective world is true, and in this sense show how the very notion of truth remains central to our efforts to know, to communicate, and to understand ourselves. This is the locutionary or constative dimension of speech acts that refers to the objective world and to how we use knowledge to describe the world.

Now, there is more than this to speech because as we have seen, we can do many things with words. In saying that 'Marion is telling Rob about last night's party' I am also interacting with someone, letting them know what happened last night, perhaps warning them about a situation that may turn out to be uncomfortable. So my speech act also engages me in an intersubjective exchange that addresses and constructs a 'we-situation', a domain that pertains to the shared world of self and other. In this interactive mode of communication my speech act is also a claim, even if not in a verbally explicit manner, that there is normative rightness in my saying so, that to act in this way when I relate to you is acceptable. This claim to the rightness of what I say to you in a given context of interaction reaffirms our relations and renews our intersubjective bond and intersubjectively recognised norms of social action. In this way we can also read the above sentences as '[I hereby can assure you that] it is raining today'; '[I am warning you that] Marion is telling Rob about last night's party'; '[I can confirm to you that] this table is red'. This is the illocutionary or performative dimension of my speech act which refers to the world of intersubjective relations between people and the norms and regulations that mediate human interactions.

The third dimension of speech acts Habermas refers to is the expressive dimension. The expressive dimension encompasses the subjective world of speakers, that which we all disclose and express about our own selves when we speak. In speech we also disclose dimensions that refer to our sincerity and authenticity as speakers, to how truthful we are or try to be as we speak. So when I say 'This table is red' I am also disclosing something about myself; as mundane as this utterance is, it contains a dimension that makes a claim about my own sincerity in telling you that I am truthful when I state that the table is red. In this dimension is the fundamental recognition of the place of the individual in the communicative act and how internal worlds of subjective experience come to bear in contexts of communication. Claims to validity also pertain to the realm of what we feel and how we engage with the world as psychological beings, holders of identities and perspectives that matter a great deal in the shared worlds we at once construct and inhabit.

Table 6.1   Speech acts and communicative competence

Mode of communication	Cognitive	Interactive	Expressive
Type of speech acts	Constatives	Regulatives	Avowals
Domains of reality	'The' world of external nature	'Our' world of society	'My' world of internal nature
Basic attitude	Objectivating	Norm-conformative	Expressive
General functions of speech	Representation of facts	Establishment of legitimate interpersonal relationships	Disclosure of speaker's subjectivity
Validity claim	Truth	(Normative) rightness	Truthfulness (sincerity)

Source: Adapted from 'What is Universal Pragmatics?' (Habermas, 1998/1976)

In this way we can read the above sentences as '[I am being truthful when I tell you that] it is raining today'; '[I am sincere in telling you that] Marion is telling Rob about last night's party'; '[When I tell you that] This table is red [I am not trying to deceive you or lie to you – or perhaps I am]'.

In his tripartite model of speech acts, Habermas binds the communicative act to an intersubjective context in which interlocutors act to understand each other at different levels of their interaction: self, self–other relations, objective world. All these dimensions pertain to the act of communication; in acts of communication there is always more than just sending or receiving messages and describing a state of affairs. As Table 6.1 shows, inbuilt in speech acts are communicative competences that express ourselves as subjects, establish and renew relations between people, and produce representations and narratives about the world, all at the same time. In doing so, these competences also produce domains of reality, corresponding to our internal, shared, and objective worlds. This model moves comfortably between microprocesses of communication and personal expression and larger macroprocesses of societal and cultural reproduction, showing how micro and macro constitute one another.

In raising and responding to validity claims about these three dimensions, we find that these claims, as much as the words that carry them, are not free-floating but pertain to specific pragmatic contexts, which define from the outset what is intelligible and acceptable for interlocutors. I turn to this problem next.

Validity, context, meaning

The tripartite model of communication presented above aims to reconnect the representational function of language to its expressive and appellative (that is, appealing) functions. The 'logos', or cognitive, function of language has been traditionally conceived as the privileged ground for validity claims, whereas the expressive and appellative dimensions tended to be considered as irrational forces. From this perspective, as I speak and represent the world through language, the relations in which I engage and the personal experiences I display are usually seen as obstacles that are likely to compromise the validity of my propositions. For example, we have all come across the idea that in being emotional, or driven by our relationships, we fail to read the world as it is.

TCA breaks away from this tendency of dismissing the rational content of our interactive and subjective lives by integrating logos, pathos, and ethos (see Chapter 10 on rhetoric for a detailed consideration of these dimensions) and demonstrating that in everyday communication speakers raise and respond to validity claims at all three levels. Habermas writes, 'we should conceive the illocutionary role as the component that specifies which validity claim a speaker is raising within her utterance, how she is raising it, and for what' (1998/1981: 110). That is to say, when we speak the illocutionary dimension has power to engage interlocutors in a relationship that can provide reasons for and understanding of what we say, why we say it, and for what we say it. Sometimes we accept the validity of a subjective or social claim and therefore also accommodate the validity of a proposition that may otherwise sound odd, strange or challenging. In social psychology we come across these claims all the time; representations make sense for individuals and communities not only because they represent states of affairs in the world but also, and at times more fundamentally, because they express identities and ways of life (Jovchelovitch, 2007). It is the subjective and intersubjective dimensions that hold explanatory power over the intelligibility and acceptability of representations that do not correspond cognitively to a state of affairs in the world, but are nevertheless redeemed as valid. Through communicative acts we exchange reasons at different levels and contextualise the rationality of our propositions, linking them to a person, to an interaction, and to a way of life.

It is in this sense that all validity claims depend on the context in which communication takes place and, as with words, on the kind of social game of which the communicative act is a part. What makes our claims intelligible and acceptable are the totality of symbols and representations, the language games and the ways of life to which we belong. We only understand the meaning of utterances if we understand that meaning cannot be separated from validity, and that to understand the meaning of an utterance it is necessary to understand its validity in relation to the language and culture in which it has a place and the communicative context in which it takes place.

Validity claims are thus linked to contexts that define the acceptability and intelligibility of claims posed by interlocutors: different ways of life and different contexts of justification shape both the meaning and the validity of utterances. This, however, does not mean that everything goes and

Box 6.2　Meaning and validity in the Brazilian Xingu

As mentioned earlier in this chapter, the Bororo Indians living in the Xingu area of central Brazil describe themselves as Arara, a tropical bird that is part of their natural environment. 'The Bororo are Arara' is a statement whose claim to validity we may find difficult to accept, for in the West we tend to think that if we are human beings we cannot be birds and vice versa. The statement, however, makes much more sense and its validity starts to hold if situated in the expressive and social world of the Bororo, in the cultural traditions they hold and the way of life they sustain. As Lévi-Strauss (1976) showed, the Bororo link human, animal, and natural worlds in a single cosmology of identifications that sustains the fuzziness of boundaries as a logical way of life. Outsiders communicating with the Bororo for mutual understanding may be compelled to accept the validity of the statement because the force of their identity and cultural claims offer good reasons for the idea that the Bororo are indeed Arara. In the language game of Bororo life, being both human and bird makes perfect sense. And at a time when the sharp separation of human life from its natural habitat seems to pose an increasing threat to the very possibility of life on this planet, the Bororo statement takes on an uncanny universal rationality.

every claim we raise is equally justifiable. It is one thing to understand what makes sense and is acceptable in a context; it is quite another to assert that what makes sense and is accepted by contexts cannot be criticised and, if necessary, dismissed. Our contemporary world is fraught with a multitude of claims to validity operating at all the three levels of Habermas's model. There are different claims about self, about the ways in which we interact and relate to each other, and about the ways in which we represent the objective world around us.

So how do we settle different claims to validity? There are a number of different ways of settling contested claims. First, we can appeal to authority and suggest that a claim is valid because it was put forward by, say, a professor, a scientist, or a priest. We could also appeal to tradition and claim that there are tested and reliable ways of thinking and acting, which have been operational for a long time and are intrinsic to our institutions and laws. Rather than argue about a new recipe for Tarte Tatin one could (probably with good reasons) just draw upon the accumulated wisdom of the traditional formula and its delicious outcome. One could also appeal to force to settle contested claims, and many governments and states have done so: dictatorships or wars are good examples of resolving contested claims using force and violence.

In TCA, the route suggested to settle different validity claims is the use of reasons. Historically, the use of reasons has been regarded as fundamental to the idea of rationality. It is in the practice of argumentation, in discursive interaction, in a conversation where interlocutors give reasons for and reasons against claims that a communicative rationality emerges and defines the validity of all claims made in all the three dimensions of speech acts. Note here that the analysis of an ideal speech situation, in which interlocutors free from coercion use reasons to settle differences, is not only central for a theory of communication but at the same time provides foundations for a theory of the public sphere. The settling of different claims through the use of reasons and the experience of achieving mutual understanding in communication that is free from coercion provides a communicative procedure for pluralistic public spheres, which is a crucial point of connection between TCA and theories of the public sphere. Settling contested claims can thus take a rational route that is *communicative* rather than coercive.

At this stage we can have a first overview of what Habermas packs into the communicative act: inherent to the everyday performance of speech acts is a system of communication between social actors that connects language, meaning, and the coordination of action with contextualised validity claims and the exchange of reasons and arguments. Because communicative performance involves three levels of self, self–other and world, it is capable of producing and reproducing the social order at the level of the person, the interpersonal, and the objective world. The three dimensions of subjective, interrelational, and objective that had been until then separated in both philosophy and the social sciences are connected again in the theory of communicative action.

The public sphere and the lifeworld

Communicative action is always context bound and that is why the concepts of the public sphere and the lifeworld are so important in TCA. The ideal speech situation is linked to, and to some extent dependent on, both notions. In the theory of the public sphere, Habermas presents the historical and normative dimensions of a societal space that enacts, or at least facilitates, the principles of communicative action. Through the notion of the lifeworld he substantiates the connection between meaning, validity, and the cultural frameworks, the practices, values, representations, and background assumptions human communities construct (Habermas, 1998/1988). Both concepts are complementary to communicative action.

The public sphere and communication

In the theory of the public sphere, Habermas offers an account of the emergence, transformation, and eventual disintegration of the bourgeois public sphere, a unique phenomenon created out of the relations between capitalism and the state in the seventeenth and eighteenth centuries in Europe. Important in understanding TCA, inquiry on the public sphere is also an inquiry into the normative ideals that guide a political community: How are decisions made and on what basis? Who participates and who doesn't? How are contested issues resolved? This inquiry traces the social and historical conditions that facilitated rational and critical debate about public issues, and how open access, genuine argument, and accountability become principles guiding decision-making in public life.

The public sphere is defined as a body of 'private persons' who assemble together and form a public to discuss matters of common concern. It is a space where citizens meet and talk to each other in a fashion that guarantees access to all. Unrestricted debate about public matters is an essential feature of the public sphere and central to understand how it relates to communicative action. Argumentative dialogue, not dissimilar to the ideal speech situation that seeks mutual understanding, is the novel central procedure introduced by the liberal model of the public sphere. Its ideal features are:

- Debate in the public space must be open and accessible to all.
- The issues at stake must be of common concern; mere private interests are not admissible.
- Inequalities of status are to be disregarded.
- Participants are to decide as peers.

These ideal features constitute the principles that regulate discursive interaction in public and provide the social foundations for the ideal speech situation that is at the centre of communicative action. The public sphere was created as a social space where arguments and dialogue are central to reach understanding and deal with difference in perspectives, a space where participants engage with each other on the basis of what they have to say and disregard inequalities in wealth, status, and power. Out of this open, unrestricted, and non-coercive discursive interaction emerges public opinion, understood as a consensus achieved through free debate about common life.

This new culture of public debate was historically linked to large societal transformations at the level of economic, social, political, and cultural life (see Box 6.3). These transformations were deeply related to tremendous social psychological transformations in society and went hand in hand with the way individuals understood themselves, their role, and competences. The new public changed society psychologically because it introduced debate, questioning, the idea that individuals could reason for themselves, produce views and solutions for what happened in society. The new public sphere of individual citizens constructed opinions, ideas, representations, values, and

Box 6.3   The Emergence and 're-feudalisation' of the public sphere

The public sphere emerged in early modern Europe as a counterweight to absolutist states. It evolved in the context of the development of early modern capitalism and the intense discussions that were linked to the rise of literacy, the emergence of new forms of civic association, and a new independent press. Habermas notes that the spread of salons and public houses in Germany, France, and England was overwhelming at the turn of the 18th century; by 1710 only London had more than 3000 pubs (public houses), each with a constant group of habitués. The new public sphere introduced a strong distinction between itself, the state, the economy, and private interests. It was conceived as an arena of free debate, unconcerned with buying and selling, for the production and circulation of discourses that could be critical of the state and markets. It challenged traditional forms of power associated with kinship, lineage, and birth rights by introducing the power of a public capable of rational debate and argumentation.

One of the key targets of this new liberal culture was the secrecy of monarchic states. The medieval style of public representation referred to the status publicly displayed by the feudal lord and was immediately linked to his concrete persona: in presenting himself he presented power. Critical discussion and debate were alien to the exercise of power and the only public face of the Renaissance state was splendour, pomp, and showing off. Yet its core, as Habermas remarks, was submerged in secrecy. The word 'secretary', which to this day refers to high office in government, expresses well the idea that to govern is to be a keeper and guardian of secrets.

It is this form of medieval representation that resurfaces in contemporary societies, leading to what Habermas calls the 're-feudalisation' of the public sphere. Today, just as before in feudal monarchic states, prestige, spectacle, and display are central features of what is 'public'. If we think about the invasion of 'celebrity culture', of the importance and space granted to the private lives of individuals in the media and the press, to the following of minute daily private concerns in Twitter, we will understand what Habermas means: instead of critical debate, spectacle; instead of focus on issues of common concern, a focus on the trivial; instead of independence and separation between state, economic power, and public opinion, clear interference, expressed in lobbying and the dominance of public relations. In all of these we can spot the disguised touch of secrecy under the light of an excessive visibility whose true aim is to take attention away from what really matters in the public sphere.

sentiments about a diversity of issues potentially questioning the actions of governments and states. Individuals and groups could think for themselves, read for themselves, and engage in conversations that sought impact and change in the institutional order of the day.

Central to what allowed public opinion to flourish and be exponentially propagated by emerging institutional channels (such as legally guaranteed free speech, a free press, and freedom of assembly) was this psychological and political subject: individuals interacting in public now could think, express ideas, have opinions, and, for the first time, have a real impact in society as citizens. The new subject of the public sphere, through rational discussion of political life, was creating a novel space between the state and society and rendering the state accountable to its citizens. The history of the public sphere neatly demonstrates how the psychological, the social, and the political are inseparable in human society.

The use of argumentative dialogue for political participation and the principle of accountability were thus the two novel conceptions introduced by the new public. The circulation of public opinion becomes itself a new political player mediating the relations between the state and the new civil society. In this context the emergence and development of mass media of communication become a key element of the public sphere (in this respect see Chapters 13–15 on mass-media health, political and science communications). Novel means of communication, in particular the consolidation of the press, publicise the interests of the new public and at the same time put the actions of the state under scrutiny, pushing processes of decision-making and political deliberation into the open.

Elsewhere I have suggested that Habermas's work should be understood as more than a historical and sociological account of the bourgeois public sphere; his inquiry on the public sphere is also a social psychological study, a powerful narrative of the transformations that occurred in the subjectivity and mentality of a new social class as it tried to assert itself and radically change the social landscape of European societies. Embedded in Habermas's theory of public life is also a theory about perspective-taking, reciprocity, and role-taking in social life, about the societal requirements for dialogue between self and other to take place, and about the need to justify and validate one's position in relation to interlocutors (Jovchelovitch, 2007). 'The public sphere as the space for reasoned communicative action is the issue that has concerned me all my life', says Habermas in his Kyoto lecture (2004). Indeed, Habermas's theory of the public sphere cannot be understood outside his theory of communicative action.

Communicative action and the lifeworld

Whereas the public sphere refers to the societal space and institutional arrangements that enable/facilitate communicative action, the concept of the lifeworld is crucial in defining the conditions for all possible communication. Drawing on the analysis of background knowledge put forward by Wittgenstein, Habermas retrieves the long-standing phenomenological concept of the lifeworld (Husserl, 1970; Schuetz, 1970) as complementary to communicative action. The lifeworld can be defined as the background horizon pertaining to the contexts in which people communicate to reach understanding. It takes shape in language and acts of communication and appears as 'a reservoir of taken-for-granteds, of unshaken convictions that participants in communication draw upon in cooperative processes of interpretation' (Habermas, 1992: 124). It refers to the unproblematic knowledge that supplements, accompanies and provides the context for communicative action: the traditions, the natural languages, the presuppositions, and assumptions that govern everyday life. While seeking mutual understanding, actors engage in processes of communication that do not disappear, but solidify in symbolic structures of meaning and understanding that become the matter of the lifeworld. In this process they come to construct and consolidate the intersubjectively recognised elements of a shared understanding about the world, which social psychologists call social representations (Marková, 2003; Moscovici, 2000; Wagner and Hayes, 2005 see also Chapter 7).

Because communicative action is dependent on situational contexts it must be connected to the lifeworld of the participants in interaction. Communication towards mutual understanding necessitates a background of common assumptions, representations, practices, and cultural meanings. This background constitutes the horizon within which the exchange of reasons and the different claims embedded in speech acts make sense and are interpreted by interlocutors.

The three structural components of the lifeworld are person, society, and culture. Each one of these produces and reproduces the lifeworld. In producing and reproducing the symbolic references, parameters, and background knowledge that enables a language game to solidify and that gives meaning and validity to a proposition, individuals develop themselves as persons, interact to produce societies, and establish the semantic contents of cultural traditions. The lifeworld provides the points of reference, the parameters, the resources against which individuals make sense of the world around them, develop the theoretical and practical competencies to deal with the everyday, and establish the communicative relations that allow for the development and reproduction of person, society, and culture.

The three structural components of the lifeworld map into Habermas's tripartite model of communication as he seeks to integrate the subjective, intersubjective, and objective in the production and reproduction of the lifeworld. Figure 6.1 tries to capture the overall theoretical structure of the theory of communicative action, outlining the tripartite model that constitutes and connects its various facets.

Consider the centre of the figure where the microprocess of communication between interlocutors – who are always situated in a context where different perspectives meet and are observed by a third party – grows exponentially to the analysis of macroprocesses involving the production and reproduction of lifeworlds. The top level of the figure indicates the components of action towards reaching understanding operating in the language of interlocutors and observer: speech acts, validity claims, and the dimensions to which they refer. The bottom level of the figure indicates the components in the production and reproduction of lifeworlds through communicative action. The double arrows indicate the co-constitutive nature of the constructs. Important to note is that the communicative act at the centre triggers a tripartite model that permeates the overall theoretical architecture of TCA: across the figure we find the three levels of the subjective (individual, expressive); the interactive (intersubjective, social rules, and norms) and the objective (the world of objects, society, and culture). Each

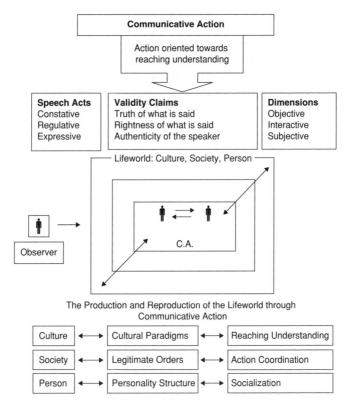

Figure 6.1   Habermas' overall model of communicative action

one of these levels can be found in our speech, in our efforts to coordinate and reach mutual understanding, and in the ways in which we construct ourselves, our public spheres, and lifeworlds.

Communicative action and strategic action

Habermas is convinced that 'reaching understanding is the inherent telos of human speech' (1989b: 287). Finding inspiration once more in Austin, who saw the orientation to reaching understanding as the original mode of language use upon which all other uses of language depend, TCA proposes that communicative action is the original type of action upon which all other forms are parasitic. To this effect, Habermas makes a very sharp distinction between communicative action and **strategic action**:

> I count as communicative action those linguistically mediated interactions in which all participants pursue illocutionary aims, and only illocutionary aims, with their mediating acts of communication. On the other hand, I regard as linguistically mediated strategic action those interactions in which at least one of the participants wants with his speech acts to produce perlocutionary effects on his opposite number.
>
> (1989b: 295)

Communicative action is action oriented towards reaching understanding whereas strategic action is oriented towards success. Communicative action aims for mutual agreement between interlocutors and the achievement of a consensus that can impact on action coordination. Strategic or purposive action is a form of acting that seeks a result in the behaviour of others. Its strategic aim is to influence, to exercise an effect on the other. If in my interaction with you my goal is to change your behaviour, this aim controls what I say, how I say it, and for what I say it. It bends my speech acts out of validity claims such as truthfulness, rightness, and sincerity, so that I can systematically distort the objective world and even lie to you to achieve my goal of influencing you. Strategic action suspends validity claims, in any one or more of the domains of reality involved in speech acts, be it the person, the interpersonal or the objective domain (see Box 6.4).

Strategic action distorts communication; it pretends to be communication when in fact it is not. It is usually drawn upon in the public sphere by power interests that impinge upon our language in order to dominate and manipulate. The concept of strategic action unpacks how the use of power – political, economic, and cultural – employs the three dimensions of speech acts to achieve effects of dominance and ideological distortion in the public sphere, in interactions and in individuals. This besieging of language by power is not just an external matter because distortion, dominance, and manipulation

Box 6.4   Communicative or strategic action?

Much of the debate about public issues today exemplifies the suspension of validity claims. Take for instance the discussions that preceded the UN 2009 Climate Change Conference in Copenhagen. A crucial few weeks before the summit, the debate was dominated by the hacking of a computer at the University of East Anglia in the UK, where an important centre for research on climate change is based. The hackers leaked emails that expressed a rather mundane and usual type of discussion that scientists engage in when analysing data. The emails were taken out of their context of scientific debate and thrown into the public domain with the intent of casting doubt on the scientific evidence that points to the man-made nature of climate change (for more on the difficulties of science communication, see Chapter 15). Because science is not a religion, its knowledge is always open to scrutiny given by reasoned argument; and scientists will question and explore data sets as a matter of course. However, this questioning was taken by strategic actors as evidence of unreliability of the data, further compromised by the alleged lack of sincerity of the scientists in question. In this case, rather than addressing substantive issues related to the body of evidence in question, campaigners seeking to undermine the case for the man-made nature of climate change focused on suspending validity about the sincerity of scientists, a tremendously effective type of strategic action. In this case the debate is derailed from its substantive focus and becomes a matter of persuading and influencing public opinion without any regard for reaching an understanding. Interests, which are associated with political and financial power, disrupt communication and block the process of argumentation so that monological actors can strategically advance and succeed in their private positions. The suspension of validity claims also suspends the act of communication, that is overtaken by a strategic goal external to mutual understanding, that is, the success of a certain position.

inscribe themselves in the way we speak and use language. It enters our very selves and becomes almost automatic through continuous use. Indeed, the concept of strategic action resembles Freire's (2005) analysis of extension (see Chapter 2): the other is invaded by self, who denies, silences, or distorts his words by persuading, by dominating, by using propaganda, and other similar instruments.

The juxtaposition between communicative and strategic action allows an examination of the distortions that bend communication out of its aims and the consequences of these distortions at the micro and macro levels. For every domain of communication that is distorted there is a consequence. In the strategic processes that bend communication out of mutual understanding we find the origins of anomy, individualism, and loss of meaning in individual lives. In the interactive domain we find disruption in social solidarity, perspective-taking, and recognition. Finally, distortions in communication in the social domain produce a diminished public sphere, whose critical function is overtaken by spectacle, celebrity culture, and consumerism.

Is TCA idealist?

Many criticisms have been levelled at Habermas's TCA, but the one that stands out as the most persistent and pervasive is the charge of 'idealism' (see Calhoun, 1992). As with the theory of the public sphere, TCA is seen as idealistic – not quite adequate to capture what really goes on in human life. It is not difficult to see why the charge is there: this is a theory that blatantly insists on the idea of mutual understanding as the basis of communication whereas even a casual glance at our social worlds would have to put this claim under scrutiny. Be it because of conditions of deep asymmetry found in unequal public spheres or the existential anxieties associated with the uncanny other, communicative action in Habermasian terms seems to be more an ideal than a practical possibility.

This criticism is not without foundation because it is difficult to disentangle the dynamics of misunderstanding in human relations (Ichheiser, 1949) from the practice of communication. The distinction between communicative action and strategic action separates from the act of communication all those forms of interaction that systematically distort it; however, many have convincingly maintained that communication and miscommunication are inexorably intertwined, and that to cast one at the expense of the other is to grasp just half of the story. In everyday life, for instance, distortion in communication seems to be the rule rather than the exception (a claim advanced in Chapter 9). Social psychologists have studied in detail phenomena such as persuasion, rumour, and deception, focusing on rhetorical processes of influencing and persuading others (Billig, 1996). Habermas excludes influence and persuasion from communication whereas these may be seen as the crux of the problem, indeed the norm when we study human communication.

However, to suggest that TCA does not examine failures and distortions in communication as integral to communication is too simplistic; it fails to capture what Habermas really suggests. Central to TCA is the analysis of social action, what holds societies together, and what makes these – and, ultimately, all human life – possible. In this, Habermas is not alone. Acting collectively created the human world as we know it, and it is in communication directed to understanding and sharing intentions that we find the origins of the human mind, collective action, and human cultures. This is true in Habermas but it is also an argument advanced by evolutionary and cultural psychologists, anthropologists, and primatologists (Tomasello, 2005, 2009; Goody, 1998; Humphrey, 1976; Jolly, 1966): joint intentionality and cooperative action play a key evolutionary role in the formation of *Homo sapiens*. There is substantive evidence to suggest precise homologies between the cooperative structure of human communication, and the cooperative structure of human, as opposed to other primate, social interaction and culture (Tomasello, 2008). An interesting question to ask here is what happens to the human inheritance of competitive tendencies? Altruistic and cooperative actions have systematically puzzled scholars surveying the evolution of human behaviour as it diverged from the ancestral line (see Chapter 11).

The central issue here is to recognise the role of communicative action in laying foundations and producing a basic platform for the specific modality of life which humans evolved. It is not accidental that language, self, and culture are among the most important sociocognitive distinctions between humans and their closest relatives. Developmental and social psychologists alike have shown that cooperation and dialogue are central for the healthy development of human babies (see in this respect Chapter 1); the self is a dialogical structure that emerges in the transitional space of communications between infant and care-taker (Winnicott, 1988, 1965). Play and game are crucial social and psychological processes that allow decentration and perspective-taking, inscribing the tension between I/Me at the heart of human self-awareness and understanding (Mead, 1932). Perspectival representations and reading the minds of others are equally central in cognitive development and the acquisition of language (Malle and Hodges, 2005; Tomasello, 2003; Olson, Astington and Harris, 1998). This allows us to speculate that cultures of cooperation and dialogue are adaptations evolved precisely to sublimate and control competitive tendencies we inherited from other forms of life. In evolving such powerful communicative tools, humans were able to pool resources and succeed collectively in establishing cultures and developing selves.

Whether societal relations distort, prevent, or destroy these evolutionary, sociocultural and psychological achievements is a completely different matter that requires a sharp analytical distinction between conditions of possibility and conditions of realisation. In this sense, there is nothing cosy in Habermas's view of communication. What we find is a clear understanding that humans live in society because they have evolved communicative skills that allow the coordination of action, the sharing of goals and intentions, and the tension between the consolidation of cultural traditions and the innovation of these traditions by every new generation, known as the ratchet effect (Tomasello, 1999). These skills created a platform of human achievements that are expressed in our psychological, social, and cultural lives (Tomasello and Rackozy, 2003; Trevarthen, 1979).

TCA and the dialogical imagination

Interestingly enough for someone consistently criticised for idealising human communication, Habermas's starting point was a deep personal understanding of the failure of communication and the fragility of communicative life forms. In pondering about the links between theory and biography Habermas (2004) provides an overview of how his own personal trajectory intersected with his theoretical concerns. He describes how his speech impediment shaped his understanding of the very social nature of human beings, his sense for the dependency and vulnerability we all share, and an awareness of the relevance of our interaction with others. His early experience gave him a sharp understanding that 'we find ourselves existing in the medium of language' and 'it is more for communicating than for describing the world that we use language'. Human life necessitates mutual understanding if it is to function at all and so does the healthy development of the human infant. Indeed, no individual person and no human community could come into existence on the basis of strategic action, misunderstanding, or deception alone. Dialogue is at the basis of mind (Vygotsky, 1994) and shapes cognitive development (Perret-Clermont, 1980; Doise and Palmonari, 1984, again, see Chapter 1).

In this deep personal motivation we find what in my view is essential to understand Habermas and his overall project as well as the equivocation of those who consider his position 'idealist'. His project aims to grasp both the nature and role of communication in a distinctive form of human life, and the normative utopias that sustain our moral and ethical imaginations. How can we make a distinction between what is essential, universal, and foundational in human life and its multiple conditions of realisation? How can we sustain a moral and ethical imagination that is committed to the practice of dialogue as a means to resolve the dissents, disagreements, and sharp differences that permeate our 'human, all too human' misunderstandings and deceptive realities? Habermas understands all too well failures in communication and the dangers these failures contain. But he shows that we can only understand why something fails if we understand why and how it works in the first place. That is precisely what Habermas has given us: a theory that binds individual and social life to an intersubjective communicative context in which the desire of interlocutors to understand each other guides the way they use reasons at the personal, interpersonal, and objective levels, raising and responding to validity claims grounded in lifeworlds and public spheres where the normative principles of equality in access, indifference to status, and rational argumentation rule over the power of interests and money.

The charge of idealism that is levelled at Habermas contains a trap whose danger rests in the acritical reconciliation with what exists and a denial of the normative utopias that fuel the dialogical imagination. It is in the tensions between the actual and the possible, explored by Habermas throughout his work, that we find the cognitive, emotional, and practical resources for understanding what is real and daring to imagine it and do it in a different way.

The psychology of self–other relations shows that while communication between self and other is indeed a thorny process, made of ambivalence and contradictions, it is absolutely necessary for the construction of individual persons and communities. Recognising the other as a person in his or her own right and learning how to take their perspective are central processes in the development of the child, in the constitution of the moral self, and in the development of our public spheres. The ontogeny of human experience is about encountering and communicating with the other, and succeeding in this encounter is paramount for human life (Spitz, 1945; Stern, 1985). Habermas's theory of communication allows us to extend these insights to a much larger conceptual landscape that projects the primacy of intersubjective experience as the foundation and ethical guide to our shared human reality.

Part II
Special Topics in Communication

7
Representations, Identity, and Resistance in Communication

Caroline Howarth

Keywords: Culture; cultural difference; encoding-decoding; identity; ideology; resistance; social representation.

> *We cannot communicate unless we share certain representations.*
> (Moscovici and Marková, 2000, p. 274)

> *Representations sometimes call our very identities into question. We struggle over them because they matter – and these are contests from which serious consequences can flow. They define what is 'normal', who belongs – and therefore, who is excluded.*
> (Hall, 1997, p. 10)

Our identities, the ways we see and represent ourselves, shape how we communicate, what we communicate about, how we communicate *with* others, and how we communicate *about* others. Hence **identity**, **representation**, **culture**, and difference are all central to a Social Psychology of communication. Take the factor of culture, as addressed in Chapter 3: Germans and Greeks differ considerably in the amount of small talk in business discussions, which is seen by Greeks as important to building up relationships (Pavlidou, 2000). American English speakers tend to be talkative and inquisitive in conversations with people they do not know well, and relatively quiet in the comfort and intimacy of close relationships, while the reverse is true for Athabascan Indians (Tracy, 2002). Added to such **cultural differences** are communication patterns relating to gender (Duveen and Lloyd, 1986), religion (Miike, 2004), class (Skeggs, 1997), language and dialect (Painter, 2008), among others. What's more, it is very difficult to untangle the intracultural nature of identity and how this impacts on communication (Martin and Nakayama, 2005). Hence communicative exchanges are 'deeply cultural', as 'groups of people will speak and interpret the actions of those around them in patterned ways' (Tracy, 2002, p. 34). One of the questions for a Social Psychology of communication is: Do these cultural patterns facilitate or obstruct communication? (See Box 7.1.)

Hence we need to examine the 'patterned ways' of speaking, interpreting, and acting and so explore the relationship between communication and identity. Interestingly, in two distinct disciplines, theories of representation have emerged as a means of examining such patterns in communication, and connections between communication, identity and **resistance**.

Box 7.1   Do cultural differences facilitate or obstruct communication?

Communication is often studied with reference to *inter*cultural differences, that is communication between people from *different* national and linguistic groups. Hence the fact that there 'are' different cultures – distinct and discrete, relatively homogeneous cultures that can be defined against one another is taken for granted in much work on communication. Following an **encoding-decoding** model (Hall, 1980, detailed below), for example, messages are seen to be encoded in the symbols and nuances of one culture which may not be accessible for someone from another culture. As Porter and Samovar (1988, p. 21) explain:

> When a message reaches the culture where it is to be decoded, it undergoes a transformation in which the influence of the decoding culture becomes a part of the message meaning. The meaning content of the original message becomes modified during the decoding phase of intercultural communication because the culturally different repertory of communicative behaviour and meanings possessed by the decoder does not contain the same cultural meanings possessed by the encoder.

Culture informs the ways we think and act in relation to everything – even the ways in which we think *about* communication. Hayakawa (1978), for example, points out how communication is represented in Western cultures, where the listener is often positioned as subordinate to the active and independent speaker. In other cultures where collective understanding is more highly valued than individual success, there are not so much different roles of the speaker and the listener, but rather a joint enterprise for meaning, empathy, and building connections with others (Fitch, 1998). This is important to bear in mind when conducting research into communication. The social sciences as a whole but especially anthropology and cross-cultural psychology have in fact fuelled a whole communications industry that examines, records, and advises on cultural difference – what to do where, how to act, how to please, how to do business, how to negotiate, how to order from a restaurant menu, etc. (Bennett, 1993). Clearly there are different cultural practices across all sorts of located and virtual social encounters, and such knowledge can be enormously helpful, as detailed in Chapter 3.

However, such intercultural texts, albeit produced with the best intentions and sometimes acclaiming the importance of intercultural respect, may often be 'somewhat inclined toward stereotyping, occasionally given to exaggerating cultural differences' (Hannerz, 1999, p. 398), offer one-dimensional accounts of culture that downplay the interconnections between culture, gender, class, and history, and possibly endorse ideologies of prejudice (Orbe, 1998). In many settings such claims of cultural difference attract an array of obstacles to successful communication, namely overstated assertions of difference/similarity, states of anxiety about difference and prejudiced attitudes (as already described in Chapter 3). Representations of 'other cultures' often impose homogenising claims of how 'our culture' compares (favourably) to others (Hall, 1997), while talk about 'our culture' may do symbolic violence to the identities and practices of minoritised groups (Orbe, 1998).

Once we accept the diversity and ongoing transformation within all cultures, it becomes very difficult to speak of 'different cultures' very meaningfully (Howarth, 2009a). However, as the literature demonstrates (Martin and Nakayama, 2005), there clearly are various cultural practices, forms of identity, different social groups, and relations of power that do lead to different forms of communication. But rather than examine different 'cultures', I suggest we see culture as something that we *do* through systems of representation, not something we have. In this way we can now examine how all cultures change and transform, meet and merge with others, clash and crystallise into distinct and sometimes hostile factions *and* contain competing representations, interests, and voices. We then begin to see communication as a political struggle (Hall, 1981) or cultural negotiation (Holliday et al., 2004), a way of presenting and re-presenting cultural knowledge in a ongoing system of negotiation – though we are not all positioned equally in this dialogue, as is evident when we consider representations of 'race' (Hall, 1988, 1997; Box 7.2).

In Social Psychology this is Social Representations Theory (SRT), as developed by Serge Moscovici (1961/2008); in Cultural Studies this is the extensive work of Stuart Hall (1980, 1988, 1997).

SRT has been described as a theory of communication since its inception. Indeed, as Duveen (2000) has pointed out, 'representations may be the product of communication, but it is also the case that without representation there could be no communication' (pp. 12–13). Representations (as common structures of knowledge and social practice produced in social psychological activity) can *only* exist in communication through the development of shared systems of values, ideas, and practices. Furthermore, **social representation** (as a psychological process that is at once cognitive *and* cultural) is *only* possible through the communication of emergent and relational identities, shifting claims to difference, and claims to commonalities. SRT studies make use of many different communicative genres: everyday talk, narratives, scientific discourse, media images, historical documents, institutional practices, cultural artefacts, advertising posters, and even drawings and weavings.

And yet, SRT does not offer a precise theory of communication per se. Rather it is a theory about the role of representations in communicative practices, particularly in the transmission of knowledge and the presentation of identities. This is valuable for a Social Psychology of communication as it highlights the simultaneously ideological and collaborated nature of communication, the relationship between communication, difference, and identity, and the possibilities for resistance and transformation within communicative exchange. However, it is in studying SRT that we learn about these aspects of communication, with a particular focus on the *social psychological* processes involved. However, by incorporating the work of Hall, as we do below, we are able to develop a much more compelling account of the *politics* of communication, consider the ideological role of the media and other public institutions in the development and dissemination of representations, and possibilities for resistant identities to emerge in communicative practices. Hall describes his approach as:

> more concerned with the effects and consequences of representation – its 'politics'. It examines not only how language and representation produce meaning, but how the knowledge which a particular discourse produces connects with power, regulates conduct, makes up or constrains identities and subjectivities, and defines the way certain things are represented, thought about, practised and studied.
>
> (1997, p. 6)

Hence, an 'articulated' account of representation that draws on both SRT and Hall proposes a more *political psychological* version of communication than either theory provides alone.[1] Furthermore it demands an integrated focus on what Moscovici and Marková (2000) call the primary genres of communication (everyday debate and conversation) and secondary genres of communication (mass communications, institutionalised discourses, and so forth).

What is the relationship between representation and communication?

Social representations are 'systems of values, ideas and practices with a two-fold function: first, to establish an order which will enable individuals to orient themselves in their material and social world and to master it; and secondly to enable communication to take place among members of a community by providing them with a code for social exchange and a code for naming and classifying unambiguously the various aspects of their world and their individual and group history'.

(Moscovici, 1973, p, xiii)

From this widely cited definition, we see that representations 'provide collectivities with intersubjectively shared means for understanding and communicating' (Duveen and Lloyd, 1990, p. 2). Because they are the codes we use to explain the past and the past is always changing to accommodate the present and support ambitions for the future, these codes (and the identities they support) are always in a process of transformation (Hall, 1988). Moscovici first employed the term *social* representation to distinguish the concept from Durkheim's (1898) notions of collective and individual representations. For Durkheim a collective representation is a 'social fact' which is imposed on us, difficult to challenge, uniform, and coercive in its effects. Social facts are more common in traditional societies, where there is comparative uniformity in belief, knowledge, and communicative practices. In contemporary society, different knowledge systems (relating to science, religion, health, economics, politics, and so forth) compete in diverse settings. As a result there is more critique, argument, and debate and so less stability in knowledge and communication. Most collective representations have now fragmented under these pressures, giving birth to more dynamic, unstable, and oppositional representational fields (Hall, 1980). Under the pressures of globalisation, meanings become highly contested and negotiated, as Lewis recognises:

Meanings becomes a battleground between and among folk cultures, class subcultures, ethnic cultures, and national cultures; different communications media, the home, and the school; churches and advertising agencies; and different versions of history and political ideologies. The sign is no longer inscribed within a fixed cultural order. The meaning of things seems less predictable and less certain.

(1994, p. 25)

Or simply, as Hall has put it, 'meaning floats. It cannot be finally fixed' (1997, p. 228). Hence the process of representation in and of itself invites social and psychological change. As Philogène's (2001) research demonstrates, 'social representations are vectors of change, because they are the medium by which we communicate new situations and adjust to them' (p. 113). Representation is something we do in order to understand the worlds in which we live and, through communicating our understanding, we convert these systems of values, ideas, and practices into a social reality, for others and for ourselves. In this process the idea or practice may be confirmed or perhaps rearticulated in some way (Hall, 1980). And representation is not something we do independently as *thinking individuals*, but something that is always a relational, collaborative process. We find in these ideas a strong resonance with Vygotsky's idea of mediation, his insistence on the social basis of thought and his attempt to understand how symbolic tools become the means for individual cognitive functions, as discussed in Chapter 1. Representation is also of course a deeply political process evident in 'thinking societies in clubs, museums, public libraries, political libraries, cafes, economic or political associations, ecological movements, medical waiting rooms, therapy groups, adult education classes' (Moscovici, 2001, p. 12). Hence the process of communication encourages both change and stability, resistance and containment in the genesis of knowledge (Hall, 1981), as we see in both primary communicative genres (as in the case of interpersonal exchanges) and secondary communicative genres (the domain of mass communications and public meaning).

Communication across science, the media and the everyday

Moscovici's own classic study of the circulation of knowledge about psychoanalysis in media and everyday discussions is generally seen as the communication of scientific knowledge into popular discourses. This can easily be related to Hall's model of encoding-decoding. This presents a powerful critique of theories that characterise mass communication as a transparent and straightforward system of inscribing and discovering the intended meaning in discourse, where audiences read off the intended meaning in media texts, for example (Hall, 1980). Hall demonstrates the 'lack of fit' between the circular process of encoding (by producers and reporters) and the decoding (by audiences), and the ways in which this opens up possibilities for polysemic values and oppositional accounts to develop. (Such a 'lack of fit' is similarly evidenced in both psychoanalytic approaches, see chapter 9, and Goffman's notion of impression management, where what is intended in a message and how it is ultimately received are never simply one and the same.) In a similar way, various studies using SRT examine 'how science manages to become part of our cultural heritage, of our thinking, of our language and daily practices ... by leaving the labs and publications of a small scientific community to penetrate the conversation, the relationships, or the behaviour of a large community and to get diffused in its dictionaries and current reading matter' (Moscovici, 2001, p. 10).

This is often described as the relationship between the reified world of science, where representations are encoded, and the consensual world of everyday conversations and commonsense, where representations are decoded (in this respect see also Chapter 15 on science communication). Just as Hall critiques studies that present this as a one-way process from encoding to decoding, we need to be critical of SRT studies that only examine the transmission of science into the everyday (Batel and Castro, 2009). Just as for Hall's encoding-decoding model, we need to see these worlds (of science and the everyday) as intimately connected and reactive to each other. Hence we also need to examine the impact of everyday knowledge on scientific discourse (Howarth, 2009b). As we see in this chapter (e.g. Box 7.2), SRT studies have examined the construction and communication of different identities – in children's stories, institutionalised practices, and school curricula, for example. We may still find that certain representations become reified as normative beliefs and practices, but that the relationship to science is much less specific. What may be more productive to a Social Psychology of communication is an analysis of the processes of reification and consensualisation (Howarth, 2006a). In a similar way to Hall's, this would allow us to examine how representations become *systemically distorted* and *naturalised* in the maintenance and defence of the dominant cultural order.

Box 7.2   Community dialogues and challenging representations that 'race'

The relationship between identity, difference, and resistance has been at the centre of my own studies on racialised identities. Drawing on both SRT and Hall, I have looked at the role of 'race' in young people's efforts to assert and communicate positive cultural identities (Howarth, 2002a). In particular I have examined the impact of racism on children's sense of self, of community, and culture (Howarth, 2006b). I have shown how 'race' may limit identities – restricting one's sense of possibility and of ambition, and how such representations may be communicated and institutionalised within the symbolic culture of schools (Howarth, 2004). In being seen in a particular way, for example, as black, brown or mixed, pupils are positioned as different, as other and, often, as *less than* in contexts of intellectual achievement and learning (Howarth, 2007). These contemporary racist stereotypes remain tied to our history of colonial relations, slavery, the denigration and economic exploitation of particular cultures, and the maintenance of white privilege and hegemony (Hall, 1997). Because these 'are widely known and shared in the culture, or among the stigmatized, it is not necessary for a prejudiced person to communicate the devaluation of the stigmatized for that devaluation to be felt' (Crocker, 1999, p. 103). Such representations, then, are *ideologically* constructed, communicated, and resisted in systems of difference and privilege that constitute and communicate the social norms and consensual beliefs of a culture. Once again, we see that values, ideas, and practices are communicated symbolically – through the media, material culture, social spaces, embodied practices, and so forth. Very little may be actually *said* for racialising stereotypes to be felt.

This research into 'race' highlights the symbolic violence of communicative exchanges that marginalise, stigmatise, and exclude others. I have also found that it is in supportive collectivities and community dialogues where such negative experiences can be discussed that identities are debated, defended, and sometimes re-made. Children and teenagers in educational and community groups – often with the explicit aim of challenging prejudice and spoilt identities – collaborate innovative ways to problematise racism, disrupt its gaze, and so rupture its hold over their identities (Howarth, 2004; see also Chapter 2). The opportunity for communicating one's experiences of identity and developing a sense of relationship and community is one that unites a number of perspectives in this book, certainly that of Freire (Chapter 2) and in the case of religion as communicative action (Chapter 12). Developing a sense of community can provide the social support and psychological resources to reconstrue threats to identity manifest in racism and other forms of bigotry (Howarth, 2009b). Thus, we can see how particular communicative practices both assist and challenge ideologies of prejudice.

Both SRT and Hall assert that communication is normative yet transgressive, individual yet shared, prescriptive yet malleable. Representations, as Abric has described, are 'consensual but marked by strong inter-individual differences' (1993, p. 75). Hall has also explored the deeply ideological and restrictive nature of representations and also their very agentic and transgressive nature. How do we explain this contradiction? Abric (1993) suggests that in communication it is not *all* of a representation that is open to elaboration, development, or contradiction. There are different constituents: the core and periphery. The core of a representation is the 'heart', the fundamental elements of a representation 'determined by historical, sociological, and ideological conditions' (p. 74). It is 'stable, coherent, consensual and historically marked' (p. 76). It resists change and is relatively continuous and consistent. The periphery is more responsive to the communicative exchanges within which it occurs. Peripheral elements are open to challenge and revision, and are 'flexible, adaptive and relatively heterogeneous' (p. 77). Hegemonic representations, similar to ideologies, are comparatively unchanging over time and so are almost completely dominated by the central nucleus of ideas. Other representations, particularly those that oppose the dominant order, are more contested and so more reactive to the peripheral elements.

These include what Moscovici defines as emancipated and polemical representations. The former 'are the outgrowth of the circulation of knowledge and ideas belonging to subgroups', separate from the main spheres of public debate. The later are 'generated in the course of social conflict, social controversy and society as a whole does not share them' (Moscovici, 2000, p. 28).[2] In a similar way Hall distinguishes between dominant-hegemonic (also 'preferred meanings'), negotiated and oppositional readings. The former are obviously akin to hegemonic representations in that they saturate commonsense and support the dominant cultural order. Negotiated readings are more complex as the reader/viewer has the potential to adopt *and* oppose dominant discourses more in line with local conditions, and so are comparable to emancipated representations. Finally, oppositional readings are related to polemical representations, but are in direct opposition and critique to mainstream beliefs and discourses.

What is also common in these accounts is a focus on the cultural embeddedness and multi-accentuality of representations, highlighting their polysemic (Hall) or polyphasic (Moscovici) nature. Hall draws on Bakhtin (1981) and Volosinov (1973) to highlight the ways in which meanings are 'accented' by those who speak them, historically and contextually contingent, and characterised by oppositional meanings and contradictions. As described above, there is always a 'lack of fit' or a tension between the processes of encoding and decoding, which fuels debate, argument, opposition, and resistance. Moscovici, also influenced by Bakhtin, takes this a little further: while there is always such a lack of fit between intended meanings and interpretations in the process of representation at the level of *thinking societies*, there may also be a 'lack of fit' between the representational systems of *thinking individuals*. Hence ambivalence, tension, contradiction, what Moscovici terms 'cognitive polyphasia', exists both at the level of psychology and at the level of culture; both in terms of what individuals say, do, and think and in terms of how representations are communicated and understood more broadly (Wagner and Kronberger, 2001). A close reading of Hall suggests he would have little to argue with here, although he would demand more analysis of the politics at stake in the polysemic nature of representation, as we turn to next.

The politics of representation

In using representations, we incorporate them into our current ways of understanding and everyday talk, through the processes of (a) anchoring and (b) objectification. Anchoring integrates new phenomena into existing worldviews in order to make the unfamiliar familiar. Anchoring involves ascribing meaning to the object being represented. 'By classifying what is unclassifiable, naming what is unnameable, we are able to imagine it, to represent it' (Moscovici, 1984, p. 30). In the course of anchoring the unfamiliar in the familiar, representations are modified. An informative example of anchoring can be found in Augoustinos and Riggs (2007): through the analysis of everyday talk they demonstrate the ways in which contemporary representations of culture are anchored in 'old and discredited social Darwinist notions of biological hierarchy' (p. 126) which present Aboriginal cultures as 'very very primitive' and white cultures as 'modern' and 'advanced'. In this way, what was non-communication (the unknown, strange, and vague) becomes communication. Too often, the anchoring process is narrowly interpreted as an individual psychological process (Howarth, 2006a);

what Augoustinos and Riggs demonstrate are the ways in which this is simultaneously a deeply ideological process.

The process of objectification produces a domestication of the unfamiliar in a way that is more active than anchoring because it saturates the idea of unfamiliarity with reality, turning it into the very essence of reality. This produces the materialisation of an abstraction. Deaux and Wiley (2007) provide a good example of this with reference to debates about immigration that are organised around the tangible metaphor of the melting pot and references to blending, mixing, forming, and the crucible. In this way images cease to be images or signs; they become a part of reality, just as 'Dolly the sheep' ceases to be an image of cloning but has come to embody the material reality of genetic manipulation (Gaskell, 2001). The media play an important role in the production, dissemination, and debate over different representations and the images on which they rest (Hall, 1997) – as do all communicative exchanges 'in social, scientific, political or religious communities, in the worlds of theatre, cinema, literature or leisure' (Moscovici, 2000, p. 111). Through objectification, images become constitutive elements of social and ideological reality, rather than simply elements of thought.

These are not, then, neutral psychological processes. By classifying a person, a thing, an event, or a nation, we are at the same time assessing and evaluating it/her. For example, Jodelet (1991) found that images such as 'decay' and 'going off like butter' were common in people's talk about mental illness. While this tells us something of the everyday experience and identity of the villagers (as close to the land and nature, Wagner and Kronberger, 2001), they also reveal the prejudice and fear of contagion that has been 'unconsciously transmitted for generations' (Marková, 2007, p. 229), communicated through collective memories and ideological practices. Similarly, in my research in Brixton, South London, for example, I have found that prejudiced representations of the poor and of black people are articulated with other representations of crime and come to form commonsense knowledge about Brixton (Howarth, 2002a). By looking at how dominant discourses manipulate values and ideas in the service of particular interests we can study the 'ideological battle' of representations.

This relates back to Hall's dominant-hegemonic readings or preferred meanings. Hall is particularly interested in the **ideological** role of the media in producing systems of representations that serve to *prefer* particular interests and identities over others, and so systematically distort particular representations and sustain systems of power and inequality. Hence he is interested in the ongoing ideological construction of reality. Similarly, Moscovici (2000) sought to answer this question: 'How do people construct their social reality?' He continues:

While the actor sees the problem, the observer does not see the whole historical solution. Marx was well aware of this dilemma when he wrote: 'Men make their own history, but they do not make it just as they please: they do not make it under circumstances chosen by themselves, but under circumstances directly encountered, given and transmitted from the past'.

(Marx, 1852/1968, p. 97)

This quotation connects different levels of representation: *microgenesis*, *ontogenesis*, and *sociogenesis*. These are terms developed in SRT, but we can see important correlations with the work of Hall. Both perspectives are concerned with the microgenetic level of communication: communication between individual actors in particular readings, encounters, and contexts. They both are profoundly interested in the ontogenesis of identities and the representations individuals have of themselves. But, crucially, for both Hall and SRT, the cultural, historical, and ideological aspects of communicative practices – that is, the sociogenetic level – frames both the ontogenetic and microgenetic levels. Hall (1981) illustrates this nicely in the quotation below, referring to the particular media portrayal of an event:

The choice of *this* moment of an event as against that, of *this* person rather than that, of *this* angle rather than any other, indeed, the selection of this photographed incident to represent a whole complex chain of events and meaning, is a highly ideological procedure.

(p. 241)

It is here, in the sociogenesis of communicative practices, where representations appear at their most ideological – pervading the media, social institutions, cultural arrangements, advertising campaigns, political discourses, and so forth. This is also where we see how different values and practices are reified and prioritised over others, how some representations (and the social groups and social identities to which they relate) are marginalised and excluded from mainstream systems of discourse and how the process of representation supports ideological systems. Hence, networks of representations support a priori hierarchies of knowledge, restrict the development of identity and sustain discourses of difference, privilege, and power (Howarth, 2004). This immediately provokes Hall's question: 'Can a dominant regime of representation be challenged, contested or changed?' (1997, p. 269) Such an approach to dominant regimes of representation is one which compares interestingly with the various mechanisms of social influence discussed in Chapter 4.

Resistance and identity and communicative exchange

Hall's question speaks to the heart of representation – as it highlights the transformative nature of knowledge, communication, and identity. This was evident in Moscovici's seminal study of the image of psychoanalysis in three subcultures in 1950s Paris: 'the transformation of knowledge as it is communicated across different groups and parts of society ... and the ways in which each social group reconstitutes knowledge according to its own interests and concerns' (Duveen, 2008, p. xii). The same is true of individuals: they take up and rework, re-interpret and re-present knowledge in a way that fits into and develops their sense of self (Howarth, 2006a; Box 7.3).

We can also relate Hall's encoding-decoding model and concept of articulation to Moscovici's distinction between propaganda, propagation, and diffusion within secondary or more formalised communicative genres (in mass communications and public institutions). Through his detailed analysis of the highly differentiated sections of the French press in the 1950s in *La Psychanalyse* (1961/2008), Moscovici gives examples of the different ways in which representations are encoded and decoded within three social groups, and the different psychological phenomena they give rise to: stereotypes, attitudes, and opinions. Most clearly, he shows how representations of psychoanalysis were encoded with stereotypes of American decadent culture and Western imperialism by the Communist Party press in order to denigrate and reject psychoanalysis as a pseudoscience. This is propaganda. Within Communist writings Moscovici found that psychoanalysis is always articulated with representations of American bourgeois culture, creating and cementing new meanings and readings (Moscovici and Marková, 2000)

Box 7.3   Possibilities for resistance and connection in multicultural settings

We have seen that representations of others pervade communicative exchanges. In Chapter 4 we have also seen that successful communication is based on the ability to connect with the other ('dialogicity'). This was something I have explored in research into intracultural identities in multicultural settings (Howarth, 2009b) – where the ability to communicate across difference is central to the identity of the group and individuals in that context. The acute intersectionality of these communities can be seen as a resource in diverse settings and an asset to global communication and community-building. For example, Bennett (1993) examines the experiences of 'constructive marginals' and their efforts to transcend the confines of essentialised ideologies of cultural difference. What we can see from this research is that the ontogenetic experience of what we might call various 'intracultural' identities (such as British Mexican or British Caribbean) can lead to a comprehensive understanding of cultural difference – particularly an understanding of the (co-)production of difference and the impact on identity. Such an appreciation and sensitivity for the power of representations to ascribe identities, limit the possibilities of self and stigmatise particular communities, is a valuable asset for communicating in multicultural settings. Indeed, some researchers have found examples in history where intracultural groups such as 'Creoles' were recognised as 'astute traders with a mastery of the finer points of intercultural negotiations' (Bird, 2009, p. 61).

In order to communicate effectively one needs to find some level of connection and common knowledge (a shared language or rules of inter-action, see Chapter 9). It is vitally important in multicultural settings to have a good understanding of the intersubjective production of cultural difference and to know how to use difference to build commonalities and not obstacles in forging intracultural relationships and successful dialogues. This requires not simply learning about 'others', but learning about the processes that *other*. As Martin and Nakayama (2007) have argued, successful communication requires 'the ability to understand what it's like to "walk in someone's shoes"' (p. 10), and to 'go through the eye of the needle of the other' (Hall, 1988, p. 30). Indeed, the more you do this, the more you learn about others, the more you learn about yourself; the more you realise that 'other' cultures are not so 'other'. The more experience you have in multicultural settings the more you realise that all cultures are deeply complex and diverse and that all cultural generalisations are problematic. This leads to an understanding that all identities are also deeply complex and constantly changing. Thus an understanding of the essentially intracultural nature of identity is valu-able for successful communication.

in ways that promote and defend a commitment to Communist politics and identity. By contrast, propagation was used in Catholic discussion to accommodate particular aspects of psychoanalysis into the existing religious doctrines and so develop particular attitudes to psychoanalysis consistent with the authority of Catholicism. Diffusion occurred in liberal debates with the aim of informing public opinion. Such liberal professionals would claim a certain sceptical intelligence and characterise out-groups as dogmatic. As Duveen explains:

> What one sees in [Moscovici's study of] *Psychoanalysis* is not only the way in which distinct social representations both generate and are sustained by different communicative genres, but that these different communica-tive systems also reveal different forms of affiliation amongst the publics drawn together around each communicative system.
>
> (2008, p. 371)

What this suggests is that different forms of mass communication are tied to different forms of groups and different identity positions. In Hall and SRT we also see that it is in social interactions and activities, in communicating with others, that representations and identities become meaningful, debated, contested, and transformed. This is because communication is central to the social psychological connections between the transmission of shared knowledge and individuals' positioning in relation to this knowledge (their identities). As Kronberger and Wagner have argued:

> Our membership in social groups constrains the ways in which we come to understand an object, and conversely, by positioning oneself with regard to an object and by the style we communicate about it, we ascertain our belonging to a particular group of people, and simultaneously distance ourselves from others.
>
> (2007, p. 177)

This focus on identity demands a connected analysis of primary and secondary communication genres: everyday debate and more formalised public discourses. Identities are often described as the stories individuals and communities 'tell themselves and which locate them in society' as Cieslik and Verkuyten (2006, p. 79) have put it. However, as they go on to point out, 'the stories available to tell are not unrestricted. ... Historical, social and political patterns limit and shape the possible group narratives or the available narrative space through which groups can manage and negotiate their multiple identities' (ibid.). Hence. it is in communicating in its broadest sense, through the media, material culture and social space, social interactions and embodied practices, that identities come alive, invite common histories to be told and establish the (constructed and so shifting) boundaries of culture, common identities, and difference. However, there are very real limits to the (co)production of identity.

The huge disparities in communication mean that we are not equally positioned in producing or contesting knowledge about 'us' or 'them' in mainstream debates. As Moloney (2007) illustrates very vividly with editorial cartoons of refugees, these 'inequities in the media access allow for the proliferation of one version of events over others, which not only reproduces the identities of voiceless groups in society but also reconstructs them' (p. 63). And such groups do not have the material or cultural capital to challenge representations of them that they see as inaccurate or destructive: the communicative genres of propaganda, propagation, or diffusion are not available to them. Her study gives a very fine-tuned analysis of the visual and textual codes used in the media that turn indirect stigma into blatant stereotypes that produce social distance between 'us' and 'them' and demonise and dehumanise the individuals and communities so represented – often in quite contradictory ways. As Hall (1997) has argued, such stereotyping 'is part of the maintenance of social and symbolic order. It sets up a symbolic frontier between the "normal" and the "deviant", the "normal" and the "pathological", the "acceptable" and the "unacceptable", what belongs and what does not or is "Other", between "insiders" and "outsiders", us and Them' (p. 258).

And at the same time, Hall reserves a place for resistance and agency against such propaganda: cultural identity, he insists, 'is a matter of "becoming" as well as "being". It belongs to the future as much as to the past' (1991, p. 225). Hence, identities are not merely imposed or ascribed; identities are also a matter of negotiation, connection, imagination, and resistance. As Duveen (1994) asserts, 'the circulation of representations around the child does not lead to them being either simply impressed upon the child, or simply appropriated by the child, rather, their acquisition is an outcome of development' (p. 112). Even in the face of negative stereotypes of self, there are the possibilities of resistance and social creativity as we find ways to co-construct and communicate more positive versions of self, community, and culture (Tajfel, 1978). This means that there is room to debate, resist and potentially transform stereotypes and practices that *other* and exclude (through a process of conscientisation, for example; see Chapter 2). As Philogène's (2001) research into representations of black Americans and African Americans has vividly illustrated, 'when new circumstances force us, as a group or a community, to rethink the present and imagine the future as part of adjusting to a changing reality' we develop to new or 'anticipatory representations' (p. 128). This links to a theme running through the book, namely the question of communication can facilitate an openness to change and aid in resisting forms of disempowerment and oppression. Hence, as Hall would say, the politics of representation always provokes a struggle over meaning and therefore is always unfinished.

Our psychological capacity to imagine alternative futures is highlighted by Moscovici in his original study:

> Social representations is an organised *corpus* of knowledge and one of the psychical activities that allow human beings to make physical and social reality intelligible, to insert themselves into groups or day-to-day relations of exchange and to free the powers of their imagination.
>
> (1961/2008, p. xxxi)

What are important here are the notions of exchange and imagination. As Hall has pointed out, communication cannot be seen as a top-down dissemination or a process were the informed élite (scientists, the Church, heads of social institutions, media gurus) inform the masses (see Chapters 2 and 14); this is simply one side of communicative exchange where particular meanings are encoded. Communication is always unstable and unpredictable because these meanings are decoded in constantly shifting and oppositional ways. We should (perhaps rather hopefully) see communication as an *imaginative exchange* that potentially leads to a qualitative change in all parties involved. As Moscovici argues, 'Communication is never reducible to the transmission of the original messages, or the transfer of data that remains unchanged. Communication differentiates, translates and combines' (2008, p. xxxii). Similarly, Hall proposes that we look for moments of negotiation, struggle and '*imaginative resistances*' where people express their discontent and agency, develop new identities, and propose alternative social relations (1960). While otherising representations can be internalised and so pose a threat to identity and esteem (Box 7.2), our intrinsic psychology and communicative capacities for dialogue, debate, and critique bring to the fore the possibilities for social and political psychological change (Box 7.3). Hence communication involves 'the double movement of containment and resistance' (Hall, 1981) or a 'double orientation' (Marková, 2000) that invites *and* contests different versions of reality through the interconnected social psychological processes of representation and identification. Hence, while representations always stem from somewhere and bring with them ideological connections to previous systems of knowing, identifying, and excluding, they are simultaneously dynamic and open to be elaborated in new, transgressive ways.

An articulated account of representation founded on both Hall and SRT draws attention to these dialectics and demands an integrated theory of the complex connections between psychological processes, relations of power, and the potential for resistance contained within and invited by communicative exchange. SRT is profoundly useful as it highlights the cultural and ideological nature of the psychological processes that sustain communication. Hall's work deepens a more political reading of representation and presents an important reminder that 'cultural meanings are not only "in the head". They organise and regulate social practices, influence our conduct and consequently have real, practical effects' (1981, p. 3). Hence, I suggest, a Social Psychology of communication requires such an articulated account of representation that highlights the ways in which communication is itself always ideological, collaborative, agentic, potentially imaginative and transformative.

Notes

1. Hall refers to 'articulation' as a practice of bringing together different theoretical frameworks in order to move beyond the limits of either theory on its own.
2. For a detailed discussion of these types of representations and illustrative examples from debates on immigration, see Deaux and Wiley (2007).

8
Rumours and Gossip as Genres of Communication

Bradley Franks and Sharon Attia

Keywords: Bullshit; cultural epidemiology; genre; gossip; minimal counter-intuitiveness; rumour; serial reproduction method.

> *Careless talk costs lives.*
> UK Ministry of Information poster campaign (1940)

Introduction

Rumours and **gossip** are often thought to be trivial, but as the above examples suggest, their content may be connected to matters of life and death for individuals and communities. The question of what rumours and gossip are, and how they disseminate, are not new to social scientists. This chapter aims to elaborate on the question of how rumours and gossip disseminate by examining their distinctive communicative and social psychological qualities. The chapter begins with a discussion of some key aspects of gossip, and suggests that it can be considered a specific genre of communication, with associated pragmatic qualities of the kind discussed in Chapter 5. We then consider some of the common methods used to study the transmission of rumours, and this allows a formulation of some of the differences between rumour and gossip, in particular concerning how rumours spread (relating to a 'viral' metaphor of the spread of cultural ideas discussed in Chapters 4 and 11), and their connection to social sense-making (discussed in connection with social representations and social influence, in Chapter 4). The final section highlights some parallels between the way in which rumours spread and other forms of culturally recurrent beliefs such as religion (see Chapter 12 for a contrasting view of some connections between religion and communication). These parallels emphasise their cognitive and emotional qualities, and relevant cultural and contextual factors.

Gossip, rumour and genres of communication

Gossip can be considered as a genre of communication – as having its own descriptive and prescriptive conventions for production and interpretation, which are understood tacitly by communicators, and which are used to evaluate the success of a particular exchange.

Traditional approaches in linguistics focused on aspects of a text in defining a genre (to qualify as an example of a genre, it would need to include specific stylistic elements – so a lecture should possess formality of address; e.g. Martin, 1987). However, a recent consensus considers genre as socially and culturally defined, in terms of the relations between aspects of text or spoken language, and communicative expectations and the specifics of the social interaction. So although there may be stylistic similarities between instances of a genre, what knits them together in the genre are their social and pragmatic qualities (e.g. Swales, 1990; Paltride, 1997; Eggins and Slade, 1997).

Luckman (1992) further argues that a 'communication genre' is a routind, interactive pattern of communication that can offer a solution to a recurrent problem or a means to achieving a recurrent goal of social life. Such a picture is developed by Gunther and Knoblach (1995) who suggest that a communication genre has three levels of structure. Internal structure relates to standard linguistic, behavioural, content, and related patterns that are constitutive of performing the ritual appropriately. Interactive context relates to patterns of ordering or sequencing the component parts of the genre (e.g. how and when components of the ritual, and the ritual itself, can be repeated). And external structure relates to aspects of the broader environment that can influence how the exchange is interpreted, what licenses different communication genres in the culture, which kinds of participants are appropriate to a specific genre, and which social activities or purposes are achieved by the genre.

The gossip genre

Eggins and Slade (1997) suggest taking gossip to be a genre is a matter of commonsense social psychology – people reliably recognise and refer to instances of gossip in everyday life, differentiating it from other forms of exchange. So people ascribe a set of characteristic and distinctive qualities to gossip exchanges, allowing them to behave appropriately in such exchanges, and to expect others to do so too.

Gossip exchanges connect to what has been called 'bullshit' (Frankfurt, 2005). **Bullshit** is not concerned with the truth value of the utterance – someone who engages in an exchange of verbal bullshit does so without regard to the truthfulness of what they are saying. It is not deliberately or necessarily false, but this is because truth or falsity is not required. What is required is a topic of exchange that cements the relationship between the speaker and hearer, and that reminds them that they are both part of a specific social group. Frankfurt explains that 'bullshit is unavoidable whenever circumstances require someone to talk without knowing what he is talking about' (p. 63). This allows that people will delay judgement on whether the communicated content is accurate, or indeed will defer making a judgement at all, if the exchange does cement group connections. This arises in part from the overall purpose of a gossip exchange in cementing group membership of the participants via the evaluation of a non-member (or members); truth and accuracy may be superseded by social and emotional demands.

The participants in gossip are usually members of the same group (relative to the target, who is usually either a member of an out-group, or whose behaviour renders them a possible future member of the out-group). Gossip also usually tends to be exchanged within status or hierarchy levels, as opposed to across them.

Bergmann (1993) suggests three qualities of gossip – acquaintance, absence and privacy: mutual acquaintance with the target of the talk, the target's absence from the exchange, and privacy of the topic about the target. Much gossip also involves 'morally contaminated material' (Bergmann, 1993: 85), so that its telling makes a more or less explicit negative moral judgement regarding the third party, and a more or less implicit shared positive moral judgement about the speaker and hearer. Eggins and Slade (1997) amplify this by characterising gossip as 'talk which involves pejorative judgement of an absent other ... which is meant to be confidential (or at least not reported back to the third party), and is about an absent person who is known to at least one of the participants' (p. 278). While much gossip *is* pejorative in character, we note below that gossip *can* also be approving of its targets. The evaluative aspect of gossip combines with bullshitting to suggest that assessing the truth of the statements or the acceptability of the judgement of the third party, may be suspended, ignored, or permitted to fall short of being fully accurate. The primary function of gossip is not to communicate something indubitably true about the target, nor something clearly accurate about their morality. Rather, it is to elicit appropriate affective and social identity responses in the hearer, thus fulfilling the social-emotional functions of gossip.

Gossip also appears to have distinctive stages. The first stage involves invitations to engage in gossip. These can (depending on the prior relationship between the speaker and hearer, the situation, and the nature of the topic and target for gossip), be more or less explicit. Bergmann (1993) suggests that initial invitations to gossip may be like 'fishing devices' – designed to persuade the hearer to take the bait to gossip without this invitation being explicit; for example, making a comment about one's own position vis à vis the topic of gossip, offering a natural invitation to generalise to others. The invitation may therefore be, pragmatically, 'off the record': if the hearer chooses not to take up the invitation, the speaker does not lose face, and a non-gossip exchange can take place. Such a tentative start to a gossip exchange may have several sources. One is in the nature of communication itself: Chapters 5, 9 and 11 have argued in different ways that communication is 'egocentric' – speaker and hearer often do not attempt to take into account the thoughts of the other, and even when they do attempt this, they are not very successful. A tentative beginning allows use of subtle signals of emotional response, verbal and non-verbal (see Chapter 3), to gradually establish an implicit agreement to engage in gossip. Once established, gossipers can use culturally agreed norms to structure the exchange and to predict and interpret the beliefs and intentions of the other.[1] A further reason is that making a pejorative evaluation regarding a target may leave oneself open to negative judgement if the hearer is not seen to agree to the terms of that evaluation. Such factors may reflect an instantiation of a principle of politeness (see Lakoff, 1973, 1976; Leech, 1983; Brown and Levinson, 1986). The original formulation of Lakoff's second rule of politeness was, 'Give options' – the speaker should leave to the hearer the decision about conforming to a particular line of talk, by employing expressions and communication markers that reflect a degree of hesitation.

Once the invitation has been accepted, there follows a sequence of what Eggins and Slade (1997) suggest are obligatory elements in gossip. The first is the 'third person focus', which introduces the target of the gossip, and will usually frame the topic or behaviour to be evaluated. The second is the 'substantiating behaviour', where the speaker or hearer provides evidence that they have the competence to judge the topic or target, and so can be relied on to make an evaluation of the target. This may involve sharing information about access to the target, and/or information about normal activity or behaviour in the relevant circumstances, so that the target can be judged to have departed from the norms. With acquaintances, colleagues, or other non-intimates, this stage establishes shared attitudes and values as the basis for shared evaluations; with intimates, it reconfirms that basis. The final obligatory component is 'pejorative evaluation', where the events, behaviours or qualities of the target outlined in the substantiating behaviour component, are commented on or judged. Eggins and Slade (1997) suggest that the shared pejorative evaluations drive the gossip forward, providing a theme around which the exchange is elaborated and developed. While it is clear that much gossip does involve such pejorative evaluation, gossip can also involve a positive evaluation of the target. Indeed, Barkow (1975) has argued that, for evolutionary reasons, we should tend to favour negative gossip about rivals and those who are of higher status than ourselves, and positive gossip about allies. So what really counts is that some social comparison takes place (see Wert and Salovey, 2004), and this drives the normative evaluation of the target and their behaviour.

The genre of gossip permits considerable variation in the extent to which the properties are met, so that gossip is a 'family resemblance' phenomenon. The intensity of evaluation may vary with the target and topic (and their importance to the in-group, and the parties to the exchange). Or the extent of bullshit might vary with the degree of the parties' membership in the group, or the degree of actual acquaintance with the target (e.g. gossip about celebrities may involve more bullshit, though mass-media saturation may give the impression that an emotional evaluation is empirically supported: e.g. De Backer, Nelisson and Vyncke, 2007). The parameters of the genre are open to variation as long as the social and emotional functions of the exchange are supported (see Baumeister, Zhang and Vohs, 2004).

An evolutionary motivation?

Eggins and Slade (1997), following Bergmann (1993), suggest that gossip has two social-cultural functions: establishing and reinforcing group membership, and exercising social control. Relatively superficial gossip can pave the way for someone to join a group by expressing shared values and beliefs; membership can then be consolidated by gossip regarding issues with stronger moral resonance, or relative to which decisions demarcate significant group divisions. The 'right to gossip' about those who express or transgress group norms is thereby earned, and partly retained through its exercise. This reflects the second function of gossip, controlling the behaviour of group members and potential transgressors, by verbally policing moral boundaries. Norm-breakers are targets of gossip, compromising their attempts to maintain group reputation and status (Emler, 2000; Wert and Salovey, 2004).

The connection with status and social groups has two further aspects. The first is that gossip does not merely involve exchange of descriptive information concerning the target – rather, the motivation for gossip and its content is intrinsically affective. Participants in gossip share emotional assessments and moral judgements of themselves, of the target, and of the topic. Since some of the information communicated may have the status of bullshit, there is uncertainty regarding the accuracy of statements. We suggest that participants tacitly vacillate between treating the content of the exchange as bullshit, so that truth evaluation is irrelevant, or treating it as something with important consequences, which requires evaluation. In the latter case, Clore and Gasper's (2008) 'affect as information' thesis may apply, in which emotion and mood are treated as evidence regarding possible evaluations. In uncertainty, they claim, affect 'fills in' knowledge gaps, acting as information to support a preferred outcome (or to contradict a dispreferred one). In gossip, where there is uncertainty regarding accuracy of elements of the substantiating behaviour (e.g. regarding a target's allegedly problematic behaviour), the affective thread of the pejorative evaluation provides a basis to form a conclusion regarding those elements (and similarly for positive evaluations). So for many cases, the evaluations of the target *appear* justified empirically to the participants, even if they would not appear so to an impartial observer. In this way, the representations of the target generated in gossip, and the associated representations of the speaker and hearer, comprise both descriptive information about them, and emotional, motivational, and evaluative assessments. These aspects of the representations are intertwined in a way that echoes the 'embodied' cognition and communication discussed in Chapters 5 and 11.

The emotional connection for gossip may reflect the evolutionary, adaptive functions of those emotions (see Chapter 12). Keltner, Haidt and Shiota (2006) argue that emotions help to solve inherently social adaptive problems, which may also be supported by specific kinds of communication exchanges.[2] In gossip, the evaluation largely relates to adaptive problems concerned with 'group governance', relating to cooperation and its management, supporting reciprocal altruism (creating emotions of gratitude, guilt, anger, envy); as well as to 'group organization', supporting a status hierarchy (engendering emotions of pride, shame, embarrassment, contempt, etc.). Such emotions enable and support social commitments, so in gossip they can inform participants about the other's mental states and can evoke appropriate responses; by being shared across individuals, and spread by rumour, those states and responses can help define group membership and structure. Ultimately, the recurrence of these emotions in connection with exchanges concerning the target and topic of gossip helps to define cultural identity, articulate norms and values, praise exemplary behaviour, and punish transgressors.

A broader evolutionary grounding for gossip is proposed by Dunbar (1992). He suggests that language itself may have evolved as a human analogue to grooming in other primates. In other primates, grooming supports the function of cementing in-group relationships. The time spent grooming is positively correlated both with the size of neocortex for that species and with the usual size of group in which it typically lives (for Old World monkeys and apes). Typical group sizes of around 50 individuals correlate with spending around 20 per cent of the time grooming. Humans have much larger typical social groupings than non-human primates – people can reliably track changes, maintain information, and sustain face-to-face relationships with about 150 people; but this predicts spending upwards of 40 per cent of the time grooming. Dunbar suggests the reason this time investment can be avoided, and that humans can inhabit even larger groups, is the capacity to use language for social bonding – broadly, gossip – purposes. Gossip allows us to share information regarding people not physically present, to cement relationships with those who are present, and to negotiate group memberships more generally. So gossip – which at first glance appears a trivial expense of linguistic effort –is seen as a major engine of the evolution of language and sociality.

Studying the transmission of rumours

In comparison to rumour, gossip is relatively well defined. Rosnow (2001) has suggested that rumours involve a group communicating in chains of transmission in order to make sense of some situation, event or issue, so as to help us cope with anxieties. In the study of rumour, perhaps the most widely used methods are **serial reproduction methods**.

Serial reproduction methods

The study of rumour transmission dates back to Stern (1902). Stern experimented on rumour transmission through a chain of participants who told a story from 'mouth to ear' without repeating or explaining the content. The story was shortened and modified through the chains of communication. Further classic work using a serial reproduction method was carried out by Bartlett (1923, 1928, 1932): asking British students to memorise and then retell an unfamiliar Native American folk story in a chain of successive tellers and listeners. Over a series of retellings of the story some culturally unfamiliar items or events were omitted. Other unfamiliar items were modified, being replaced by more relevant and familiar items. Bartlett hypothesised that contents repeatedly transmitted accorded with cultural expectations or prior knowledge, mentally represented as schemas. So schema-inconsistent information was more difficult to represent and recall, and thereby less likely to be transmitted.

Further work by Gordon Allport and Joseph Postman during the Second World War was driven by concern about the damaging effect of false wartime rumours on national morale. Allport and Postman (1947) employed the serial reproduction method, asking participants to describe an illustration

Box 8.1   Bartlett's classic studies

Bartlett is perhaps most noted for the classic text 'Remembering' (1932). This suggested that remembering is a dynamic, inferential process – constructive rather than merely reproductive – and thus it essentially involves distortion. Bartlett asked participants to reproduce material, such as folk tales and drawings, in order to explore the transformations that occurred in individual or group memory over time. When asked to recall information from memory, people tend to remember only a few salient details of an experience, so that they reconstruct the missing pieces in accordance with the expectations driven by knowledge frameworks of stereotypical objects or events, known as schemata.

To Bartlett, and some of his followers, a schema was viewed as an abstract knowledge structure that controls attention and the reconstruction of memory, and enables recognition and recall of objects and events from past experience (see Abelson, 1981). Bartlett suggested that schemas are not fixed, but rather flexible frameworks that allow us to preserve past experience and use it appropriately to cope with 'the demand, issued by a diverse and constantly changing environment, for adaptability, fluidity and variety of response' (Bartlett, 1932, p. 218). Schemata direct selective attention to a manageable segment of stored knowledge in order to deal with the overwhelming amount of information in the environment (see also Schurr, 1986). In this way, individuals deal effectively with complex tasks (Fayol and Monteil, 1988, Lord and Foti, 1986 in Taylor et al., 1991) cope with problems, goals, or select information to support action (Leigh and Rethans, 1983; Whitney and John, 1983).

Bartlett also studied the psychological basis of cultural change, and the effects of cultural contact, using the idea of constructive memory. He examined how alternative versions of the same stories took on different, conventional versions in different cultural groups. Bartlett explained this via two processes: conservation and constructiveness. Conservation involves borrowing content from another culture on the basis of resemblance, and constructiveness involves new information being combined with old so as to fit into cultural schemas. Operating together, these processes act to both stabilise and transform the cultural item.

Bartlett's analysis thus went beyond analysis of the transformations of content on the individual level to suggest an account of culturally driven transformations in what he called the social constructive processes of memory – a process whereby a group of people collaboratively and dynamically construct meaning. He thus demonstrated that transformational processes in cultural transmission were both cognitive (i.e., employing individuals' psychological 'determining tendencies') and cultural (i.e., based on 'group difference tendencies' of societies). Bartlett gives the example of the contact of migrating groups with native populations, in which new cultural contents are introduced, and when individuals later return home, they bring new cultural items back with them (Bartlett, 1923).

Recent studies have further explored Bartlett's notion of 'group driven tendencies' using the serial reproduction method. These studies explore the effects of memory processes on emerging contents of various kinds of cultural items. One area focuses on group stereotypes, and examines the role of expectancy-based memory biases on the repeated communication of stereotype-relevant information. Kashima (2000) presented an initial participant with a narrative involving information both consistent and inconsistent with traditional gender stereotypes. This participant was tasked to reproduce the story for a subsequent participant, who then reproduced it for another participant, and so on. Early in the chain, stereotype-inconsistent information was likely to be recalled, while nearer to the end, this pattern had reversed.

in a chain of communication. Only 30 per cent of the details were retained after the first five to six transmissions. They concluded that 'as rumour travels it ... grows shorter, more concise, more easily grasped and told' (Allport and Postman, 1947a). These findings, repeated across settings and contents, led to the formulation of 'the basic law of rumour': the strength of Rumour *(R)* varies with the importance of the subject to the individual engaged in transmission *(i)* multiplied by the ambiguity of the evidence related to the subject matter *(a)*; i.e. $R \approx i \times a$. However, this 'law' lacked detailed empirical grounding, was criticised for ambiguity regarding 'importance', and for ignoring the emotional content and context of rumour (see Pendleton, 1998; Rosnow, 1980).

Rumour, media and content analysis

Interest in rumour transmission flourished during the Second World War. Knapp (1944) used media analysis to analyse over a thousand rumours and distinguished between three types: 'pipe dream rumours', expressing wished-for outcomes; 'fear rumours', expressing feared outcomes; and 'wedge driving' rumours, aiming to weaken group solidarity or interpersonal relations. He also suggested that rumours serve to interpret the world in a meaningful way, give expression to human motives, and, at a societal level, express as well as meet the emotional needs of the community.

Shibutani (1966) analysed 60 occurrences of rumours taking place from 1839 to 1960. He concluded that at the centre of serial transmission lies the element of distortion. He also coined the notion of 'improvised news', suggesting that rumours act as a collective problem-solving tool in times of ambiguity and uncertainty – so that, if news from official channels is limited, people tend to improvise to fill in the gaps.

Recently, DiFonzo, Bordia, and colleagues have studies explored rumour transmission via computer-mediated communication (e.g. Bordia, 1996; Bordia, DiFonzo and Chang, 1999; Bordia and Rosnow, 1995). For example, they analysed rumour-related content in Internet discussion groups and observed ongoing rumours in online discussion for a period of one month (Bordia and DiFonzo, 2004). Most statements were 'sense-making', acting as a focal point for further discussion. This reinforced their earlier findings that rumours can involve a group effort to reduce anxiety via social sense-making, and that they often emerge in contexts where there is uncertainty and little credible information (DiFonzo and Bordia 1998, 2000; DiFonzo et al., 1994). These findings corroborate Shibutani's (1966) earlier analysis.

Rosnow (1991, 2001) similarly argues that rumours attempt to deal with anxieties and uncertainties by creating and circulating information to interpret things, address anxieties, and provide a rationale for action. Rosnow, Yost and Esposito (1986) distinguish two types of rumour: 'wish' rumours invoke hope for a certain end, while 'fear' or 'dread' rumours invoke feared results. When anxieties and uncertainty increase, people who spread rumours are less likely to verify the information on which they are based (Rosnow, 2001).

Studying rumours experimentally has involved planting them in controlled situations (e.g. Smith, 1947; Schall, 1950; Rosnow et al., 1986; Scott, 1994 in Pendleton, 1998), studying those already in circulation (e.g. Kapferer, 1989; Kimmel and Keefer, 1991), or planting them in uncontrolled situations. Schachter and Burdick, (1955) planted a rumour in a school, suggesting that some examinations were missing, and found that the transmission of rumours doubled in a class where ambiguity and uncertainty had been increased by one of the girls being removed unexpectedly from class.

Rumour, gossip and genre

There seems to be a range of similarities and differences between gossip and rumour. The central role for managing uncertainty via rumour echoes the role of bullshit in gossip. In both cases, empirical uncertainty combines with a disposition towards believing something that is in line with prior affective and motivational tendencies. Hence, people fill in gaps in their beliefs in part based on the nature of the social and emotional factors that motivated the communication in the first place. However, the way in which uncertainty figures does, of course, differ: in bullshit and gossip there is deliberate game-playing with uncertainty, while in rumour the uncertainty may not be deliberately invited.

The differences between rumour and gossip relate to the way that rumour's other core aspects of content and function are not restricted in the way they are for gossip. If a core function of rumour involves sense-making in conditions of uncertainty, this differentiates it from the specific role of gossip in facilitating social comparison and evaluation of group membership – though there may, of course, be overlaps in cases where whole groups of people struggle to make sense of their identity and social comparison in conditions of rapid change.

Similarly, rumour is not restricted to evaluating the qualities and behaviour of another person or group of people, but can involve a vast array of topics. Nor is it merely concerned with reinforcing groups and cultural norms. And, finally, it does not typically involve communication between individuals who are self-defined as a member of an in-group, nor of similar status levels.

The connections between gossip and rumour may also be fluid – for example, through serial exchanges, what started as gossip may come to resemble less evaluative judgement about others, or what was not gossip may become gossip as detailed information about situations or people becomes open to interpretation. Rumour per se, therefore, is unlikely to constitute a genre of communication; it is more likely a category of informal diffusion or propagation of ideas, in which specific exchanges draw on particular genres including gossip, narratives, and other forms of informal exchange.

Rumour, gossip and pragmatics

Given that communication genres are culturally defined, a major aspect of their explanation falls under the rubric of pragmatics (see Chapter 5). And the roles of bullshit and making sense under conditions of uncertainty suggest that this will involve an inferential approach to communication.

Inferential approaches to pragmatics have their base in Grice's (1958, 1975) theory of conversational implicature (see Chapter 5). The cornerstone of this is the Cooperative Principle, which states that interlocutors should 'Make your conversational contribution such as is required, at the stage at which it occurs, by the accepted purpose of direction of the talk exchange in which you are engaged'. It has been argued by some that this principle as it stands does not cover all genres of communication – for example, where exchanges are typically unequal or not fully collaborative, or where the strategic goals that direct the individual intentions of one party are less cooperative than those of the other. Indeed, Holdcroft (1979) reformulated the principle to allow for variations appropriate to different genres: 'Make your contribution to the discourse such as is required, at the stage at which it occurs, by the purposes you have in entering into, or which you have accepted as the purposes of, or which are the generally accepted purposes of, the discourse in which you are a participant' (Holdcroft 1979, 139).

Another option arises from relevance theory; Unger (2004) has suggested that genre information can be accessed so as to provide information for detailed fine-tuning of expectations of relevance. Such recalibration can concern not only expectations regarding the content of the specific interpretation, but also regarding how the exchange will unfold. Unger suggests that a Gricean picture would require separate, prior recognition of genre before the process of interpretation begins (and so would require a finite list of possible genres to choose from, which is not empirically tractable). By contrast, his account integrates genre as simply another kind of (admittedly, social and cultural) information taken into account during utterance interpretation.

Regardless of this subtlety, it is clear that gossip and rumour involve inferential processes of understanding, in which the interpretations generated are underdetermined by the empirical information, and so are in part directed by the affective and motivational dispositions of the interpreters. This has the further effect, which Sperber (1994) has argued is defining of all cultural transmission, of implying that every communication involves a transformation of content. Inferential communication means that, through repeated chains of communication in rumour, we would expect incremental changes of content, which may however be limited by underlying mental dispositions of communicators. This balance between change and stability is, as we have seen, a central theme in research on the transmission of rumours.

Why are rumour and gossip so contagious?

We now turn to the cognitive and social psychological qualities that seem to make some ideas more likely than others to be retained and spread through gossip and rumour. These include qualities of the content of the ideas, their emotional qualities, and their social-cultural qualities.

Contagious thoughts?

One way of understanding the transmission of rumour is via the **cultural epidemiology** of representations theory of Sperber (1996). Sperber uses the metaphor of disease contagion to suggest that representations act like viruses, spreading through minds in a non-random way. Some ideas die at the moment of their creation, whereas others survive and spread. He suggests that some ideas are 'easier to think' about, easier to communicate, and therefore more likely to spread and 'infect' other minds. The question that arises, is 'why and how some ideas happen to be contagious' (Sperber; 1996; p. 1). Sperber's answer focuses both on the susceptibility of minds to particular kinds of representations, and the process of mind-to-mind communication (i.e., the pragmatic inferential process: see Chapter 5). Such susceptibility is based on the claim that cognition involves specialised, presumably evolutionarily specified learning devices or mental modules (see Hirschfeld and Gelman 1994). Such special-purpose devices constrain the contents of culture which are acquired and transmitted (Hirschfeld and Gelman 1994; Pinker 1997; Sperber et al., 1995; Boyer 2000, 2001; Sperber and Hirschfeld, 2004).[3]

An important suggestion as to why some beliefs are more culturally robust is offered by Boyer (1993) regarding religious representations. He suggests that cross-culturally recurrent aspects of religious beliefs are based on the special purpose representations noted above, but they involve systematic violations of the ontological expectations of these representations. Religious beliefs are '**minimally counter-intuitive**' – they are not bizarre, maximally counter-intuitive, nor are they mundane: rather, they involve the negation of a fragment of the intuitive beliefs upon which they draw. For example, it may be that a recurrent way of representing a 'spirit' is as an entity that possesses all of the ontological qualities of a human being, but has the physical quality negated (Atran, 1990; Boyer, 1994). Similarly, Sperber (1996) argues that the success of religious representations lies in their 'evocative' quality – they are paradoxical, in systematically deviating from ordinary expectations, but still relevant, in being closely related to the representations from which they depart. They thereby generate 'relevant mysteries' – holding a promise, but not admitting a final interpretation. People may arrive at specific interpretations based on emotional and motivational states or on deference to authority in specific settings, interpretations which may not therefore generalise beyond those settings (Franks, 2003).[4] Atran (2002) suggests that part of the success of minimally counter-intuitive concepts arises because they remain associated with the day-to-day world, so that they can regularly be evoked. If an idea is unusual but not massively implausible, we are more likely to remember it, and it is more likely that we will share it with others.

So, could the transmission advantage of counter-intuitive contents be implicated in the spread of rumours and gossip? We have suggested that a core aspect of rumour and gossip may be the bullshit-related tendency to suspend judgement about the accuracy of information transmitted; and this echoes the indeterminacy of a counter-intuitive representation. And we have noted that the resolution of indeterminacy in the interpretation of counter-intuitive religious representations is often temporary and driven by prior emotional and motivational dispositions – exactly as noted for gossip and rumour. Combining these ideas, it might be hypothesised that the transmission success of gossip and rumour is connected to the extent to which they reflect minimally (but significant) counter-intuitive deviations from cultural expectations of conduct, or deviations from previous knowledge of a situation.

An example regarding the memorability of rumour and gossip is provided by the 'Underground Propaganda Committee' (UPC), established by the British military in the 1940s to create and disseminate rumours as defensive weapons against the expected Nazi invasion of England. During the Second World War, this committee developed the science of 'engineering' rumours to become more spreadable using the help of international networks (see http://www.psywar.org/). Similarly, the American Office of Strategic Services (OSS – later to become the CIA), began crafting their own counter-rumour-weapon strategies using the help of Knapp. Knapp's work was adapted in 1943 as a manual for rumour engineers, suggesting that successful rumours should be easy to remember by following a stereotyped plot and remaining connected to the interests and circumstances of the group. It was also suggested that successful rumours exploit the emotions and sentiments of the group.

Contagious emotions?

Rumour and gossip appear to have important emotional qualities. The uncertainty and indeterminacy surrounding the contents of many contents of rumour and gossip, may lead to their being 'relevant mysteries', which evoke special fascination and interest, including an emotional response.

Knapp's analysis (1944) classified rumours on the basis of the emotion they arouse and the effect they have on the receiver. 'Wish' rumours are those that raise one's hopes and desires, perceived as generally harmless; 'bogies' tend to induce fear and anxiety, whereas 'aggressive' rumours have the effect of dividing groups. Moreover, the uncertainty itself may give rise to using emotions as if they were information, which then reduces the doubt.

There is also a further parallel with religion. We have suggested that gossip may comprise a distinct genre – as a type of communication ritual that can be a part of a transmission of rumours. At an individual level, religious ritual may recruit emotion to support the temporary reduction of doubt and uncertainty (Franks, 2003). And Whitehouse (2000, 2002) has argued that 'imagistic' rituals – those which involve heightened emotional arousal – provide a stronger basis for recall and transmission of religious ideas and shared group identity than rituals with lesser arousal. At group level, emotional arousal in sequential performances, can involve socially polyphonic movements, so that 'synchronized affective states among group members in displays of cooperative commitment converge people expressions ... to public sentiment' (Atran and Norenzayan 2004, p. 718). And many religious rituals address existential anxieties by means of 'rehearsals' which recreate the same existential threat within the ritual, while permitting its removal via the communal sharing of the ritual experience – that is, collectively satisfying the emotions that motivate religion in the first place. Rumour and gossip can, we suggest, have a similar role as ritualised means of rehearsing, confronting, and talking about threatening, 'dread' contingencies. This promotes rumour's function as a means of social sense-making under conditions of perceived or actual threat and uncertainty, as discussed earlier (e.g. DiFonzo and Bordia, 2004).

Rumours motivated by existential threats may be exemplified by the attempts of US President George W. Bush's administration to explain the motives for invading Iraq. It is arguable that the propaganda machinery, which included careful rumour-engineering, used fear to enhance specific explanations, especially when linked to the 'global war on terror.' In practice, they suggested that the war was unavoidable: a confrontation between the US military and al Qaeda terrorists who, if not defeated in Iraq, would soon be attacking the USA.

Contagious contexts?

Rumours and gossip spread markedly under some conditions or cultural contexts, but less so under others. As mentioned regarding Bartlett's work, they need to 'fit' prior cultural beliefs – that is, comprise schema-relevant information. In recent years, cognitive anthropologists have developed Bartlett's idea that schemas are not inert 'cognitive maps' but complex knowledge structures which direct experience of the present, inform expectation of the future, and play an important role in the (re)construction of past memories (D'Andrade, 1992). Such 'cultural models' are argued to be taken-for-granted intersubjective views of the world, shared among members of a society (D'Andrade, 1995; Holland and Quinn, 1987; Shore, 1996). They influence the transmission of ideas by guiding people's attention to some ideas rather than others, and provide a context of ambient ideas relative to which new ideas are transmitted and interpreted.

As suggested earlier, studies show two conflicting tendencies – schema-relevant information is better remembered and transmitted in comparison to schema irrelevant information. However, although experiments show that stereotype-inconsistent information is more likely to be recalled in general, towards the end of a communication chain this reverses, and stereotype-consistent information is more likely to be recalled. This tension suggests that the most memorable information will reside between being entirely consistent and entirely inconsistent with pre-existing expectations from cultural context – resembling the 'minimally counter-intuitive' beliefs discussed above.

It is not, however, merely the context of other cultural ideas that influences the dissemination of rumour and gossip. It is also the availability of technologies for transmission. Ideas spread better when there are more social facilitators to communicate them, and when there are means of communication that promote repetition and retention. Modern advances in communication technologies facilitate the electronic diffusion of ideas in ways that humanity has not seen before (see e.g. Jenkins, 2006). Given this, the mass media offers huge capacity to spread rumours and gossip, leading to 'media contagion' (Marsden, 1998). Positive rumours spread via the media may act as rapid advertising campaigns, while negative rumours and gossip may still be stabilised because of their spread (Knapp, 1944). This is not to say that the media are the cause of those rumours – rather, they constitute a specific set of vectors of transmission that can usually precipitate gossip's spread. Such 'media contagion' may also be implicated in the spread of ideas around terrorism. Media publicity devoted to terrorism acts as a contextual vector offering selective and sensationalised information, including false rumours, that can incite and coerce. It might be viewed as not reducing the likelihood of such attacks, and perhaps even precipitating their spread (Marsden and Attia, 2005).

Box 8.2   Rumour and sacrifice representations in Israel

In 2005, a few months after the disengagement from the Gaza strip, an experimental study to explore the transmission of ideas relating to religious sacrifice and commitment was conducted within Israeli culture.

The study (Attia, 2010: unpublished) involved a serial reproduction method, in the form of an online, worldwide web association test which invited participants to 'play' a continuous trial of associations around the concept of religious sacrifice and commitment relative to God, the state, and the Jewish people; these themes being drawn from a prior media analysis. The study's duration was just over two weeks, with a total number of 1005 participants.

Once the first participant completed a set of associations – having three layers, each unpacking the previous – these associations then became options for subsequent participants who could either select from those existing options or create their own new associations. These then became options for selection by subsequent participants, and so on. This dynamic aspect of the study meant that as participants entered new chains of associations, a network of associations grew, generating web pages that became options for subsequent selection. As more participants play the game, a complex hypertext network of web pages linked by chains of associations thus emerged.

Findings revealed that via the emergence of the dynamic associative networks, themes consistent with cultural schemata, expectations, or scripts relating to Jewish sacrifice and commitment tended to reappear or re-emerge, but in slightly different versions, creating clusters of stable representations whose content varied around several core concepts. Consistent with Sperber's epidemiology theory, these core concepts appeared to act as centres of representational gravity which constrained and directed the construction of new representations – these are the most salient 'cognitive attractors'. Moreover, while those core concepts clearly had an overall cultural success as indicated by their being retained at the end of the experiment, their specific 'popularity' ratings had varied during the experiment. This suggests that the relative preponderance of an idea is a dynamic quality rather than being static, and in particular that it is highly influenced by context. This can be illustrated by the difference in popularity of an idea (as something that is associated with 'sacrifice') before and after an 'explosive' violent event which occurred at the time of the experiment. The following graph illustrates the results of first-hand associations regarding sacrifice and commitment to god as suggested by Israeli Jewish respondents (comprising 70 per cent secular and 30 per cent religious participants); these results, in particular, the increased use of themes of 'blind faith' and 'self sacrifice and love for the land' coupled with a decreased use of 'belief in the connection between the Jewish people and the land of Israel', and the notion that sacrifice concerns 'political ideology and religion'.

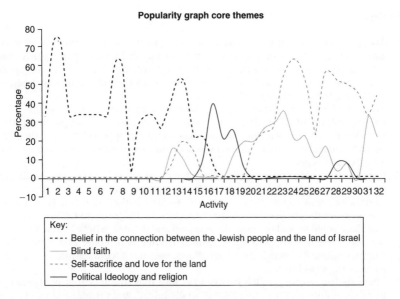

Figure 8.1 Popularity graph core themes

Note: The fire like sign around activity point 20–1: indicates involved a significant flare up of violence between settlers and security forces.

Each core there, marked in color, refers to many different ways of expressing the same meaning.

The activity axis refers to 66.5 days of the experiment documented twice a day.

Conclusions

This chapter has suggested that the core difference between gossip and other forms of cultural transmission lies in the tacit knowledge of the 'rules' that govern the gossip genre. Rumour, by contrast, is more fluid, involving the transmission of ideas by many informal means. We have also suggested that both gossip and rumour can entail the 'contagious' spread of ideas, in part because they may involve suspending belief about accuracy and rely on emotional states to drive their full interpretation. This results in interpretations that can help people to make sense of a changing world and other people, but ones whose accuracy may be subordinated to specifically social and emotional functions, which themselves may be grounded in evolutionary dispositions. The connections with mass media suggest further that the importance and impact of rumour and gossip are likely to increase rather than diminish in the future.

Notes

1. The suggestion is that gossip has associated with it a set of normative collective intentions to interact in a specific way (see Chapter 5). Once participants enter into an exchange governed by such collective intentions, the task of interpreting the other's intentions and beliefs is simplified, since they can in part be predicted by those norms (see Chapter 11).
2. This offers a way of expanding Luckmann's claim that communication genres support fulfilment of recurrent social goals or solution of social problems. Here the idea is that one way they do so is via recruiting appropriate emotional and motivational states, which are themselves connected to solving recurrent evolved, adaptive problems.
3. It is not essential to endorse such a view of evolved special-purpose representations in order to motivate the idea that minimally counter-intuitive beliefs are easier to think about and communicate. What is essential is that such beliefs minimally diverge from deeply held beliefs that are epistemically intuitive to their holders – and these could as well be culturally acquired and defined beliefs. McCauley (2004; see also Barrett, 2008, and Upal, Gonce, Tweney and Slone, 2007) calls them 'counter-schematic' beliefs. In what follows, we intend 'counter-intuitive' to subsume both possibilities.
4. There are interesting parallels between the idea that counter-intuitive representations are attention-demanding and culturally robust, and the idea from social representations theory that social sense-making often revolves around an attempt to make the unfamiliar familiar by relating novel entities or ideas to what is already culturally well rehearsed (e.g. Moscovici, 1973).

9
Empty and Full Speech

Derek Hook

Keywords: Empty speech; founding speech; full speech; the Imaginary; *méconnaissance*; phatic communication; the Other; speech acts; the Symbolic.

Introduction

Despite the frequency of psychoanalyst Jacques Lacan's recourse to the key terms of classic communications theory (notions of entropy, signal, noise, redundancy, and so on), communication studies has yet to adequately explore the critical potential of psychoanalytic thought for the analysis of communication. The aim of this chapter is to highlight the distinctive contribution that psychoanalysis makes to understanding the *transformative* potential of communication. More specifically, I will show that psychoanalysis provides a unique means of distinguishing two fundamental registers of communication. The first of these occurs along the '**imaginary** axis'. This is the domain of one-to-one intersubjectivity that serves the ego and functions to consolidate the images subjects use to substantiate themselves. The second register – far more disturbing and unpredictable – occurs along the **symbolic** axis. It links the subject to a *trans-subjective* order of truth, it provides them with a set of socio-symbolic coordinates, and it ties them into a variety of roles and social contracts. Importantly, it entails the radical alterity of what Lacan refers to as 'the Other'.

Psychoanalysis provides an instrument that enables us to distinguish the noise of everyday *imaginary* (or '**empty**') **speech** from the disruptive potential of a form of *symbolic* (or '**full**') **speech** capable of delivering truth and effecting change in its speakers. One of my objectives here is to provide an outline of the instrument in question, namely Lacan's 'L-schema' which, as I will show, helps us to isolate the key elements underlying potentially transformative instances of communication from those more suited to imaginary forms of misrecognition. Also at stake is the importance of a distinctively psychoanalytic contribution to communication, an approach which grapples with the unconscious dimension of such phenomena.

The triadic structure of dialogue

Let's begin with a basic assertion: any dialogue, any form of intersubjectivity, needs to be grounded in something other than the standpoints of its two participants. This is evident in the case of two people from very different backgrounds who meet for the first time and are able to understand one another simply because they speak the same language. Communication, as such, always entails *a third point of reference*. This idea seems affirmed if we extend our example to consider the case of *misunderstanding*. For reasons of accent, dialect, and so on, we would be right to expect misunderstandings in the interchange between persons who speak the same language but come from different countries. That they might overcome these difficulties, identifying the problematic words or meanings in question, only affirms what I am referring to as the principle of the third.

Constant recourse to some extrasubjective point of reference is necessary for communicative interaction to function. This third point typically functions implicitly, discretely, such that it *feels* as if there really are only two perspectives involved in any dialogical interchange. Then again, when meaning breaks down, the importance of this third point becomes far more overt. Such an external authority – say the role of an expert – provides a means of resolving deadlocks, a point of arbitration, an extrasubjective position of adjudication. We might diagrammatise this factor of communicative interchange – the fact that something stands apart from and anchors the dyadic interchange of one-to-one intersubjectivity – in the form of a vertical superimposed upon the horizontal axis of intersubjective dialogue (Figure 9.1). The vertical represents the *symbolic axis* of human exchange; it necessarily includes reference to an external third point, and it is to be contrasted to the *imaginary* axis of one-to-one dialogues that emerge between any one person (or ego) and their like others (or alter egos). The psychoanalytic name for this third point – which functions as an amassed collection of social conventions and laws, as the embodiment of the authority of the 'rules of the game' – is the **'Other'** (capital 'O' so as to distinguish it from like others [alter egos]).

This third point thus supplies a standard of intelligibility, and, in addition, a *principle of appeal* which holds out the prospect of symbolic mediation. If intersubjectivity were merely a matter of two conversing subjectivities trying to make sense of one another in the absence of such a symbolic Other, then conflicts would be intractable. Two opposed perspectives, each unable to make recourse to anything other than the terms of their own frame of reference, would surely result in the all-or-nothing struggle for recognition. We are here in what psychoanalysis understands as the imaginary register, a domain as much characterised by the ego's self-love as by the limitless potential for rivalry and aggressive conflict. This is a characteristic of the imaginary axis of subject-to-subject interactions: each participant is locked

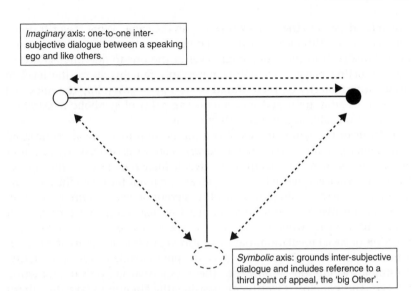

Figure 9.1   Symbolic and imaginary axes of communicative activity

into the concerns and perspective of their own ego. Two important parallels with evolutionary theory (as discussed in Chapter 11) should be pointed out here. First, the concept of a third point or Other interestingly relates to the notion that symbolic culture acts as an external theory of mind. Second, the idea that in the imaginary axis subjects are locked into the perspective of their own ego, resonates with the concept of egocentric communication elaborated in evolutionary psychology. (Problems of egocentrism are also a vital concern in the theory of communicative action; see Chapter 6).

The third as point of appeal

The competitive nature of team sports provides an exemplary case of the domain of imaginary intersubjectivity. Both sides want what the other side does: to win and for the other to lose. This provides a nice sketch of the narcissistic ego-logic of the imaginary register: despite the likeness, the equivalence between players, there is ultimately no real concession that the opponent is as deserving of recognition as oneself.

Now although things sometimes get out of hand in such contests, these imaginary interchanges are virtually always put on hold by the appearance of the referee. The aggressive confrontation with an opponent is often thus bypassed; calls for verification from the Other take precedence. Protestations of unfairness, appeals for a decision ('Penalty!', 'Offside!'), are instead addressed to the figure who oversees the game. What is worth stressing here is that this Other – who embodies the rules of the game – cannot be assimilated into the 'horizontal' level of the one-to-one interactions of the competing players. The Other necessarily remains above the level of dyadic intersubjectivity; there would be no way of grounding the rules, the function of arbitration and judgement, the point of symbolic registration ('Goal!', 'No goal!'), if this were not the case.

In terms of the symbolic axis of communication then, we are concerned with something more than merely *taking another's perspective*, which, after all, would hardly remove us from the dyadic imaginary level of intersubjectivity. So, what is often taken as an ideal of communicative efficacy – the attempt to 'see something from the other's point of view' – is not necessarily a goal of effective communicative change. Our diagrammatic representation makes this evident: when it comes to the symbolic axis, we are looking to a function of social mediation that is *not itself a psychological element, not itself a type of subjectivity*. There is no easy stepping outside of ego-subjectivity, no simple assumption of 'how the other sees it' that succeeds in bracketing my ego. This paradox is worth emphasising: the attempt to take the other's point of view occurs *via one's own ego*, so the very gesture of 'opening up to the other' really only reaffirms my ego (i.e. the logic here is that of *how I think they see it*).

Before leaving the above example we should draw attention to a type of truth-of-consensus that is in operation here. As every follower of sports knows, what 'counts' according to a referee's decision does not necessarily reflect the actual state of affairs; it is what has been declared by the referee that stands as the historical record. There is an overriding 'meta-truth' at work here; even if we disagree with the referee's decision, we do not dispute the rules of the game, the referee's mandate to implement them. It is this symbolic factor, the framework of convention, of consensual rules and regulating principles, which means that it is possible to transform the state of 'egos at war' into genuine social ties.

Why the use of symbols implies an addressee

When I do something stupid (spill a cup of coffee, etc.), why the need to express myself in *socially codified* terms? How come even my most 'brute', immediate 'non-mediated' responses take on an immanently *symbolic* form ('Oh God!', 'Oops!')? There is an obvious resonance here with Wittgenstein's famous maxim, 'there is no such thing as a private language'. We might take this idea one step further though, by asking the following: Why is it that even in my most private moments I nonetheless utilise 'public language' (or signs, or gestures), that I remain caught up in the process of making meaning – at least potentially – for some Other?

A related line of questioning: Who are the epitaphs on tombstones addressed to? The most obvious answer is that they are addressed to the loved ones of the departed person, their immediate community. Then again, it would seem that such epitaphs are also addressed to an audience that is beyond the amassed subjectivity of the 'here and now'. It is for this reason that this notion of the Other cannot be viewed as the equivalent of social psychology's 'generalised other': we are not merely dealing with an aggregate of subjectivities here. Something else is present in the Other, an element of the historical beyond; the Other is always characterised by the prospect of a future exceeding our own situation.

For psychoanalysis, even an internal monologue presupposes a field of reception. We might say then that each instance of speech presupposes a listener, a 'frame of listening'. Emphasising the importance of this role of the Other adds a degree of complexity to how we may have understood the determining role of *the receiver* of given communication. The message I send is always in part a function of *whom it is sent to*. This recipient plays a determining role in its success; they make something of it, recognise some-thing in it, and through it, they make something of me. This sets up a kind of reverberation, not only the anticipation of *how I might be understood*, but also in the terms of the feedback effect of *what I might have meant* now that I am aware of how the other has apprehended my words. This gives us a better grasp of the *return*-effect of a signal; a better appreciation of how one's message is only half (if even that) of what is effectively communicated.

This facet of the Other, the factor of 'how I am heard', always entails the potential of over-interpretation. We approach here the traditional emphasis in Freudian psychoanalysis on the ambiguity of meaning and intention, slips of the tongue, and so on. The breadth of how I might be heard always exceeds the more delimited field of what I (consciously) intend to say, whether by virtue of the tonal variations of my voice, my accent, or the 'materiality' of how I speak (patterns of pronunciation, enunciation, etc.).

Miscommunication as the rule

Goffman's (1959) theory of impression management likewise calls attention to how the complex signalling machinery of human interaction always leaves the message-sender open to a type of double-reading (see Chapters 3 and 17). This is the distinction between the (relatively controlled) expres-sions they consciously use, and the expressivities they inadvertently 'give off'. Goffman adds that a fundamental asymmetry underlies interpretative exchanges, which, in his view, gives *the listener* a distinct advantage. This differential arises as a result of the interpretative latitude afforded the recipi-ent of communications, who is able to scrutinise any of the multiple (and *unintentional*) forms of expressivity given off by the person who is speaking.

This directs us to a structural necessity of the fact that communication works at all: the 'bandwidth' of a speaker's potential meanings is always larger than the bare minimum needed to deliver a message.

We have then a stronger thesis here than the idea that ambiguity and misunderstanding are inevitable byproducts of communication. It is not simply that successful communication is beset by an omnipresent horizon of potential misunderstandings. Rather, 'successful communication' is never itself certain, secure, but is rather something of an accident, the unlikely outcome of a potentially huge range of signals, over-readings and ambiguous significations present in each communicative situation. That we may have progressively learnt to screen out the seemingly redundant or inadvertent components of everyday communication does not detract from the idea that pure uncomplicated communication remains a virtual impossibility. This line of discussion sheds some light on the psychoanalytic assertion that our communicative attempts are always qualified by types of failure, by an overarching impossibility; after all, it is this very impossibility of us ever fully, transparently 'saying it all', understanding one another, that keeps us talking.

Symbolic registration

The fact of such an Other interlocutor provides a means of understanding declarative statements, the function **speech acts** (Chapter 5), whose performative 'telling function' always exceeds the literal meaning of the words spoken. Likewise, when public oaths are made, when someone states a fact 'for the record', or makes a verbal contract before a series of witnesses ('I swear to tell the truth, the whole truth and nothing but the truth'), we have more than the intersubjectivity of speech, but a type of registration, a making of history. The implication of this idea is that communication, particularly in its performative, declarative, and institutional capacities, is constantly involved in types of symbolic registration.

A nice series of examples of *not* informing the Other is supplied by Pinker (2007). He describes a number of scenarios in which a degree of deliberate ambiguity is utilised such that symbolic registration is put on hold. In each case the key protagonist is involved in a risky gambit, and the use of ambiguity enables them to 'save face' in Goffman's (1967) phrase, so as to potentially preserve an existing set of social roles. In the first example, a driver who is pulled over by a police officer for an infraction hands over his driver's licence along with a 50 dollar bill, suggesting that 'maybe the best thing would be to take care of this here' (Pinker, 2007, p. 374). The benefits of such a strategy are immediately obvious: rather than the danger entailed by a more explicit offer of a bribe – which of course is itself illegal – his ambiguity provides an alternative explanation should the offer be rebuked. It thus suspends the full implications of this act: the Other has not as such been properly informed of what has gone on.

A second example concerns the enactment of the sexual come-on, as in the line quoted by Pinker in which a potential suitor asks his partner after a date: 'Would you like to come up and see my etchings?' That the partner can decline the (implicit) offer smuggled into this question by taking it literally – 'Etchings really aren't my thing' – means that the embarrassment of a failed pass can be avoided.

In both of these cases the fact of being able to offer something in a tacit manner – of momentarily bypassing the symbolic registration of the event – is vital. Stated in a more direct way, the bribe, the pass, would have changed things. The definition of the situation would have been different, as indeed would the *relationship* between the two individuals. In the case of an explicit bribe, the act becomes a crime; the offer of sex in the case of the dating friends likewise changes the roles of the protagonists. Let us imagine that the couple in question worked together, and that she was not interested in a sexual relationship. This is the benefit of not informing the Other: things can go on as they were, the participants can preserve the dignity of the social roles they had prior to the encounter in question.

Empty speech

As crucial as speech is, it often leads us nowhere. This poses a question: How are we to understand those types of everyday communication in which a great deal is spoken by the participants, but effectively nothing is heard, nothing new is learnt? We might link this to the sense one sometimes has of two people talking *but of each effectively talking only to and of themselves.*

This type of interpersonal communication is well depicted in an episode of the US TV show *The Sopranos*. The lead character, Tony, is forced to take a hiatus from his therapist, and struggles to find a suitable listener to take her place. It quickly becomes apparent that her replacement, an old friend of Tony's, is not up to the task: although initially he listens, he uses the pauses in Tony's speech to insert stories and complaints of his own – in other words, he listens and responds with his ego. Their resulting conversation is like a comedic parody of a dialogue: their respective narratives hardly connect; they speak over one another, paying little if any attention to what the other is saying. We have the situation, thus, where two speakers, seemingly involved in a dialogue, are actually involved in two self-enclosed monologues, each using the other as the mute audience to a story they are telling themselves about themselves.

In such exchanges each participant is locked into a narcissistic closed-circuit of ego-speech in which the only thing that matters is *how this communicative content affects them.* Such an ego-centred or 'imaginary' dimension of communication is not merely an anomaly, an irritating aspect of everyday speech that blocks true dialogue. This 'empty speech' should be viewed rather as a constant tendency within communicative exchange, an impasse that is *inherent to intersubjective dialogue itself*. To this we should add the qualification that this imaginary dimension is not only a problem; it is also absolutely necessary, it is a precondition for dialogue to occur at all. Empty speech affords a means of connecting with others, it calls out for the recognition that they can provide, it contains the prospects of a type of imaginary mediation – that one might be understood, loved – but it is, in itself, insufficient for transformation, for symbolic forms of truth.

Box 9.1   On empty speech and bullshit

There is an interesting resemblance between 'empty speech' and Frankfurt's (2005) conceptualisation of bullshit, also discussed in Chapter 8. Frankfurt's philosophical analysis asserts that bullshit is neither simply careless, unplanned talk – the bullshit of advertisers and politicians is, for example, often carefully crafted, strategically designed – nor merely a case of lying. An effective lie, after all, maintains some proximity to what is true, not only in the sense that successful lies are often interwoven within a series of truths, but in the more fundamental sense that the liar presumably needs to know what is true in order to design their deception. Says Frankfurt: 'The liar is inescapably concerned with truth-values ... he must design his falsehood under the guidance of truth' (2005, pp. 51–2). For Frankfurt this is not the case in the 'empty talk' of bullshit, which is produced without any concern for the truth. It is this detachment from the frame of the truthful – which even lies must remain strategically connected to – that particularly vexes Frankfurt, hence his argument that bullshit is more the enemy of truth than are lies. With bullshit it is more a case of *fakery* than outright falsity, more an instance of *bluffing* than of intended dishonesty, which means that the bullshitter need not necessarily get things wrong, or even that what they say is factually untrue. Essentially anything goes – truths and falsities alike – in the narrative that the bullshit artist spins, so long as it serves their interests.

What Frankfurt misses is the factor of ego-benefit, the ego-gratification that comes from speech of this sort. In short, his analysis would be sharpened by adding the observation that this is essentially *ego-led speech*. With this hypothesis we are better placed to account for the omnipresence of this type of talk, and indeed, for its overriding purpose, namely its *ego-substantiating function*. Hence the psychoanalytic idea that a subject *speaks himself or herself into being*, into believing he or she is a substantial entity: this is the notion of empty speech as a way of shoring up, lending consistency to, an ego; talking here is a project of imaginary *self-making*.

Having evoked a sense of empty speech and its rudimentary objectives, it helps to turn to a consideration of the *form* of this type of speech. Although speech holds out the potential of truth, it brings with it also the trappings of illusion; it enables us to believe what we invoke. This is the imaginary aspect of language which functions to thus supply an illusory object-status to what is in fact insubstantial. One is reminded here of the seductive charms of rhetoric as discussed in Chapter 10: the greater your powers of expression, the more I *feel* that I know *exactly what you're talking about.*

An appreciation of the representational illusion that language is capable of is evident in the notion of reification (discussed also in Chapter 7): the idea that the functioning of discourse gives practical object-status to postulates ('personality', 'intelligence', 'femininity') that have no independent, material existence beyond the explanatory frameworks of meaning that call them into being. One of the objectives of clinical psychoanalysis in bringing to the fore the symbolic aspect of spoken interchange is that it may help momentarily dissipate the illusory, figurative properties of language. It is in this respect that Lacan (2006) presents us with an opposition between two different forms of truth. On the one hand there is what is true within the confines of a given discourse (within the horizon of a particular mode of knowing, a type of intelligibility). On the other there is the truth made apparent by the pact established by the speech-situation itself: the designated roles conferred by a particular interaction, for example, or a consensus established as ratified by a form of symbolic registration (as in the case of a referee's decision).

The image-making capacity of empty speech leads us away from difficult truths and introduces a set of systemic distortions into the subject's communications, distortions of what an ego *would like to hear and believe.* Hence the links so frequently found in psychoanalytic texts between subjective truth and that which disturbs, discomforts, causes pain. Authentic speech, intimates Lacan (1998), provokes anxiety, certainly so inasmuch as it is directed at a non-subjectifiable Other, an Other who can never be second-guessed, and who is always in part unrecognisable, impossible to anticipate. There is an abiding suspicion in psychoanalysis that what furnishes the ego with a comforting image of the world, or gratifies its inherent narcissism, necessarily involves a swerve away from reality. This is a theme we will return to, the idea that there are few subjective truths that do not emerge without running against the grain of resistance.

An important psychoanalytic maxim to bear in mind when analysing intersubjective communication: talk is continually conditioned by the tendency (on the part of both speakers) to affirm the ego, to protect and insulate it against what it finds unpalatable, and to mobilise defences against hearing anything too disruptive. These defences involve an epistemological dimension, namely the systematic distortions whereby the ego hears on the basis of what is already 'known' by, pertinent to, or reflective of its own interests. This is the imaginary function of *immediate comprehension,* which entails an insistence on attributing ego-centred meanings as a means of understanding. We might then overlay Piaget's long-standing concepts of assimilation and accommodation – which distinguish between the cognitive operations of fitting new experiences into existing schemas and the construction of altogether new structures of understanding – with a properly psychoanalytic dimension: we may as such speak of *imaginary* assimilation and *symbolic* accommodation.

This underlines once again the challenges behind communicating at all: in sending a message the subject is typically more concerned with affirming an ideal image of its ego, with winning the gratifications of the recognition of others, than with what is being communicated per se. Frankfurt's (2005) example of a Fourth of July orator who goes on in bombastic fashion about the greatness of America, its illustrious and heroic history, is instructive in this respect. What this speaker really cares about is *what people think of him,* as a patriot, someone who reflects deeply on the origin of his country. The listener's disposition is likewise conditioned – the case, one might say, of 'having an ego for ears' – by how what is being said might serve to affirm their ego, what they know, what they might be able to tell about themselves.

The L-schema

We may now turn our attention to the L-Schema, which extends the basic diagram of communication offered above (see Figure 9.2). We can treat the schema as a diagram of communication where Subject (S) and ego (o) – two facets of the individual contained on the left-hand side – are conversing with another ego (o') (on the top right). As established above, any ego to other interaction brings into play another principle of Otherness, the 'big Other' (bottom right). We are thus able to account for the four corners of the Schema. Importantly however, the schema is used both as a means of mapping the communication between two subjects (two egos) and as a depiction of the four nodal points of *a single subject's subjectivity.* Given the psychoanalytic emphasis on the split nature of the subject and upon the fleeting quality of unconscious events which suddenly emerge and then disappear, it is not surprising that the individual is viewed here as *a set of relations* rather than as a single, unified entity. This affirms something reiterated above, namely that there is always a split between what an ego means to say (an individual's conscious intention), the act of speaking (the fact of the enunciation itself) and how they are heard (the place of the Other).

One question often comes to the fore in considerations of the L-Schema: if we assume that the ego is the seat of identifications, the functional basis of the rational individual, then why does it appear only in the third position

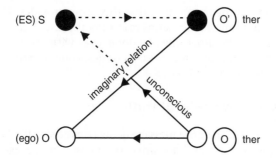

Figure 9.2 The L-Schema
Source: Lacan, 1988, 2006.

of the schema (at the bottom left)? In this respect it helps to trace the communicative event as a movement across the positions of the schema. There is an initial moment of speaking (at S) which connects the subject to an other, an *alter ego* which supplies the images and desires that will provide the basis of the subject's ego (the ongoing process of identifications that give it its 'identity'). This is a point worth pausing over: such an 'identity' maintains always an alienating destiny. With the ego it is never the case of an original or integral 'me' but instead an amalgamation of images and reflections that have been taken on so as to lend a degree of bodily and psychological coherence.

It is by virtue of this outside-in nature of the ego's constitution that, for psychoanalysis, a form of alienation proves an inescapable condition of human subjectivity. There is thus a structural basis to the psychical and epistemological trend to misrecognition. This is what underlies the *méconnaissance* of distorted forms of knowing that are always routed via others, and that are delimited by the ego's habit of understanding on the basis of what is already 'known' by, or reflective of, given ego-interests. This provides an answer to the question of why the alter ego (o') comes first: because, simply put, as the originating source of the subject's identifications, *it does come first.* We have then the conditions for a constitutive form of aggressivity with an other who is always more authentic at being me, oddly, than I am. Such a narcissistic rivalry is part and parcel of any primary identification, a foundational element of human subjectivity.

There is no easy means of transcending this deadlock. The imaginary content of the ego is always already derived from the other, which means that any attempt to assert the status of my existence or my desire *as primary* necessitates the elimination of this other. Of course to eradicate the other means that one loses the basis of one's own identifications, and along with it, the possibility of the recognition that this other provides. The impasse is writ large: if I am to make any claims regarding the uniqueness, the authenticity of my desire, the other must be done away with, as the enemy of my self-realisation. Then again, this other is of desperate importance, for without them my ego has no existence.

The trans-subjective order of truth

More important then than the message being conveyed is the *implicit request made for recognition*. Such an imperative, on the side of message-senders and receivers alike, routinely supersedes the possibility of any real communicative gains or change. This imaginary deadlock is not, however, completely unsurpassable: the type of 'third-party appeal' discussed above enables the establishment of forms of convention and agreement, providing thus the basis for a properly *trans-subjective* order of truth. We might take the example here of legal conflicts, or, more particularly, the apparent intractability of divorce battles. Things get hopelessly muddled in such a rivalry of competing egos; there are two conflicting versions of events, each of which is anchored into its own self-interested subjective reality. The only thing that can be ascertained with any certainty here is the principle of the relevant law. The idea here is that *the structure of communication itself* involves such a reference point, that it establishes an order of truth, and provides thus the basis for a genuine and potentially transformative social contract.

Back then to the L-Schema: having discussed the other–ego (o'–o) relation, we may now turn our attention to the diagonal that bisects this axis, that is, to the Other–subject (O–S) relation. As opposed to the empty speech of the imaginary axis, this relation holds out the possibility for viable communicative change. The S is the speaking subject, who, by communicating within a given socio-symbolic context and by necessarily utilising the codes, signifiers, and language(s) supplied by the Other, constantly produces more in their communicative attempts than what they had meant. We should as such be wary of treating the subject as the first or most important term in this four-part structure. After all, the moment of speaking is always already conditioned by the factor of the Other, by the fact of the symbolic system which I draw upon to express myself, and in terms of which I am heard. The starting point of the schema would thus be – counter-intuitively, as always – at the bottom right, in the fourth position of the diagram, the only position, incidentally, that emits signals in two directions. It is the source of the ego's constant attempt to understand its symbolic location, its social role(s) (the O–o trajectory), and the necessary precondition for any attempt to use language, to express one's self in symbolic terms (the direction of O to S).

The arrow from the bottom-right to the top-left thus gives us the unconscious vector of the diagram. This diagonal implies that the conditions of the symbolic *speaking the subject* is a condition of speaking at all. This vector also, incidentally, implies that the unconscious must be understood via the symbolic order, via the fact of the trans-subjective factor of the Other, a fact which entails a far stronger societal dimension than is typically accorded the notion of the unconscious. There is, of course, considerable resistance to this field of unintended messages and meanings enabled by the Other. What the L-Schema illustrates is that this Other-subject line of transmission is continually disrupted, denied, or bypassed by the production of ego meanings. This current, crucial to the production of subjective truth and change, is constantly detoured, rechannelled by the cross-axis (o'–o) of other–ego exchanges. The dotted diagonal line connecting the middle of the diagram to the top-left corner indicates as much: the truth-potential of Other meanings produced on this axis is continually deflected. The possibility of any ego-disruptive or symbolic speech is continually rerouted and assimilated into the ego's characteristic function of misrecognition.

Full speech

We now tackle the task of characterising 'full speech'. Ron Howard's (2008) film *Frost/Nixon* dramatises a series of interviews carried out in 1977 between the British journalist David Frost and the former US President. The film stages the encounters between the two men as a desperate affair of two egos in crisis, indeed, as a bout – Nixon's aide even likens the interviews to a boxing-match – as a 'struggle to the (symbolic) death'. The stakes of such a symbolic demise are real: Frost's career is in free-fall; he risks enormous debt and professional humiliation in his attempt to record these interviews with a man who, in turn, is aggressively intent on using the exchanges as a means of restoring his image, potentially returning to politics.

What accounts for much of the film's dramatic tension is that, prior to the final interview, Frost seems completely outclassed. Nixon has at his disposal all the rhetorical devices of the smooth-talking politician; he is in his element in front of the TV cameras. When the filming begins, the beleaguered Frost, by contrast, becomes a virtual irrelevance: his interrogative skills are swept aside and he is reduced to a stage-prop that allows Nixon (very nearly) to vindicate himself. We have thus an exemplary instance of empty speech: the 'little other' of Frost amounts to no more that a patsy, a means to Nixon's grandiose self-narrativisation.

How then does this type of speech tip over into something different? Given his vitriolic assertions of innocence, his declared intent to 'set the record straight', why does Nixon go on to admit error, and culpability in the Watergate scandal? Why the apparent apology for 'letting the American people down' – which, until that point was inconceivable for the recalcitrant Nixon – and the declaration, a perfect instance of the *act* of saying something effectively making it so, that 'My political life is over'? (see Box 9.2).

Box 9.2   Unexpected disclosures – Nixon's admissions

Nixon's admissions come at a very particular moment in his discussion with Frost, as Frost transcriptions of the famous interviews make clear. After repeated assertions of his innocence ('... you're wanting me to say that I ... participated in an illegal cover-up? No.' (Frost and Zelnick, 2007, p. 244)), Nixon considers the emotive question 'How do I feel about the American people?', and then changes tack to recall an earlier event:

I didn't expect this question frankly though ... I think I said it all in one of those moments when you're not thinking ... I had a lot of difficult meetings those last days before I resigned and the most difficult one, and the only one where I broke into tears [was when] ... I met with all my key supporters just a half-hour before going on television ...

... And, at the very end, after saying, 'Well, thank you for all your support during these tough years' ... And I just, well ... I sort of cracked-up; started to cry; pushed my chair back and then I blurted it out, I said, 'I'm sorry, I just hope I haven't let you down'.

Well, when I said, 'I just hope I haven't let you down', that said it all.

I had.

I let down my friends.

I let down the country.

I let down our system of government and the dreams of all those young people that ought to get into government but think it's all too corrupt ...

Yep, I ... I, I let the American people down, and I have to carry that burden with me for the rest of my life.

My political life is over.

I will never yet, and never again, have an opportunity to serve in any official position ...

And so I can only say that, in answer to your question, that while technically I did not commit a crime, an impeachable offence – these are legalisms.

As far as the handling of this matter is concerned, it was botched up, I made so many bad judgments.

(Nixon, cited in Frost and Zelnick, 2007, pp. 246–7)

Five aspects of full speech

Before turning to consider the above example, it is important to make a few qualifications. It is crucial, for a start, to maintain some distance from the assumption that truth simply emerges here in the form of an encapsulating statement. If, as Lacan emphasises in his later seminars, subjective truth, the truth of desire, *can only ever be half-said*, then moments like the one pinpointed above are events, openings up onto profitable and transformative sayings without representing 'the whole truth'.

From a strict psychoanalytic perspective the answer to why Nixon made such unexpected admissions has little to do with the structure of an interpersonal two-way dialogue. We should thus bracket a series of banal psychological speculations (such as Nixon's need to 'come clean', or the interpersonal skills of the interviewer), viewing this outcome rather in terms of how the imaginary dimension of empty speech slipped momentarily into the symbolic register of full speech. Now although there are good reasons to question such an assessment – to query whether Nixon's comments really qualified as full speech, as paradigmatically different from empty speech – many of the characterising features of full speech can be illustrated by means of this example.

We have, first, the factors of error, surprise, the unanticipated (i.e. what Nixon *had not meant to say*), each of which represents a route to a difficult, previously unacceptable disclosure. Put differently, we have a speech-moment – as in the case of the typical Freudian slip – in which the subject speaks *beyond himself or herself* (beyond their ego), and ends up saying more than they had meant to. In such cases there is something *Other* in one's speech, something which seems not to have been said by one's self, or adequately integrated into the field of one's own conscious (ego) identity.

Second, there is the disruption of ego-to-ego speech which occurs when it becomes apparent that it is the *Other* rather than the 'little other' that one is speaking to. That the Other provokes anxiety, upsetting the operations of ego-speech, is an important consideration here. When Frost comes to occupy the position of this Other – the role of the 'confessional interlocutor' of History, of the expectant American People – *this itself* is a precondition of Nixon's unexpected admissions. Frost himself, as 'little other', could not precipitate such a destabilisation. Furthermore, the confessional nature of Nixon's speech could not effectively have been achieved 'intrapersonally' by Nixon – the structure of confessional communication necessitates an Other. Confessing – a theme also of Chapter 11 – cannot function without this element of symbolic registration, without alerting an Other as to what has been done.

Third, we have the performative dimension of Nixon's comments, the fact of their illocutionary force as speech acts, the consideration, in other words, of the 'what is done' by virtue of what he says. Full speech has the capacity of being able to bring about change in the speaker and the situation. This is clear enough in Nixon's declaration that his political career is over, a statement that makes what it says to be so. It is apparent also in Nixon's acknowledgement of wrongdoing, an acknowledgement which confirms the events in question – and his own complicity therein – thus committing these facts to the official historical record.

Fourth, a different relation to truth has been established. It is not only that something about the structure of the (intersubjective) situation has been changed by virtue of what Nixon has said. Something *about himself* and his own relation to his past has also changed, been brought into a different relation to truth. So, whereas in empty speech there is a gap between the ego content of what is enunciated and the position of enunciation (what is said does not chime with the truth of the subject), in full speech the subject articulates their position of enunciation (their speaking-position of desire) despite its discordance with the ego. This links to another characteristic of full speech: rather than the imaginary self-making of empty speech that operates to assure and comfort us, full speech resembles a 'coming undone' of this ego typically accompanied by anxiety and resistance. Truth here takes the form of that which disturbs, destabilises.

A fifth consideration includes the role of full speech as a type of **founding speech**. The fact that full speech entails the making of an elementary pact (of speaker and interlocutor), that it implies a contract, the acknowledgement of certain reciprocal obligations, is crucial. In this respect one should draw attention to the precise conditions immediately preceding Nixon's confession. Surrounded by his most loyal supporters, and about to confront the big Other of the expectant American people, Nixon reaches breaking-point at the moment that he is forced to confront not merely his own compromised symbolic position, but the fact of a failed pact, an abused bond. What is effective and powerful in full speech has much to do with this establishment of a *new order of relationship between myself and my other/Other interlocutors*, a relationship that is 'ratified', confirmed by the very conditions of speaking themselves.

Speech devoid of content

Lacan shares with Austin (1962) at least two vital commitments in his approach to speech. The first of these is a resolutely non-psychological stance which does away with any reference to the intentionality of inner states. Lacan concurs, secondly, with the pragmatic imperative of breaking our fixation with the *constative* dimension of language, that is, with the assumption that the functioning of speech is best evaluated with assessments of truth and falsity. In other words, speech should not be viewed as a chiefly descriptive means whose primary task is to name or represent, and whose efficacy can thus be based on its degree of factual accuracy. Although such properties are vital to language as a communicative modality, they do not best pinpoint its ability to facilitate and convey communicative meaning. As argued above, this fecundity of meaning-making harbours illusions; it functions to create effects of certainty, stability, and ego-coherence, to reify both its speaker and their objects.

Empty speech, we could say, has an alienating, inauthentic destination, even if composed of factually true fragments. Full speech, by contrast, may be made up of less than convincing elements despite the fact that its end-point is one of revelation. The implication is that the truth-potential of full speech should have little to do with the *empirical* truth-value of its contents. The paradox of this situation is that empty speech is often exceedingly full of non-substantive ego-supporting contents (full of bullshit, we might say) – it is heavy on content but light on substance. So, while empty speech is typically loaded with insubstantial materials, symbolic full speech is often stripped of content, purified of imaginary trappings. This is an idea which resonates with Jakobson's (1960) concept of **phatic communication**, with the idea of essentially meaningless exchanges that function simply to main-tain a social bond, to keep communicative channels open and effective. Lacan draws on Mallarmé in this respect, who, he says:

> compares the common use of language to the exchange of a coin whose obverse and reverse no longer bear any but eroded faces, and which people pass from hand to hand 'in silence'. This metaphor suffices to remind us that speech, even when almost worn out, retains its value as a *tessera* [a ticket, a password]. Even if it communicates nothing, discourse represents the existence of communication; even if it denies the obvious, it affirms that speech constitutes truth; even if it is intended to deceive, the discourse speculates on faith in testimony.
>
> (Lacan, 2006, p. 209)

The contract of communication

It is important that we grasp the truth-potential of full speech. What Lacan has in mind is not simply a truth of verification; it is a truth which relies upon neither the correspondences of form nor of content. In the exam-ple of a worn coin passed between people, what matters is neither the detail of its content nor how it is handed over. What is important is that this (essentially meaningless) object is exchanged so as to maintain the *contract of communication itself*. The *tessera* that Lacan refers to is a 'dumb element'; the fact of its exchange, however, confirms a contract, a bond, a pact (one has paid the price of admission; one knows the password). Full speech is thus true not by virtue of its content or its form, but *by means of the symbolic contract that is set in place* between subjects. Full speech has absolutely nothing to do with sincerity, with the subjective authenticity of the speaker. What makes an oath legally binding is not that I perform it enthusiastically or with a sense of piety – I can quite easily reel it off like an automaton – but that it binds me to the law. Bluntly put: what seals a deal is not my inner psychological state, but my signature. My word here is indeed my bond, but as *the mark of a contract*, not as an index of psychological meaning. Representational efficacy is not then what installs such a pact. Be it the case of signature, thumbprint or oath – the minimal signifier can be essentially meaningless – it is *the mark* of the promise that counts to confirm a contractual relation, to alter a given symbolic constellation. (This emphasis on the non-psychological is by no means to dismiss an analysis of the psychological – or, 'imaginary' – aspects; it insists rather that an analysis of communication must take into account symbolic factors that cannot be reduced to the psychological.)

We cannot then view empty speech merely as pointless and inauthentic as compared to full speech as the authentic position of enunciation; to do so would reduce full speech to an expressive modality. Unexpectedly, empty speech may be a necessary precondition for the event of full speech, certainly so if it provides the means whereby speech becomes increasingly unmoored from the objectives of truth and sense. This would accord with the psychoanalytic conviction that the (relatively) undefended 'nonsense' of free-association is a necessary route of access to subjective truth. The prattle of empty speech is a precondition for the truth-potential of full speech to emerge. Just as the truth-potential of full speech is always at risk from the disruption of empty speech, so it is that in the midst of the babbling of empty speech a moment of full speech may erupt, a pulse from the Other may break through (the o'–o axis of the L-schema).

Box 9.3 Heidegger's truth in discourse

Commentators have linked Lacan's notions of full and empty speech to a variety of philosophical theories, the most notable being Heidegger's (1927) opposition between *Rede* (or discourse) and *Gerede* (idle talk). In the case of *Gerede*, Heidegger has in mind a type of intelligibility on display in everyday communicative interchanges. If we break the contents of communication down into *the objects that it focuses on* (the objects that we speak about) and *the claims or positions we assert* relative to such objects, then idle talk is preoccupied with the latter. *Gerede* is that mode of communication in which our interest in making claims or establishing positions relative to this object overrides any insight into the object itself. Rather than attempting to grasp the object for what it is, the communicative interchange remains preoccupied with what is asserted *by means of* the object in question. Such objects are thus passed about on the current of such activities (claiming, arguing, asserting) without themselves ever being adequately understood. Our talk thus becomes increasingly unsubstantiated, cut adrift both from its objects and from any adequate epistemological grounding.

If *Gerede* contains a rudimentary sense-making ability then so does *Rede*, but of a higher order. The notion of *Rede* is accorded an important place in Heidegger's philosophy. He considers it to be both a foundation for language, and the means for the articulation of a superior type of intelligibility. *Rede* must be separated from mere assertions about things, from a focus on properties and attributes. We are here interested in how things might be disclosed in their Being. *Rede* is thus never simply *about* something. It imparts to us rather a given object *and the necessary framework of understanding* that enables us a more significant apprehension or appreciation of the object. So, on the one hand we have an assertion about something (*Gerede*), a strategic speech act, and on the other a framework that underlies and enables this speech act to work (*Rede*) and that makes possible a deeper intelligibility of things. This, incidentally, bears a striking similarity to an ideal of pedagogy and communicative efficacy that can be read out of the work of Freire (Chapter 2) and Vygotsky (Chapter 1): the notion that one needs to do more than communicate a detached piece of information, that one needs to convey with it the broader frame of comprehension that allows one to adequately apply this information.

In view of the transformative function of communicative discourse we might identify a tacit convergence of three very different thinkers. There is the commitment to discourse (or *Rede*) as able to reveal the truth, to disclose the 'Being-there' [*Dasein*] of its objects in Heidegger. In Vygotsky, too, via his notions of mediation and symbolic tools, we find a commitment to particular forms of discourse that are able to teach new abilities. This is the crucial distinction between a mere *assimilation* of new contents and the *accommodation* of new socio-cognitive skills that transform pre-existing competencies. In Lacan the notion of full speech provides a case of communicative interaction that disrupts the constant reiterations of ego-attributions and ego-affirmations in favour of disruptive types of knowledge the subject didn't know they had.

Symbol-as-pact, symbolic-as-law

Grasping full speech requires that we add a key qualification to what is meant by 'the symbolic'. We are not concerned here simply with symbolisations, with representation in its semiotic dimension, but with relations of convention as they install laws, customs and bonds. It helps here to approach the symbolic via the structural anthropology of Levi-Strauss, as a system of exchanges. The symbolic thus denotes the effective operation of collective customs and institutions which work not by reference to the intrinsic meaning of symbols, but on the basis of how they locate subjects, by generating the symbolic coordinates that enable such subjects to take up positions in social reality. The exchange of symbols cements certain pacts. As the recipient of a gift from the mafia knows very well: what matters in accepting such a gift has little to do with its intrinsic qualities, and everything to do with the links and obligations thus established between the parties concerned.

For Lacan, then, the platform established by virtue of a spoken exchange installs a code of sorts, 'rules to play by' as we might put it, a series of consensual parameters that characterise the implicit contract of communication itself. The first extralinguistic facet of this agreement concerns the fact that *there can be communication*, that a communicative attempt is possible, and that, presumably, some understanding can in principle be achieved. The second facet concerns the fact that speech does indeed represent a viable route to truth, despite the fact that this route possibly involves the contradiction of what has been accepted. Third, despite the fact that deception is a constant possibility of all human speech engagements, a given communicative exchange nonetheless entails an aspect of 'good faith' (*bona fide*), apparent in both the elementary trust one exhibits towards what one is told (there is always the potential that something genuine, authentic is being said), and in the implicit pledge one makes in speaking (that I have committed this act of saying something to you). (This constant possibility of deception is likewise a factor emphasised by evolutionary approaches; see Chapter 11.)

These then are the meta-communicated components of any speech situation, components that are not dependent on the content of what is said, or upon the frame of mind, the psychological conditions under which the speaking occurs. They nonetheless install a rudimentary social bond, a 'kinship of communication' that ties both participants into their shared socio-symbolic world. Communication is thus involved in the constant renewal, the reinstantiation of the social contract itself. What this means in turn is that empty gestures (asking 'Can I get you anything?' when the expected answer is no) are important communicative acts. The same holds for rhetorical questions which ask after what *they know not to be the case* ('Are you OK?' when someone clearly is not). Despite being redundant at the level of literal content, such questions, like empty gestures, nonetheless add something to the communicative exchange. They move a social bond along, they strengthen an interpersonal tie; more than just fostering a relation, they secure and reiterate certain roles.

The case of politeness is of interest here inasmuch as it tells us something about the *meta-communicated context* of what is being communicated. So, what is polite about the roundabout way of asking someone to do something, say the request 'Would you mind passing me that book?' Taken at a purely literal level, this is a request as to whether the recipient objects to being asked something. What makes the request polite is its indirectness, the very fact that *it does not work at the level of literal meaning*. By couching the request in these terms I make apparent the fact of *my relation to the content*, i.e. that I respect their prerogative to turn down my appeal, and so on. Indirectness, in other words, itself communicates something. It signals to the hearer, as Pinker stresses, that an effort has been made, that their feelings, their situation has been taken into account.

Conclusion

If it is the case, as Evans (1996) suggests, that communications theories based on modern linguistics typically prioritise *conscious intentionality* and *dyadic* models of exchange, then, as I hope to have shown, a psychoanalytic orientation certainly has something new to offer.

It is easy enough to anticipate a series of critical remarks that may be directed against the above psychoanalytic approach to communication. A first predictable charge, that psychoanalysis is either too arcane in its theory, or not scientific enough, can be dealt with by pointing to its value as a *conjectural* theory that is helpful in the making of hypotheses and predictions in respect of various communicative failures and successes. Important here is to emphasise how concepts like the Other, the imaginary, full/empty speech, unintended expressivity both link to other theoretical frameworks (impression management, cognitive and evolutionary psychology, the ideas of Heidegger and Vygotsky) and are in fact useful, practicable concepts.

A second and more pertinent criticism is that the model of communicative change advanced here is specific to the realm of clinical psychoanalysis and is not as such generalisable beyond this domain. True as this is when it comes to issues of applied clinical *practice*, it seems less of a problem when it comes to the attempt to theorise reoccurring deadlocks within communication, in anticipating how many ego-to-ego ('empty') communicative attempts run aground.

The analytical vocabulary of psychoanalysis helps distinguish between messages sent to others and to the Other, emphasising thus is specific to the dimension of symbolic registration. It likewise draws attention to the constant contract-making dimension of symbolic exchanges, highlighting furthermore the importance of founding speech, making apparent how everyday interchanges entail types of reciprocal role designation. Such concepts may help sensitise us to certain of the recurring trends within communication, to the fact, for example, that various types of imaginary assimilation tend to prevail over the possibility of hearing or learning something new, over the prospect of change (or what I have called 'symbolic accommodation'). They alert us to how demands for recognition within ego-to-ego interchanges routinely override the effective exchange of communicative contents, warning us, similarly, of the perennial tendency to aggressive rivalry as it occurs within imaginary communiqués.

The overriding importance of these concepts, once used in combination, concerns the theorisation of communicative change. Ultimately, what psychoanalysis warns is that it is only under the conditions of properly *symbolic* communication that one might facilitate the accommodations of real communicative change, as opposed to the pseudo-changes of imaginary assimilation that work to sustain a given status quo.

10
Communication as Rhetoric and Argumentation

Martin W. Bauer and Vlad P. Glăveanu

Keywords: Argument; audience; celebratory; composition; deliberative; delivery; ethos; invention; judicial; logos; metaphor; metonymy; non-European rhetoric; orator; pathos; persuasion; question; rhetorical situation; style; the three musketeers of rhetoric; tropes.

Introduction

Rhetoric represents an old stock of knowledge that offers the practical tools for speaking in public and for social communication more generally. Rhetoric is both an art and a science that everyone, in different contexts of daily life – at home, at school, at the market, at the workplace and so on – draws from, more or less consciously. At the same time rhetoric can mean many things to many people and, most importantly, many different things all at once. There is an ongoing *'rhetoric about rhetoric'* that positions it either among the most valuable skills a person could have (the Queen of Liberal Arts, oldest of the humanities, precious capability, practical logic, etc.), or among the most detestable activities someone could engage in (sophistry, deception, specious reasoning, obsession with **style** over content, loaded language, empty discourse, a form of idolatry, and a poisoning of the mind, etc.). Rarely can one find neutral accounts of rhetoric as the discipline concerned with how people use **arguments** in persuasive forms of communication or, in more specialised depictions, how people use non-literal meanings (for example in irony, sarcasm, etc.). In this chapter we will distinguish between at least four meanings of rhetoric:

- the act of **persuasion**: persuading others by form and content;
- a didactic system: set of rules, a hygiene of speaking (a morality);
- a method of analysing the available means of **persuasion** (critique);
- a worldview: the 'rhetoricality' of all human activities as based on discourse.

Implied by the last point above is the fact that rhetoric is something we constantly 'do', talk about and cannot avoid. Like ubiquitous computing, rhetoric is everywhere, noticed and unnoticed. To realise this one needs only to consider the *vocabulary* of rhetoric that includes terms such as: **persuasion**, situation, exigency, speaker/**orator**, topic, **audience**, **invention**, argumentation, example, paradigm, public life, forms of rationality, arrangement, eloquence, **style**, **metaphor**, memory, location and vivid images, **delivery**, etc. These are all words we commonly use and very few of us are aware of just how rich their history is and how they link us to the development of rhetoric as a discipline. To raise awareness of this, this chapter will therefore start with a brief historical perspective on rhetoric and reveal how the 'ups' and 'downs' of its trajectory reflect larger socio-cultural contexts. The very old 'roots', located in Greek and Roman Antiquity (BCE), need to be revisited in order to appreciate classic rhetoric and its tenets. The discussion will later focus on the 'anatomy' of **arguments** or the classical canon of rhetorical analysis: the **rhetorical situation**, the genres, the faculties. Processes of **argument** construction and **delivery** will be approached by looking more closely at the three main dimensions of rhetorical communication – **logos**, **ethos** and **pathos** – and their interdependence. Finally, modern echoes in the study of rhetoric will be presented, including interrogations about the existence of **non-European forms of rhetoric**, and conclusions drawn about the relevance of a 2500-year-old tradition for our present concerns.

The past and present of rhetoric

The origins of rhetoric, the *second oldest profession*, are commonly traced to events in Sicilian Syracusae during the fifth century BCE, where after the fall of two tyrants property claims needed to be made in public courts by former owners. Eloquent people, who came to be known as 'Sophists' or the 'bearers of wisdom', made a living out of representing these cases before the judges and juries. They developed techniques for speaking on behalf of other people, which became one of the many meanings of the term 'representing', that is, standing in for somebody else. Ever since, rhetoric has been many things to many people: the art of **persuasion**, a heuristic to find the adequate means of **persuasion** in a situation, a canon of teaching, the science of **style**, a morality of public speaking, an élite practice, a playful form of entertainment, a ploy of manipulation. The historical path of rhetoric, at least in the West, is a sinuous one. Its times of ascent and times of decline correspond to major eras in Western history and reflect their dominant ideas about knowledge, truth, and discourse (see Box 10.1). It therefore comes as no surprise that philosophers differ in their take on rhetoric and psychologists involved more recently in this area are trying to build upon philosophical presumptions that often contradict each other.

Box 10.1   A potted history of rhetoric

The history of rhetoric is characterised by phases of waxing and waning. To simplify matters, one could say that rhetoric has so far had three main historical periods.

The first is represented by axial **Antiquity (400 BCE–100 CE)** when the classical canon was defined. Based on the work of the Sophists, Plato, Aristotle, Cicero, and Quintilian, among others, different conceptions about rhetoric emerged. In general, rhetoric was considered to belong to public life (which at the time excluded women, children, slaves, and 'barbarian' foreigners) and to be an important part of the education of young men (teaching them how to speak effectively). This included the polemic of Socrates, as recorded by Plato (1994) in the dialogue 'Gorgias', against Sophistry (i.e. the pleasing of listeners rather than the pursuit of truth), and Eristik (i.e. the tricks of appearing to be right even when you are wrong). This suspicion of the true expert against the skilful amateur persists in modern polemics against 'spin doctoring' and 'bullshitting' in public life (see Frankfurt, 2005).

With the fall of the Roman Empire, rhetoric receded into obscurity, to revive in the **late Middle Ages and Renaissance (1200–1600)** when ancient sources, in particular Aristotle, were rediscovered in part via Islamic and Jewish scholarship in southern Spain (including some false attributions of an ancient source to Cicero, with significant beneficial consequences; see Yates, 1966). Rhetoric was inherited from late Roman times as a key part of the classical curriculum of education, the liberal arts' *trivium*, alongside grammar and logic (see Marrou, 1984).

With the Reformation, Enlightenment, and the Age of Science, rhetorical concerns declined once more. This decline can be accounted for in many ways, including the emergence of a scientific ideal of 'no rhetoric' (the *'nullius in verba'* motto of the Royal Society of London, meaning 'take nobody's word for it'), the lack of public occasions for conversation under absolutist regimes, and an emerging division of labour between specialised fields of activity, i.e. science, the law and the arts, and industry. Overall, the cult of mathematical formalism in pursuit of an objective truth and that of a romantic view of the authentic, subjective expression, squeezed the third culture, that of adequate public communication, into oblivion. In the early nineteenth century, Heinrich von Kleist seems to have complained about the rather strict division between people who deal with **'metaphors'** and those who feel comfortable working with 'formulas'. For him, those able to handle both **metaphors** *and* formulas were 'few and between' and did not represent a category in itself.

Only the **post-Second World War revival** (see Perelman and Olbrechts-Tyteca, 1988; Toulmin, 1958; Bitzer, 1968; Meyer, 1994, 2004, 2008) recovers an appreciation for argumentation and **persuasion** which recognises both the rules of formal logic and the quest for authentic expression as special cases of a more complete rhetoric.

Throughout its history, the reputation of rhetoric oscillated between a symptom of corruption and a marker of freedom. For Kant, in the tradition of eighteenth-century Enlightenment 'rhetoric, the art of using people's weaknesses for one's own aims – no matter how good these may be in intention or even in fact – is unworthy of any respect whatsoever. Moreover, both in Athens and in Rome, it came to its peak only at a time when the state was hastening to its ruin, and any true patriotic way of thinking was extinct' (Emanuel Kant in 'Critique of Judgement', c.1800). This view is shared by Schopenhauer's (1864/2009) mid-nineteenth-century playful tract against rhetoric, where he exposes 38 tricks on 'how to appear right even when wrong' – an antidote against rhetorical deception. By contrast, McGuire (1986), in reviewing the concerns of social psychology with attitude change, suggested that times when rhetoric is valued are also times of freedom of speech and liberty for individuals. As such, the enemies of rhetoric are the enemies of liberty more generally. The valuation of rhetoric expresses a 'republican spirit' of speaking out against the undue accumulation of power (on the history of rhetoric consult Kennedy, 1980).

But what was rhetoric for its founding fathers, the Greek and Roman thinkers of Antiquity, and how can their conceptions inform our modern understanding of persuasive communication? Classical definitions include at least four examples, each stressing different elements of the *rhetorical tradition*:

1. Rhetoric is the art of deception and manipulation of an ignorant public. According to this polemic of the Greek philosophers Socrates and Plato (427–347 BCE) against Gorgias (485–380 BCE), sophists have no true expertise and little concern for truth, showing preoccupation only with immediate pleasure and gratification. In a modern unflattering characterisation, the 'bullshitter' (Frankfurt, 2005) seeks effect before truth, and in that respect is more dubious morally than the liar who remains entangled with the truth. A more appreciative take on the Sophists' concern for timely and adequate public speaking is presented by Poulakos (1999).
2. Rhetoric is public reasoning, and a heuristic of finding the best means of **persuasion** for a given occasion considering all the constraints. Public discourse seeks to persuade an **audience** and swing an agreement. This is

the meaning advocated by the Greek philosopher Aristotle (384–322 BCE), who cultivated the view that 'true and just ideas are necessarily stronger' if expressed under conditions of public debate (see Aristotle, 1991 and 2007 editions). This idea foreshadows Habermas's power-free discourse in the public sphere (see Chapter 6 on communicative action in this volume).

3. The Roman republican senator Marcus Tullius Cicero (106–43 BC) was sceptical about theory. He favoured practical experience and the virtues of the speaker. The 'good person, speaking well' (*vir bonus, bene dicendi*) expresses the Roman ideal of an honourable man and speaker who receives the trust of the community because of his proven virtues.

4. Finally, rhetoric is the art of speaking well, or eloquence. With Marcus Fabius Quintilian (35–95 CE) Roman rhetoric became pure eloquence, the art of speaking well (*ars bene dicendi*). This was at the time of the empire, when the function of public speaking was reduced to ornamentation. Rhetoric is here the literary concern of cultivating expression and **style** for pleasure. The concern for the form of speech overshadows the concern for what to say.

In conclusion, Plato stressed the malleability and the weakness of the **audience** which the Sophists are exploiting; Aristotle stressed the force of the **argument** in the situation, while not ignoring other elements; Cicero and Quintilian focused on the strength of character of the speaker and his/her **delivery**. What this brief historical account illuminates us about is the *diversity of conceptions* around rhetoric that can and do, implicitly or explicitly, inform modern thoughts on the topic. Those who continue to reject rhetoric may well be adopting a Platonic view of it as the purposeful deceit of weak souls. Of course this position raises further questions about what is actually 'true', who holds the 'truth', and how the 'truth' can be validated. Neo-positivist scientism is based on this fundamental dichotomy between truthfulness and falsity, where scientific methods and discourses are on the side of the former while rhetorical means and strategies belong to the latter. Despite such radical positioning, nobody can deny nowadays the importance of studying persuasive communication. Psychologists have well taken on the task of revealing the mechanisms that underpin this important social process with the means of science: experimental demonstration. Ancient ideas about the role of speaker attributes, **styles** of **delivery** and **audience** characteristics, resurface in studies of 'empirical rhetoric' within an experimental paradigm (see Box 10.4 about the Yale programme for example).

But above and beyond these aspects, probably one of the most insightful and lasting contributions to the study of rhetoric has been made by Aristotle (see the 1991 and 2007 editions), who over two millennia ago explored multiple rationalities (Hoeffe, 2003). In his view there is a rationality of logic (the construction of syllogisms based on certain premises), a dialectic rationality (helping us to conclude based on uncertain premises), a *practical rationality of rhetoric* (belonging to a discursive public life and the elaboration of common sense), and even a rationality of poetic expression (the value of theatre for the regulation of emotions). Most importantly, all these rationalities need to be understood in their respective domains of production. As for rhetoric, although Aristotle can be said to have emphasised its logical aspect (**logos** – the **argument**), he did so without neglecting the emotional side (**pathos**; the mark of sophist practices) or the qualities of the speaker (**ethos**, a vivid concern for Roman thinkers). The importance of this synthesis will become even clearer as we discuss next the 'anatomy' of classic rhetorical **arguments**.

The classic rhetorical canon

Classical rhetoric (see Barthes, 1970) is a didactic system that is 2500 years old and which describes a canon of five concerns: the situation, the genres, the faculties, the figures of speech, and the forms of proof.

First, the *rhetorical situation* is defined by four variables. An issue is in the air that needs addressing, a **question** is raised, a problem needs to be solved (the *exigency*). Timing is crucial. Oftentimes speakers face a 'now or never' type of situation. There is a right moment to speak out, a window of opportunity, and speaking too early or too late might jeopardise the effect (something referred to as *kairos*). Rhetoric also leads us to ask: who is the *audience*? Every utterance is directed towards a particular **audience** and, in fact, the speaker addresses a certain image that he or she constructs about who the **audience** is, what they want to hear and how they want to be spoken to. This is a crucial idea since the **arguments** built for an 'imagined' **audience** need to persuade the 'real' **audience**; any major misappreciation in this regard can prove to be extremely counter-productive. Finally, the **rhetorical situation** also includes the *speaker* or **orator**, his or her competences, dispositions, and limitations. The speaker must decide how to present him or herself in the situation (the *persona*, mask) given the exigency, the *kairos*, the **audience** and what he or she wants to say. The **audience** is invited to trust the *persona* projected by the speaker, and it is in this interplay between real and imagined speakers and real and imagined **audiences** that the fate of persuasive communication is decided. Indeed, the gap between real and imagined **audiences** and real and imagined speakers is a key issue for recent rhetorical analysis (see Meyer, 2008). A **rhetorical situation** thus means the optimal path through five constraints: to construct **arguments** that fit the problem at hand and to accomplish their **delivery** at the right time by a speaker with specific strengths in relation to a particular **audience** (see Bitzer, 1968).

We can conclude from the above that **persuasion** is the function of the total social situation, not just of words alone. Let's take an example of a particular **argument** in order to understand this important claim:

> *Smoking is bad for your health;*
> *You are a smoker who wants to live long;*
> *Therefore you had better give up smoking.*

Few would disagree that this is a convincing **argument** on paper at least, and yet its clarity and logical strength are by no means enough to achieve **persuasion**, i.e. smokers giving up smoking. The **rhetorical situation** in this case is constructed around a specific kind of exigency: the problem of the contradiction between a long life and smoking, or that smoking is a burden on the health system. How persuasive is the **argument** above with regard to this exigency? Well, that would depend, on the one hand, on who the speaker is. An ex-smoker would probably be more convincing than a non-smoker and certainly more than a person who lit up a cigarette while making the point, or a 'closet' smoker whose secret habit has just been revealed. What about the timing? Time and place for this kind of speech are not to be disregarded. It is one thing to deliver the **argument** during a class at school and another to give this speech in the waiting room of a lung cancer specialist.

Second, in continuing with the basic concerns, classical rhetoric distinguishes between three *genres* (see Table 10.1). *Deliberation* takes place in the public arenas of politics. It advises on a particular course of action on the basis of usefulness, expediency or nuisance. Its main concern is the future. *Judicial* discourse has its privileged place in court, in front of a jury or a judge. Its purpose is to accuse or defend a person on the basis of what is right or wrong with regard to the law, statutory or recognised tradition. Its main focus is on what has happened, the actions of the past. Finally, *celebratory or epideictic* rhetoric occurs at funerals and festivals. The purpose is to

Table 10.1 The three classical genres of rhetoric and their distinctions

Genre	Audience	Criterion	Purpose	Time	Reasoning
Deliberative	Assembly; Politics	Useful Nuisance	Advise on a course of action	Future	Example
Judicial	Judges, Jury Court	Right, just wrong [Justice]	Accuse; Defend	Past	Enthymeme
Epideictic	Spectators Funeral; Celebration	Beauty Honour	To honour To censor	Present	Comparison Amplification

honour or censor a particular person through comparisons and amplifications of his or her deeds. The main focus is the present of those attending the event, aiming to encourage and reinforce common morality or simply to entertain. It is worth noting that an analysis of genres allows us to classify speech occasions without any order of preference between them. The issue is not whether **deliberative** rhetoric is 'better' than epideictic rhetoric. What this classification does is to call to our attention the fact that each format needs to be assessed in its own terms; each serves a typical situation and we need to adapt our speech according to its features. So, for example, it helps the speaker immediately to recognise whether he or she is talking in the parliament or in front of a court to generate the right **arguments** and find the adequate tone.

Third, classical rhetorical education has focused on *five skills* (or faculties) that need to be taught:

1. *Invention* means finding the best **arguments** for the occasion and supporting the creativity for doing that. Here lies one of the most important paradoxes of rhetoric: how to convince people of a 'new' claim based on what they already know and want. Rhetoric is always to a large extent redundant, catching people where they already are. This is not a gratuitous observation since it relates to an important interrogation: is **persuasion** an imposition from outside, like brain washing, or an elicitation of what people already are or have – in terms of knowledge or motivation – but might not be aware of? This is a topic of historical debates, for example over the genre of religious preaching as indoctrination or enlightenment (see Chapter 12 in this volume). Once invented, **arguments** need to be presented.

2. *Composition* advises on how to construct the storyline, order the points coherently with a beginning, a middle part with facts, propositions, and balancing the pros and cons, and ending with a conclusion (advice that is still useful for essay writing!). The beginning and the ending should be able to raise attention and passion, while the middle should focus on demonstrating the point in question.

3. *Style* explores the uses of figurative, non-literal speech. Here rhetoric historically merges with the study of literature and advises us, for example, to use a 'plain' **style** to teach, 'medium' to delight and 'grand' to move an **audience** (where plain, medium, and grand refer to the density of use of rhetorical figures in speech or writing). Elaborate classifications of rhetorical figures or *tropes* have emerged from this analysis of stylistic features (see Box 10.2 concerning the non-literal use of language), and concern with such groupings and naming of figures can often make rhetoric a rather boring and unedifying exercise.

4. *Memory* **training** was crucial at a time when notepaper did not exist or was hard to obtain. Speakers were advised in 'mnemotechnics' on how

Box 10.2   Rhetoric and non-literal language

Among the considerations of **style**, the master **tropes** of **metaphor** and **metonymy** received much attention in classical and modern rhetoric. These key figures of speech allow one to go beyond literal meanings and to extend the repertoire of verbal expression.

Metaphor allows for the transfer of a set of characteristics from a source to a target domain. Speaking of an 'English rose' when referring to a woman, the speaker makes an attempt to transfer floral beauty and delicacy (source) onto a woman, typically born in England (target). An age-old debate rages over whether this metaphorical transfer from a source to a target is purely ornamental and attention grabbing (substitution theory) or fundamental for our understanding of the world (interaction theory). Areas of ignorance are often explored metaphorically with lasting effects, and new insights thereby gained are not lost when the **metaphor** is later dropped (see Ricoeur, 1978, p. 45). **Metaphors** offer potentially innovative concepts that create new insights through the entailment and implication of attitudes and connotations. Knowing that 'time is money' has all kinds of implications for our relations to time: we now like to use time well, save it, invest it, and we despise those who waste or 'steal' it; and all this on the back of a **metaphor** (see Lakoff and Johnson, 1980).

Metonymy allows us to substitute a word for an associated word. Famously, in Britain one speaks of the 'Crown', while not referring to a piece of precious metal worn occasionally by the monarch, but to the unwritten constitution of the country. The crown is worn by the monarch in formal sitting, and this sitting is a constitutional arrangement. Thus the 'Crown' is a part of the body of the monarch, and the monarch is the 'constitution' by association. This feature of language extends widely the possibilities of symbolic meaning: a crown (signifier) is not just a piece of metal (signified).

Figures of speech, and there are many more than these master **tropes**, are a main point of focus for rhetorical concerns and on all these notions it is useful to get further guidance in Corbett and Connors (1999) and in Sloan (2001). A playful illustration is Queneau's 'exercises in **style**' (2009), where the writer offers 99 versions of a most banal occurrence in a bus by making use of and also illustrating rhetorical devices.

Figures of speech are classically considered a matter of **style**, and Aristotle recommends they be used with care and not in excess. The hygiene of minted words requires that they are clear and not far-fetched; they shall not be ludicrous or obscure, but elegant (in the sense of concise and surprising) and appropriate for the **audience**; vulgarity shall be avoided as shall mixed **metaphors**, where multiple sources are projected onto a target.

A modern version of such rhetorical hygiene was offered in the twentieth century by neo-positivist thinkers. Inspired by a scientific-mathematical outlook and in a fight against political ideologies of the day, they declared everything 'non-sense' which did not hold up to a strict logical analysis of truth value: every statement must be true or false, otherwise it is non-sense. This exercise attempted to purify the use of language to an ideal of formalism where every expression was literal and without ambiguities, in other words, illustrating a 'zero-degree' rhetoric. Similarly, and maybe derived from such philosophical preoccupations, the 'plain English movement' for example (see Orwell, 1946) militated against the use of **metaphors**, long words, the passive voice, foreign expressions or jargon. What it favoured were literal meanings, short and clear words of the English vocabulary and the active voice (except when breaking these 'rules' was absolutely necessary).

to memorise complex **arguments** in the absence of written prompts on the pulpit. The most famous advice urges the speaker to consider that memory is contextual and to identify locations (method of *loci*) in his/her visual field, to place ideas in these locations, and to further associate ideas with vivid images (*imagines agents*). Imagination supports memory and the need for memory encourages vivid imagination. It is arguable whether modern advertising, which places glamorous women in beautiful locations in association with consumer products, goes much beyond this 2000-year-old recipe. The change lies in the fact that not only the speaker's memory is supported but, once the image is externalised and visible to all, the **audience** also gets help for remembering. In a marvellous essay Yates (1966) demonstrated that medieval cathedrals, with their vivid images of heaven and hell, are mnemonic designs to remind the paperless preacher what he needs to say. By extension, most visual forms of artistic imagination are props to support our collective memory for important ideas. In this conception art is a key element of the moral community reminding us of what is important.

5. Finally, ***delivery or action*** summarises the preoccupations with the actual speaking in front of the **audience**, the bodily attitude, the tone of voice, the breathing, speed and pacing of the utterances. Mnemonic techniques and elocution training remain today very much part of the preparation of actors who in turn dispense advice to public speakers in management seminars.

Within the faculty of **invention**, rhetoric distinguishes between three means of **persuasion** or proofs. **Ethos** or character refers to the efforts of presenting the speaker in a favourable light by projecting his or her prudence, goodwill and virtue. Credibility and trustworthiness are ancient attributes of speakers that persuade. It remains open whether the speaker truly 'is' or only 'displays' these characteristics for the occasion, which is indeed a matter of controversy for classical authors. **Pathos** refers to the attempts to induce emotions and lead the **audience** towards a desired judgement. These include appeals to anger, fear, love and hate, shame, kindness, pity and envy. And finally **Logos** refers to the practical **arguments** of which there are two types: *enthymeme* and paradigm (or example). Both are logically deficient but sufficient for purposes of public speaking. The relative weight given to these three means of **persuasion** has been debated for centuries and defines different traditions of rhetoric. The Sophists, attacked on this by Socrates and Plato, focused on **pathos**, the Romans, with Cicero and Quintilian, highlighted the **ethos** of the speaker, and Aristotle brought logic into public communication. More precisely, Aristotle stressed the need for balancing all three considerations although, at a time when others privileged either **pathos** or **ethos**, his ideas might have appeared to favour the **logos** (see Braet, 1992). This notion of 'balance for a purpose' is neatly personalised in the 1844 French romantic novel of 'The Three Musketeers' by Alexander Dumas (see Table 10.2). The swordsmen Aramis (= **logos**), Athos (= **ethos**), Porthos (= **pathos**) are brought together by d'Artagnon (= exigency) to save the honour of the Queen in a race against time (= kairos) and under the unifying slogan *'all for one, and one for all'*. We shall take this story as an illustration of the rhetorical principle that **arguments** alone will not do, neither a good person, nor the appeal alone; only when devolved in conjunction is **persuasion** likely to be achieved.

Table 10.2 Basic forms of rhetorical proofs as personalised in *The Three Musketeers*

Rhetoric	Personification	Fictional character
Exigency	D'Artagnon	Young and naïve, passionately in love; 'the new kid on the block'; wants to impress his girlfriend by protecting the Queen from the machinations of MiLady and the devious Cardinal Richelieu; he is in need of competent help
Logos	Aramis	The intellectual of the group; a mix of soldier and monk; introverted; ambitious and without scruples; least popular character; ends up in Church Service as a Bishop and makes politics as General of the Jesuits
Ethos	Athos	Gentleman, landed aristocrat, likes the quiet life, virtuous, well behaved and noble character;
Pathos	Porthos	A gentleman who lost his fortune; colossal and a clown, courageous and loyal, a passionate womaniser.

Argument construction

Rhetorical analysis cannot and should not stop at describing the structure of persuasive means (i.e. **logos, ethos**, and **pathos**) but needs to understand how they are produced in everyday interactions, when and with what kind of effect. An implicit question takes shape: How to best construct our persuasive communication? If, according to Aristotle, rhetoric is the art of finding the adequate means of **persuasion** for a given situation, then analytical knowledge is only a prop in that process.

Logos or enticing the mind

Perhaps the aspect that has received most attention from theoreticians and researchers from Antiquity onwards, the **logos** is concerned with the content of the message, with the **argument** to be developed. And it is from Antiquity that ideas come about how an **argument** based on **logos** could be constructed with the help of deduction from a feasible, conventional premise (*enthymeme*) and/or induction from an example (*paradigm*). Let's take these in turn.

The *enthymeme* avoids boring the **audience** by following a principle of economy: much can remain implicit. From unproven assumptions, conclusions can be drawn. Assumptions are common places, commonly taken for granted and no longer questioned. But what logically is a deficient form of reasoning appears as virtuous in public speaking: to be brief, to avoid distraction, to respect the **audience** by not boring them; in sum a commitment not to say more than is necessary (what Voltaire allegedly hinted at when he said 'the secret of being boring is to say everything'). *Enthymeme* will make use of an established fact without further queries. This can either be a traditional commonplace of the community ('though shall not kill'), or a constructed commonplace (e.g. by repeating a verbal association between things). This second situation is famously represented by the association between Saddam Hussein and al Qaeda activities, in the build-up to the Iraq War after 9/11. Soon enough, this repetition led to the unquestioned assumption that the two were in fact related and as such constituted the premise for further **argument** construction, namely that an attack on Saddam Hussain would be an action against al Qaeda.

The other form of classical proof is the *paradigm* or *example*, the single case inference. It is recommended to start an **argument** with a case or to end an abstract **argument** with an illustration. The case can be factual, based on real historical events, or fictional – either literally possible (a parable) or literally impossible (a fable). The purpose of the case is to suggest the general validity of a claim through illustration, or the opposite, to refute a general claim by counter-example. Both moves are logically insufficient, but the power of the example is widely present in public communication. Modern uses of examples are the stories of 'good practice' in social policy and the myriad of case studies mobilised in management training. The cases of success or failure of businesses make for strong **arguments** of what needs to be done and what is to be avoided.

Modern revivals of rhetoric have focused on the uses of **arguments,** and authors like Toulmin have put forward analytical tools for understanding 'practical reasoning' in contrast to logical **arguments** (see Box 10.3).

Box 10.3   Rhetorical argumentation

To rescue argumentation from the formal logic of deduction and induction as the sole arbiter of viability, Toulmin (1958) – among others – suggested schemes for analysing practical argumentation. The idea is based on the analogy with the human body, where a common number and structure of bones gives rise to a multitude of physiognomies depending on how the flesh stacks up. The general anatomy of practical argumentation consists of six basic elements. From data a claim is inferred, with or without qualification. This inference is supported by a warrant, and a warrant might be further buttressed by a backing. A rebuttal can specify particular conditions, which again might be backed by a rule. An **argument** can be more or less complete, or some of these elements remain implicit.

Data 'A = B' >>>>> 'so, presumably', >>>>> 'likely' [Qualifier] *Claim* 'A = C'
'since' *Warrant*   'unless' *Rebuttal*
'on account of' *Backing*   'on account of' [*Backing*]

To take Toulmin's example, the statement *'Harry is born in Bermuda, therefore he is British'* entails an implicit **argument** that is more elaborate. In a more explicit form the statement might read as follows: Harry was born in Bermuda (data), so he is presumably (qualifier) a British citizen (claim), since 'born in Bermuda' will generally mean 'being British' (warrant) following legal statutes of the place (backing), unless both parents were aliens (rebuttal). This scheme is useful for empirical research of argumentation because it gives a framework of what to look for and it allows us to specify what is implicit and what is explicit in any given statement. With this tool, **arguments** in public debates – for example over issues of genetically modified crops or stem cell research – can be typified following their effective structure and degree of explicitness (see Liakopoulos, 2000).

Developments in the analysis of argumentation stress its peaceful nature and rejection of violence in the settling of confrontations. Argumentation is the continuation of conflict by peaceful means, and as such this kind of analysis aims at classifying the means available for argumentation and their source of power (see Perelman and Olbrechts-Tyteca, 1988). The revival of rhetorics after the Second World War can be seen as a reaction to the experience of global warfare in the twentieth century and the search to clarify alternative strategies in an emerging global public sphere.

Ethos or establishing trust

It goes almost without saying that the *persona* or the 'source' has a great impact on the persuasiveness of any communication. The speaker, who can be an individual or an organised group or political party, a business corporation or even a nation, needs to construct a reputation as truthful and trustworthy in order to secure the goodwill of the **audience** (of employees, shareholders and consumers, etc.). This process is at the core of modern corporate communication where public relations experts aim to present the corporation at its best. Nowadays this aim is summarised as corporate social responsibility (CSR), and expresses care about the environment, business ethics, fare trade, employee welfare, local community impact etc. Important to note, the corporation needs not only to 'do' good but to be 'seen' doing good. And since 'being seen' can outweigh the actual doing, it is often the case that the good is not done (just promised or mimed) or, equally, that when good is done it is done for ulterior motives (the instrumentality of doing 'good'). What do ancient rhetoricians have to say about this gap between real **ethos** and projected **ethos**?

For Aristotle, in order to be perceived as truthful you would need to demonstrate practical wisdom, virtue and goodwill. Importantly, this impression arises from the conduct of practical argumentation and from an explicit belief in the power of good **arguments** (see chapters on communicative action). Cicero listed even more virtues that, according to him, would carry the speaker's credibility: *prudentia* (prudence, including *memoria* for the past, *intelligentia* for the present and *providentia* for the future), *justicia* (justice), *fortitude* (fortitude) and *temperantia* (temperance). These perceived virtues are residuals of past actions in the interest of the community; the credible speaker is thus rooted in the community and has its trust. This is all, of course, hard to attain and demonstrate, but easily lost. Quintilian made a more direct link between being a good man and being skilled at speaking. This 'ideal **ethos**' contributed to the decline of rhetoric accused of being preoccupied with **style** over substance (see also the chapter on 'empty and full speech').

Classical rhetoricians also list practical props, by which **ethos** can be gained or lost in the moment of speaking. In order to modulate credibility one can try to express modesty, to refer to established authorities and associate oneself with prestigious others (something that modern psychology refers to as 'basking in reflected glory'; Cialdini and colleagues, 1976), to attack the opponent's character (argument *ad hominem*), to put oneself into a better light and so on. At the same time one should not make the mistakes of overusing rhetorical figures or being bluntly inconsistent with past action and statements since these features shed serious doubts about the person's good intentions. Also the criteria for credibility do change over time (and can vary according to geographical place) so it is always useful to reflect upon what can make someone look more successful and trustworthy in any particular context (age, wealth, social status, education, past success, etc.).

Pathos, or moving the audience

It is tempting to assume that if a person manages to look credible and to construct 'solid' **arguments** then he or she will be able to move the **audience** in the desired direction. As it happens, this is not always the case. More is needed for **persuasion** to succeed and this rests with the capacity to stir emotions and to appeal to the deepest passions, concerns or needs of your **audience**. Despite the Stoics' plea to 'persuade without pandering to affect', the Sophists were certainly not mistaken when they emphasised the role or importance of **pathos** for **persuasion**. And, because their work involved also teaching others the skills of their 'trade', we now have a generous list of props to construct 'pathetic' **arguments** including: *captatio benevolentiae* (initial appeal to sympathy), *adhortatio* (promises for the future), *ominatio* (prophecy of evil, prediction of disaster), *descriptio* (vivid description of consequences of action/non-action), *cataplexis* (threatening retribution/punishment for ill doing), *energia* (having vigour of expression), *climax* (using and ordering triplets by dignity; e.g. the good, the bad, the ugly), *synonymia* (repeating the same issue with different words), etc. To this list modern social psychology can add a lot more since one of its main concerns rests in knowing **audiences**, their representations, attitudes, behaviours, needs and emotions in general (evolutionary) and in particular (cultural). From here to manipulating the **audience** in persuasive communication is only a small step, easily made by specialists working in applied fields (advertising and consumer psychology, political psychology, health psychology, etc.). This risk of manipulation continues to taint the field with a threat of moral dubiousness (see also the chapter on social influence).

Modern echoes of rhetoric

Since the 1960s we have enjoyed a general revival of rhetoric if not an era of pan-rhetoricality. It is an age in which rhetoric and especially the investigation of it flourishes once more, including through scientific studies. The demarcation between 'truth seeking' and rhetoric has faded; not, however, the emphasis put on 'truth seeking'.

Experimental social psychology took up the topics of **persuasion** and attitude change (see Box 10.4; see also Chapter 4 in this volume) with various degrees of success, argumentation analysis became popular again, and efforts are being made to compare different types of rhetoric with one another and even to order them on a scale analogue to temperature (where certain forms of discourse – for example, scientific – are at a '0 degree'

Box 10.4   The Yale programme of an 'empirical rhetoric' and its discontents

During the Second World War, social psychologists started an empirical programme of determining the best combination of **audience**, speaker and message features to maximise effects on audience attitudes (Hovland, Janis and Kelly, 1953). The effort is known as the *'Yale Programme of Communication and Attitude Change'*. Attitude change on many topics was induced by varying experimentally the alleged speaker characteristics (source of high and low repute), varying the message characteristics (positive or fear appeal, one-sided or two-sided information), and varying the audience features (in-group, out-group, active or passive participation, persuasiveness as a personality factor). This research paradigm was part of the post-war revival of rhetoric under the names of **persuasion** and attitude change. It impressed widely with its experimental logic and was part of the quest for a magic key to successful communication. Hovland (1959) advocated the combination of experimental and field studies. It impacted on the Total Propaganda of the Cold War mobilisation and became a milestone of communication research.

However, the programme yielded contradictory results, and did not provide the 'magical key' of **persuasion** (see Lowery and DeFleur, 1995). For example, conflicting conclusions over the effectiveness of 'fear appeal' were never settled. It resurfaced as a veritable 'politics of fear' after 9/11/2001 to rally support for national security policies (see Rampton and Stauber, 2003). The Yale model overestimated the power of the source considered as a bundle of features in isolation, which led to a rediscovery of the obstinate and active audience vis-à-vis a particular source (Bauer, 1964). As a programme of empirical rhetoric, it was found lacking. According to Perelman and Olbrechts-Tyteca (1988, p. 12), the Yale paradigm takes for granted the persuasiveness of experimental demonstration – the very problem which the analysis of **persuasion** needs to clarify. The Yale programme was not able to understand why someone is successful or not in persuading others of their results. Finally, for Billig's later project of a 'rhetorical social psychology', the Yale programme neglected the key rhetorical process of inventing **arguments** that persuade in particular situations. The quest for general laws of **persuasion** led to an obsession with message arrangement and neglected the creative, heuristic, and improvised nature of **invention** in each persuasive communication (see Billig, 1996).

rhetoric for using unambiguous language, and other forms of discourse deviate from this point of absolute comparison).

The regained interest in rhetoric, however, raises some essential questions about the meaning of communication itself and how a history of understanding rhetoric comes together with the necessities of applying rhetorical tools in marketing, in politics and elsewhere. Is communication an act rooted, as its etymology suggests, in *communio* and *communitas*, the importance of coming together, of conversing and chatting in order to build social relations, to consolidate community life? Or is it mainly a strategic effort to achieve some specified success, to convince, win **arguments** and change the 'minds and hearts' of others in a predetermined direction? These are, of course, rhetorical questions in themselves, meant to make us more aware of the *double-nature* of communicative acts, independent even from the actual intention of the speaker. The revival of rhetoric clearly reminds us of the basics: communication is as much about content as it is about relationships between people.

What is rhetoric in the present context? Following a recent definition by Meyer (2008 and 2010), it is the negotiation of the *difference between individuals on a given question*. It is a game with questions and answers, where answers make questions disappear or not. The classic 'ingredients' of the **rhetorical situation** are still important: the individuals (speaker, audience members), the expediency (a given **question**), etc. And yet there are many attempts to offer a new synthesis with additional concepts: the key idea of difference, of the distance between speaker and audience (between what either side believes, what they want, how they feel, etc.), and the need to negotiate, to navigate this difference if **persuasion** is to succeed. We have to remember that the distance here is mediated by the imagined *persona* of the speaker and of the **audience** that we made reference to earlier in this chapter (see also Chapter 9 in this volume). This meshing of both classic structural elements and processes is what characterises the modern echoes of rhetoric, exemplified by:

- Buehler's *triarchic model of speech* (the 'organon model' of language, 1934) which postulates that all forms of communication take place in the sender–receiver–object triad. In this model, objects or states of affairs of the world are represented as 'symbols' (bearing information about the world), as 'symptoms' (expressing the state of the sender), or as 'signals' (appealing to the receiver to act). The main functions of language are therefore those of representation, expression, and appeal and they persist in every single utterance in everyday life, though specialisations might tip language use towards one or the other of these functions. This idea has been taken up in Luhmann and Habermas's account of communication in the context of a functionally differentiated society.
- Austin's (1962) *speech-acts* (see also Chapter 5 in this volume) highlight performative speech as forms of acting and changing the world in contrast to speech as constative or merely describing the world. Austin stresses the many things speech 'does' and so reacts to the contemporary

attempts to restrict language to its descriptive function. Speech acts fail not because they are 'false depictions', but because they violate common expectations, they are infelicitous in relation to conventions. Speech acts operate on three levels which invite comparisons with the traditional notions of **logos**, **ethos**, and **pathos**, respectively. One can 'do' words as locution ('saying it'; its literal and grammatical correctness), as illocution ('in saying it'; to formulate a promise or give an order in a conventional and recognised manner), and as perlocution ('by saying it' we elicit a non-conventional reaction from the listener which might be our hidden agenda: by promising we gain a vote).

- Luhmann (1984/1995) sees communication as a cascaded triple selection of information (**logos** – translating thoughts into words), utterances to gain attention (**ethos** – selection controlled by the ego considering and respecting the alter), and responses (**pathos** – selection controlled by the alter who can agree, disagree with, or ignore the message). Communication as such is an improbable human interaction that, in order to be more likely, needs to be propped up by mutual constraints. These constraints can be the language that fixes meaning, circulation technologies that focus attention, and general symbolic systems that allow interactions to follow an exclusive concern at the expense of all other concerns, for power, profit, justice or love.

- With Habermas (1987; see Chapter 6 in this volume) we emphasise the contrast between strategic, single-minded actions and communicative action, between actions oriented towards success or towards reaching a common understanding. Habermas distinguished between three forms of success-oriented actions, again associated with the triad of **logos**, **pathos**, and **ethos**. Instrumental action is world-oriented and makes claims that are judged on being true or false, working or not working, etc. Dramaturgical action is subject-oriented and claims are judged on the authenticity of the expressive self. Finally, normative action has an intersubjective appeal and its claims are judged on their consistency with morality and community norms. By contrast, communicative action invests all three claims with equal importance, which again echoes the Aristotelian concern for balance among the '**three musketeers of rhetoric**'.

It is perhaps not surprising that in almost all modern approaches to communication one can identify a similar *conceptual core* in the triadic form: sender–receiver–message; **ethos–pathos–logos**; utterance–response–information, and so on. As tempting as it might be to think that we are tapping into a universal feature of human communication, we must always remember that these ideas all emerged in a Western historical context. Their generalisation outside of this cultural sphere is for the time being a hypothesis that deserves serious investigation rather than being taken as an established fact (see Box 10.5 for a discussion).

Box 10.5   How universal is rhetorical theory?

Rhetorical theory and analysis is mostly the product of the Græco-Roman tradition of Western intellectual history, rescued by Islamic scholarship through the Western Dark Ages. This tradition provides the analytical apparatus to analyse the **rhetorical situation**, the types of persuasive argumentation, the necessary training to become a good **orator**, the concerns for stylistic features, and the genres of public communication. To what extent is this an ethnocentric view of public communication? To what extent is it a universally valid analysis?

This question increasingly concerns researchers who compare Arabic, Indian, Chinese, African, and other **non-European traditions** of public communication, often done as comparative literature, but increasingly as comparisons of all communicative genres of public life (see Kennedy, 1998; Lucaites, Condit and Caudill, 1999). Certainly this is a big question to which we can only allude here. In principle, we can see how answers to this question might play out in either of two ways.

First, we can imagine a comparative rhetorical analysis taking as the commonplace the three classical dimensions of public **persuasion: ethos**, **pathos**, and **logos**. Is it that Chinese or African rhetorical tradition privileges one over the other of these dimensions, as the Sophists opted for **pathos**, the modern scientists for **logos** and the Romans for **ethos**? It might be that Chinese rhetoric in the tradition of Confucius privileges the **ethos** of the speaker over **logos** and **pathos**. Who is speaking outweighs what is being said, and pandering to emotions is discouraged.

Or might it be the case that Chinese or African traditions of public communication need to be analysed with entirely different categories to understand what is going on? There might be more than three dimensions – or entirely different dimensions – of **persuasion** at work in these cultural contexts. Rhetorical acts need to be understood as a function of different constraints V, W, X, Y, Z etc., of which we have little understanding if we try to immediately assimilate them into **ethos**, **logos**, and **pathos**. Be that as it may, this is an open question with a pressing exigency in a rapidly globalising world.

Conclusion: Why do we need rhetoric today?

As we come to an end, the benefits gained from studying rhetoric and especially from recuperating what might seem to be 'old and stale' ideas about **persuasion** in public communication are hopefully self-evident. And yet let us consider at least two important consequences, the first directly related to academic teaching, the second to the larger scale of everyday life and everyday interactions.

In a modern academic environment, the construction of novelty and the capacity to innovate are both highly praised and encouraged through institutionalised systems of rewards and penalties. *Claims to innovation* are constantly made and academics at all stages in their career need to persuade others of their originality and the value of their ideas. This is particularly true for the study of communication. Knowing the tradition is useful, as it enables us to identify false claims to innovation. The informed student can easily 'call the bluff' of imposters who reinvent the wheel and present 'old wine in new bottles'. However, calling the bluff of old hats sold as new ones is an easy party game when ignorance of traditions is ripe. More important is the other side of this critical capacity.

Knowing the debates and the analytical tools with which classical rhetoric has tried to understand the act of **persuasion** is important if the renewed research interest in this topic is to make any real progress. Progress will only arise if we know of past mistakes and gain a clear understanding of where past attempts hit the hard rock. In order to make any progress with rhetorical theory and investigations of public discourse, it is important that we carry the past knowledge lightly, playfully, while at the same time remaining mindful of its achievements.

Finally, we should also keep in mind the predicament of an ambitious pig farmer. He wants to be practical and raise many pigs to sell on the market, and for this he needs a 'theory of raising pigs'. One day his wife discovers that pigs are animals, mammals to be more precise, and it is therefore useful to know biology to start with. The same must be true for all those enthusiastic and practically minded students of communication who want to know all about making everybody's lifestyle healthier, about how to sell the latest consumer products, or how to manage better the reputation of a corporation, or save us all from climate change and global warming. The practical concerns of life are not so clearly separable from the theoretical ones, and the old–new theory of rhetoric *was and can be* put to good use in the most varied of circumstances. As the social psychologist Kurt Lewin allegedly said, 'there is nothing more practical than a good theory', and this is especially true when that good theory is a theory of rhetoric!

11
Evolution and Communication

Bradley Franks and Japinder Dhesi

Keywords: Adaptation; cues, cultural niche construction; culture; deception; egocentric/egocentrism; signals and signs; theory of mind.

Introduction

The connections between communication, **culture**, and cognition are complex, and some insights into these connections arise from evolutionary approaches. One such recent insight is that, as Tomasello (1999, p. 78) notes, 'Humans inherit their environments as much as they inherit their genomes'. Equally striking is the possibility that genes and culture may interact, perhaps that they have a symbiotic relationship and constitute a 'double helix' (Levinson, 2005). This chapter will introduce some key issues in the evolutionary analysis of communication and cultural transmission; it suggests that much everyday communication is strategic, geared towards persuading others and achieving adaptive goals, even when it does not appear so to the parties to that communication (contrasting with the ideas discussed in Chapters 6 and 12). The principal argument is that evolutionarily inspired accounts of communication and cultural transmission can further benefit from insights from 'embodied' cognition (such embodiment also has an impact on how we view the basic processes of communicative exchange; see Chapter 5). Cognition, on such a view, is simultaneously 'extended' beyond the skin into the environment, and 'grounded' by intrinsic connections to action, emotion, and bodily experience, leading to an **egocentric** view of communication (a similar conclusion is reached on the basis of a different perspective, in Chapter 9). Wheeler and Clark (2008) suggest a 'triple helix' of culture, evolution and the 'outwards'-facing aspect of embodiment; we suggest a need to integrate this with an account of the 'inwards'-facing aspect of embodiment; and this leads to a view which bears similarities to that offered by Vygotsky (discussed in Chapter 1).

Evolution and communication

This section explores the contribution of evolutionary theory to our understanding of communication.

Basic processes of communication

Evolutionary analyses (e.g. Hauser, 1997) suggest three principal ways in which animals convey information. **'Cues'** are generally associated with enduring qualities of physical appearance or another aspect of phenotype, which involve no immediate cost for the organism because they are usually permanently 'switched on'. A typical example is pigmentation in poisonous prey species acting as a warning to potential predators. **'Signals'** are contingent responses to changing aspects of the environment, which, since they can be switched on or off, carry a cost for the organism; for example, vocalisations indicating presence of predators, or birdsong to attract mates. **'Signs'** are not *designed* to be communicative by evolutionary processes or by the intent of the organism, but are *treated* as informative by others; for example, a track left by prey or predators. All three communication types arise in human communication and cultural transmission.

Connections between signals and audience responses can be coupled to varying degrees. Cheney and Seyfarth (1990) offer a widely discussed picture of vervet monkeys' alarm calls in response to predators. Vervets typically encounter three kinds of predators (pythons, eagles, leopards), and evade each in specific ways (e.g. running up a tree away from a leopard). They also employ a different alarm call for each kind of predator, and conspecifics, on hearing an alarm call, immediately enact the appropriate evasion without first checking on the presence of the predator. The conditions for the evolution of the alarm call were, arguably, simultaneously ones in which a specific predator was detected *and* in which taking specific, appropriate evasive action arose. Millikan (1996) suggests that alarm calls of various species are both *descriptive* – indicating the presence of a specific predator, and *directive* – an imperative to avoid that predator in a specific way. The calls evoke what Millikan (2004) labels 'pushmi-pullyu' representations in the hearer: not solely a description of the predator, nor solely a motivation to action, but both; they 'tell in one undifferentiated breath both what is the case and what to do about it' (Millikan, 2004, p. 20). The connection between these aspects of the representation is direct; it does not depend on making an inference. Such a view is generalised by embodied accounts of mind, going beyond description–action relations, to suggest that a far wider range of representations involve intrinsic relations between descriptive information about objects, and affective and motivational orientations towards them.

Motivations driving communication

Evolutionary analyses suggest a range of adaptive purposes or motivations for communication. The settings in which these motivations arise and are addressed provide cost–benefit ratios for communication; to make an adaptive contribution to solving problems, the costs of communication need to be reliably outweighed by the benefits of doing so.

There is a more or less standard catalogue of motivations underlying higher primate communication. They relate to: sexual advertisement (indicating one's availability and quality as a potential mate); status/rank, territorial defence, conflict management and conflict resolution (indicating one's willingness to fight to defend territory, one's potential danger in doing so, and then one's response should this be reciprocated); social integration (expressing contact or group membership); parental care (e.g. demanding parental care and offspring activity) (Buss, 1999; Tooby and Cosmides, 1990). Such a catalogue seems readily extendable to human beings, and, although it would be difficult to claim that it was exhaustive, it strikingly maps directly onto demarcations offered by evolutionary accounts of the social functions of emotions.

Deception and communication

One important evolutionary aspect of communication concerns **deception**: conveying misinformation to the receiver in order to achieve specific ends. Deception is a way of convincing the receiver of the message that the sender has specific qualities that differ from the ones that the sender actually has, and so 'persuading' the receiver to act in a way that would benefit the sender.

Maynard Smith and Harper (2002) suggest that signals may act either as 'indices' or 'handicaps'. Indices are honest because their expression is physiologically constrained (e.g. calls with a low frequency that can only be produced by large bodies); they cannot be faked even though their production cost is relatively low. Handicaps are honest because their expression is costly, so that high-quality individuals suffer a lower relative cost for production than low-quality individuals. Zahavi and Zahavi (1974) note that mate selection provides a set of adaptive problems where it may pay the displaying sex – usually, the male – to attempt to fake being of higher genetic quality than they actually are, to improve their chance of being selected by the choosing sex (usually, the female). If for lower-quality males, the cost of faking a 'high-quality' signal is higher than the potential reproductive benefits, females can take the presence of the signal as an honest indicator of quality. Only higher-quality males could produce the signal without creating greater costs for themselves. So peahens prefer to mate with peacocks with larger, more brightly coloured tails, which may indicate mate quality. But a weaker male with a huge beautiful tail would not survive long, since it could not easily escape predators. The benefit for a weaker male (in mating with more females), would be smaller than the cost of faking (a higher predation risk). The benefit for a stronger male would outweigh the increased predation risk since they would remain able to evade predation. So the 'handicap principle' proposes that the cost of the signal to the sender provides assurances to receivers that the signal is honest (Zahavi and Zahavi, 1974).

Miller (2002) details a similar analysis for human beings. He argues that there has been a co-evolutionary process: because males became adept at producing dishonest signals to indicate their worth as mates, females became adept at detecting deception. It will pay females to respond only to ever more extreme indicators of quality, and so it pays males to generate more extreme signals. Miller suggests female mate selection may therefore often be geared towards 'neophilia', requiring ever new indicators of quality.

Stable physiological qualities may be, for human beings (unlike other species), open to intentional faking (e.g. cosmetic surgery), and can be transformed into a dishonest signal from one that was, in the past, constrained to be honest. They may also function as handicap (e.g. the cost of cosmetic surgery restricts its availability). So human cultural indicators may blur over time the boundaries between honest and handicap signals. Neophilia in communication regarding mate attraction and status may thereby be an important engine for cultural innovation. Signalling quality in humans may involve signalling status via cultural means, and so there may be a reciprocal premium on assessing the reliability of status indicators (Buss, 1999). Indeed, Dhesi (unpublished) postulates an evolved competence in virtue of which humans represent hierarchical social relations, namely a *Folk Politics*, drawing on evidence from ethology, primatology, evolutionary psychology, cognitive psychology, and developmental psychology (Barkow, 1975; Boehm, 1991; Buss, 1991; De Waal, 1998; Edelmark and Omark, 1973; Smith, 1988).

Trivers (2000) further considers *self*-deception – the active misrepresentation of reality to the conscious mind – as directly analogous to deception between individuals. Trivers claims that this could be adaptive since not being aware of one's true motivations may permit one to engage in more successful deception of others. If true information is represented consciously, it is more likely to 'leak' out to others via communication. And if that information concerns competitive motivations, its availability to others may reduce the likelihood of success. Self-deception supports creation of a 'self-serving world' of self-enhancing misrepresentations of personality, attitudes towards others, personal narratives, and social relations which reinforces an egocentric view of communication (see below): we make little attempt to ensure others understand us because we assume we are understood even where it is obvious to outsiders that we are not. The presumption of being understood allows us to make limited efforts towards actually being understood.

Overall, evolved qualities of communication relate important aspects of mental and cultural representations to solving core social adaptive problems. It is therefore largely *strategic* – aimed towards outcomes which depend on the agreement, compliance, cooperation or deception of others – even when it seems otherwise to the participants.

Embodiment, evolution and communication

Wilson (2002) notes various claims regarding embodiment of mind. The ones deployed here relate to the view that cognition is 'extended' beyond the skin into the environment, and that representations are 'grounded' by intrinsic connections to action, emotion, and bodily experience.

Views of extended cognition have been developed in various ways, relating to distributedness, externalism, and situatedness (e.g. Shore, 1996; Lave, 1988; Winograd and Flores, 1986). Clark (1997) has argued that many aspects of the environment (artefacts, processes, other people) can function as body-external aspects of mind (e.g. as memory, processing, and so on), and so should not be viewed as separate, but as equal components that interact to generate 'mind'. 'Mind' emerges from the local interactions of brain and body with the environment. As Dennett (2002, p. 1) puts it, *'minds are composed of tools for thinking that we not only obtain from the wider (social) world, but largely leave in the world, instead of cluttering up our brains with them'*. There are different 'strengths' to this thesis, but the broadest picture will suffice here.

Wilson notes that action-guidance is a major function of the mind/brain, and embodied views construe perception, representation, memory, and inference as geared towards selection and anticipation of desired events, and avoidance of negative events. Approaches have been offered in terms of pushmi-pullyu representations (Millikan, 1995), action-oriented representations (Clark, 1997; Franks and Braisby, 1997), and florid representing (Dennett, 2000). A related thesis is that experiential and bodily states (including perception, emotion, and motivation) play a role not only in the processing of information about those states, but also in the processing of concepts in the absence of direct experiential input. Conceptual representations incorporate aspects of emotional, embodied, and perceptual experience, without a separate inferential link between these aspects and more 'descriptive' contents (Lakoff and Johnson, 1980, 1999; Barsalou, 2008; Vigliocco, 2006; Clore and Huntsinger, 2007; Damasio, 1995).

Embodiment then faces in two directions simultaneously: 'outwards' towards the world, and 'inwards' towards non-descriptional states of mind and body. But this is not to suggest distinct phenomenal realms of representation contents or types reflecting these different directions. Rather, every representation is held to possess content that reflects the intertwining of the two faces: it is simultaneously *extended* and *grounded*.

Communication: Embodied representations

The mental representations involved in communication appear embodied in the two senses we have noted. Regarding 'inwards'-facing, they are partly constituted, directed, and constrained by adaptive function(s), and the emotional and motivational states that help to achieve those functions by

Box 11.1   Embodiment: externalism and grounded cognition

Externalism

The predominant conception of cognition in cognitive science and Anglo-American philosophy of mind and language has been individual-istic – that cognition is an 'internal' property of individuals, which can be studied by abstracting it away from physical and social environments (Zerubavel, 1997). This 'methodological solipsism' (Fodor 1980) has increasingly come under attack. Doubts about internalism and individu-alism were originally raised by Putnam (1975) and Burge (1979), who questioned the extent to which such a view could account for mental content and meaning. They argued that the content of a person's men-tal states depends causally and ontologically on the properties of the ecological and social environment in which that person was located. So changing environments necessarily changes the content of thought. Those who reject individualism are known as externalists. In recent years externalism has taken a more radical turn in the 'extended mind thesis' (Clark and Chalmers, 1998), which holds that not only are the *contents* or meanings of beliefs located 'outside' the individual's head, but that mental *processes* may also extend beyond the boundary of the skin of the individual agent. The implication is that mental content and process depend on *relations* between the individual's internal states and processes and the external states and processes. To paraphrase Putnam, 'mind just ain't in the head.'

Grounded cognition

Consider the following results: participants exposed to words associated with stereotypes of the elderly walked more slowly than participants in a control condition (Bargh, Chen and Burrows, 1996). Participants asked to nod their head (as in agreement) while listening to persuasive messages held more positive attitudes towards message content than participants asked to shake their head (as in disagreement) (Wells and Petty, 1980). Such results have been explained by grounded cognition theories, which reject standard theories of cognition that assume that knowledge is represented by abstract amodal symbols stored in memory. Grounded cognition asserts that mental representations and processes are intrinsically grounded in the body (e.g. Lakoff and Johnson, 1980) or the brain's modality-specific systems for perception (e.g. vision), action (e.g. movement) and introspection (e.g. emotion) (Wilson, 2002). There is increasing supporting evidence from cognitive psychology and neuro-science (see Barsalou, 2008; Vigliocco, 2008).

driving appropriate cognitions and actions. Concepts – mental representations employed in categorising the world – incorporate not only descriptive information about the object of representation (e.g. features of the object), but also affective and other embodied information regarding it. Moreover, Clore and Gasper (2008) suggest a role for 'affect as information' in social inference. Where there is uncertainty in judgement, affect 'fills in' the gaps, acting as information to support a preferred outcome (or contradict a dispreferred outcome). Rather than forming a restricted set, representations with such a 'pushmi-pullyu' structure are widespread, and the extent to which they incorporate a 'push' or a 'pull' may be variable.

The representations involved in communication also have an 'outwards'-facing, extended aspect – they depend on the presence and interaction of other people in appropriate ecological and cultural contexts for their content, elicitation and fulfilment. Keltner, Haidt and Shiota (2006) argue that the emotions involved have specific adaptive functions, helping to solve inherently social problems, overlapping with those motivating communication noted above. Problems of reproduction relate to mate selection and retention, supporting sex (relating to desire), attachment (love), and mate protection (jealousy); and to offspring protection, supporting attachment (love) and care-giving (compassion). Problems of group governance relate to cooperation and its management, supporting reciprocal altruism (emotions relating to gratitude, guilt, anger, envy); and to group organisation, supporting a dominance or status hierarchy (emotions of pride, shame, embarrassment, contempt, awe, disgust). Keltner et al. argue that, via enabling and regulating social commitments, emotions have functions at individual, group, and cultural levels.

In sum, representations of the social and ecological environment are integrated with emotional states that are connected to solving key adaptive problems. Communication in pursuit of the adaptive functions, which draws on those representations, is thereby integrated with the emotional states that drive their solution.

'Theory of mind'

It is often claimed that the major difference between human and non-human communication is human use of recursive syntax: the generation of infinite possible structures via finite rules of grammar and a lexicon (Hauser, Chomsky and Fitch, 2002). Together with **'theory of mind'**, this is often taken to produce essentially human qualities of communication (e.g. Sperber and Origgi, 2000). The addition of theory of mind certainly complicates communication but, as argued in Chapter 5, the extent to which people can and do take into account others' representations in communication is limited.

The motivation towards sharing mental states is, of course, *not* the same as the achievement of that motivation (as the motivation towards eating food is not the same as finding a meal). To make progress on this issue, we need to unpack the notion of 'sharing of mental states'. Gardenfors (2008) suggests that such intersubjectivity comprises, in order of increasing complexity, the capacity to represent others': emotions (empathy); focus of attention; behavioural intentions; desires; beliefs and knowledge (the latter encompasses theory of mind). Separating out these capacities empirically is complex, and has spawned intriguing and contested work in developmental and comparative psychology (e.g. Povinelli, 2005; Tomasello, 2008).

From an embodied perspective, such decomposition is harder to envisage 'downwards' from *theory of mind* through to empathy; although empathising or sharing desires may arise without simultaneously sharing beliefs, the reverse is less likely. If beliefs are intertwined with embodied states, then entertaining someone else's beliefs may necessitate entertaining those other states as well. But one may empathise with another without entertaining their intentions, desires or beliefs; one may entertain their desire without sharing their intentions, and so on 'upwards'. Indeed, Bermudez (2002) has suggested that what *appears to be* representation of 'higher' mental states and use of *theory of mind* in communication, may actually involve exchange of 'lower' signals of emotional, motivational, and desire states. Detecting and responding to such signals regulates interaction and communicative turn-taking. When they indicate that the interaction is failing from the perspective of one party, there may be an attempt to understand the other's beliefs, followed by resumption of communication, and so on. Attempts to deploy theory of mind may thus be failure-driven.[1] Furthermore, there is general agreement among psychologists that theory of mind skills require two kinds of cognitive processes: specialized representational capacities to capture mental state knowledge; and executive selection processes in order to use such knowledge to predict and explain behaviour (Leslie et al., 2004, 2005; Wellman et al., 2001). Given that the deployment of theory of mind is costly, failure-driven use would also prove to be a more economical use of cognitive resources.

Hence, achieving goals via activities such as communication that *appear* to involve shared beliefs may instead involve coordination of intentions around a joint behavioural outcome. This relates to the possibility, discussed in Chapter 5, that joint or collective intentions and beliefs relative to an outcome can be entered into without the participants actually sharing beliefs or knowing the other's beliefs, or indeed sharing the same intention for wanting to achieve the outcome. *Coordinated action* and *coordinated intentions* around a joint goal are not the same as, or reducible to, *shared actions* and *shared intentions*. Many adaptive interactions appear thus: in mate selection, parent–offspring interaction, social hierarchy relations, the actors may have divergent intentions and beliefs regarding the interactions, but if those intentions and beliefs converge around achieving the goal, there is little reason for the actors to enquire into the detailed contents of others' minds.

Evolution and cultural transmission: Communication

An evolutionary approach not only clarifies communication, it also informs the conceptualisation of culture.

Characterising culture

A pretheoretic characterisation of culture is as an acquired and patterned set of beliefs, practices, and artefacts largely shared by a group or community, that is disseminated horizontally within age or peer groups, and transmitted with limited change vertically across generations. Cultural change possesses two countervailing tendencies: one towards directed, non-random cultural innovation; the other towards conservatism or inertia regarding change of core aspects.

Cultural transmission and cognition

Discussing evolutionary accounts of culture and communication raises issues regarding their underlying views of the mind (see also Chapter 8). The most widely adopted evolutionarily inspired view of mind is 'massive

Box 11.2   Gene-culture coevolution

There are, broadly, three evolutionarily inspired accounts of cultural transmission: memetics, epidemiology and gene-culture coevolution. Memetics and epidemiology have been discussed in Chapter 4, so we will limit ourselves here to discussing gene-culture coevolution. Gene-culture coevolution or 'dual inheritance theory', is a branch of theoretical population genetics. Conceptually, gene-culture coevolution is a hybrid between memetics and cultural epidemiology. Like memetics, it seeks to account for cultural change via processes of Darwinian evolution. Unlike memetics, gene-culture coevolution theorists argue that genetic and cultural evolution are not independent but interdependent. For gene-culture coevolutionary theorists there is reciprocal relationship between culture and genes. Like cultural epidemiologists, these theorists believe the success of cultural items may depend on psychological factors. Unlike cultural epidemiologists, these theorists don't focus on the role of mental content or modularity in cultural evolution. Instead, Boyd, Richerson, and their collaborators have modelled how psychological biases can have a stabilising role in cultural transmission, favouring, for instance, prestige or conformity.

modularity' (e.g. Tooby and Cosmides, 1992; Sperber, 1996; Carruthers, 2006). This views mental faculties as special-purpose representing-and-processing devices (modules), 'designed' by evolutionary pressures to contribute to the solution of specific adaptive problems confronted by our ancestors in the 'environment of evolutionary adaptedness'. Hypothesised modules include *Theory of Mind* – interpreting human behaviour in terms of mental states (Avis and Harris, 1991; Tomasello et al., 2003); *Folk Biology* – categorising and explaining living kinds in terms of biological principles (Atran, 1995, 2002; Gelman and Hirschfeld, 1999), and *Folk Sociology* – sorting conspecifics into categories (Hirschfeld, 1996).

But massively (or even largely) modular minds may not be compatible with embodiment. Modules are traditionally defined in terms of their information-processing content, which is given either by the domain properties alone or by those properties circumscribed by an adaptive function (see Gelman and Hirshfeld, 1998; Barrett and Kurzban, 2007). Such definitions typically incorporate descriptive content, omitting embodied states of emotion and motivation (see Box 11.3). This is acknowledged by Tooby, Cosmides and Barrett (2007) who note the difficulty of retaining modularity when adaptive functions suggest cognition and emotion/motivation are interpenetrating. Modularity also sits uneasily with extended cognition, since mental modules' essential structure arises from the 'proper domain' of problems encountered in the EEA, which likely differs from modern

Box 11.3   The embodiment of social cognition and communication

Hirschfeld (1996) has posited an evolved Folk Sociology, governing our capacity to sort conspecifics into inductively rich categories, and acquire and communicate knowledge about such categories (see also Astuti, 2001; Gil-White, 2001). We have seen how representations involved in communication are embodied: intertwining descriptive aspects with emotions, motivations, and action dispositions. But the widely adopted evolution-inspired view of the mind as modular does not appear to be compatible with such embodiment. This poses a challenge to Hirschfeld and colleagues' proposal of a Folk Sociology (as one such mental module). One example of how social group information processing is embodied comes from priming research. As noted in Box 11.1, Bargh et al. (1996) found participants primed with the elderly stereotype walked slower down a corridor than control participants. Presumably, the social category priming activated the stereotype of the elderly which in turn activated action schemas resulting in the embodiment effect of walking slower. Other research has shown embodiment effects of priming other social categories on behaviour including rudeness and aggressiveness (Dijksterhuis and Bargh, 2001). A second example of embodiment effects is the role of emotion in social group information processing. It was noted earlier that emotions are intertwined with embodied cognition, and communication may help solve specific adaptive problems including problems of group governance and group organisation (Keltner et al., 2006).

A Folk Sociology also overlooks the fact that in certain historical and cultural contexts social categories (e.g. race, sex, and caste) entail not only categorizing individuals into groups but also a ranking of these groups within a status hierarchy from superior to inferior, as in a Folk Politics (Dhesi, unpublished). And there is evidence that representations of social status are embodied. For instance, relative status rank influences verbal and nonverbal behaviour patterns. Leffler et al. (1982) found that participants randomly assigned to high status spoke more often, claimed more direct space with their bodies, and intruded upon their partners by means of touching and pointing, than participants assigned to low status. Representations of social status are also intertwined with emotions. Keltner et al. (2006) propose that emotion such as pride, shame, and awe help to support status hierarchies (see also Caprariello, Cuddy and Fiske, 2009).

In sum, an explanation of the communication of information pertaining to human social relations needs to account for how our mental representation of social groups and social status incorporate not only descriptive information but also embodied content.

environments. By contrast, extended cognition suggests that significant aspects of structure and content may emerge from the interaction of a more flexible mental set-up with current environment. The result may, as Wheeler and Clark note, echo modularity if the environment promotes this, but modularity may not be a preferred mode of cognitive organisation.

Cultural environments, communication and extended cognition

Communication leads to the simultaneous change and retention of cultural items over generations of transmission. Tomasello, Kruger, and Ratner (1993) make the telling observation that cultural items are cumulative: the use and interpretation of an item by one generation inputs to its use and interpretation by subsequent generations. This is labelled the 'ratchet effect', since the items are 'ratcheted' in each generation. For ratcheting to work, arguably, new generations represent the intentions and other mental states that previous generations brought to an item, so as to employ it in a similar way. By deliberate action or accidental misinterpretation, cultural items change gradually through successive transmissions, and the outcome may be an item that differs markedly from the original. Neophilia, noted earlier, exemplifies ratcheted communication: the new can only be seen as new against the background of the old.

A broadening of the concept of a cultural belief is offered by Laland, Odling-Smee and Feldman (2000), who note that animals – including humans – change their environments to create 'niches', and some such changes can alter subsequent requirements on **adaptation**. This creates the possibility of the evolution of psychological qualities based on the prior construction of cultural 'niches'. **Cultural niches** then set up new feedback cycles, which lead to spiralling changes to the constructions, and so on. This parallels ratcheting: each new generation exposed to a niche can add to and alter the behavioural and psychological aspects of that niche. As Odling-Smee, Laland and Feldman (2003, pp. 260–1) suggest, much human niche construction is 'guided by socially learned knowledge and cultural inheritance, but the transmission of this knowledge is itself dependent on pre-existing information acquired through genetic evolution, complex ontogenetic processes, or prior social learning'. Cultural niches can incorporate artefacts, patterns of belief as well as ritualised patterns of activity and communication.

This provides a way of understanding extended, embodied cognition in a specifically evolutionary setting: ecological and cultural environments impact on cognition because they constitute adaptive niches. Mind and culture are thereby intrinsically coupled. So understanding communication and culture in evolutionary terms reinforces the view that the representations and processes involved are embodied.

Embodied communication, evolution and culture

This discussion raises three issues: whether humans possess an adaptation for culture; the connections between communication, culture, social relations, and theory of mind; and the scope for culture to have an impact on thought.

Culture and adaptations

Some approaches suggest humans possess evolutionary adaptations 'designed' for culture, while others suggest that culture is a byproduct of adaptations 'designed' for other purposes. Modularity theorists tend to suggest the latter: adaptations respond to inputs from outside their proper domain which allows them to be 'colonised' by culture.

An alternative is that humans possess one or more adaptations whose principal function is the generation of culture. Tomasello (2008) suggests that the difference between chimpanzees and humans lies not in possession of 'theory of mind' per se, but of a specific type of theory of mind: whereas chimpanzees appear able to consider conspecifics as possessing mental states in competitive situations, they are unable to do so in collaborative situations. Humans, by contrast, do both. Tomasello suggests that human culture involves the generation and maintenance of joint or collective intentions for collaborative action; the motivation to form collective intentions is a psychological primitive, irreducible to individual intentions and beliefs (see Searle, 1996). Tomasello nonetheless takes a relatively untroubled view of verbal communication and the sharing of individual beliefs and communicative intentions. 'Mind-reading' abilities are grounded in sharing collective intentions and beliefs, in Tomasello's view. So culture – as a repository and means of communicating about collective intentions and beliefs – instantiates individual human adaptations for sharing mental states; culture is both an adaptive means and end.

By contrast, Hauser (2005) suggests that what separates humans from other primates is inhibition. Humans are able to regularly inhibit, delay, or suspend action towards an attractive goal. This places a premium on executive function, and being able to plan so as to not act immediately on affective and motivational states. Human culture adds the symbolic communication, marking, and sharing of inhibitions.

The picture presented here shares something with Tomasello and Hauser. However, its foundation is the two egocentric limitations of mind in communication and social interaction. First, that embodiment may lead to egocentric ways of thinking: representations that have first-person affective attachments which prompt biased 'online' interpretations of others, their intentions, and so on. Second, that communication is egocentric: the extent to which we try to and can take into account others' beliefs and intentions while communicating with them 'online' is highly limited. We present a stark picture of egocentric limitations, to problematise the widespread assumption of universal and successful inferences to others' mental states under normal online processing conditions. The view here is that this is neither universal nor always successful (see also Bermudez, 2004; Gallacher, 2001; Hutto, 2004). This does not deny possible variations in the prevalence and accuracy in deployment of 'mind-reading' across components of intersubjectivity, across individuals, communication aims or contexts. Additionally, these limitations appear most prominent in 'online' processing (while interacting or communicating with a person). When 'offline' – when planning interaction or communication, or thinking reflectively afterwards – they may diminish, and indeed online limitations may only become apparent offline. Keysar (2007) suggests that this limitation on online communication may arise from theory of mind being a relatively recent evolutionary adaptation that is not well integrated with other faculties such as working memory (for a contrasting view see Birch and Bloom, 2004).

In sum, humans may have an evolved motivation to share mental states with others, perhaps based on a psychological primitive of joint intentionality. But this is coupled with egocentric limitations on its fulfilment. These egocentric limits may be made apparent in social interaction, and this may lead us to attempt to circumvent them. But the tools to do so may not be available from within individual cognition and social relations.

The argument here is that symbolic culture provides tools for beginning to circumvent egocentric social relations and communication (see Chapter 9 for a similar conclusion from a different perspective). Culture may thus be thought of as failure-driven in its origins and operation. The adaptive ends relate to social relations and shared internal states; culture offers important sets of means for achieving those ends. We now turn to two areas where this has significant implications.

Communication and culture (1): External theory of mind and ameliorating egocentrism

Cultural niches can alter the range of representations available for communication, along dimensions of 'content' and 'form'. Regarding content, culture has the potential to reduce the egocentrism of representations, encouraging a decentred embodiedness via expressing sharedness or by schematising representations (by abstracting across different perspectives). In this way, it may encourage decoupling of the descriptive aspects of a representation from the embodied aspects; for example, it may ameliorate the affect associated with 'hot' individual cognition and social relations, leading to 'colder' cognition. We return to this below.

Regarding form, culture can provide representations which are publicly available, and relatively enduring, allowing them to be recurrent, repeated, and available across a range of individuals. They can thereby function as an 'external' resource for cognition, permitting engagement with their contents, which is offline from the interactions with those who produced those contents. The possibility has been discussed elsewhere of cultural artefacts functioning as an external memory, or as provision of external processing resources, for example books or computers (see Clark, 2003, 2008; Hutchins, 1995). The specific suggestion here is that this form interacts with the content, so that culture offers an 'external theory of mind': a resource indicating how minds and social relationships can and do work, how communication works, how emotional responses are to be managed, how plans and projects are to be prosecuted, etc. For example, linguistic culture can offer the start of sharing of individual beliefs and intentions by virtue of the fact that its products are public and offline.

This echoes the Vygotskyan idea (see Chapter 1) that the mediation of individual thought by cultural tools prompts a qualitative change in that thought; in this case, the specifically social psychological aspects of individual cognition – and the related social relations – are transformed by the mediation of cultural tools. Via the generation of cultural products which embody collective intentions, we can enhance the possibility of sharing beliefs and intentions across individuals. So *possessing* theory of mind per se is a prerequisite for the generation of culture, since it provides the motivation to generate collective intentions, and to share individual beliefs and intentions with others; but culture is a prerequisite for theory of mind's full *use*, since it helps to ameliorate the egocentric limits on individual and social thinking.

The publicness of symbolic culture connects with the amelioration of egocentrism, first, because the production of offline, written communication is less egocentric in that it can be in a sense non-social at the time of production (the audience is not physically present, so their immediate responses do not need to be taken into account, even if the message is being framed with beliefs about their ultimate responses in mind). Second, it offers the possibility for reflective sharing of individual beliefs and intentions, because cultural artefacts can encode representations of those beliefs and intentions in an external memory as a theory of mind resource. Third, their publicness allows for the conversion of joint or collective intentions into shared individual intentions (or at least, greater explicitness in the articulation of individual intentions in relation to joint intentions). Finally, it offers opportunities to learn from role models and descriptions, as patterns for bringing information concerning theory of mind from reflective thought into online communication. It thereby offers not only ways of enhancing our offline theory of mind capabilities, but also of attempting to use them in online interaction (e.g. in detecting and responding to deception).

Symbolic culture generally, and external theory of mind in particular, connects to the social adaptive functions towards which communication is often directed, in part because cultural representations (as representing collective beliefs and intentions regarding the nature of the communication and social interactions) can enhance the possibility of sharing the mental states involved. This is because the normative qualities[2] of culture constrain the operation of communication exchanges, leading to two implications. First, the mental states involved may be more predictable because their nature is culturally prescribed; for instance, collectively shared implicit propositions such as a man asking his date if she'd like to come up for a coffee (instead of a direct invitation for sex). Second, mental states may be inferable with more accuracy because their communication and signalling is culturally prescribed; for example, emotional display rules (see Chapter 3). In this way, cultural norms regarding communication can govern the way in which mental states are intended to be shared and might actually be shared.

Additionally, there appear to be institutionalised cases of collective intentions which prescribe specific relations between individuals, dyads or small groups (and their shared beliefs and intentions) on the one hand, and those collective beliefs and intentions on the other. For example, it seems part of the expectations governing the institutions that one is honestly trying to communicate and share beliefs and intentions when one enters into a marriage, or enters into initiation as a priest, or writes a cheque to pay for goods; these are all assumed to involve honest signalling or communication of intent and belief. Those individual intentions and beliefs can be 'read off' the institutional norms for the activities, so that others can make strong assumptions about the mental states of the actors. The norms appear to regulate both the content of appropriate mental states, and the intent to honestly communicate them. This view of institutions draws on Searle's (1996) thesis that institutions are established by collective intentions that impose a social function on some entity or action; and that this imposition and its operation depend on 'background' conditions. In these cases, one of the social functions is an *external theory of mind* function regarding the content and communication of individual mental states; and the background conditions include relevant adaptive functions and their embodied mental states.

Institutional arrangements thus codify and constrain individual intentions, thereby limiting changes to collective intentions (and related individual intentions), via ratcheting processes. This makes the core cultural phenomena of institutions (and their associated collective intentions and patterns of individual intentions) relatively resistant to change over time.

Communication and culture (2): External theory of mind and recalibrating embodied thought

By communicating an external theory of mind in normative terms, symbolic culture offers the possibility of recalibrating the relations between descriptive aspects of mental representations and emotions, motivations, and other qualities. There are two kinds of case. One is where the components of the representation remain fundamentally intertwined but the affective aspect is heightened or diminished. A second is where the intertwining between descriptive and non-descriptive aspects of a representation is altered, decoupling the connection to some degree or rendering it contingent.

The first case is exemplified by hyper-expression and hypo-expression that have been discussed in connection with cultural display rules for emotions (e.g. Ekman, 2000). Culture not only offers different representations of these relations, but also different ritualised means of managing them. The finding that culture has an impact on the tendency to attempt to adopt the perspective of the other, and success in doing so (Wu and Keysar, 2008), supports this contention.

The second case is exemplified by cultural niches that support the development of 'cold' cognition – that is, where the embodied qualities of emotion and motivation are relatively decoupled from the descriptive qualities of representation, resulting in thought that prioritises the "rational". Some cultural representations in external theory of mind depict the connections between emotion and action, or between motivation and action, as less intrinsic than in fully embodied mental representations. They may instead depict those connections as *contingent* on context, or on inferences about causes of motivations, or about consequences; that is, on normatively relevant factors. The normative framing of such factors in external theory of mind can then encourage the decoupling of descriptive and non-descriptive aspects of representations, prompting more *inferential* connections between them via rewards and punishments encouraging the inhibition of behaviours and affective responses, which might otherwise be more or less automatically connected with beliefs. In fact, presenting context, motivation, affect, descriptive belief content, action, and consequences as separate appears a consequence of the technology of a major vehicle for culture: writing. The linear, sequential nature of writing systems makes it virtually impossible to present such information in parallel or as indissolubly linked. Poetry attempts this, but in doing so gives rise to massive interpretive indeterminacy. Given that writing was the major source and repository of symbolic culture for over 500 years, the presumption of such decoupling is part of at least Western culture in that period, reaching its peak in Enlightenment views of human rationality.

However, communication of external theory of mind by symbolic culture does not *inevitably* lead to decoupled, 'cold' cognition. Indeed, some cultural niches – for example, mass visual media – might lead to a *lack* of decoupling. Repeated exposure to violence on film, television, and in computer games arguably results in low emotional regulation, desensitisation, hyper-expressivity, etc. (e.g. Anderson and Bushman, 2002). The principal means connecting individual representations and mass media representations may be *non-inferential–imitation* (e.g. Hurley, 2002): mimicking both the behaviour and the underlying emotional/motivational/mental state of a role model. In visual mass media they are presented as indissolubly coupled, and may be imitated as such, given the hypothesised functioning of 'mirror neurons' (e.g. Gallese, 2001).

Summary and conclusions

In this chapter we have shown how current evolutionary accounts of communication, cultural transmission, and cognition can benefit from theories and research on embodied cognition (both the inward and outward-facing aspects). We have suggested that understanding the mind as embodied connects with egocentric cognition and communication, which itself sets up culture as a means for solving the adaptive problem of 'reading' others' minds. The result suggests a more piecemeal account of the connections between mind and culture than often envisaged, generating interdependent relations between the two. It also suggests that characterising culture in terms of sharedness of beliefs is insufficient, and that normative, collective intentions are an integral part of culture. This makes it harder to see how evolutionary approaches could relate to either mind or culture separately from the other (as opposed to considering their evolution as an interdependent system).[3] It thus seems clear that we need to build on recent developments in understanding the interactions between genes, culture, and mind, while expanding our conception of the mind to take in its embodied aspects, and being sensitive to the interdependencies between each of these components.

Notes

1. Speech acts (Austen, 1958; Searle, 1978: see Chapter 5) may be a way of expanding the range of signals taken to directly express internal states. They move away from emotional and related signals to ones that express intentions and planned actions, away from immediate behavioural intentions to future-oriented planning. Of course, such conventionalised expressions are easier to fake than emotional indicators.
2. The normative qualities of collective intentions are discussed by for example, Gilbert (1989) and Searle (1996). Entering into a collective intention leads to a joint commitment to a form of action or thinking, which may be related to a common project. Viewed in this light, they can provide 'desire-independent' reasons for action (Searle, 2001), by contrast with adaptive intentions, which are 'desire-dependent'.
3. The current approach gives a reason why much symbolic culture has *content* relating to shared beliefs in the context of adaptive goals. Other approaches offer reasons why culture might in large part *comprise* shared representations, but no real reason why it should be *about* shared representations.

Part III
Applied Areas and Practice

12
Religion as Communication
Edmund Arens

Keywords: Communicative action; community; memory; narrative; religious-communicative practice; ritual; strategic action; transcendent reality.

Introduction

The practice of religion and communication are profoundly connected with one another. Religion makes use of different forms of communication, aimed at disclosing reality and creating **community**: prayer and preaching, worship and witnessing, reading and listening to sacred texts, singing and sharing, prophetic discourse, **ritual** practice, and theological reflection. This chapter seeks to sidestep this apparent variety of forms of communication, to ask if there are qualities of communication distinctive to religion. For example, is religious communication essentially strategic or a means of advancing understanding and community (i.e. a case of either **strategic** or **communicative action**, as discussed in Chapter 6)? Is the core of religious communication *expressive* or *effective* – to reiterate the distinction dealt with in Chapter 3 – and, furthermore, reiterating the concerns of Chapter 4, is religious communication ultimately qualified predominantly by its *contents* or its *processes*? This then is the central question of this chapter: Does religious practice primarily aim at maintaining and legitimating existing structures of communication or is it more directed at transformation (see Chapter 2 on power and empowerment)?

This chapter takes the following four steps. First, following Ninian Smart, different dimensions of religious communication are presented. Second, three illuminating views of ritual practice are sketched. The third step deals with religion and communicative action. Here Jürgen Habermas's changed understanding of their interrelation and relevance is addressed. I conclude by pointing out some significant forms of **religious-communicative practice**. The central argument will be that, as an exemplary form of communicative action, religion involves the creation, sharing, and replication of community.

Dimensions of religious communication

In his book *Dimensions of the Sacred* (1996) Ninian Smart provides an impressive anatomy of the world's beliefs. In his attempt to reach a cross-cultural phenomenology of the world's religions he outlines seven dimensions of religious practice. According to Smart, religion first involves a doctrinal or a philosophical dimension, that is, it is related either to theological doctrines or philosophical ideas. Second, a ritual or practical dimension is implied in that religion involves activities such as worship, meditation, pilgrimage, sacrifice, sacramental, and healing rites. A third realm is called the mythic or **narrative** dimension: each religion has its own stories concerning its Gods, founders or primary heroes. The fourth aspect refers to the experiential or emotional dimension. It highlights both the fundamental experiences of the founders and the experiences and emotions stimulated by and emerging in spiritual and ritual activities of the believers. The fifth dimension has to do with obligations and imperatives – this is the ethical or legal dimension. The sixth dimension is about the social and organisational component, and it relates to the roles of religious specialists, the social placement, and the patterns of organisation of religions. Finally, a seventh dimension concerns the material or artistic facets of religious practice; religion expresses itself in a variety of material and artistic creations, for example, temples, churches, mosques, monasteries, statues, books, and icons.

As we have seen in Chapter 5, speech act theory has made some important clarifications concerning the interrelation of language and action, or communication and interaction. The philosopher John L. Austin introduced this approach to communication which was subsequently elaborated by John R. Searle. Austin (1962), who found that in ordinary language, people perform different actions by speaking. By uttering a sentence a speaker performs the 'locutionary act' of saying something, and, at the same time, he or she in general performs an 'illocutionary act' which determines the intersubjective direction of the locution. The illocutionary act decides whether the utterance is a question, a wish, a complaint, a command, or a statement etc. While the illocutionary act is performed *in* saying something, the 'perlocutionary act' refers to the consequential effects which may be achieved *by* saying something. Austin had a special interest in institutional speech acts like baptising, ordaining, marrying, or swearing in. If these acts are performed by the appropriate persons in the right context with the use of the right words they enact or perform the action and thereby constitute a social fact. Searle (1969) elaborated the double structure of speech acts containing, on the one hand, a propositional aspect or propositional content, and, on the other hand, an illocutionary part aspect which indicates what is done in the speech act and how it shall be understood by the hearer. Searle outlined the rules by which speech acts are constituted and regulated.

He emphasised the sincerity rule by analysing the presuppositions and obligations of 'promising'.

On the basis of insights achieved by pragmatic semiotics, speech act theory, theories of text, communication, and action, I made the proposal to differentiate between five dimensions of linguistic communication (Arens, 1994). These include an intersubjective, an objective, a textual, a contextual, and an intentional dimension. Communication takes place between subjects, who communicate with one another about something. This means that communication first implies individuals or groups who 'do things with words' (Austin, 1962), who engage in social relations and, second, at the same time articulate propositional contents (Searle, 1969). A third dimension of communication refers to the *texts or* other *media* which are used in the communication process. Further, the local and social contexts of communication are relevant. Finally, the intentions or aims of the subjects involved have to be taken into consideration.

Applying the first dimension to religious communication, the relevant *religious subjects* (those who follow the religion) have to be taken into account. They comprise, on the one hand, religious authorities, specialist, or office bearers; and, on the other hand, their addressees, the laity, the ordinary believers, support groups, and communities. The second dimension, *religious contents*, include propositions or statements about **transcendent reality**, especially God or Gods, about cosmic reality, its origin and end, about the creation and salvation of human beings and humankind. These religious contents are encoded in stories, creeds, doctrines, commandments etc. Third, a variety of *texts or media* are used in religious communication: images and icons, spoken and written texts, sounds, and music etc. Sacred Scripture is an important medium of communication, of distribution and of storage (Sandbothe, 2001) for many religions. However, the human body and the human being is probably the first and foremost medium (Faulstich, 1997) as a vehicle for experiencing and communicating religion – for example, kneeling in prayer. Fourth, *religious contexts* have to be taken into account. These are surroundings where religious communication practices take place: sacred places like temples, churches or mosques, burial and celebration places, and also social and cultural contexts in which religious communication occurs. In view of the fifth dimension, it has to be acknowledged that the intentions or aims of religious communicators are manifold.

Religious subjects clearly have different aims; priests are inclined to preserve and to pass on the religious heritage, whereas prophets usually adopt a more critical attitude towards existing traditions, conditions, and institutions. Moreover, there are intentions implied in religious speech acts like prayer and preaching, ritual, and liturgy. Additionally, I mention comprehensive religious aims with regard to God's adoration by the believers, to the preservation of the cosmos and to the salvation of human beings.

These overall aims allow a differentiation between theocentric, cosmocentric, and anthropocentric religions.

Views of ritual practice

Religious communication is ritualised in many ways, allowing the study of rituals to make an important contribution to unfolding the structure and practice of religion. Three significant approaches to ritual will be sketched. We outline the work of social anthropologist Victor Turner, who studied the rituals of passage and the characteristic features of what he called the 'ritual process' (Turner, 1969). Turner determines three phases of ritual process, in which the religious dimensions and meanings of rituals simultaneously become evident. The rituals of passage are, first, always about one's removal from a given position in the group, community, or society. Second, they are about a transitional phase in which the ritual subject no longer has their old, abandoned social role, but does not yet have a new status. In the third condition the passage is fulfilled, a new place or status is reached, a new fixed position inside the group, community, or society is gained and occupied. According to Turner, the middle or 'margin' phase which he designates as 'liminality' provides the key to understanding the ritual process. Marginal persons are neither here nor there; they are situated between socially fixed positions and are not integrated into the social structure. From this perspective they appear as outsiders. However, in the condition of liminality something fundamental happens for ritual subjects. They have the experience of an alternative form of human relations that is opposed to the social structure. Turner calls this 'communitas'. While the social structure represents a hierarchically arranged system of fixed positions, the *communitas* is an unstructured and relatively undifferentiated communion of equals. In the intermediate stage of statuslessness, an egalitarian community is experienced and practiced. The 'margin' condition of spontaneous, concrete *communitas* comes into opposition with the status system of the norm-regulated social structure. For Turner, the religious quality of the marginal position in complex societies is conserved in religious performances and institutions. The quality of transitional religious life appears now especially in monastic orders and communities which try to institutionalise liminality or *communitas*.

Religious Studies scholar Catherine Bell regards ritualisation as a creative act of the production and reproduction of the past (Bell, 1992). Ritualisation, in her view, represents a strategic procedure by which the agent is endowed with ritual competence. Bell focuses on the relation between ritual and power: ritual both empowers and exercises power at the same time. In *Ritual. Perspectives and Dimensions* (1997), Bell outlines characteristics of ritual-like activities: formalism, traditionalism, invariance, rule-governance, sacral symbolism, and performance. Performative enactments communicate on different sensory levels. They acquire their dynamic through their framing. The latter enables them to create a 'world' of their own in which the participants are involved. Being involved in ritualisation, according to Bell, people are not aware that they in fact (re-)construct traditions and meanings. They consider themselves as creative without realising that for the most part they simply respond to the given which they pass on at the same time.

Anthropologist Roy Rappaport in his masterpiece *Ritual and Religion in the Making of Humanity* (1999) sees the fundamental task to ritual as generating acceptance. Insofar as this happens, ritual 'is *the* basic social act' (Rappaport, 1999, p. 138). He suggests that, in rituals, encoding, formality, invariance, and performance go together. (This strongly parallels the discussion in Chapter 9 of symbolic phenomena in communication; that is, the importance of conventions, roles, and performative or demonstrative acts in knitting together the social fabric of a given community or institution.) Rappaport insists that 'by taking ritual to be a mode of communication some of its strangest features ... become clear' (1999, p. 50). He regards rituals as embedded in what he calls 'liturgical orders'. Liturgical orders combine physical and verbal components. Rituals are multivocal enactments. Additionally, liturgical orders always contain some formulas which are put in hierarchical order. Those which occur at the peak of a liturgical order, in Rappaport's view, consist of extremely invariant creedal statements. He calls these creeds 'Ultimate Sacred Postulates' (1999, p. 168). This is what is decisive about Rappaport's approach: he considers the ultimate postulates as *products of performative acts* – so that the truth of liturgical orders is not discovered, but is in fact constituted by the performance itself. Consequently, what is at stake here is the question of the creative power of ritual. By the enactment of ritual or liturgical order, divine word and divine order are created and established. Thus religious ritual for Rappaport is creative, performative, and productive. Ritual and religion play an eminent role 'in the making of humanity'.

Religion and communicative action

The philosopher Jürgen Habermas has developed a comprehensive and influential communicative theory of action (as discussed in Chapter 6) (Habermas, 1984a, 1987). According to his normative approach, based on philosophical reflection and on reconstruction of the core of communication, communicative action is the original 'dialogical' mode of human communication and interaction. Communicative action is the cultural basis of human life and living together, whereas instrumental action is appropriate to deal with natural resources and material conditions (though it is often also applied to other people, problematically in Habermas's view). Communicative action is oriented at intersubjective understanding and agreement. It either aims at reaching a consensus of the speaker and the hearer, or it articulates a given or presupposed agreement. If the consensus is questioned or lost, communicative action will be replaced by strategic action, a mode of communication oriented at success of one or other of the parties. Habermas regards strategic action as a deficient 'monological' form of social action in which the other is not recognised as a communication partner but is used merely as an instrument or a tool in order to reach one's own individual or collective goals. However, he also claims that a new consensus can be achieved by argumentative discourse, a form of communication which explicitly addresses and discusses the different validity claims which are implied and raised in each party's speech acts. These validity claims refer to the truth of the propositions which are asserted, the rightness of the relations between the communication partners, and the truthfulness of the speaker's utterance. Discourse, in Habermas's view, has the formal structure of an 'ideal speech situation'. This kind of free, equal, and unrestricted communication, on the one hand, exceeds the capacities of the 'real communication community'. But, on the other hand, the 'ideal speech situation' or 'ideal communication community' provides the goal of communication, towards which instances of real communication can aspire, and relative to which they can be evaluated.

For much of his work, Habermas took the view that religion and unrestricted communication are incompatible. In *The Theory of Communicative Action* (1984a, 1987) he developed a sophisticated theory of society, action, communication, and rationality alongside a rudimentary theory of religion. He then understood the development of religion in a social-evolutionary framework. (Habermas, 1984b) His position contained the central thesis of the 'linguistification of the sacred' (Habermas 1987, pp. 77–111). In brief: speech or communication replaces the sacred. According to Habermas, religious-metaphysical worldviews become untenable in the process of social rationalisation and the formation of modern structures of consciousness; they become, as he calls it, 'obsolete'. The stage of social evolution reached in modernity differentiates the dimensions of moral-practical rationality, once combined in religion, into societal justice and morals. In his view, the religious ethic of brotherliness cultivated especially in the Judaeo-Christian tradition, entered into 'a communicative ethic detached from its foundation in salvation religion' (Habermas, 1984a, p. 242). Thereby, the religious ethic is both superseded and retained in a secular form.

According to Habermas, religious practice had not only an ethical orientation, but also a ritual shape. It became obsolete when it passed its functions of social integration and expression over to communicative action. The authority of the sacred was substituted by the authority of consensus. Thus, communicative action was released from sacredly protected normative contexts. The result is that religion belongs to a past stage of humanity, which has in the meantime been superseded by modernity. In the course of modernisation, religion lost its cognitive, expressive, and moral-practical content; it was transmuted into a communicative ethic. Free and unrestricted communication thus takes the former place of religion.

Religion in today's society

Habermas's view of religion has changed significantly in the last two decades. This became obvious in his Frankfurt Peace Prize speech on 'Faith and Knowledge' (Habermas, 2005) in October 2001. In his speech he made it clear that religion has not disappeared from today's secular society. For him, the menacing dimension of religion had become conspicuous with the terror attacks of 11 September 2001, when the 'tension between secular society and religion exploded' (2005, p. 327). Nevertheless, in contrast to a fundamentalism that has become terroristic, there are also religious forms and religious communities that deserve the description 'reasonable'. Habermas now acknowledges that the boundaries between secular and religious reason are more fluid than he first envisaged. The 'determining of these disputed boundaries should therefore be seen as a cooperative task which requires both sides to take on the perspective of the other one' (Habermas, 2005, p. 332).

Cooperation, to be sure, presupposes communication – indeed, Habermas reiterates that the resources of religion and its semantic potential have to be translated by philosophy. But he nevertheless accepts in the meantime that faith and knowledge, religion and reason, theology and philosophy are not simply antipodes of which one pole belongs to the future, while the other has disappeared from the present. Secular and religious rationalities are inextricably linked to one another; each, in a reciprocal manner, communicates something about the other, both benefit from the productive dispute with the other. Religion, in Habermas's changed view, is of course connected with and has to do with communication. 'From the very beginning, the voice of God calling into life communicates within a morally sensitive universe' (2005, p. 336). Even those who, like Habermas himself, do not believe in the theological premises of the concept of creation, can nevertheless understand and approve of some of their consequences. The discourse between religious and secular forms of communication essentially concerns a socially pressing agreement about human practice.

One should note, however, that Habermas decisively opposes an 'unfair exclusion of religions from the public sphere'. He holds that the secular should remain 'sensitive to the force of articulation inherent in religious languages' (2005, p. 332). Inherent in religion is thus a communicative potential that is of undeniable importance, especially in the post-secular age of globalisation and genetic technology, in which both aggressive forms of fundamentalism (which may seek to limit technological change) and rapid scientific-technological transformations pose serious challenges to what has been dubbed our contemporary 'risk society'. Given the seemingly unbridgeable differences of social and cultural worlds that appear to share no common language, and the polarised positions generated by the possible biotechnological production of 'human nature' (Habermas, 2003), one begins to appreciate that the communicative potential of religion is not merely a private matter. On the contrary, it belongs to the realm of public communication and social discourse – it is part of the public sphere (Habermas, 2008).

Religion as intersubjective practice

Within a communicative approach, I suggest that the following claims can be made: religion is itself a constitutive communicative practice, which is genuinely intersubjective and agreement-oriented. Empirically, religions contain and practise 'hybrid' forms of communication with different combinations of communicative and strategic elements. Within a particular religion a variety of forms of communication take place, in the form of speech acts enacted by its members. These speech acts go along with non-linguistic actions – for example gestures and other types of behaviour (see Chapter 3 for dimensions of nonverbal communication). All these performances or 'doings' are embedded in a comprehensive life practice. Such life practice is carried out on the part of – as well as within – a communication community. Religious communities of communication in these actions give expression to their obligations to and responsibility in view of their belief in a transcendent reality. And doing so, they create, maintain, question, and change community.

If the agreement-orientation represents the distinctive feature of communicative action, then religious practice itself can be viewed as communicative – if and insofar as it is directed at a reality in which people do not deal with one another strategically, do not functionalise, and misuse the other as an instrument for one's own purpose (see Box 12.1). Although factually religious people, groups, and institutions often act strategically, from a normative point of view, religious practice in its 'ideal' shape – which by adherents (e.g.) of empiricist approaches is called idealistic – is thoroughly communicative. Genuine religious action is oriented at a reality, in which people mutually recognise, associate with, and experience each other in solidarity and in so doing act together. This community-related and agreement-oriented character of religion is thrown into sharper relief when contrasted with the motives and functioning of other 'non-natural' beliefs such as magic. Whereas religion represents an intersubjective, consensus-dependent, and agreement-oriented practice originating in and linked to communities, magic has a tendency towards strategic-instrumental and rather mono-logic dealings with the external, social, or inner 'world' (Theissen and Merz, 1998).

It is important to note that communicative-religious action does not solely offer inspiring rhetorical force (as Habermas sometimes proposes); rather, it is also semantic – it discloses and names a reality. This reality for human life and basis for living together brings forth a crucial semantic dimension, namely, the dimension of promise. It is the promise of a relieving and reconciling liberation from political, social, physical, and psychic bondage and mortality's grip. In such religious speech and communal practice we find both a semantic and a performative-practical surplus. Of course, this surplus can be translated into philosophical speech, but cannot be transformed without residue. In communicative-religious speech and action, according to my understanding, there are different potentials involved: a *creative*, that is, a reality-disclosing potential; an *innovative*, namely a reality-transforming potential; and an *anamnestic* potential of **memory** and remembrance. The latter provides a means whereby a given community becomes aware of and tries to do justice to the reality of the victims of history (Peukert, 1984; Arens, 2007). From the perspective of the religious communities, such

Box 12.1   Is religion an instance of strategic behaviour?

Critics of religion of either Marxist or Darwinist origin regard religion as a means of strategic behaviour or communication. Karl Marx considered religion as an expression of the real misery and at the same time as a helpless and futile protest against this misery. In religion the subjugated people sought consolation and relief by belief in a better afterlife. Religion is thus thought to be a strategy to reduce the pain of the given miserable conditions, to render them more endurable. As religion does not really change the unbearable social conditions or liberate people from the condition of exploitation, it is not simply an ineffective strategy; it is, furthermore, profoundly ideological, an instance of false consciousness. Hence Marx referred to religion as the 'opium *of* the people'. Lenin underlined that religion is a strategy used by the ruling powers to keep their predominant position and to keep the masses under control. That's why he called religion 'opium *for* the people', that is a drug to sedate the masses, to immobilise them and to make it impossible for them to revolt against their exploitation and oppression.

Darwinist conceptions view religion as an evolutionary strategy, a means of adapting to an uncontrollable environment. Religion aims at bringing order into a chaotic and hostile world. By sacrifice and submission to natural or supernatural forces the chances for biological survival and reproduction grow for the community. Richard Dawkins asserts that 'the selfish gene' (Dawkins, 1976) aims at utmost replication and reproduction, insisting that it both stimulates and steers the process of evolution. According to him, all living organisms except human beings are steered only by their genes. In the case of human beings, a cultural counterpart emerges, which he calls 'meme'. The replication of memes takes place through imitation (Greek: *mimesis*). Memes are drummed into people fundamentally by education. For Dawkins, religious ideas and enactments belong to the most wicked memes. Religion along with its associated 'God delusion' – which can take either an active or passive form (Dawkins, 2006) – is thus viewed as a byproduct of evolution. Dawkins regards religion as a complex of highly dangerous memes and describes it as a 'virus'. In these terms, religion is understood as intellectually obsolete, morally reprehensible, and educationally unsound. In Dawkins's view, religious education can be labelled 'indoctrination'; religion is thought to lead to fanaticism, fundamentalism, and absolutism. That's why this infectious virus with its strategy to replicate and to spread has to be fought against and to be stopped by atheist enlightenment.

Other evolutionary approaches to religion, such as that of Pascal Boyer (2001), provide a very different view, one in which religion has natural origins and is culturally transmitted, but where it is not necessarily concerned solely with strategic communication. For Boyer, religion produces and stabilises socially minded behaviour, for example, cooperation and community.

innovative-anamnestic religious action can be understood as communicative faith practice. Religion is performed in the communicative practice of people who in their communicative, communal, and critical actions communicate either *with* or *about* a reality – in the theistic religions, with or about a reality called 'God'. This dimension of religious communicative practice – its ability to foster and extend substantive community bonds – helps to ensure that religion is more than merely opium for the masses but is also a means of creative, innovative, and anamnestic societal practice.

Religious-communicative practice

The monotheistic religions of Abrahamic origin – Judaism, Christianity, and Islam – articulate two basic forms of religious-communicative practice: the act of witnessing and of confessing (Arens, 1995). Witnessing points to the reality of God in a most personal way; the transcendent reality is made accessible via self-involving action of the witness. In his or her own action and by his or her own person the witness discloses and makes visible what is of utmost importance and relevance. The witness acts as a 'human medium' (Faulstich, 1997). He or she gives testimony and communicates in order to convince others of this reality. Witnessing is either missionary, or diaconal (in the other's service), or prophetic, or pathic (taking place in suffering). In the last case, witnessing (Greek: *martyria*) becomes martyrdom. On the one hand, for the believers and the believing communities, martyrdom is often regarded as the ultimate act of faith – giving one's life for the truth and for others; on the other hand, martyrdom seems to be a highly ambivalent action, as can be determined in the assessment of suicide attacks. From the outside, they appear as acts of false fanaticism, as utmost strategic actions with the aim to produce as many victims as possible.

Witnessing is thus basically agreement-oriented – it aims at convincing. This contrasts with confessing, which does not aim at convincing; rather, it willingly gives expression to an already realised common conviction. Confessing involves achieving consensus, or rather, performing and thus communicating it; it requires agreement, which manifests itself in the confessional text, for example the Jewish *Shema Israel*, the Muslim *Shahada*, or the Christian Creed (Rappaport, 1999). The consensus and commonality once professed is actualised in the acts of confessing or professing. (See Chapter 9 for a discussion of the public dimension of confessional activity.)

Besides these elementary actions of faith practice which are characteristic of monotheistic religions, various other forms of religious-communicative practice can be traced across a variety of religions. The Abrahamic religions are interwoven with witnessing and confessing practices which function in a mutually supporting and overlapping manner. I would like to point to five human practices which occur, although not exclusively, in religious contexts and are performed by religious people: the practices of remembering, narrating, celebrating, proclaiming, and sharing.

The past made present: Remembering

Remembering is a fundamental individual and collective practice which links us to our personal and communal past. Our memory forms, contains, and communicates answers to questions such as who we are, where we come from, where we belong to, and what makes up our identity. As individuals, communities, and societies we are unable to exist without memory (Ricoeur, 2004). Religions also depend on traditions and practices of remembering, indeed religion can be considered 'as a chain of memory' (Hervieu-Léger, 2000). This relates first to biographic memory which forms our personal identity, second to 'communicative memory' which links us to our contemporaries, and third also to 'cultural memory' (Assmann, 2006). In the latter, the formative and normative events of the collective past which 'must not be forgotten' are kept in mind. The cultural memory of a group, society, or religion is enacted above all in festivities and ritual celebrations. They take place in extraordinary times at specific dates. 'Dates give history a ritual dimension: they become anniversaries' (Smart, 1996, p. 160). Religious remembrance includes the memory of the dead, and the memory of those who have been victims and have suffered unjustly. According to Critical Theory and Political Theology, it should not be restricted to the memory of one's own history but include the whole history of suffering. Remembrance thus becomes 'memoria passionis' (Metz, 2005) and it is enacted as 'anamnestic solidarity' (Peukert, 1984).

Individual and collective memory may of course be perverted by focusing on the 'victor's history' (Benjamin, 2005), may as such be used to the ends of strategic self-assertion and self-praise, becoming an instrument thus of the forgetting or denigrating of others. In these cases, the provocative and productive 'dangerous memory' of the founding figures, the true tradition or the truthful remembrance, often claimed by the prophets, is required.

Telling God's story and faith stories: Narrating

Religions not only remember the founders and paradigmatic figures of their religious traditions; they also recount their formative and normative actions in stories. Indeed, an elementary content of many such narratives is the cosmic event 'in the beginning' when the Gods or God created the world. The origin of humankind and of death, as well as the beginnings of one's own tradition, are narrated and enacted in myths and stories (Smart, 1996). They reach from creation-myths and myths of primeval times to foundational stories (Eliade, 1985). Narrating arguably plays an important role in the development and maintenance of both personal and social identity and religious identity. In a way, we are what we have been told and what we tell our children, friends, contemporaries, and fellow believers; Bruner (1991) speaks of 'the narrative construction of reality'. Narrating furthermore is an important element in educational and therapeutic processes (Bruner, 2002); narrative analysis provides a relevant tool for qualitative social research (Jovchevolitch and Bauer, 2000).

Judaeo-Christian faith has a 'narrative depth structure' (Metz, 2005). Religious-communicative practice involves the narrating of stories of promise, liberation, exodus, faith, and hope. Through these stories the semantic content of religion is communicated, preserved, and passed on. Narrating faith stories implies their interpretation and contextualisation relative to contemporary situations of communication and action. Indeed, narration makes an invitation to imagine the present situation in the light of the faith story and to act in a particular way. Telling God's story and faith stories is thereby a prime example of communicative-religious practice because religion lives, remains alive and is handed down in these stories; its contents and intentions are remembered and actualised by and in them.

Festivities and liturgies: Celebrating

Another form of social and religious-communicative practice, mentioned already, is celebrating (Turner, 1982). Service to God or worship in Christianity and other religions has the character of celebration. Liturgical celebration is a powerful expression of participants' experiences of community, of their communal interconnectedness; it is an expression and practice of *communitas*

(Driver, 1991). Liturgical action creates, strengthens, and transforms community (see Box 12.2). This enables us to highlight a theme running through this book – a theme which, incidentally, again emphasises the importance of a social psychological approach to communication – that is, the priority in various sorts of communication on bonding, substantiating community ties and identities (see e.g. Chapter 7 on rumour and gossip, Chapter 13 on health communication, and Chapter 9 on symbolic aspects of communication).

To be sure, ritual celebrating may not only establish *communitas*, but can also become neurotically compulsive in the Freudian sense; it can degenerate

Box 12.2   Components and varieties of liturgies

Liturgies are very complex forms of communication. They comprise a variety of speech acts, e.g. lecturing, preaching, confessing one's sins, and confessing the common faith (i.e. saying the creed), praying, praising, and thanksgiving. They further contain a number of gestures, (e.g. blessing, making the sign of the cross, beating the breast, and bowing). At the same time, different postures are taken up such as standing, kneeling, or sitting. Liturgies also include other nonverbal modes of communication and action, e.g. offering, eating (communion), and walking (processions). In the Christian tradition, diverse forms of expression and celebration have been emphasised by the various churches and particular church segments. In high churches, liturgies appear to be multivocal and multimedia sacred enactments or 'sacred plays' involving sacred texts, sounds, and images. High church liturgies make use of hymns, chorals, holy water, incense, bread, and wine etc. These elements are interwoven with an opulent and often colourful ritual performance which communicates by way of a variety of sensory means and appeals to all human senses.

In the Roman Catholic and Anglican tradition the verbal components of liturgy are closely linked with the sacramental ones: the prayer service is the first part of the worship followed by a second part of the liturgy, called the 'eucharist' or the 'Lord's Supper'. In the Reformed churches, the liturgy seems rather sober and intellectual; the main emphasis is on verbal communication. The written, lectured, and preached 'Word of God' is at the centre of the worship service whereas the corporeal, motion-related, expressive, and emotional parts of liturgical action and interaction have been restrained. This restriction has been introduced for theological reasons, because worship by the Reformed churches has been regarded first and foremost as a celebration of God's saving word and action. Consequently, worship must be prevented from degenerating into magic practices and a display of 'self-righteous' human works.

into magical effective-thinking and spiritless ritualism and thus becomes strategic action (Bell, 1992). Liturgical celebration is constantly threatened with corruption and can turn into the demonstration of religious power. In this case, it brings about different kinds of criticism. This criticism contests either the very possibility and validity of liturgical action in general, or it aims – like the prophetic criticism of the cult – at 'true worship', at the proper relation of liturgical-ritual and ethical-communicative action. In true worship, strategic power relations can often be interrupted and transgressed. An imaginative participation and embedding into a greater or even unlimited community of memory and hope is experienced and anticipated. Hence, an opening or widening of agency is understood to take place. Celebrating is a central religious-communicative practice in which God's saving reality and surpassing action is remembered, actualised, narrated, praised, and performed.

Spreading the good news: Proclaiming

A further form of religious-communicative practice is proclaiming. Thereby, religious content and meaning is communicated in order that it will be shared. Proclaiming makes known the meaning of a religion and is in this respect informative. This happens, of course, in the sense of an engaged and evocative communication, which intends that the addressees make what is communicated their own. Proclaiming may take the strategic form of proselytising, that is, the attempt to convert others to one's own religion. Anyway, it emphasises impressing the prevailing religious message upon the addressees while taking into account the situation of its listeners, and is thereby capable of being fruitful. There is thus a missionary element within proclaiming or proselytising: it aims at persuading people into a religion or – in the case of those who already possess religious conviction – at reinforcing, defending, strengthening, or perfecting such conviction. Of course, missionary proclaiming can degenerate into a strategic instrument. Such distortion occurs when proclaiming is turned into indoctrination, coercion, and enslavement. Religious fundamentalism uses proclaiming or proselytising for its own purposes. In this case, the strictly traditional 'Word of God', taken literally from 'Holy Scripture', is proclaimed against the seemingly godless modern world. Fundamentalism is rooted in rigid communities from which it pursues its proselytising strategy of gaining influence and of 're-conquering the world' (Kepel, 1994).

Besides the missionary aspect – that is, the attempt at converting others – another important moment of proclaiming is encountered in the Abrahamic religions. It led to their qualification as *prophetic* religions. In fact, prophetic proclaiming is an indispensable element for Judaism, Christianity, and Islam. The prophet is first of all the one who proclaims God's word and will. Prophetic action is performed in speech acts, symbolic and subversive actions. The Biblical prophets have been called the inventors of social criticism; they first and foremost criticise their community 'from within'

(Walzer, 1987). They raise critical objections against the prevailing political and religious powers in the name of God. They intervene in God's 'lawsuits' with the world or with idols and they take God's side. For the Biblical prophets, God's side is at the same time the side of the powerless, the poor, the discriminated against, and excommunicated. Prophetic practice uncovers social and religious injustice and oppression, articulating God's objection to it. Prophetic proclamation also announces God's promise of a new, just, and benevolent order. Prophetic practice comprises opposition and resistance to the political, social, economic, and religious injustice taking place. However, it accompanies the condemnation of unbearable 'sinful conditions' with the 'heralding of a new world' (Comblin, 1990).

Solidarity, charity, and compassion: Sharing

A significant form of communicative-religious practice is sharing; this is a general term for what in Christianity is called charity or *caritas*. Such practice of benevolence, compassion, pity, and solidarity is central for all religions; it belongs everywhere to the ethical, communicative core of religion. The practice of sharing creates, strengthens, and transforms community in particular ways. All religions have their ideas about how the goods of the earth – the material as well as the spiritual, the social and also the communal goods – are to be shared (see Box 12.3).

Box 12.3   With whom shall we share?

For Muslims the practice of charity (Arabic: *zakat*) is one of the main religious obligations. It belongs to the five 'pillars of Islam'. Paying the obligatory social tax, giving alms, doing voluntary charity, and sharing with the needy shows the solidarity with and attachment to the global Muslim community (Arabic: *umma*). In Buddhism benevolence, mercy, or compassion (Sanskrit: *karuna*) belong to the characteristics of the Buddha and are the decisive virtues of Buddhists; Buddhism extends mercy to all living beings and calls for compassion with all creatures. Both Judaism and Christianity acknowledge the obligation to share the goods of the earth, to assist the needy, to help the poor, to be in solidarity with the weak, and to establish a just social order. For Judaism, charity (Hebrew: *zedaka*) does not only mean giving alms but is considered as an attribute and an essential activity of God Himself.

Despite their common appeal to share, the different religious traditions are not unanimous in view of the reach and the limits of charity and solidarity. This remains a debate both within and among religions. Factually, sharing has often been limited to one's own family, relatives, or fellow believers. Exclusivist and fundamentalist religious circles combine strong in-group solidarity and in-group charity with hostility and aggression against the people of other faiths who, for fundamentalists, are nothing but unbelievers. However, great founders of world religions and religious leaders like the Buddha, the prophets of the Old Testament, or Jesus of Nazareth proclaimed and practised unlimited, universal compassion, solidarity, and charity. For Muhammad, Allah is first and foremost 'the Merciful, the Compassionate'.

The worth of the spiritual goods of the different religious traditions can be discovered in the course of interreligious encounters. By participating in the worship of other traditions or by taking part in common celebrations, through everyday dialogue, and by way of theological discourse, religious people are able to get to know, to appreciate, and perhaps to share at least in part the spiritual wealth of other religions. Thus, the question 'With whom shall we share?' may be answered on the spiritual level by developing modes of interreligious 'inter-active universality' (Askari, 1991).

According to the German theologian Norbert Mette (1994), sharing should not be understood 'in the sense of occasional conduct, but rather as a definite form of living and dealing with each other. It is the expression of a deep-reaching consciousness of solidarity' (p. 182). It enables people to mutually engage in a liable, reliable, and lasting life practice. 'Sharing, thus understood, is the most radical form of communicative practice, in that those involved share with and participate in one another' (Mette, 1994, p. 182).

The communicative-religious practice of sharing further means to aim at both understanding other religions and searching for an agreement with the participants of other faiths and beliefs. In many instances it inspires and hopefully facilitates the possibility of interreligious encounters. At its purest, it can be said to resist any hegemonic operation, to exclude such dominating tendencies, instead performing an acknowledgement of the others which is able to transgress boundaries and transform narrow or restricted conceptions of oneself and the other. The communicative-religious practice of sharing is directed at mutually experiencing and exploring the possibilities of interreligious communication, understanding, and agreement in the face of the creative, communicative, and liberating reality of God.

Conclusion

This chapter has claimed that religion is communication. On the one hand, religious communication takes place in ritual practices. On the other hand, rituals need to be embedded in communicative and critical practices and they need to be reflected within the horizon of communicative approaches. The normative theory of communicative action developed with Habermas, by its sharp distinction between communicative and strategic action, is a productive starting point for understanding religion as communicative action. Applying the theory of communicative action to religion enables us to unfold the contents and the processes, the intentions and the aims of religious-communicative practice, to differentiate among fundamental communicative faith practices, to relate them to each other, to show that they aim at understanding and agreement, community and solidarity, and to contrast them with strategic practices oriented at one's own goal or gain.

13
Mediated Health Campaigns: From Information to Social Change

Catherine Campbell and Kerry Scott

Keywords: Civic journalism; collective action; edutainment; dialogical critical thinking; health communication; health communication strategies; journalism of conversation; journalism of information; KAB (Knowledge + Attitudes = Behaviour) approach; mediated health campaigns/communication; networked journalism; social capital; transformative social spaces; social identity.

Introduction

Health communication campaigns seek to promote healthy behaviours and to build healthy communities. What social psychological pathways are most likely to lead to healthy behaviours and healthy communities? What **health communication strategies** are most likely to facilitate these social psychological processes? How can the media best be used to promote health-enhancing psycho-social changes in individuals, communities and the wider societies in which they are located, particularly in relation to the socially excluded groups who suffer the poorest health?

In this chapter, **health communication** is understood to include any form of communication that seeks to empower people to take control over their health, through promoting one or more of the following: health-enhancing behaviour change; the appropriate accessing of health-related services and support; the development of health-enabling **social capital**; the facilitation of **collective action** to tackle obstacles to health; and the development of health-related social policy (at the local, national and/or global levels of influence). A variety of strategies have been developed to tackle these goals. These include didactic health education campaigns which target vulnerable groups with information about health risks; community strengthening approaches which seek to promote health-enhancing social participation in vulnerable communities; and health advocacy approaches which target powerful decision-makers who have the economic and/or political power to tackle and transform unhealthy social environments.

The first aim of this chapter is to map the evolution of health communication campaigns from their roots in information-based health education towards 'community strengthening' and 'social change' approaches. Information-based health communication targets individuals, seeking to persuade them to change their behaviour through providing them with factual information about health risks. Community strengthening approaches target communities, seeking to build 'health-enabling' social settings through facilitating health-enhancing dialogue and social participation by community members (Campbell and Murray, 2004; Stephens, 2008).

The second aim of the chapter is to examine the potential of various forms of **mediated health communication** – including **edutainment, civic journalism**, and the internet – to facilitate the development of healthy community contexts. It is framed by the World Health Organisation's definition of health as a state of 'physical, mental and social well-being, and not merely the absence of disease or infirmity'. Particular attention is given to the potential for mediated communication to help people tackle various threats to health and well-being, including gender violence in the context of HIV/AIDS, child poverty, human rights abuses, supporting children with autism, and breast cancer.

Health communication: From social cognition to collective action

Historically, health promotion has been driven by 'social cognition' models of behaviour, seeking to promote behaviour change by changing peoples' knowledge and attitudes. Such approaches assume that health-related behavioural intentions result from the decisions of rational individuals, on the basis of sound information about health risks. These approaches are underpinned by varying elaborations of the **KAB approach** (Knowledge + Attitudes = Behaviour). This model holds that if a person has information about a health risk (such as lung cancer), and a negative attitude to it (e.g. lung cancer is a bad thing), s/he will form an intention to behave in a way that reduces that risk (e.g. avoiding cigarettes), with behaviour change often following from behaviour-change intentions.

Such approaches view human beings as rational individuals, capable of making sensible behavioural choices on the basis of sound information. A generation of health communicators have poured money into information-based awareness-raising programmes, such as media campaigns, counselling, and workshops to build health-related skills such as assertiveness in relation to refusing risky engagement with illegal drugs or unprotected sex. While such approaches have had some successes in limited contexts, on the whole their results have been disappointing (Ogden, 2007). Few smokers, heavy drinkers, or fast drivers are unaware of the potentially health-damaging impacts of their behaviour, for example.

Crossley (2000) points to three types of factors that undermine the assumption that people will necessarily make rational and well-informed decisions about their health: unconscious factors, socially constructed peer norms, and power inequalities arising out of social relations such as gender and poverty (see Box 13.1). Against this background, there is growing recognition of the limitations of traditional health promotion in favour of community-strengthening and social-participation approaches, which focus not only on educating people about health risks, but also facilitating the types of social participation most likely to empower them to resist the impacts of unhealthy social influences. A growing body of evidence shows that participation – in community groups, voluntary associations, and civic and political life, as well as informal networks of friends, neighbours, or family – can be a powerful positive influence on health and well-being (Wallack, 2003).

Box 13.1   Why do people knowingly engage in health-damaging behaviour?

Three sets of factors lead people to engage in unhealthy behaviours, even when they are in possession of accurate factual information about health risks and how to avoid them. The first are *unconscious factors* – outside of the individual's rational and conscious awareness – that nevertheless exert a profound influence on their behaviour. Research has found that socially isolated gay men in Norway are more likely to engage in unprotected sex than their more socially connected peers, with skin-to-skin contact symbolising unmet needs for intimacy. Over-eating may sometimes be driven by unmet needs for love and nurturing. Some young women use the strategy of under-eating to increase their sense of control over their lives. The second factors relate to *socially negotiated peer norms*. While levels of cigarette smoking are falling among many groups in the UK, they are rising among teenage girls in Scotland, where smoking is often a key criterion for membership of particular friendship circles. Peer influence often drives abuse of illegal drugs and alcohol. Finally, *socially structured power relations* undermine the likelihood that people will engage in health-enabling behaviours. Gender, poverty, and social isolation make smoking a compelling behavioural option for many lone mothers in England, battling to cope with the overwhelming demands of their daily lives. The social construction of masculinity often leads men to ignore early signs of health problems, and to delay accessing vital health services when illness threatens. A combination of poverty and economic dependence on men leads many African women to engage in unprotected sex, despite sound knowledge of HIV/AIDS and a keen desire to avoid infection.

See Crossley (2000) and the references therein for an account of the research in this box.

The individual behaviour change approach to health communication generally overlooks the health-enhancing benefits of participatory forms of communication. Against this background, a new generation of health communicators are seeking to understand the psycho-social pathways between participation and health, and how best to facilitate these.

In addition to providing the intrinsically health-enhancing benefits of social support (Berkman, 1984), social participation is health-enhancing because it links people into communication networks that they can use to develop critical understandings of the social and psychological circumstances that place their well-being at risk. In this chapter such networks are said to provide '**transformative social spaces**', namely supportive social settings in which people are able to engage in critical dialogue with trusted peers and that ideally lead to the development of actionable understandings of obstacles to their health and well-being, and strategies for tackling these at the individual, community, or even macro-social levels. In ideal circumstances, such critical understandings inspire and empower people to collectively renegotiate the social norms that drive their behaviour and to engage in forms of personal or group activism that actively challenge the circumstances that place their health at risk.

Social inequalities and health

Various interlocking social inequalities impact negatively on health. In many social settings it is those with the most limited access to economic and political power who are also the most unhealthy. Within this context, redistributive social policies – which increase people's access to economic resources and social and/or political recognition – are often seen as a necessary condition for narrowing the health gap between rich and poor, and in improving the health of groups who have limited access to social power in particular contexts, including women, children, the elderly and the disabled (WHO, 2008).

However, social elites seldom voluntarily give up economic or political power in the absence of assertive and vociferous demands from less powerful groups. Unfortunately, the very people who must provide this assertive and vociferous 'push from below' often have limited opportunities and resources to do so. Moreover, poverty and other forms of marginalisation often foster a sense of disempowerment and fatalism among the excluded. Before members of socially excluded groups are able to demand substantive changes in the unequal social relations that undermine their health, they need to come to see themselves as active agents capable of acting positively to improve their lives and to increase their control over their health and well-being (Gaventa and Cornwall, 2001). Against this background, this chapter examines how health communication might best facilitate the development of 'transformative social spaces' in which members of marginalised social groupings can participate in the types of communication, dialogue, and action that facilitate the development of confident and empowered identities and equip people to take better control of their lives and their health.

Theoretical framework

To be human is to engage in dialogue with others in the ongoing challenge of giving meaning to our lives. Through communication we construct the social identities that govern our behaviour and experience, and negotiate the 'recipes for living' that drive our actions and shape our health and well-being. The symbolic interactionist perspective (Mead, 1962) emphasises the role of social interaction and dialogue in constructing the social identities that influence the behavioural possibilities and constraints available to us. These are often associated with our membership of and position within hierarchical social groups. The assumption underlying the arguments made in this chapter is that health communication is effective to the extent that it provides opportunities for people to renegotiate these identities in health-enhancing and empowering ways. To improve their health, people need to engage in critical reflection and dialogue, develop new insights into the way unequal social relations limit their health and life chances, and brainstorm strategies through which they might begin to resist these negative impacts.

Communication and power

Within unequal societies, there is an overwhelming tendency for unequal power relations to perpetuate themselves, with communicative possibilities and outcomes tending to reinforce the position of dominant social groups in the vast majority of social interactions (this is a theme present also in Habermas's critique of strategic as opposed to communicative action, see Chapter 6). One mechanism through which this happens is that marginalised social groupings become trapped in self-limiting understandings of their place in the world, and of their potential for action – forms of 'power-knowledge' (Foucault, 1980) that often lead to fatalism and passivity.

However, in principle, the exertion of power always goes hand in hand with the possibility of resistance (Foucault, 1980, see also Hook, 2007). Foucault speaks of the 'micro-capillarity' of power. Rather than being a monolithic force, power operates through a complex array of 'meticulous rituals' (Foucault, 1975). Since communication is a key medium through which the meticulous rituals of power are continually enacted and reenacted, the possibility always exists that in ideal social circumstances, groups of marginalised actors may develop the insight, agency, and confidence to refuse to engage in communicative styles and acts that undermine or disempower them. Key to this process of refusal is the process of reformulating their social identities and their associated sense of their place in the world in ways that challenge the negative social relations that compromise their dignity and well-being (see Chapter 7 for a discussion of the role of communication in shaping social identities). The task confronting health communicators concerned with challenging the social hierarchies that lead to health inequalities is to provide 'transformative social spaces' for the development of such resistance.

From didactic to participatory communication

A generation of programme evaluations suggests that information-based health-promotion approaches, discussed above, have had remarkably limited impact on the behaviour of their audiences (Wallack, 2003). Information is often a very weak determinant of behaviour change, particularly among marginalised social groups whose freedom to control their behaviour may be limited by wider social conditions such as poverty or gender.

Furthermore, individuals are not 'empty vessels' that can be 'filled up' with new information. All human thinking takes the form of a process of dialogue – a communicative form, we might say – the process of debate or argument and counter-argument, conducted both internally and between individuals (Billig, 1996). In his account of 'the thinking society', Billig argues that people are engaged, individually or collectively, in a constant process of weighing up different points of view. People constantly evaluate new sources of knowledge both in terms of preexisting assumptions, habits, custom, ideology, and tradition, and also in terms of the often contradictory motivations that influence their behaviour as they move from one social setting to the next.

Health-related behaviours are not simply the result of individual knowledge and skills imparted to passive audiences by active health communicators. They are nested within complex social structures in which people collectively appropriate and construct new meanings, identities, and behavioural possibilities from one moment to the next in response to the challenges they face in their lives. For this reason, effective health communication needs to facilitate situations that constitute a microcosm of 'the thinking society' by encouraging target audiences to participate in the processes of dialogue and debate through which identities and behavioural possibilities are created and recreated.

Building transformative social spaces

How can the types of social spaces most conducive to empowering dialogue best be characterised? Fraser (1990) argues that in unequal societies, the public sphere tends to be dominated by men rather than women, and the wealthy rather than the poor, and to provide limited space for ethnic minorities to exert influence (see Chapter 4 for more on the topic of social influence). Marginalised groups tend to lack the confidence, skills, and social legitimacy to advance their needs and interests. For this reason, she posits the concept of 'counter-publics', which refers to safe separate spaces in which marginalised groups can retreat to develop and 'rehearse' the types of critical arguments they will eventually take into the dominant public sphere as part of the project of challenging the power of dominant groupings and demanding their share of symbolic and material social power.

What psycho-social processes need to take place within these 'counter-public' spaces, best equipping marginalised groups to make effective demands for social recognition? Paulo Freire (2005) answers this question with his concepts of **dialogical critical thinking** and praxis, through which people are able to reflect on and transform their existing understandings of themselves and their place in the world, and act to improve their life circumstances (see Chapter 2 for a more detailed account of Freire's work). It is through such reflection that excluded groups are able to deconstruct their existing self-limiting knowledge and develop understandings of how their taken-for-granted assumptions are shaped by oppressive power relations and by worldviews that support the interests of the dominant social classes.

Such reflection informs the development of new ways of making sense of the world, and more empowering understandings of the possibilities of alternative social relationships. Ideally, participatory dialogue and reflection also lead to an enhanced sense of confidence in one's ability to change one's social circumstances, as well as the identification of existing individual and group strengths, skills, and capacities to contribute to the fight for social change. Identification of strengths and skills is part and parcel of the collective formulation of feasible action plans to challenge limiting social relations. Finally, and ideally, effective dialogue leads to the identification of potential support networks that marginalised communities can draw on to enable them to put these action plans into practice.

The latter point is based on the insight that marginalised groupings are often not able to tackle the social settings that undermine their health without significant assistance from outsiders who have the economic and political power to assist them in achieving their goals. Bourdieu (1986) argues that limited access to social capital (which he defines as durable networks of socially advantageous inter-group relationships) is a key factor in perpetuating poverty and other forms of social disadvantage, hindering people from improving their life circumstances. Facilitating the development of 'bridging social capital' – linking health-vulnerable communities to actors and agencies outside of their community with the power to support them in improving their health, well-being, and life chances – needs to be a key aspect of any health communication programme that seeks to strengthen the capacity of excluded groups to withstand or ameliorate the impact of harmful social relations on their lives. A key challenge currently facing health communicators is to develop better understandings of how communication strategies can facilitate links between marginalised communities and powerful and supportive outsiders (e.g. health or welfare professionals, political leaders and policymakers, powerful economic actors, various local, national, and global networks of support).

A growing research literature points to links between social capital and health. In addition to 'bridging social capital' discussed above, positive health has also been associated with 'bonding social capital', understood as norms and networks of solidarity and mutual support within marginalised communities. In view of evidence for links between both forms of social capital and health, Wallack (2003) argues that a key challenge facing health communicators is to develop 'community strengthening' communication strategies that go beyond the simple transmission of health-related information, seeking also to facilitate the development of bonding and bridging social capital in their target communities. This is one of the key themes in this book, connecting theoretical perspectives as diverse as psychoanalysis (Chapter 9), social representations theory (Chapter 7), and notions of communicative action (Chapters 6 and 11), namely the idea that one of the strongest aspects of communicative change resides in building social links, establishing communal networks, and fostering horizontal ties.

The remainder of this chapter discusses various forms of mediated communication in the light of their ability to facilitate the processes of health-enhancing critical dialogue, reflection, and social capital construction outlined above.

Mainstream media

There is no doubt that the mainstream media (commercial and public television, newspapers and radio designed to reach large audiences) play a key role in providing those who can access them with information about health risks, as well as providing advice about individual behaviour change strategies. However, as already argued, while information is a necessary condition for behaviour change, it is not a sufficient one. To what extent do these media facilitate transformative social spaces, in which people are able to engage in dialogue about their health and the social inequalities and/or pressures that enable or undermine it?

According to Hodgetts and Chamberlain (2006), the mainstream media tend to approach health from an individualistic and biomedical perspective. Health-related news stories and advertisements overwhelmingly frame health as a biomedical issue. They tend to place responsibility for change on the unhealthy individual, masking the crucial role played by unequal social environments in shaping health, and in preventing many members of disadvantaged groupings from engaging in health-promoting behaviour. Furthermore, the media often favour sensationalising stories of diseases, focusing on the health problems of individual footballers' wives or pop stars rather than locating the occurrence and distribution of health within the context of wider political and policy debates. In this way, the mainstream media reduce public understanding of and support for the need to tackle many health issues through redistributive social change.

Another limitation of traditional health communication stems from its expert-driven nature. Socially excluded groups, along with carrying the greatest burden of disease, also lack symbolic power or 'voice' – the power to contribute their views to the debates that shape public understandings of local realities and social challenges. In the mainstream media, journalists and health experts decide what counts as a health issue, and how marginalised groups will be presented to the public (this idea connects with many debates discussed in the field of science communication, see Chapter 15). Marginalised groups tend to be 'spoken of' by health professionals and members of government rather than having the opportunities to speak for themselves. They have little influence on the way they are represented in the media, generally situated as passive targets for advice and aid, often entrenching their own sense of disempowerment and fatalism. Excluding their perspectives from the creation of media messages can lead to incorrect, non-representative and biased coverage of issues. Moreover this exclusion often leads to health promotion messages that fail to resonate with the lived realities of the target group and are ultimately ineffective.

Examining how the media might play a more positive role in advancing the health interests of marginalised groups, Hodgetts and Chamberlain (2007) distinguish between a '**journalism of information**' and a '**journalism of conversation**', with the latter opening up greater possibilities for the facilitation of dialogue about health, the positioning of health as a social as well as an individual issue, and the inclusion of the voices of the marginalised in shaping representations of health and health-relevant social relations. A 'journalism of conversation' abandons the concept of the journalist as a detached and neutral observer holding an objective mirror to reality. Instead, it views the journalist as a collaborator who works with representatives of the lay public to produce stories that reflect a wider range of voices than those of the middle classes from which most journalists and newspaper readers are drawn. Such a 'journalism of conversation' opens up the possibility of more socially contextualised understandings of health, and positioning health issues as contested and socially constructed, rather than as the reflection of uncontroversial biomedical 'facts'. This form of journalism favours increased interactions between journalists, their traditional audiences and the social groups that form the topic of news stories or documentaries. Rather than simply viewing people as consumers of media and advertisements, the collaborative journalist views them as citizens with a stake in the key social, political, and economic debates that shape the social relations in which they live.

What strategies might health communicators use to locate current representations of health as individual and biomedical issues within wider understandings of the social structuring of health and illness? How might they draw marginalised social groupings into a more active engagement in shaping media representations of their lives? How might health communication encourage socially excluded groups to see themselves as experts in their own lives, as well as citizens and agents capable of acting in ways that increase their access to good health? The following sections focus on some examples of media strategies that have sought to tackle these challenges.

Edutainment

Edutainment involves the intentional placement of educational content into entertainment communicated through television, radio, music, or theatre (Singhal and Rogers, 2002). This approach to health communication constitutes a compromise between two extreme positions: those who believe the media should transmit accurate information about health free of commercial interests or distorting ideology, and those who argue that the mandate of the media is to make money and entertain viewers.

The South African television soap opera *Soul City* is an excellent case study of a programme with mass-based appeal – averaging up to 14 million viewers on prime-time television. *Soul City* aims to increase critical public reflection and dialogue about HIV/AIDS, antiretroviral treatment, and sexual health, in ways that serve as a springboard for the renegotiation of health-damaging sexual norms, as well as promoting the development of a social environment that is supportive of health-enhancing behaviour change. Below, *Soul City* series 4 is taken up as the focus of discussion. *Soul City* series 4 sought to tackle gender-based violence, with survivors of violence being at particular risk of HIV/AIDS (Usdin et al., 2002).

Pre-production research found that most South Africans regarded domestic violence as a private matter, in which outsiders should not intervene. The programme specifically sought to challenge this view, positioning violence as the result of socially structured gender inequalities, and providing audiences with ways in which they might respond and intervene. The programme worked hard to model behavioural opportunities for action. Thus, for example, one episode depicted people ignoring a man beating his wife. Later she stood up in a community meeting, accusing others of knowingly allowing the abuse to continue. Later, when her husband again tried to beat her, villagers surrounded the couple and banged pots, stopping the man. The rationale underlying this demonstration of community agency was to suggest that everyone had the capacity to challenge this practice, and to model ways in which they might do it.

A domestic violence hotline number was embedded in the programme, targeting both victims and concerned outsiders. The storyline also modelled various options for survivors: for example, moving out of home and involving the police. It showed both these options working well and badly for women to promote a realistic sense of the possible consequences of action.

For aggressors, the programme sought to develop critical thinking of violence as a choice made by men, rather than an inevitable response to angry feelings.

Some of the goals of the series were informed by ideals of health advocacy (see Box 13.2), an approach to health communication that seeks to target powerful economic and political actors and policymakers who have the power to create more health-enabling social environments. In this regard, the series was also used to raise public awareness of the South African government's slow progress to implement a Domestic Violence Act. Public marches were organised to coincide with the programme. Parallel

Box 13.2   Health advocacy: Targeting 'the power gap'

Health advocacy is an approach that regards ill-health as the result of a 'power gap' rather than an 'information gap' (Wallack, 1994). Strategies seek to persuade powerful people to promote health-enabling social environments through campaigns to:

- pressurise politicians to develop policies and budgets that promote access to health care by marginalised groups and reduce discrimination against women, the elderly and the disabled;
- encourage pharmaceutical companies to lower the costs of life-saving drugs in poor countries;
- 'name and shame' industries associated with polluting factories, unsafe working conditions, or employment practices that discriminate against women;
- challenge commercial companies that target young people through cigarette and alcohol advertisements.

Health advocacy is often implemented as part of a comprehensive toolkit of strategies to facilitate change, and efforts to target leaders often go hand in hand with grassroots activism. A frequently cited US example is the 'Million Mom March', which sought to promote public awareness of the dangers of guns that kill thousands of children every year. This campaign combined a public event involving the mass mobilisation of 'ordinary citizens' and the very successful mobilisation of media publicity. Starting with one mother's outrage at watching a high-school massacre on television, the campaign ended up involving thousands of mothers in a march on Capitol Hill in Washington, DC. This was a highly publicised event seeking to use the symbolic power of motherhood as a way of lobbying politicians to work towards stricter gun control to protect their children.

workshops were held for journalists to improve the quality of their reporting of domestic violence, and training materials were developed for police called in to intervene in abuse cases.

Widespread firsthand audience participation in producing the programme was minimal compared with alternative media strategies such as civic journalism discussed below. However, the latter necessarily operate on a much smaller scale in individual communities. Furthermore, while firsthand participation by audience members in designing programme messages is ideal, in reality, participatory health and development projects often find it difficult to involve the most marginalised community members, particularly women, who may be housebound due to domestic responsibilities or other gender-based restrictions on their freedom of movement. Edutainment strategies of this nature offer a means of reaching such groups. Furthermore the entertainment format has the power to attract viewers (e.g. male abusers) who might otherwise resist explicit efforts to get them to think critically about their behaviour.

Civic journalism

Various forms of civic journalism (also called public journalism and citizen journalism) involve the collaboration of journalists and members of the public in constructing media outputs. Like *Soul City*, this approach also seeks to generate critical reflection on the impact of social structures on health, as the first step towards political action to tackle health inequalities. Such awareness is seen to be necessary to counter the individualism of mainstream reporting in which the poor and the marginalised are unfairly stigmatised as suffering ill-health due to individual factors such as bad behaviour, general fecklessness, or lack of motivation, masking the social circumstances that prevent them from being healthy. It also seeks to encourage members of excluded groups into dialogue about their health among themselves, as well as giving them a voice in public debates about how to tackle obstacles to their well-being, and involving them in efforts to challenge and renegotiate the way they are represented.

Many civic journalists collaborate with marginalised groups, not only in producing news stories, but also in promoting their involvement in social participation through public policy formation and democratic political processes. Aside from including community voices in the process of news production, they are also expected to be active in the community, convening public meetings, and working with citizens to think of the most effective ways to tackle community problems and advance community interests (Wallack, 2003).

Latin America has a rich tradition of citizen–professional collaboration in media projects, including radio, print, dance, murals, puppets, loudspeakers, and theatre. These projects tend to be grounded in Freirian principles of democratic interaction, dignity and solidarity, in communities previously disabled by alienation, passivity, or silence. Radio Estella del Mar (REM), founded by Catholic Bishop Juan Luis Ysern, is a radio programme run on these principles through partnership between professional broadcasters and local community members (Rodriguez, 2003). REM is a network of six community radio stations in southern Chile, an isolated region which was of interest to the Pinochet government because of its rich natural resources. Ysern sought to build grassroots awareness of the value of these resources, as well as the capacity and confidence of local people to make self-benefiting decisions about which mining proposals to accept and which to reject. His starting assumption, present also in Freire, was that the aim of communication is the co-construction of meaning rather than the transmission of information. The station holds discussion fora on issues such as **social identity**, culture, communication, empowerment, and democracy. Emphasising process over product, it seeks to build cross-generational memory and community interactions to feed community reflections on the role they can play in taking control of their lives and futures.

Hodgetts and colleagues have conducted various studies seeking to carve out a role for civic journalism in New Zealand. They seek to promote public understandings of health as a political issue as well as a technical and biomedical one, and to give the poor a greater role in shaping how they are viewed in the wider society, as well as a greater voice in debates about how to tackle the social inequalities that undermine them (Hodgetts and Chamberlain, 2007). They challenge the media's tendency to construct a public of consumers rather than community-oriented citizens interested in sharing, caring, and advancing the common good. One study (Barnett and Hodgetts, 2007) reports on the activities of the Child Poverty Action group which sought to challenge dominant negative representations of resource-poor parents. The group's work examined media reports on child poverty, highlighting the conceptual split between the working poor (represented as 'deserving'), and the unemployed poor (represented as 'undeserving'), which failed to take account of the cycle of poverty which trapped many families. It also challenged media stereotypes of poor people spending their meagre resources on cigarettes and gambling rather than on their children. The group convened meetings with parents of children in poverty, who, given the opportunity, were strong self-advocates, refuting claims that they were uncaring parents, and presenting themselves as morally worthy citizens battling with difficult circumstances.

Networked communication

The internet is increasingly said to be a health communication tool that is sustainable, dialogical, and inclusive of marginalised voices. It is said to provide unprecedented possibilities for laypeople to participate in the construction of media representations of their worlds, to engage in dialogue about political and social issues of concern, and to mobilise collective action to challenge social injustices.

Any such opportunities are obviously strictly limited to the relatively privileged two billion of the world's seven billion citizens who are currently online (Internet World Stats, 2009). Furthermore, certain levels of 'media literacy' are necessary for people to make optimal use of the internet's potential. However, what can it offer those who are fortunate enough to have the necessary access and literacy? Beckett (2008) is enthusiastic about the potential of the networked public sphere to act as a force for positive social change. He argues that the internet is pulling together a diverse and increasingly sophisticated audience, keen to participate in shaping their own representations, and their own lives. His research in Western Europe suggests that young people and ethnic minorities are decreasingly interested in traditional television or newspaper communication styles, including their narrow interpretation of politics in terms of the activities and debates surrounding parliaments and traditional political parties. Such approaches are rejected for failing to reflect the diversity of voices that increasingly constitute the global public sphere. A growing number of people are more interested in finding out about the world through online news aggregates, friends, and social networks than from television or newspapers. In abandoning traditional forms of public communication in favour of diverse satellite and digital media, they tend to be highly technically skilled in finding information that resonates best with their own social interests and cultural concerns.

Against this background, Beckett outlines a model of '**networked journalism**', involving a high degree of interaction between the media and the public in the production of the news, an approach which provides a useful starting point for thinking about more collaborative ways of using the media to promote health-facilitating social participation. This approach regards news as the outcome of high levels of cooperation and engagement between journalist and reader. At the early stage of a news story it would be made up of publicly generated material in a fairly unprocessed form. However, what starts off as a report on an event (e.g. a factory fire) could evolve into another story (e.g. about unsafe working conditions), as a wider range of people (e.g. factory workers, union officials, industrial health consultants) get involved in constructing the story of the event. In this model the journalist acts as facilitator and mediator among participants in a story-building network, rather than simply as author representing the event in question. This model further illustrates Hodgetts's distinction between a 'journalism of information' and a 'journalism of conversation or collaboration'.

Online patient communication

Health websites and online discussion fora (message boards, journals, e-mailing lists and blogs) for those coping with disability or illness are growing steadily in popularity. Some research depicts these as a positive source of support, solidarity, and activism – as deeply empowering for parents of autistic children, for example. Internet communication provides many parents with a vital opportunity to develop meaningful and constructive representations of the deeply complex and stigmatised condition of autism, often in the face of the failure of the health and educational systems to offer their children the types of support and understanding they need. However, other literature on the role of the Internet paints a more complex picture. Orgad (2006) weighs up these complexities in her discussion of Internet use by women with breast cancer.

Much has been written about the way in which biomedical treatments and approaches neglect the emotional and spiritual needs of cancer patients through an excessive focus on their physical tumours and complications, leaving many patients feeling alienated and unsupported with potentially very negative implications for their health (Crossley, 2000). Orgad's findings suggest that women with access to online communication often find it an invaluable tool in learning to cope with breast cancer and in generating vital support from similar others. Many women have used online communication to share experiences and to communicate with others in co-constructing life narratives in which they start to frame their experiences in ways that are meaningful to them. Through this process they are often able to regain a sense of control over their lives, a vital component of psychological healing.

However, Orgad argues that these positive possibilities are limited by the tensions and contradictions inherent in online communication as well as constraints from wider social structures. The 'disembodied anonymity' of online communication allows users to share personal stories with a high level of openness, but also creates relationships characterised by distance, which avoid the 'emotional price' extracted by conventional give-and-take interactions in the real world (Orgad, 2006: 20). The structure and form of online patient communication can increase a sense of closure and control, but can also constrain stories to a predetermined and limiting formula. Orgad found that online postings tended to be constructed within unwritten rules, dictating that stories should focus on hope, optimism, success and survival, discouraging scripts that did not fit in, such as stories of hopelessness, anger, death, and broader social discontent.

A further constraint of online communication, particularly relevant to the concerns of this chapter, is its contribution to what Orgad refers to as 'the privatisation of illness experiences' – the construction of illness as a predominantly intimate, individual and domestic drama. Through effectively containing patient voices within anonymous and disembodied internet spaces, online patient communication reduces the potential for patient experiences and issues to be heard offline, by policymakers, health professionals, and others in the general public, where they could have broader social and political effects.

The much-heralded possibilities of networked communication for health and social change are limited in many ways. While internet communication certainly opens up some possibilities for increasing the power of ordinary people to frame debates about their health and well-being, these opportunities are limited to those who have access to this form of communication. They may be shaped and constrained by powerful and limiting social representations about social reality, health and healing – which arise either from dominant forms of power-knowledge in the wider society, or from dominant groups within the internet site itself, as Orgad's case study shows. There is also the worrying potential for the Internet to fragment audiences. In the face of the sheer volume of material online, audiences may become segmented into groups that only access sites representing their particular interests, with not enough networking or engagement between different Internet sites. Furthermore, the controversial rise of potentially health-damaging websites, such 'pro-ana' (websites that support anorexic lifestyles) websites in which anorexic girls trade tips on how to evade parental or hospital surveillance of their diet and behaviour, raise a host of complex questions about what constitutes health-related empowerment, and about the role of the internet in this process.

Conclusion

There is growing interest in the potential impacts for 'community-strengthening' approaches to provide opportunities for people to develop a critical awareness of the social roots of many health threats, as well as bonding and bridging networks of health-enhancing solidarity and support, as the first step to working collectively towards health-enabling social change. This chapter has been framed by a conceptual framework which maps out some of the psycho-social pathways between social participation and health, drawing on Paulo Freire's (2005) argument that sustainable and long-term individual behaviour change is most likely to occur when people work collectively to understand and tackle the social circumstances that place their health at risk. Against this background, various forms of mediated communication have been examined, highlighting their potential for providing 'transformative social spaces' for critical reflection, dialogue, and social capital construction. In ideal circumstances, such reflection, dialogue, and networking enables people to develop actionable insights into the links between social inequalities and ill-health, an increased sense of agency to challenge the negative impacts of social inequalities, and strong networks that might facilitate action at the individual, community, and – ideally – even macro-social levels.

Ideally, the development of such dialogue, agency, and solidarity paves the way for the political and economic changes necessary to *challenge* the unequal social relations that place disadvantaged people's health at risk.

However, large-scale social change is often a long-term process whose outcome is by no means certain. A parallel interim measure may be that of health-vulnerable groups working together to develop practically feasible ways of *ameliorating* the impacts of negative social relations on health rather than changing them.

Few of the strategies outlined above have been formally evaluated, and this chapter has sought to map out the psycho-social mechanisms underlying their potential impacts rather than to engage with the programme evaluation literature. It is particularly difficult to evaluate such programmes, given the two kinds of challenges that face health communicators who see their role as more than simply transmitting information, seeking also to facilitate the forms of dialogue, empowerment, and social capital construction that are believed to impact on health. The first outstanding challenge is that of developing more detailed and fine-grained insights into the complex and multilayered pathways between communication strategies and processes of individual and social change. The second challenge is that of developing research tools and research designs that are able to identify and track the types of complex and multilayered individual and social processes that we have discussed in this chapter. These are often unpredictable, and may unfold over longer periods of time than those available to the average programme evaluator, as well as taking complex and indirect forms and routes to health-enabling change, that are not immediately evident. Furthermore, the pathways between communication and health may take different forms in different local settings. In such a context, Auerbach et al. (2009) argue that complex health communication programmes will often of necessity have to be guided by frameworks and models that have 'sociological plausibility', rather than being backed up by quantifiable evidence of the kind that would be preferred in the more linear, cause-effect, input-output models of behaviour change underpinning traditional public health evaluation research for example.

Despite the outstanding difficulties of providing an evidence base for community-strengthening and social-change approaches to health, the evidence for the links between social inequalities and ill-health is undeniable. Furthermore, within the international 'social determinants of health' field there is widespread acknowledgement that tackling health inequalities is likely to be an infinitely complex and long-term process, and involve careful and concerted action on many fronts, from the micro-local to the global levels (WHO, 2008). It is in this context that the concept of 'transformative social spaces' has much to offer those seeking to advance community-strengthening approaches to health. On their own, one-off health communication campaigns are unlikely to constitute a 'magic bullet' capable of tackling the complex interface of unconscious factors, peer norms, and social inequalities discussed in Box 13.1. However, the patient and sustained efforts of activist health communicators – with careful targeting of efforts at both marginalised communities and the powerful actors whose decisions impact on their lives – constitute one important level of influence in a long-term multilevel process of social change to reduce health inequalities.

Acknowledgements

Alice Clarfelt, Flora Cornish, Angela Curtis, Elaine Douglas, Andrew Gibbs, Jing Jing Liu, Barbara Osborne and Warren Parker provided valuable feedback on our first draft.

14
The Social Psychology of Political Communication

Matthew C. Nisbet and Lauren Feldman

Keywords: Agenda-setting; deliberation; framing; hostile media effect; knowledge gap effect; miserly public; polarisation; political trust; priming; public opinion; social trust.

Introduction

Political communication is formally defined as the exchange of information, messages, and symbols between institutions, elected officials, social groups, the media, and citizens with implications for the balance of power in society (McLeod, Kosicki, and McLeod, 2007). In a recent article summarising the state of the field, Bennett and Iyengar (2008) trace research on the social psychology of political communication across several intellectual traditions. One strand, as they note, connects closely to early twentieth-century sociologists such as Gabriel Tarde and Paul Lazarsfeld. These pioneers inspired research on how interpersonal conversations and community contexts shape individual news choices, opinions, political decisions, and participation (see also Chapter 4 on social influence). Theorists such as John Dewey, Jurgen Habermas, and Niklas Luhmann have contributed significantly to how the examination of these processes might be evaluated in the context of an idealised vision of public **deliberation** and participation while drawing attention to important power imbalances (see also Chapter 6's discussion of communicative action). A third influential tradition derives from work by theorists such as Murray Edelman, Harold Blumer, and Erving Goffman. The focus by these scholars on how political language and symbols lead to the selective definition and interpretation of policy issues and social problems anchors contemporary research on **framing** and media influence (see also Chapter 7, on social representations theory). Another major strand of research derives from the cognitive revolution in social psychology, with general theories of information processing and persuasion applied to the study of political communication (as in Chapter 4 on social influence).

This chapter reviews and integrates several of these major strands of scholarship. A specific emphasis, similar to other chapters in this text, is that when it comes to the prospects for facilitating social change in society, political communication is rarely a level playing field. Even in the most vibrant democracies, government officials and powerful interest groups are often able to steer news and public attention to key political issues while also simultaneously defining them in advantageous ways. However, applying theories developed from this research is also the starting point for creating the political conditions that might catalyse social change and wider public participation, addressing social problems and injustice, and rebuilding public trust. Across countries, media and political systems have changed dramatically and will continue to evolve in unexpected ways. Despite these changes, the several decades of research reviewed in this chapter offer a set of guidelines for how to communicate about complex problems and issues; how to structure media presentations; how to strategically design messages; and how to effectively reach and empower citizens.

Political communication, the media, and public perceptions

Even today, many public officials, commentators, and journalists still define the public in overly idealised and inaccurate terms. This still dominant perspective conceives of **public opinion** and behaviour as consisting of individual judgements arrived at on an issue, candidate, or government leader after conscious and knowledgeable deliberation. The key component of this assumption is that the wider public possesses both the motivation and the ability to understand the complexities of policy debates and to draw connections between their preferences and the specific positions of candidates and officials (a similar assumption, historically, has shaped health communication, see Chapter 14).

Yet a preponderance of evidence from the public opinion literature finds that the public is generally more 'miserly' than fully informed. Whether a person is making a choice about a political figure or buying a car, research in social psychology shows that individuals are far more likely to 'satisfice' than 'optimise' their use of information, relying on available heuristics as a means to process new information, form attitudes, and reach decisions (Fiske and Taylor, 1991). Specific to political opinions and behaviour, the **miserly public** tends to rely as short cuts on ideology, social identity such as religion, and the information most readily available to them via the media and interpersonal sources (Nisbet, 2005; Popkin, 1991). As a result, rather than directly persuading or shifting the direction of public preferences, much of the influence of political communication occurs *indirectly*, activating and intensifying existing preferences and views. There are indeed some citizens who change their minds during the course of a campaign, but these so-called 'switchers' are rarely the idealised well-informed and deliberative voters.

Rather, people who change their preferences have been found to be the least knowledgeable, the least attentive, and the least politically sophisticated.

Given the nature of how the miserly public forms opinions and reaches decisions, power in politics more generally turns on controlling media and public attention to different issues while simultaneously defining – or framing – these issues in selective ways. By setting the agenda of issues the public considers most important, the news media shape the criteria that the public uses to evaluate candidates, leaders, and institutions. In addition, by strategically framing issues around certain dimensions of a debate at the expense of other considerations, the news media and various political actors create causal stories for the public about who or what might be at the root of a problem and what should be done in terms of policy options and political actions.

Agenda-setting: shaping public priorities. One of the most common findings in political communication is the ability of the media to direct the focus of the public to certain issues over others. The media 'may not be successful most of the time in telling people what to think', famously observed Bernard Cohen in 1963, 'but it is stunningly successful in telling its readers what to think about' (p. 13). Subsequent research on the **'agenda-setting'** effect of the media has provided overwhelming evidence that the issues portrayed in the media shape the issue priorities of the public. By giving attention to some issues over others, the media influences what the public perceives as most pressing and most important (Iyengar and Kinder, 1987; McCombs and Shaw, 1972; McCombs, 2007). Even as changes in the media system and political campaigns over the past decade have created many more news and information choices for citizens, public opinion research continues to show an almost direct one-to-one correlation between the issues dominating the overall news agenda and public attention (see e.g. the Pew News Index, 2009).

Researchers explain the agenda-setting influence of the media by way of a memory-based model of opinion formation which assumes that: (a) some issues or pieces of information are more accessible in a person's mind than others; (b) opinion is to a large degree a function of how readily accessible these certain considerations are; and (c) accessibility is mostly a function of 'how much' or 'how recently' a person has been exposed to these certain considerations (Kim, Scheufele, and Shanahan, 2002; Scheufele, 2000). In surveys, for example, when individuals are asked to describe the issues of most concern to them, they search quickly across their short-term memory, and are most likely to draw upon those issues that are most readily salient and therefore easily recalled. Research shows that accessibility is typically a direct function of news exposure: the more attention an individual pays to the news generally or to a particular news outlet, the more likely it is that their perceptions will track the agenda of issues portrayed in the news or at the individuals' specific preferred news choice.

Priming: Why the news focus matters. Media agenda-setting effects matter because they 'prime' public evaluations. The issues that receive the heaviest coverage in the news are not unexpectedly the standards by which the public tends to evaluate a candidate, a political party, institutions, or a corporation (Iyengar and Kinder, 1987). Psychologically, **priming** effects derive from the memory-based model of opinion-formation discussed earlier. For example, when voters are asked in the context of a campaign to evaluate competing candidates and parties, if national security is a dominant focus at the time in news coverage, then the public are on average more likely to give weight to this issue over other issues. Under these conditions, voters are more likely to favour the candidate who is perceived as best able to deal with national security. If news attention switches to a different issue, then the evaluative criteria applied by voters are also likely to shift, and under these conditions a different candidate may gain in the polls (Scheufele, 2000).

Research on priming offers clear implications for communication strategies and initiatives that might seek to achieve social change in society. Candidates, elected officials, and corporations have a strong intuitive if not formal sense of how the news media can prime public evaluations. Therefore, if an organisation or group can elevate news attention to an issue, politicians and powerful institutions are more likely to take action on these issues in order to protect their public image. Media priming also helps explain why major corporations have invested heavily in social responsibility campaigns. Over the past decade, with rising news attention to issues such as climate change, fair trade, and labour practices, corporations now recognise that consumers are more likely to give greater weight to their perceived social record on these issues. As a result, companies such as British Petroleum and Wal-Mart have combined real changes in corporate practice with advertising, media, and branding campaigns to promote their environmental and labour records.

Framing: Defining meaning and solutions. The news media and political strategists not only have the ability to shape public priorities, but they also often 'frame' attention around only certain dimensions of a complex issue while ignoring others. When an elected official or journalist 'frames' an issue, they communicate why the issue matters; who or what might be responsible; and what should be done in terms of action (Entman, 1993; Gamson and Modigliani, 1989). Frames are an unavoidable aspect of political communication. They are used by audiences as 'interpretative schema' to make sense of and discuss an issue; by journalists to condense complex events into interesting and appealing news reports; by policy-makers to define policy options and reach decisions; and by experts to communicate to broader audiences (Scheufele, 1999). (See also Chapter 7's discussion of Social Representations Theory and also discussion of schema in Chapter 5, Pragmatic Theory, cognition, and social relations.)

In terms of psychological accounts of the influence of framing, Price and Tewksbury's (1997) applicability model argues that a message frame is only effective if it is relevant – or 'applicable' – to a specific existing interpretive schema acquired through socialisation processes or other types of social learning. Specifically, an issue has been successfully framed when there is a fit between the line of reasoning a message or news story suggests on an issue and the presence of those existing mental associations within a particular audience. Alternatively, if a frame draws connections that are not relevant to something a segment of the public already values or understands, then the message is likely to be ignored or to lack personal significance (Scheufele and Tewksbury, 2007).

Complementing these psychological accounts, sociologists such as William Gamson have promoted a 'social constructivist' explanation of framing. According to this research, in order to make sense of political issues, citizens use as resources the frames available in media coverage, but integrate these packages with the frames forged by way of personal experience or conversations with others. Media frames might help set the terms of the debate among citizens, but rarely, if ever, do they exclusively determine public opinion. Instead, as part of a 'frame contest,' one interpretative package might gain influence because it resonates with popular culture or a series of events, fits with media routines or practices, and/or is heavily sponsored by élites (Gamson, 1992; Price, Nir and Capella, 2005).

In everyday conversation, news coverage, and in strategic messages, the latent meaning of a frame is often translated instantaneously by specific types of framing devices such as catchphrases, metaphors, sound bites, graphics, and allusions to history, culture, and/or literature (Gamson, 1992). For example, in the UK and Europe, Greenpeace has used the term 'frankenfood' to redefine food biotechnology in terms of unknown risks and consequences rather than the industry-promoted focus on solving world hunger or adapting to climate change. Similarly, in the US, anti-evolutionists have coined the slogan 'teach the controversy', which instantaneously signals their preferred interpretation that there are holes in the theory of evolution and that teaching rival explanations for life's origins is really a matter of intellectual freedom (Nisbet, 2009b).

Perhaps no other area of political communication research has received more attention and direct professional application than framing. Over the past decade, academic scholars have joined with government agencies, not-for-profit organisations, and advocates to examine how seemingly intractable policy problems such as poverty or climate change are currently framed in political discourse and how new frames of reference might catalyse wider public attention, understanding, and action (see Box 14.1 for discussion on climate change). This process begins with audience research techniques such as in-depth interviews, surveys, and media content analysis that

Box 14.1 Framing and climate change

Survey analyses depict the American public for the most part as still largely divided and disengaged on climate change, despite overwhelming expert agreement about the urgency of the problem. Advocates for policy action on climate change – including environmentalists, political leaders, and some scientists – have sought to rally support among Americans by framing the issue in terms of a looming environmental disaster or 'climate crisis.' To instantly translate their preferred interpretation, these advocates have relied on vivid depictions of specific climate impacts, including hurricane devastation and famous cities under water due to future sea-level rise. In a leading example, publicity for Al Gore's documentary on climate change's effects, *An Inconvenient Truth*, dramatised climate change as an environmental Frankenstein's monster, including a hurricane-shaped plume spewing from a smoke stack on its movie poster and a trailer telling audiences to expect 'the most terrifying film you will ever see'. Yet this line of communication was effectively reframed by sceptics of climate change as liberal 'alarmism'. This challenge – rendered easier because the target of ridicule (Gore) was a partisan figure – quickly activate a counter-interpretation of lingering scientific uncertainty and the heuristics of partisanship and liberal media bias. The result is a public that is unsure about the scientific basis for man-made climate change and ambivalent about proposed policy actions (Nisbet, 2009a).

To generate greater wider public engagement on climate change, communication experts have suggested that messages about the issue need to shift away from an exclusive emphasis on environmental disaster and include new frames that are personally relevant and acceptable to broader and more diverse segments of Americans. Over time, these new meanings for climate change, argue experts, are likely to be key drivers of public engagement and, eventually, policy action.

One suggested strategy is to frame climate change not just as an environmental issue but also as a public health problem, calling attention to the scientifically well-understood linkages to asthma, allergies, infectious disease, and the health risks of events such as heat waves or severe flooding. A focus on public health also shifts the visualisation of climate change away from remote arctic regions, peoples, and animals to more socially proximate neighbours and places such as suburbs and cities. Research involving in-depth interviews with representative segments of Americans finds that when climate change is introduced as a health problem – with information then provided about climate policy actions that will also lead to health benefits – this reframing of the issue is positively responded to by a broad ideological cross-section of respondents (Maibach, Nisbet, Akerlof, Baldwin and Diao, in press).

systematically identify the metaphors, examples, and mental frameworks that the public, journalists, and experts use to understand, discuss, and make choices about the issue. This research then informs government agencies, organisations, expert institutions, and media producers on how to better reach specific groups within the general public, build trust, and adapt their communication efforts to motivate greater attention, understanding, and participation (see Frameworks Institute, 2009; Nisbet 2009b for overviews).

Knowledge, civic engagement, and the news media

The news media and campaign strategies do not just have indirect and subtle influences on our perceptions through processes such as agenda-setting, priming, and framing, but they are also important sources of informal learning on the part of the public. Across countries, an engaged and public affairs-savvy citizenry is widely idealised as critical to a fully functioning political system. In this tradition, political knowledge is the glue that holds together civic culture. As Delli Carpini and Keeter (1996) review, individuals with greater levels of political knowledge are on average more politically tolerant, hold stronger support for democratic principles, are more likely to participate in politics, and are better able to draw connections between their policy preferences and their support for specific political candidates.

The knowledge gap effect. Given the importance of political knowledge, scholars have devoted considerable attention to how and under what conditions individuals learn about politics from the news media. In one major implication for civic engagement, rates of learning from the news media appear to be substantially different across audience segments. Specifically, there is evidence of a persistent **knowledge gap effect**, whereby information from the media is more easily acquired by segments of the population with higher socioeconomic status (SES) and more education (Tichenor, Donohue, and Olien, 1970). As news attention to a social problem or political campaign increases over time, it serves to widen – not narrow – gaps between the information-rich and information-poor, the latter segment disproportionately comprised of lower-status individuals. Moreover, given the strong connections between knowledge and forms of participation, studies show that these gaps in information also lead to correlated gaps in participation (Eveland and Scheufele, 2000). The reality of the knowledge gap phenomenon, therefore, reinforces status quo differences in resources and participation within society, and poses challenges to using the news media to catalyse social change.

Why is it easier for members of socially advantaged groups to learn about political affairs from the new media? On the one hand, their existing levels of knowledge and media habits increase the ease and efficiency with which they can process and learn new information (Price and Zaller, 1993). Individual differences in motivation also play a role. According to several scholars, disparities in knowledge accrue because of differences in the perceived utility of information: higher SES segments find news and public affairs information more relevant and compelling and, as a result, pay more attention to it (Kwak, 1999).

The structure of a particular country's media system also contributes to disparities in knowledge. For example, in cross-national comparisons, researchers find that the market-driven model of the US media system produces lower levels of hard news knowledge and wider knowledge gaps than are found in European countries which utilise a public service model (Curran, Iyengar, Lund, and Salovaara-Moring, 2009; Iyengar, Hahn, Bonfadelli, and Marr, 2009). In Finland, Denmark, and the UK, for example, publicly funded news programming airs during prime-time evening television hours and across multiple time slots, thereby making it more accessible – sometimes incidentally so – to a broader audience; in contrast, in the US, commercial television networks broadcast news in the early and late evenings, and reserve prime-time for entertainment content (Curran et al., 2009). As such, news consumption in the US is more clearly confined to those with sufficient motivation or preference for public affairs.

Another factor related to the knowledge gap, especially in terms of public understanding of highly technical or complex issues, is the level of political controversy. Analyses of survey data by Bonfadelli and Bauer (2002) finds that in European countries with greater levels of political controversy over biotechnology, news coverage of the issue expanded beyond just élite print outlets to include coverage from the tabloid press and television, broadening the news audience for the issue and thereby lessening gaps in knowledge. But there was one key related factor. Specifically, in countries that had greater parity across citizens relative to SES, controversy served to narrow knowledge differences among citizens. But in countries with wider disparities in SES, controversy had little impact on gaps in knowledge across segments of the public. Bonfadelli and Bauer reason that in countries with greater SES disparity, news organisations 'ghettoise' coverage to just a few élite outlets, even under conditions of political controversy, with other media channels paying far less attention to the topic, diminishing opportunities for learning among lower SES segments.

Learning across types of media. Besides differential gains in learning by social status, studies have also focused on differences in the potential for civic engagement across print, broadcast, and online news users. Newspaper reading, in particular, has traditionally been associated with greater levels of civic engagement. Studies have found that newspaper readers tend to have a stronger sense of community and national identity, and a richer network of overall social connections (McLeod et al., 1996). Newspaper coverage is also particularly good at identifying broader thematic issues or problems of potential concern that may require citizen action or involvement (Stamm, Emig and Hesse, 1997). Through similar means, consumption of quality sources of public affairs television has also been found to have a positive impact on these dimensions of civic engagement, though to a lesser degree than newspaper use (Scheufele, Nisbet, and Brossard, 2004).

While these findings concerning traditional media effects are well documented, views still diverge on how Internet use may shape wider public participation and influence in society. Specifically, many scholars fear that the Internet likely strengthens rather than shifts traditional patterns of political communication effects, reinforcing gaps across countries between the resource rich and the resource poor, while exacerbating cleavages based on ideology or political identity. The conclusion is that, at societal level, the Internet likely promotes status quo power structures and political gridlock, and may actually further widen disparities in civic engagement (Dimaggio, Hargittai, Celeste and Shafer, 2004; Nisbet and Scheufele, 2004; Norris, 2001).

There are different factors that might account for the reinforcement effects of the Internet. First is the miserly way the public typically use the media. As explained earlier in this chapter, the availability of media information does not necessarily lead to the use of that information. Citizens who do choose to take advantage of Internet-based political information sources are likely to be characterised by their personal resources – including time, money, and technology skills – as well as by motivation, including confidence and feelings of efficacy (Norris, 2001). Consider also that the most influential and widely consumed content online is still produced by traditional news organisations, large media companies, powerful interest groups, and government agencies or institutions. These entities maintain a disproportionate control over the agenda of issues attended to and discussed online, disproportionately influence how these issues are framed, and despite calls to do otherwise, continue to cater to high SES audiences. This reality is unlikely to change anytime soon, despite increased capability through blogs and other digital applications for individuals and independent media to convey information. Even as the media system rapidly evolves, studies find that traditional newspaper coverage – distributed in print and online – still remains at the core of the news and information ecology, serving as the major source for original reporting on problems and policy debates, with newspaper reporting driving the agenda and discussion at cable news, blogs, and other new media (see Knight, 2009 for a discussion).

Though research points to the many problems and barriers to wider learning from the media about politics, this same scholarship suggests several initiatives that might narrow disparities across audiences. First, as Eveland (2003) suggests, whether it is print, television, or online media, it is important to think about how attributes that vary across these media may facilitate different modes of learning and knowledge gain. As he describes, dimensions such as interactivity, user control, narrative structure, and textuality need to be examined carefully by researchers and media producers, with each of these attributes potentially facilitating greater learning on the part of wider audiences.

Second, looking to the future, Bennett (2007) and others have argued that in order to widen the net of informal learning, media producers need to consider a new generation of audiences who arrive at public affairs content with very different expectations. Specifically, younger audiences have a unique set of issue priorities from their older counterparts, with a stronger preference for more globally focused topics such as the environment, poverty, or human rights and far less interest in conflict-driven coverage that focuses on traditional ideological cleavages. Younger audiences also expect their public affairs media to be 'participatory', meaning that they want to be able to actively comment, recommend, share, and contribute to coverage; and they want direct information on how they can become politically involved on the issue. (See also discussion of participatory journalism in health communication, Chapter 14.)

Third, other scholars have argued for increased investment in school-based programmes that provide a 'civics media literacy' curriculum for students from lower socio-economic backgrounds. Research shows that participation in a civics media literacy curriculum promotes increased student news use at home and increased discussions about politics with their parents. As a result, evidence indicates that these types of programmes not only boost student attention and learning about politics, but have similar influences on their lower SES parents (McDevitt and Chaffee, 2000).

Political deliberation and social interactions. If there are many limits and biases in public knowledge of politics, what exactly then should be the role of the public in decision-making? Should government and other organisations consult the public on questions of policy and what might be models for doing so?

Participatory and deliberative theorists argue for enlarging the civic role of ordinary citizens by engaging them directly in deliberations about public policy (Barber, 1984; Fishkin, 1995; Matthews, 1994). Deliberation, when it takes the form of reasoned and open-minded discussion, is expected to increase tolerance for opposing viewpoints, deepen awareness and understanding of one's own political preferences, increase involvement in civic and political life, promote greater efficacy and **social trust**, and increase the efficiency and effectiveness of policy (for a review, see Delli Carpini, Cook, and Jacobs, 2004).

Several scholars have investigated the impact of deliberation on public opinion and civic engagement by bringing citizens together to talk about public issues in controlled environments, both in face-to-face 'deliberative polls' (Fishkin and Luskin, 1999) and online (Price and Cappella, 2002). These studies have found that formal deliberations about political issues can increase knowledge about politics, enhance the quality of public opinion, and foster attitudes and behaviours consistent with political participation. Moreover, informal, everyday political conversation, as it occurs unprompted among ordinary citizens, is associated with similarly positive outcomes, such as opinion quality, civic and political participation, and political knowledge (Nisbet and Scheufele, 2004; Scheufele, Nisbet, and Brossard, 2004).

When specific features of the discussion environment are examined more closely, however, findings emerge that may temper this optimism. Political disagreement, which features centrally in most definitions of deliberative democracy, may actually serve to deter people from participating in deliberative exercises (Hibbing and Theiss-Morse, 2002). Moreover, when disagreement is aired, any benefit it has for increasing political tolerance and fostering more informed opinions may be outweighed by its potential to induce ambivalence and political inaction (Mutz, 2006).

The idea that political discussion will contribute to more reasoned opinion is itself challenged by the social psychological tendency towards group **polarisation**, which occurs when members of a group, following discussion on some topic, move towards a more extreme point in the direction of the initial opinion taken up by the group (Moscovici, 1985a). Group polarisation is problematic to the extent that it leads diverse social groups to adopt increasingly extreme and oppositional viewpoints, thereby interfering with the ability to agree upon solutions to collective problems (see also Chapter 4).

Group polarisation is an increasing concern of the online environment. Cass Sunstein (2001) has been most vocal about these concerns, arguing that the Internet makes it easier for individuals to selectively expose themselves to like-minded viewpoints, and, as a result, the potential for group polarisation and extremism is exacerbated online. The discrepancy between Sunstein's (2001) view of the online discussion environment and Price and Cappella's (2002) more optimistic findings regarding the value of online deliberation reflects an important difference between the democratic *potential* of deliberation – both in online and face-to-face environments – and how it actually plays out in the real world. When the conditions are right – whether those conditions be the purpose of the deliberation, the type of participants involved, or the rules governing interactions – deliberation can offer substantial democratic benefits. What Sunstein reminds us, however, is that these conditions are not always realisable in the real world of political conversation.

Public evaluations of the political system and the news media

The media and communication campaigns not only influence public choices, learning, and discourse, but they also play an influential role in shaping public trust in institutions and fellow citizens. As discussed in this section, this has significant implications for the ability of citizens to work cooperatively to solve social problems.

Social and Political Trust. Among the key perceptions shaped by the news media and by political campaigns are social trust and political trust. Described as the 'chicken soup of social life', social trust is the belief that the world is a generally benign place and that other people are generally well motivated (Uslaner, 2000). Social trust helps alleviate concerns of individuals that others in society will simply pursue their own narrow interests instead of working towards a greater good. **Political trust** complements social trust by assuring individuals that institutions and their officials work towards a common good, that government services are reliable and responsive, and that, if need be, government can step in effectively when problems are so great that they exceed the capacity of individuals or organisations to solve them on their own (Nee and Ingram, 1998). Both forms of trust enable individuals in society to work together, view certain expectations or outcomes as predictable, and build feelings of overall solidarity and identity.

Unfortunately, over the past two decades, across national settings, there has been a remarkable decline in overall social and political trust. A number of factors account for the overall decline in trust including scandals that drive a loss in public confidence, an absence of efforts at effective trust-building on the part of major institutions, and the increasing complexity and diversity of modern societies. Scholars, however, also note that as news coverage, especially television, has increasingly covered politics in terms of conflict and win-at-all-costs strategy, this stylistic focus has promoted widespread public cynicism about the intentions and goals of elected officials (Cappella and Jamieson, 1997; Mutz, 2006). In the US, a growing number of conservative media outlets have openly attacked government institutions and promoted fear of specific social out-groups such as immigrants or Muslims, likely further undermining overall political and social trust (Jamieson and Cappella 2007). Other researchers point to heavy TV news attention to crime as undermining social trust across communities, while entertainment media use displaces opportunities citizens might have to connect with others (Putnam, 2000; Morgan, Shanahan, and Signorelli, 2008). Yet other scholars contend that not all media are the same relative to political and social trust, and dispute direct evidence for a time displacement influence (Moy and Pfau, 2000). According to this line of research, use of quality public affairs news – especially newspaper reading – is found to promote political and social trust, enhancing the readers' connections to institutions and their community members (Shah, Kwak, and Holbert, 2001: Shah, Yoon, and McLeod, 2001).

As solutions to the decline in political trust in democracies, scholars and practitioners alike have called for the need for new types of dialogue-based initiatives that bring a diversity of citizens into direct contact with government officials and their institutions (Einsiedel, 2008; McComas, 2006; Yankelovich, 1991). They have also emphasised the use of digital media tools to increase government transparency and to sponsor direct citizen interaction. Others have pointed to the need for research on effectively reframing how the role of government is discussed relative to major problems such as poverty, explanations that also counter the free market as a government alternative (Nisbet, 2009b).

Media trust and perceptions of bias. If the media have contributed to a loss in confidence in government, journalists and their news organisations have also suffered their own significant decline in public perceptions. Across national settings, there is an ever pervasive belief in various forms of media bias. In the US, over the past two decades, the dominant belief regarding media bias is that that the mainstream news media favour liberal causes and political candidates. Yet, when researchers conduct content analyses to search for systematic patterns of partisan bias in coverage of elections, across studies they are unable to find definitive evidence (D'Alessio D. and Allen, 2000). If social scientists using the best tools available to them find it difficult to observe hard evidence of liberal bias, why are beliefs among the public so widespread? Moreover, across country setting and issue, what

Box 14.2   Perceptions of media bias: The Israeli–Palestinian conflict

The hostile media effect was first demonstrated reliably by Vallone et al. (1985) in the context of news about the ongoing conflict in the Middle East between Israelis and Palestinians. Undergraduate students from Stanford University, who self-identified as either pro-Arab, pro-Israeli, or neutral on the issue of the Israeli–Palestinian conflict, were recruited to participate in an experimental study. Subjects viewed a selection of US network news coverage detailing the events leading up to a 1982 massacre of Palestinians by a Lebanese militia group and the questions of Israeli responsibility in its aftermath. Results showed that students who characterised themselves as pro-Israeli saw the news as biased *against* Israel, whereas pro-Arab students saw the news as biased in *favour* of Israel. Thus, both groups saw the news coverage as hostile to their own position, whereas neutral viewers perceived the coverage as relatively balanced.

What might explain such discrepant perceptions? According to Vallone et al. (1985), when individuals are heavily invested in an issue – whether the Israeli–Palestinian conflict, climate change, or gay marriage – they tend to see that issue in black *or* white terms. Objective news, however, by representing both sides of a controversial issue, portrays the issue in a shade of grey (i.e. as both black *and* white). Thus, in the eyes of partisans, giving facts on both sides equal weight constitutes a hostile bias. In addition to this *evaluative* explanation, Vallone et al. (1985) also provide evidence for a *perceptual* explanation for the hostile media effect, whereby partisans actually see completely different stimuli. This latter mechanism, often termed 'selective categorization,' has emerged, in recent research, as the more well-supported explanation for the hostile media effect (Schmitt, Gunther, and Liebhart, 2004).

The hostile media perception presents news organisations and professional journalists with a nearly impossible job as even fair, balanced coverage of controversial issues will be perceived as biased and antagonistic by members of the groups being covered. Perceptions of hostile news coverage may also contribute to a broader mistrust of media and government institutions and, in so doing, undermine faith in the democratic process. Tsfati and Cohen (2005) demonstrated these relationships in a study conducted among Jewish Israeli settlers in the hotly contested Gaza Strip. At the time of the study, in 2004, the Israeli government had proposed a plan under which Jewish settlers would be relocated and Israeli Defence Forces withdrawn from Gaza. A survey of Jewish settlers facing displacement from Gaza revealed that they saw news coverage as providing an unfair, negative treatment of their group, despite a content analysis that showed a relatively balanced – even positive – treatment (Sheafer, 2005, cf. Tsfati and Cohen, 2005). Moreover, the settlers' hostile media perceptions were associated with weakened trust in the Israeli media as a whole and in Israeli democracy, as well as with heightened intentions among the settlers to use violence to resist their possible relocation.

explains the difference between subjective perceptions of media bias and objective indicators relative to coverage?

In research on perceptions of the news media, credibility is understood as a subjective assessment, influenced by the partisan or ideological background of the audience and the claims about bias that might emanate from trusted sources such as political commentators or like-minded friends. In the US context, these claims are typically focused on a liberal bias charged by conservative elites, and reinforce a widespread belief among conservative-leaning audiences (Watts, Domke, Shah, and Fan, 1999). Audiences, then, do not typically assess story content on its own merits but rather on the basis of preconceived notions about the news media – often stemming from journalists' tendency in many stories to cover and reflect on their own potential liberal bias. A number of other studies have also suggested that individuals' expectations for bias in a news source or in the media, more generally, are likely to influence their perceptions of bias in news coverage (Arpan and Raney, 2003; Baum and Gussin, 2007).

Perhaps the most crucial determinant of perceptions of bias in the news, however, is the extent to which news coverage is seen as disagreeing with one's own views. Individuals who feel most strongly about an issue tend to see their own side's views as being more a product of objective analysis and normative concerns, and less influenced by ideology, than the other side's views (Robinson, Keltner, Ward, and Ross, 1995). This human tendency translates directly to judgements about the media. In a range of studies, when news audiences who hew to opposing sides on an issue are given the same news coverage of the topic to evaluate, both view this identical coverage as biased in favour of the other side (Gunther and Schmitt, 2004; Vallone et al., 1985). The phenomenon is commonly referred to as the **'hostile media effect.'** Researchers believe that the explanation for this hostile media effect is selective categorisation: opposing partisans attend to, process, and recall identical content from a news presentation but mentally categorise and label the same aspects of a story differently – as hostile to their own position (Schmitt, Gunther, and Liebhart, 2004).

The original hostile media effect assumes that news coverage is inherently balanced. The *relative* hostile media perception (Gunther, Christen, Liebhart, and Chia, 2001) relaxes this assumption, making it applicable to news that is slanted in favour of or against a particular issue. In the presence of the relative hostile media effect, supporters and opponents of a given issue perceive bias in a consistent direction (i.e. leaning towards one side), but each group perceives coverage as significantly more unfavourable to their own position relative to those in the other group. In other words, partisans perceive *less* bias in news coverage slanted to support their view than their opponents on the other side of the issue.

Interestingly, then, whereas the implication of the original hostile media effect is a partisan public perceiving media bias where none was present and thus potentially rejecting useful information, the implications of the relative hostile media effect are somewhat different. Of consequence here is that partisans will fail to recognise bias in news that *is in fact* biased, in instances when that bias is congruent with their pre-existing views. This bias against news bias is troubling. Americans' trust in news sources has become deeply polarised in recent years – with Republicans, for example, attributing more credibility to the conservative Fox News and less to most other news organisations than Democrats (Pew Research Center, 2008). In other countries, similar perceptions of a Left or Right bias to news – or alternatively a bias relative to national or ethnic identity – exist.

In each context, as news – particularly on cable TV and online – is infused with increasing amounts of opinion and ideology, this may make it even easier for partisans to validate their personal political beliefs by accepting at face value information that comports with their views while rejecting information that advocates for the other side. Thus, the relative hostile media effect may not only reflect partisan divides in news perceptions but may also contribute to the further polarisation of political attitudes and knowledge across political systems.

Conclusion

The findings from political communication research may make it very easy to simply critique the news media, campaigns, and the public. Indeed, there is an unfortunate 'dismal science' aspect to the field: the more things change in political campaigns or in the media system, the more they appear to stay the same relative to reinforcing power imbalances, ideological cleavages, and public alienation. Yet if anything, this research should not be viewed narrowly as a direct indictment of the interaction between the media and our political systems, but rather as a powerful resource for working towards social change.

If this is going to happen, however, there need to be far more collaborations and connections between research theorists and practitioners. Scholars have an obligation to translate and articulate the implications of their research so that it can serve as a blueprint for professionally oriented students who want to tilt the communication playing field in favour of social change within their communities, countries, or cross-nationally. This research can also help clarify for journalists and political leaders the norms, ethics, and goals of political communication, focusing their practices and strategies on the factors that promote a functioning political system. Across countries, initiatives built on the foundation of theory and research will be necessary to restore and maintain public faith in government and the media.

15
Science Communication

Jane Gregory

Keywords: Boundary work; deficit model; dominant model; popular science; public engagement; public understanding of science.

'True descendants of Prometheus, the science writers take the fire from the scientific Olympus, the laboratories and the universities, and bring it down to the people.'

New York Times journalist William Laurence, 1943

'... if the UK is to take full advantage of the opportunities for creating wealth and improving quality of life offered by scientific discovery and technological development, it is crucial that we develop new approaches to bring scientists and the public together in a constructive dialogue to explore emerging issues.'

UK Government Office of Science and Innovation, 2006

'Scientists and engineers can change the world, but first they need to get over their "serious marketing problem".'

Google co-founder Larry Page, 2007

Introduction

A common stereotype of the scientist is of someone withdrawn from society and isolated from its values (Haynes, 1994; Howard, 2007). However, modern science rarely generates knowledge and products from such individuals: instead, it is a collective enterprise, organised via collaboration and competition among groups that may be multidisciplinary and geographically dispersed (Wagner, 2009). The professional norms of the scientific community demand that knowledge and practice be open to scrutiny, conducted without prejudice and shared widely (Merton, 1968). So science is, ideally, a public activity, and secrecy, private ownership, and personal knowledge are the hallmarks of invalid knowledge. Scientists function not so much through a profession, bound together, for example, by common accreditation, nor as a trade, bound by common skills, but as a community in which a wide diversity of knowledges, practices, objects, and people are held together by communication. (The idea of a community-formed-by-communication is one of this book's central motifs; see for example Chapter 12's discussion of religion as communication, and Chapter 7's discussion of how the representations of marginalised communities can bolster threatened identities.) According to sociologist of science John Ziman, 'the fundamental social institution of science is ... its system of communication' (Ziman, 1984, 2002).

The extent and limits of this community-formed-by-communication are a core concern in science studies (Shinn and Whitley, 1985; Collins, 1981; Gieryn, 1995, 1999; Lewenstein, 1995; Hilgartner, 1990, Wagner, 2009). The scientific community occupies social space, consumes resources, and contributes ideologies and products to a society which may give and receive these with varying degrees of enthusiasm. The negotiation between science and society for science's licence to practise is one that extends the scientific community into the spheres of politics, business, and everyday life, blurring the traditional distinction between the professional communication among scientists and public communication with non-scientists (Hilgartner, 1990; Wagner, 2009). However, the term 'science communication' usually refers to this public communication, from scientific experts to laypeople, of the cognitive content of science; and its products are labelled '**popular science**'.

Characterising popular science

What does popular science look like?

Authors, publishers and readers collude in shaping the character of popular science. Unlike professional scientific communications, it tends to be produced by individuals rather than by groups; and it also claims to be the latest thing, or to intimate the future, where professional science acknowledges its own imminent obsolescence. Professional science 'makes a contribution to' or 'takes a step towards'; popular science already knows the answer. It dispenses with detailed data, graphics, and references to other works that typify professional science communication, and instead conceals this evidence of human endeavour to speak as if with the voice of nature itself (Fahnestock, 1993; Bucchi, 2004).

Nature does not tell us what to do, and nor does science communication: in this regard it is different, for example, from health communication (see Chapter 13) and risk communication, both of which aim to guide behaviour and decision making in particular contexts. Popular science can be merely spectacular or amazing (a quality sometimes called 'gee-whizz'): it does not have to be meaningful or comprehensible. Bucchi (2004) identifies the idea of science as very complicated as a widespread conception, if not an outright ideology, of science communication; scientists are therefore very clever. Bucchi dates this ideology to the early twentieth century, when the sudden expansion of the newspaper industry in Europe coincided with the scientific crisis of the 'new physics', and scientists laboured to explain relativity theory and quantum mechanics to laypeople in the popular press. The metaphor of 'translation' is often used to describe this work, and it provides opportunities for skilled translators such as journalists.

Box 15.1　Popular and professional communication

This box compares one professional and one popular book produced by members of a knowledge community of specialist scientists. One name appears on both covers: Peter Irving is an early-career consultant gastroenterologist at a London teaching hospital (2010). He has published extensively in peer-reviewed journals. In 2006 he was co-editor of the book *Clinical Dilemmas in Inflammatory Bowel Disease*: 'evidence-based guidance to answer more than 60 controversial clinical questions … providing quick but detailed answers … for all medical professionals involved in the care of patients with IBD …' (Irving et al., 2006). In 2008 Irving was co-author of *Inflammatory Bowel Disease: The Facts*. It 'offers practical advice … in a clear and accessible style, written by leading authorities in the field … [it] is written primarily for sufferers … it discusses modern approaches to the problems … and provides an up-to-date and evidence-based factual guide to the disease' (Langmead and Irving, 2008).

Epistemic status	*'Dilemmas'*	*'Facts'*
Date	2006	2008
Literary style	'Quick but detailed'	'Clear and accessible'
Discursive mode	Controversy, questions, speculation	Authority, answers, instruction ('straight from the experts')
Readership	Professionals	Laypeople
Sales ratio (Amazon rankings)	1	10
Contributing authors	100	4
References	1200	0
Exclamation marks	Very few	Many
Numerical tables and graphs	Yes	No
Illustrations	Diagrams and photographs	Drawings
Scope claimed	Modest, partial: 'selected with a view to covering many of the areas'	Ambitious, complete: 'all the information you need'
Time horizon	'Inevitably, the book will soon become out of date'	'modern … up to date'

The ideology of the 'clever scientist' co-constructs the less clever or ignorant layperson. Jurdant (1993) notes that popular science texts are often explicit about what the reader is presumed not to know, or is mistaken about, as a preamble to reducing ignorance and correcting misconceptions. Laypeople are expected to be surprised by the revelations of popular science; and they are reminded of this by a litter of exclamation marks (!). So science communication often has a moral or normative dimension: it presumes that the public knows little *and should know more* about science. This has been characterised as the **'deficit model'** of the **public understanding of science** – where the unsatisfactory deficit in the public's knowledge is in comparison to what scientists know, and it can be 'fixed' by communicating science.

Jurdant (1969) also notes a broader ideology of science communication: it is scientistic, and works to advertise the fundamental values of science: empiricism, reductionism, materialism, hypothetico-deductivism, the reliability of scientific truth claims and the authority of those who make them. Jurdant also characterises popular science as the autobiography of science: it is the story that science tells about itself. Science communicates itself to laypeople as idealised and ideologically pristine, despite the inevitable compromises of everyday practice. So popular science, as science's public story, often enhances and tidies up the scientistic aspects of science; for example, by drawing direct lines between experiment and discovery when the route might have meandered, or by foregrounding facts in public when dilemma and controversy may characterise the professional milieu. Latour (1987) characterises this as the epistemological 'Janus face' of science, contrasting internal and external relations. Some scientists maintain a feud with constructivist sociologists of science because of the sociologists' exploration, outside of the boundaries of the scientific community, of the epistemological contingencies of scientific knowledge (Pinch, 2001).

What does science communication do?

Explicit in scientists' discourse about science communication is a commitment to enlightenment ideals of knowledge as a public good; and sharing

Box 15.2   The functions of popular science

- Practical: transferable knowledge and problem-solving skills
- Political: power, order, and stability
- Enlightenment: entertainment, education, and culture
- Publicity: ideology and product marketing
- Boundary work: establishing authority through identity and difference
- Reflexivity: explaining to oneself
- Public relations: reputation management and community-building

it gives science value as culture (Gregory and Miller, 1998). They argue that popular science can be useful knowledge, and that scientific epistemology provides skills for everyday problem-solving. For popularisers on the political Left, science communication also empowers individuals and nations (e.g. Crowther, 1967); from a more conservative perspective, popular science displays an orderly, law-abiding natural world, emphasising stability (e.g. Polanyi, 1962).

Science communication also serves professional purposes for scientists (Shinn and Whitley, 1985; Nelkin, 1995; Shortland and Gregory, 1991; Gregory and Miller, 1998). When scientists communicate science, they can gain individual enjoyment, material rewards and fame, and it can enhance their own understanding of their subject. Some scientists use the communications infrastructures of the public sphere to enhance communication with their own colleagues, and with other experts. But they are also contributing to the larger enterprise of establishing and maintaining a space for science on the cultural and social map (Gieryn 1999). The collective ethos of science means that individual scientists are always acting as representatives of their community, and so are obligated beyond their personal interests. Peer pressure to enforce this obligation has been identified by Dornan (1990) as the 'unwritten rules' of science communication. These demand that before stepping into the public sphere, the scientist must first have a reputation as a credible researcher, and their research should have already been published in the professional literature; the popularising activity should not detract from or take priority over research activity, and they should stay clearly within their own area of expertise; they must refrain from criticising science or in any way damaging its image; and they should avoid extremes of opinion.

These rules contribute to the many ways in which science communication does what Gieryn calls '**boundary work**' (Gieryn, 1983, 1999). Boundary work is social interaction that is undertaken to confer identity and difference, and to embed the social relations that emerge from these differing identities. Scientists, like other expert professions, deliver knowledge and applications to society in return for professional and personal resources. Unlike most other expert professions (e.g. lawyers or car mechanics), their work is undertaken away from the public's gaze, and so assent to the provision of those resources is negotiated via the representation of science in the public sphere. A lay community for science must exist for the professional community to deserve the adjective and all it implies. So the public are deliberately exposed to science in ways that reinforce the social necessity of science and that emphasise the specialness of its knowledge and practitioners, legitimating scientists' needs and products.

Popular science, then, is, in many ways, pure publicity. When a monarch undertakes publicity with displays of regalia, the material of power returns to

Box 15.3 Popular science case study: Fred Hoyle

> Professor Fred Hoyle is my hero. I understand only about one word in ten of what he is saying, but ... he is a man to be admired extravagantly.
>
> Daily Express, 1965

The British cosmologist Fred Hoyle (1915–2001) published academic papers from the 1930s and popular science from the 1940s. He wrote science fiction novels and short stories, a screenplay and a libretto, and very many newspaper and magazine articles. He gave lectures on radio and many interviews to journalists, and was a household name during the 1950s and 1960s. He made two major scientific contributions. The first was a cosmology called steady state theory (1948), which was always controversial and which was rejected after 25 years in favour of big bang theory. Hoyle vigorously popularised steady state theory in a variety of media. Hoyle's second achievement was the theory of the formation of the elements in stars. This work was immediately welcomed and celebrated by colleagues, and Hoyle never popularised it. So Hoyle popularised his own work only when it was not gaining acclaim in his professional sphere.

In later life, Hoyle developed a biological theory of the universe. It was gradually marginalised in the professional press, and thereafter it flourished in the public sphere. The most strident criticism he attracted during his career was from biologists, in response to his popularisations of biological ideas which were deemed to be beyond the realm of his expertise.

Hoyle's science fiction often contains early but highly elaborated versions of his unpopular scientific ideas. In the novels, his colleagues found these ideas interesting and worthy of discussion; when the same ideas later appeared in the professional literature (expressed in tentative terms and garnished with tags of novelty), colleagues rejected both the ideas and Hoyle. So fiction served as a 'safe house' outside of the rules of professional science.

At high points in Hoyle's popular career, his citations in the professional literature were at their lowest; and points of high popularising activity coincide not with scientific achievement or productivity or in their wake, but with Hoyle's campaigns in the political sphere for institutional resources. That Hoyle's popular works were widely bought, read, and enjoyed by laypeople was both incidental to his motivation and essential to his exploitation of the public sphere.

Source: Gregory, 2003a, 2005

Box 15.4   Popular science case study: evolutionary psychology

Evolutionary psychology emerged as a label for a novel academic configuration in the 1990s. Drawing on sociobiology, social Darwinism, and neuroscience, among other fields, it applied neo-Darwinian ideas about the evolutionary history of humans to problems in psychology. After some initial academic activity, popular science provided a space for the definition and display of this new activity, and, once constituted there, evolutionary psychology flourished in the professional literature, 'magnified' by its public excursion.

Scientists who had become 'visible' through popular works became media subjects, with journalists covering their professional activity. A series of public lectures at the London School of Economics generated news events. Publishers buoyant on a popular science boom generated books and publicity for books. In the public sphere, academics, including those outside the neo-Darwinian paradigm, and other commentators such as political journalists, engaged with the questions of evolutionary psychology, expanding and diversifying its scope and generating controversy.

Boundary work was active on many fronts, for example in detaching the novel field of evolutionary psychology from earlier academic attempts at the same problems, and in regard to the extension of evolutionary psychology as science into policy-making on social problems such as rape and gender discrimination. Social scientists resisted the scientists' invasion of their territory by working the boundary from the other direction, asserting their expertise about the same social problems in popular books and newspaper articles.

Journalists wrote articles for laypeople, such as articles about dating for women's magazines. Academics in evolutionary psychology who popularised their work reported that while they had no idea who read their popular accounts, they had written them for other academics and opinion leaders.

Source: Cassidy, 2005, 2006

the palace at the end of the tour. Scientific knowledge, however, is an immaterial good: the lecturer still has it, but the audience also take it home with them. In the early nineteenth century, when scientists were newly labelled and founding their profession, fears about empowered masses in evolving democracies crystallised into a persistent tension between exhibiting knowledge that is both esoteric enough to earn scientists expert status, and sufficiently clearly valuable and meaningful to gain public attention and generate esteem. This tension is reflected in the classic popular science scenario in which social boundaries are maintained while knowledge is displayed. Difference and/or separation between the scientist and the layperson can be emphasised by the architecture of the nineteenth century lecture hall (often with the physical barrier of the lab bench between lecturer and audience), or contemporary linguistic conventions or even styles of dress (such as the white coat of the hospital doctor, who needs a very obvious identifier since, unusually among scientists, he or she routinely interacts with laypeople) (Gregory and Miller, 1998; Fahnestock, 1993; LaFollette, 1990). This holds the public close but no closer – what Gieryn calls 'protection' in his classification of boundary work: one group holds on to another, but at arm's length, so as to emphasise separation but at the same time exploit proximity (Gieryn, 1995).

The dominant model of science communication

In 1990, Hilgartner identified a widespread and culturally **dominant model** of science communication (Hilgartner, 1990). In this 'dominant view', science communication is represented by a linear model in which scientists send information to the public either directly or via mediators such as journalists. However, unlike the classical sender-transmitter-receiver model (McQuail, 1987), Hilgartner's model also expresses social relations: it is vertical, with the scientists at the top. As the sole source of information, scientists control both its quality and its flow. They set the epistemic 'gold standard', and pass selected nuggets of high-quality knowledge on to journalists who should deliver the information as faithfully as they can. The final destination of this knowledge is a receptive but passive public at the bottom of the epistemic heap (the classic expression of science communication to the public is that it is about 'bringing it down to their level'). The role of the journalist as mediator maintains a separation between scientists and the public, and allows the journalist to stand as scapegoat for communication failures, such as public misconceptions or lack of political interest (Hilgartner, 1990).

Hilgartner notes that this model is both grossly oversimplified and a sophisticated political resource. The public sphere is open to all, and science communication is as visible to other scientists as it is to laypeople; the dominant model neglects this communicative traffic both among scientists in the public sphere, and from laypeople to scientists. The separation the model implies between professional and public communication is instead, Hilgartner argues, a continuum of communications, with grant applications, journal editorials, and research newsletters occupying a middle ground, around which boundaries are mobile and deployed tactically by the many professionals who people the space between science and the public. And journalists are not the hi-fidelity transmitters of the early engineering models: they select, frame, interpret, represent, challenge, and speculate. However, the political value of the dominant model lies exactly in its rhetorical separation of public communication from the epistemically pure scientific knowledge:

> A concept of purity requires one of contamination, and the notion of popularisation shores up an idealised view of genuine, objective, scientifically certified knowledge. Furthermore, the dominant view establishes genuine scientific knowledge as the exclusive preserve of scientists; policymakers and the public can only grasp simplified representations.
>
> (Hilgartner, 1990)

Thus scientists are the arbiters of which forms and items of popular science are legitimate, because good, useful or image-enhancing popular science can be recognised as *science*, and any knowledge compromised by its excursion into the public sphere can be rejected as merely *popular*, and blamed on intermediaries. Science remains pristine, while at the same time scientists can exploit the 'quick and dirty' qualities of the public sphere to accomplish professional gain in ways that would be inappropriate in the professional sphere. For example, they can talk across the strict disciplinary boundaries of the professional press, and jokes, mockery, and outlandish ideas all find space in public – and can be effectively disowned if expedient when the scientist returns to the professional sphere in the privacy of the laboratory (Collins and Pinch, 1979; Gregory, 2003a).

The boundary work of legitimation and discrediting that science communication performs makes popularisation a risky activity for scientists. Careers can be magnified by legitimate popularisation, and shrunk by transgressions, with these categorisations being applied inconsistently and post hoc: the 'unwritten rules' are enforced for political convenience. Sanctions can include exclusion from professional communication, so that 'excommunication' is an appropriate description of the punishment (Goodell, 1977; Gregory, 2003a).

The academic field of science communication

History

Historical as well as local contingencies apply to the boundaries between legitimate and transgressive popular science: in the UK, the 1950s provided a positive environment for popular science; the 1960s less so; and the 1970s were very risky, with the flag kept flying by a few 'visible scientists' (Bauer et al., 1995; Goodell, 1977). Scientists retreated from the public sphere, which became a combative space for journalists and other mediators. New social movements emerged for human rights, the environment, health, and war, often challenging scientific authority with alternative worldviews – which, under the terms of the dominant model, scientists could then ignore as irrelevant to science (Gregory and Miller, 1998). In 1969, the editor of the

New England Journal of Medicine, Franz Inglefinger, declared that no research could be published in his journal if it had already been exposed in public, and the practice spread. For scientists, who needed publications to secure their careers and for whom interaction with journalists could be fraught, this 'Inglefinger rule' provided a welcome release from the pressures of the public sphere (Nelkin, 1995).

Academic interest in science communication was sporadic and dispersed before the 1980s. In France, issues of 'la culture scientifique' are a longstanding feature of sociological and cultural discourse (Laszlo, 1993; Jurdant, 1969, 1993; Caro, 1993); in the USA, science communication courses arose in the agricultural colleges to support the implementation of new farming technologies during the 1930s Depression. Worldwide, risk communication emerged as a technical discourse in the 1970s in response to social frictions around the deployment of technologies such as nuclear power and vaccinations. In the 1980s, scientists in the English-speaking world and elsewhere institutionalised growing concerns about the costs of their withdrawal from the public sphere, and urged each other to communicate with the public (e.g. Royal Society, 1985). The subsequent frenzy of science communication activity has been characterised as a new social movement: the movement for public understanding of science (PUS) or, as it has become known in the US, scientific literacy. The PUS movement was dominated, at least explicitly, by the idea that the point of science communication is to transfer knowledge to the public (Gregory and Lock, 2008; Lock, 2009).

Research

The PUS movement gave a boost to science communication research, in particular in three areas: knowledge and attitudes of laypeople about science; relationships between laypeople and experts; and the quantity and character of the media coverage of science.

Public knowledge and attitudes

Surveys of public knowledge about and attitudes towards science repeatedly show that laypeople get very few questions right when asked factual questions about science (Gregory, 2003b; Bauer, 2008). This has fuelled the fire under the 'deficit' approach to science communication, even though surveys carried out before and after the PUS movement's campaigns show little difference in the public's levels of knowledge about science. Lewenstein identified that more communication about science is expected to lead not just to greater knowledge among the public, but also to more positive attitudes towards science (Lewenstein, 1993); analysis of survey data shows that this is not necessarily the case (Bauer, 2008). Studies also show that attitudes to science are rarely monolithic: one individual can be very positive about gene therapy but object strongly to GM foods, for example (Bauer and Gaskell, 2002).

Controversy has also raged over the suitability of surveys to measure the public understanding of science (Bauer, 2008), perhaps partly because survey results tend to show a public that is immune to the efforts of the PUS movement.

Laypeople's expertise

In contrast to the survey research, qualitative research has explored interactions between individual or small groups of laypeople and experts (Irwin and Wynne, 1996). It identifies that, in areas of science relevant and meaningful to them, laypeople can become highly expert, and develop the competencies to engage with professional sources and deploy professional tools (Irwin and Wynne, 1996; Epstein, 1996; see also Collins and Evans, 2007 and Djurodie, 2003). Social psychological research explores the space that is characterised as empty in the deficit model, and finds there a lively and complex world of personal and social representations of science, where shared meanings and symbols of science and technology enable and express lay attitudes and responses (see Chapter 7, also, Jovchelovitch, 2007; Bauer and Gaskell, 2002). Researchers such as Wynne and Stocking note that ignorance of science can be actively constructed and deployed by laypeople in sophisticated ways for social purposes: for example, in the workplace, technical ignorance can be a mark of respect for an expert colleague, and a patient who does not want information about their treatment can be demonstrating trust in their healthcare institutions (Irwin and Wynne, 1996; Stocking 1998).

Media coverage of science

A strong theme in the PUS movement is a concern about media coverage of science as scarce, sensationalist, and inaccurate (Gregory and Miller, 1998). Research has looked at particular mass media stories (such as the 'gay gene' or cold fusion, or themes such as risk) as well as wider, longer-term trends in coverage (e.g. Miller, 1995, Lewenstein, 1995; Hornig, 1993; Bauer et al., 1995); it also explores the production of science in the media, looking at journalistic practice and values, and the use of sources (Hansen, 1994; Allan, 2002, 2009; Bauer and Bucchi, 2009). Most studies are about news and on print media, although some look at the science content of television (Gopfert, 1996; Hansen and Dickinson, 1992).

In general, this research shows that the amount of science content in the news media is more than anecdotal evidence suggests, with variation being consistent with the usual pressures on news space. Particular sciences and technologies come and go in news coverage, consistent with political or business interest, or with salience in the public sphere more generally: for example, Bauer noted the 'medicalisation' of the UK media, with biomedical sciences emerging as the dominant public discourse of the sciences of the late twentieth century (Bauer, 1998). On TV, natural history dominates science coverage, lending itself readily to moving pictures (Gopfert 1996; Leon 2007).

On the question of accuracy of science news, 'accurate' has become a contested term. Complainants on this point tend to refer to the professional literature as the 'gold standard'; research suggests that what is identified as inaccuracy in science reporting would be understood as 'angle' among journalists or as 'framing' among media scholars – that is, emphasising those aspects of a story that are most appropriate for its new medium and audience, and recasting it in an appropriate rhetoric (Allan, 2002, 2009).

New models, new understandings

All three areas of research problematise the deficit and dominant models. Qualitative studies of lay–expert interaction produced the 'contextual model', in which locally constructed, personally relevant scientific knowledge is generated more through the life experience and personal interest than it is from the emissions of scientists. The contextual model, embedded in social relations, defines science not just as knowledge but also as a social institution, so that questions of authority, trust, and values are significant (Irwin and Wynne, 1996).

The shortcomings identified by Hilgartner in the 'dominant model' have been variously addressed. The missing continuum is modelled by Bucchi (2004), whose model is a series of lenses of decreasing diameter. The largest lens represents communication among specialists; they then shrink along the continuum, where they represent, for example, training materials, until the final, smallest lens is public communication. Bucchi explains:

> [T]he purpose [is] to emphasise the growing solidity and simplification acquired by a scientific fact, level after level, until it becomes like a ship in a bottle: to be admired for its perfection but impossible to relate to its original components.
>
> (Bucchi, 2004)

Lewenstein (1995) breaks the linear mould, and considers the multidirectional dimensions of science communication, and the versatility and independence of its actors. His detailed study of the 'cold fusion' claims of 1989 shows not only the public and journalists, but also scientists, playing multiple roles, interacting in many directions and with a variety of media, picking up and passing on information and comment about science. This 'web model' shows a complex sphere of interactions in which networks of institutions, ideas, and actors produce science and science communication. The mass media provide infrastructure in which this variety of communications can proliferate, but Lewenstein stresses:

> The model suggests that analysis of the role of the mass media in science cannot be accomplished in isolation, but must be an analysis of the complexity of interactions among all media.
>
> (Lewenstein, 1995)

Lewenstein's web model is consistent with developments in the mainstream of communication studies, where network models dominate our understanding of contemporary communications infrastructures and behaviours, with the Internet blurring roles and genres (Luhmann, 1995; Castells, 2000). These networks link the laboratory to the journal to the press release to the newspaper to the Internet to the laboratory; or the thought-experiment to the radio discussion to the science-fiction film to a corporate R&D department to a TV commercial; and they thrive because their products are, at some point, mass-consumed in a global market. Most forms of collective life in technological societies take advantage of these networks, science among them. But networks are open to diverse interests, thus ruling out absolute control by scientists of the public image of science, and making inevitable some broader social control not just of the representation of science but also of science itself (Wagner, 2009).

Genres of popular science

Science communication happens in many popular media and fora, some of which have only recently come to the attention of scholars. In part, popular science suffers from the academic neglect afforded to many forms of 'low' culture: B-movies, the 'yellow press', and fairground marvels among them (Kirby, 2009; Schmidt Kjaergaard, 2009). Science communication studies of popular communications such as these also suffer from the emphasis in science communication on the transfer of knowledge, and cartoons, superhero comics, and computer games are not expected to do this (Locke, 2005). The dominant model allows these genres to be classified as about something other than science.

Popular science books have received some attention (Turney, 2007; Lewenstein, 2009); so too have science-related films (Jones, 1998, 2001; Kirby, 2009; Flicker, 2003). Images and stereotypes of science have been studied, though visual media present similar challenges to science communication researchers as they do to students of other images (Nieman, 2001; Howard, 200X; Flicker, 2003). Science fiction has been studied as a literary genre more than as a form of popular science (Luckhurst, 2005; Roberts, 2005).

Science museums have been studied as sites of science communication (Bicknell and Farmelo, 1993; Schiele, 2008). In particular, the problem of the representation of science via its material culture has been controversial. At the same time, 'hands-on' science centres, which use physical models that visitors can use to recreate experiments that illustrate scientific principles, have been criticised for decontextualising science, detaching it from both history and society (Gregory and Miller, 1998). These science centres tend to be curriculum-led and thrive on state-funded school visits. They are a good example of where science communication and formal education interact, and their work is often labelled 'informal education.'

An emerging genre for professional science communicators is the press release. Through the 1990s, scientific institutions developed an appreciation of the benefits of media coverage, and found ways of professionalising their interactions with journalists. Now very few research institutes in Europe are without a press office (Gopfert, 2007), which typically works closely with the journals that publish their scientists' research, coordinating press releases and respecting embargoes. Thus publication in an esoteric journal can also mean exposure in the mass media for an author who thereby brings their work, their institution, and their journal to the attention of opinion leaders, policy-makers, and the public, without ever having to step out of the laboratory. Journals' prestige is now measured, at least in part, by the amount of media coverage it can attract.

The Internet-based journalism that arises from the press releases of high-prestige international journals has come to dominate science reporting, giving science coverage a uniformity across media outlets which tradition-ally have thrived on being different from each other. This homogeneity worries some critics who see this managerial input from press offices as a threat to the democratic potential of journalism (Gopfert, 2007; Kiernan, 2006; Trench, 2009). At the same time, scientific research is increasingly undertaken in private institutions such as businesses, and their news is not press-released in order to protect it from competition; so it is exempted from journalistic scrutiny in any case (Gregory et al., 2007).

From 'deficit' to 'dialogue'

In the twenty-first century, science communication is adapting to a world in which new communications technologies are disrupting traditional hier-archical social relations in favour of spontaneous and dynamic horizontal networks. At the same time, in post-Cold War Europe, the political tendency to escape the Left-Right dichotomy in favour of a 'third-way' approach has set the context for novel approaches to many aspects of social life, includ-ing the relations between science and society (Adonis and Mulgan, 1994; Giddens, 1998). An important principle of the 'third way' in the UK was the enhancement of democratic interaction between the public and policymak-ers, and one approach to this has been to reconfigure science communica-tion as 'consultation', **'public engagement'**, and **'dialogue.'**

In this dialogic approach to science communication, science becomes a matter for negotiation among interest groups, only one of which comprises the experts themselves: in dialogue, the potential is not so much for one specific party to have influence on another, but for all parties to cause and be subject to change (see Chapter 2). The canonical content of science is not open to negotiation, or to being changed by laypeople; instead, dialogue refers to policy issues, values, and personal preferences. (There are simi-larities here with Vygotsky's views on educational guidance [see Chapter 1], where shared dialogue of sorts [mediation] is necessary in learning, although the validity of the scientific concepts themselves are not open to question.) A doctor–patient interaction consists not so much of a doctor telling a patient about their condition and what treatment they will get, as the doctor and patient sharing their experience of the patient's medical condition, and the patient using public sources such as the Internet, and of them working out together what treatment options might be for the best. This situation can be an uneasy one: the boundaries demarcating science from the public, speakers from listeners, and professional science from science communication, have been worked from both sides, and many interests are served by keeping them exactly where they are. So despite the democratic potential of dialogical communication (a theme present in Chapters 2 and 6), and like traditional science communication, the agenda is invariably set by the more powerful actors; and participants risk encountering an agenda-setting and facilitation process that feels more like mob management than enhanced citizenship. For some critics, these exercises, which are often labelled 'public engagement', are a polite but diminished form of democracy compared to the street protests and grass-roots campaigns they are often designed to preempt (Elam and Bertilsson, 2003; Levidow, 2007; Lezuan and Soneryd, 2007). This managerial aspect explains why public engagements are often organised and experienced as exercises in public relations (Beder, 1999; Gregory et al., 2008).

A key focus of government-sponsored public engagement in the UK has been near-market technologies, such as nanotechnology and GM crops (Stilgoe, 2007; Thorpe and Gregory, 2010). In a global marketplace with an economy dependent on innovation, the public serve not just as the labourers of the early industrial era, but also as consumers of products, and as citizens of a global community in which innovations and the science that generates them are to be accommodated. Public engagement with emerging technologies gives them 'a place in life' (Lazzarato, 1996), transforming possible future science into common sense, and both markets and publics emerge ready for innovation. Through talk, promises of new technologies become products in themselves, and, by raising hopes and fears, do affective work to engage laypeople with science (Thorpe and Gregory 2010). This affective work displaces the rationality of traditional scientistic discourse, and dispenses with cognitive content such as facts; and it is done most powerfully by media and genres that deploy visual image and soundtrack. (This affective dimension to communication is not to be ignored; see Chapter 10 on rhetoric and Chapter 11 on evolutionary theory). Mellor (2009) includes these among 'the taken-for-granteds of popular science' when she argues for the potential of semiotic analysis in science communication research.

This situation is a long way from the contexts represented by the dominant model of science communication and the deficit model of the public understanding of science. Scientists are not distinguished from laypeople in public engagement: they too are citizens of the innovation economy; and their expertise is not so special when the dialogue focuses not on the knowledge content of science but on emotions, values, and promises. Innovation demands and creates social change, and dialogue involves social interaction, so public engagements about emerging technologies are delivered by social scientists. When the fortunes of the innovation economy are at stake, science communication is not about science but about society (Thorpe and Gregory, 2010).

Conclusions

At this point, it is worth taking another look at the quotations at the start of this chapter. From half a century ago, science journalist William Laurance's words sum up the 'dominant model' of science communication, casting scientists as gods on a mountain-top, whose 'fire' the science writers brought 'down to the people.' This model is deeply entrenched in scientific culture and remains, for scientists, the 'common sense' of science communication. By the turn of the twenty-first century, though, in the Anglophone world at least, the gods had been coaxed down from their mountain and onto the commons, at least occasionally, to enter into dialogic communication with the public, especially on policy issues of economic significance; and scientists, many now in the commercial sector, are adopting – and urging each other to adopt – corporate-style communications strategies such as public relations. Science communication has not so much changed as diversified: it is not only about the transfer of the facts of science from scientist to laypeople in order to achieve particular configurations of social relations; it is also about direct approaches to the social relations of science, without resort to factual content, via the affective content of messages about the value, promises, and uses of science. Affect travels readily in mass media, and is more amenable to mass consumption than facts. In the 'network society', where networks function 'broadband', in multiple modes, and roles and boundaries are blurred, science communication serves not only the traditional interests of science as a profession, but also the interests of governments, businesses, and media institutions; as well as those of the public who, as legitimators, subjects, customers, and citizens of a scientific society also inscribe and frame an emergent popular scientific culture that continues to variously defy, exploit, and enjoy the scientists' epistemological and ideological hegemony over the natural world.

Glossary of keywords and definitions

Accommodation: In developmental psychology accommodation refers to the cognitive operation whereby new experience cannot simply be assimilated into existing structures of understanding but necessitates the construction of altogether new structures. In studies of social influence, accommodation refers to the process whereby a majority accepts the minority view resulting in an alteration or innovation of mainstream thinking.

Adaptation: An inherited and reliably developing characteristic of a species which evolved via natural selection because it helped to solve (directly or indirectly) a problem of survival and/or reproduction during the period of its evolution.

Affect-laden interpretation: The idea that the representation and interpretation of meanings are imbued with and guided by emotional and motivational states.

Agenda-setting: By giving attention to some issues over others, the media influences what the public perceives as the most pressing and most important social problems.

Argument: A feature of logos in classical rhetoric, reaching a persuasive conclusion on the basis of either deduction or induction.

Assimilation: In the terms of developmental psychology, assimilation refers to the cognitive operation of fitting of new experiences into existing structures of understanding. In studies of social influence, assimilation refers to the process whereby a minority accepts the majority view and joins mainstream thinking.

Attitude: A psychological relation to a given object of knowledge. It is measured by evaluative positioning of a person on a scale in relation to an attitude object. The application of abstract values to a concrete object results in an attitude. Attitudes include an image of and a disposition to approach or avoid the object.

Audience: The recipient group or addressee of a given communication. The study of rhetoric emphasises that this group has certain expectations and characteristics, and that the audience is in many respects effectively a projection of the speaker.

Belief: A proposition, statement, or doctrine held by one or more individuals.

Boundary work: Activity that identifies difference, and establishes understanding of the significance and practical consequences of that difference among the differing groups. In science communication, it most commonly establishes the difference between expert authorities and non-expert subjects of that authority.

Bullshit: Informal communication that is not concerned with the truth value of the utterance – someone who engages in an exchange of bullshit does so without regard to the truthfulness of what they are saying (Frankfurt, 2005). Bullshit is not deliberately or necessarily false, because truth or falsity is not required.

Celebratory speech: One of the three genres of classical rhetoric, celebratory statements are concerned largely with the present. By celebrating, praising or censoring given events or persons, the speaker pleases (entertains) or reinforces the aspirations (moral discourse, conduct of honour) of their audience.

Civic journalism (also called public journalism and citizen journalism): A journalistic style in which news stories are produced through collaboration of journalists and members of the public.

Code model: A model of communication that assumes that semantics and pragmatics involve automatic, context-free associations between words and meanings. It supports the idea that language offers a 'conduit' for the transfer of identical meaning from speaker to hearer.

Collective action: Forms of activism in which groups of people work together to ameliorate, challenge, or resist the impacts of individual, community, or wider social circumstances that place their health at risk.

Collective intention: Joint or collective intentions place more than one individual as the subject or agent of an activity or belief (e.g. 'we intend'), and have a normative quality, which commits the members of the 'we' to act or think in an agreed way. The relation between collective intentions and individual intentions is a matter of debate.

Compliance: The act of yielding to a normative expectation on the basis of its legitimacy, or to avoid negative consequences.

Composition: One of the five faculties of classical rhetoric, composition concerns the structure of persuasive speech, and the factor of continuity across the beginning, middle, and end of a public speech or a piece of writing.

Communicative action: A term used by Habermas to refer to a 'dialogical' mode of communication oriented at intersubjective understanding and agreement. For him, communicative action is the basis of cooperative human existence. It either aims at reaching a consensus of the speaker and the hearer or it underlines and articulates a given agreement. Communicative action can be broadly understood as all linguistically mediated interaction where participants jointly seek mutual understanding.

Community: A presupposition for human life which is both enabled and shaped by a variety of communication practices. According to Habermas, the 'real communication community' where everyday communication, action, and interaction occur has to be differentiated from the 'ideal communication community' or 'ideal speech situation'. The latter both provides the goal of free, equal, and unrestricted communication and the critical standard for the evaluation of factual or real communication.

Conformity: An individual's or group's act of changing a perception, opinion, attitude, belief, and/or behaviour to align with the mainstream of opinions, attitudes, beliefs, and behaviours of a dominant group (majority influence).

Conscientisation: The development of critical consciousness or critical thinking (translated from the Portuguese *conscientização*), where consciousness extends beyond an appreciation of facts to a critical assessment of them within a system of relationships. Conscientisation cannot be arrived at individually but only through a social process – dialogue.

Conversational implicature theory: A pragmatic theory that proposes that hearers make inferences (implicatures) regarding a speaker's meaning, based on the assumption that the speaker is attempting to follow a principle of cooperativeness, even if they appear not be.

Conversion: In theories of social influence, conversion refers to the changing of beliefs, opinions, cognitions, behaviours, or customs by members of a dominant group to align with a minority.

Cues, signals, and signs: Animals (including humans) communicate in three principal ways. **Cues** are associated with enduring qualities of a species' phenotype, designed to be informative, and do not impose any immediate cost for the animal. **Signals** are contingent responses to aspects of the environment, designed to be informative, can be switched on or off, and carry a cost for the organism. **Signs**, unlike cues and signals, are not designed to convey information but are treated as informative by others.

Cultural difference: The ideological construction of differences between cultures. This frequently invites stereotypes about 'us' and 'them' and evaluations that present certain cultures as superior. In practice, when we examine cultural differences we often find that there are more similarities than differences across cultures, and therefore it is difficult to separate cultures as distinct.

Cultural epidemiology: The theory that the spread of cultural ideas is analogous to disease contagion. The most contagious ideas may have specific psychological qualities, which give rise to raised levels of interpretive activity because they are inferentially indeterminate. They are more likely to be communicated and to be retained (Sperber, 1996).

Cultural niche construction: Humans occupy a special ecological niche – a 'cultural niche'. Niche construction refers to the processes through which organisms construct and modify their environments and thereby change the selection pressures to which their descendants are exposed. As cultural processes operate faster than natural selection, it has been argued that culture has greatly increased the niche construction capacity of humans and has played a critical role in human evolution.

Culture: (1) In the Social Representations tradition, culture refers to a broad collection of values, ideas, and practices (i.e. a network of representations) that defines a particular group or community, such as the British community or a student community. Culture is thus produced in and struggled over in communicative practices. (2) In nonverbal communications research, the dominant form of culture that features is 'national culture' (e.g. British, North American, Japanese cultures). Intercultural, cross-cultural or transcultural communication occurs between individuals from different national cultures. Importantly, however, there are technical variations of communication, such as subcultural (different groups who share characteristics of a general culture) and interethnic (individuals of the same race but from different ethnicities). (3) From an evolutionary perspective, culture is an acquired and patterned set of beliefs, practices, and artefacts largely shared by a group or community, disseminated within age or peer groups, and transmitted with limited variation across generations. Symbolic culture can thus act as an external or 'offline' resource for cognition which serves as a means of achieving adaptive ends relating to social relations.

Deception: The communication of misinformation to the receiver in order to achieve specific ends beneficial to the signaller and possibly costly to the receiver.

Deficit model: A model of public understanding of science in which low levels of laypeople's knowledge of science (in comparison to the levels of knowledge among professional scientists) should be remedied, either through formal education or through science communication.

Deliberation: Reasoned and open-minded discussion that is expected to increase tolerance for opposing viewpoints, deepen awareness and understanding of one's own political preferences, increase involvement in civic and political life, promote greater efficacy and social trust, and increase the efficiency and effectiveness of policy decisions.

Deliberative argumentation: One of the three genres of classical rhetoric, deliberative statements are concerned with the future and address a decision-making audience who will make or at least legitimate a decision. The objective in deliberative statements is to exhort or dissuade a future course of action.

Delivery (or eloquence): One of the five classical faculties of classical rhetoric. In late Roman times, eloquence was the defining feature of rhetoric (Quintillian).

Deviance: In the study of social influence, deviance refers to an act or behaviour that violates prevailing group norms.

Dialogical critical thinking: The process through which people engage in debate and discussion about the social roots of their individual life challenges and how these might best be challenged or resisted.

Dialogue: Reciprocal conversation between two or more actors implying two-way and ongoing communication where *both* actors learn from and are changed by the process (as opposed to *anti-dialogue* which is characterised by monologue, vertical relationships, manipulation, objectification, cultural invasion, and domestication rather than transformation). For Freire, dialogue is to 'devote oneself to the constant transformation of reality' (1974/2005, p. 104).

Display rules: Culturally determined rules about which nonverbal behaviours are appropriate to display. These relate particularly to emotional expression (e.g. happiness, anger, grief), although the full range of nonverbal behaviours is subjected to display rules. In many cultures display rules are gendered.

Dominant model: A model of science communication that is structured by a vertical hierarchy in which scientists, at the top, dispense 'pure' knowledge to journalists below, who then faithfully pass it on to a receptive public. The classic expression of the dominant model is that when scientists talk about science to the public, they are 'bringing it down to their level'.

Doxa: Opinion or an unsubstantiated view; awareness of the presence of things or phenomena without a critical perception of them (as opposed to *logos*, knowledge that is based on evidence and reflection).

Education: For Freire, education is 'communication and dialogue' (1974/2005, p. 126), and requires both interlocutors in the process (the educator and educatee) to seek knowledge rather than to simply extend information from one person to the other. The role of the educator is 'to attempt to move towards a new way of thinking in both educator and educatee, through the dialogical relationship between both' (Freire, 1974/2005, p. 112).

Edutainment: The intentional placement of educational content into entertainment communicated through media including television, radio, music, or theatre.

Egocentric/egocentrism: In the terms of developmental psychology, the term 'egocentric' refers to children's inability to see the world from another person's perspective. Egocentricism more generally refers to a mental disposition which results in a failure to take into account the perspective of others. Miscommunication between interlocutors may arise as a result of an 'egocentric default'.

Egocentric communication: The idea that people do not regularly attempt to take into account other people's mental states during conversation and that, even when they do attempt to do so, they are not very successful. This contrasts with the ability to think about these things reflectively, separate from the process of communication.

Elementary cognitive functions: Innate cognitive functions that we share with animals, made up of the 'natural' processes of reactive attention, associative memory, and sensory-motor thinking.

Empty speech: The overriding imaginary function of empty speech is to affirm and substantiate images the subject has of themselves, to mobilise defences against hearing what would prove too disruptive. It is a way of lending consistency to an ego; talking here is a project of imaginary *self-making*. The image-making capacity of empty speech leads the subject away from difficult truths and introduces systemic distortions into the subject's communications.

Encoding-decoding: In the study of representations, encoding-decoding refers to a circular process by which mass communication is imprinted with meanings (codes) and read through the meanings salient to different audiences. There is often a 'lack of fit' between the processes of encoding (or the production of communications) and decoding (the reception and interpretation of communications). Both processes feed into, and sometimes challenge, each other. Encoding-decoding occurs in different communicative genres:

> **Diffusion**: Attaching new ideas into familiar knowledge in a seemingly neutral manner, characterised by sceptical intelligence. Little obvious attempt is made to confirm or deny new ideas.

> **Propagation**: The association of the unfamiliar to particular beliefs established by central authorities (such as the Church). This works as a system of accommodation as new ideas are adapted in order to fit in with current practices of particular groups.

> **Propaganda**: The ideological manipulation of new ideas to support and defend the political interests and identity of a particular group (such as a political party) and so denigrate the beliefs and values of others.

The notions of encoding and decoding are also important in a very different social psychology tradition, namely the study of nonverbal communication. The notions of encoding and decoding here draw attention to how individuals perceive, interpret, or understand nonverbal behaviours or communication and how individuals express nonverbal behaviours.

Ethos: One of the classical means of rhetoric, ethos focuses on the credibility of the speaker. The speaker's credibility persuades on the basis of personality and/or competences (prudence, goodwill, and virtues) that embody the aspirations of the moral community he or she addresses.

Extension: The transfer of scientific knowledge and skills. Freire, in critiquing agricultural extension programmes in Brazil, equates extension with cultural invasion through the imposition of one particular vision of the world.

Founding speech: The 'pairing-effect' of reciprocal forms of naming which involve the interdependence of speech acts, as in the case of uttering 'You are my wife' which locates me in a symbolic role and position relative to the person I am speaking of. Importantly, such forms of self-designation always entail reference to an other, and to the Other.

Framing: The tendency for the news media and political actors to focus on only certain dimensions of a complex issue while ignoring others. This selective 'framing' communicates why the issue matters; who or what might be responsible; and what should be done in terms of action.

Full speech: A type of speech capable of delivering unanticipated unconscious effects of truth and effecting change in its speakers. More specifically, full speech transforms the speaker in the act of speaking, and it typically involves aspects of 'what one had not meant to say'. Not only does full speech establish a new relation to truth, it also establishes a *new order of relationship between myself and my other/Other interlocutors*.

Genre: A routinised pattern of communication that has implicit, culturally sanctioned rules governing the appropriate way of engaging in that type of communication, with whom and with which consequences.

Gossip: A special case or genre of rumour, in which people exchange potentially ungrounded, evaluative views about an absent party, often driven by emotional motivations, with the function of promoting normative social control and social comparison in general.

Health campaigns, mediated: Efforts to support healthy behaviours and healthy communities using communications media such as radio, television, print, and the Internet.

Health communication: Forms of communication that empower people to take control over their health, through promoting one or more of the following: health-enhancing behaviour change, the appropriate accessing of health-related services and support, the development of health-enabling social capital, the facilitation of collective action to tackle obstacles to health, and the development of health-related social policy (at the local, national, and/or global levels of influence).

Health communication strategies: These include didactic health education campaigns which target vulnerable groups with information about health risks; community strengthening approaches which seek to promote health-enhancing social participation in vulnerable communities; and health advocacy approaches which target powerful decision makers who have the economic and/or political power to tackle and transform unhealthy social environments.

Health-enabling community contexts: Social environments which enable and support the likelihood that community members will behave in health-promoting ways.

Higher cognitive functions: Cognitive functions that are uniquely human, which originate in social interaction, and are the products of mediation. Vygotsky groups together here 'processes of mastering the external means of cultural development and cognition, e.g. language, writing, counting' and processes such as 'selective attention, logical memory, concept formation' (Vygotsky, cited in Rieber and Robinson, 2004, p. 550).

Hostile media effect: The tendency for individuals who feel strongly about an issue to view media coverage of that issue – regardless of its objective content – as biased or 'hostile' against their position.

Identity: An individual's sense of who they are in relation to others around them. This simultaneously incorporates a sense of belonging and shared knowledge and a sense of difference and individuality. Different forms of identity and so different types of social groups lead to different communicative genres.

Ideology: A system of hegemonic representations that sustain the dominant cultural order. It is hence useful to examine the ways in which communicative practices operate ideologically through the systematic manipulation of knowledge in the service of power and the defence of unequal social relations.

Illocution: Is the act performed in saying something (e.g. making an apology, an observation, a bet, a promise, etc.). Rather than focusing upon the content of what has been said, we are here concerned with what the act of saying something does, how a situation is changed by virtue of the speech act.

Imaginary, the: The domain of one-to-one intersubjectivity that serves the ego and functions to consolidate the images subjects use to substantiate themselves. The imaginary is as much characterised by the ego's self-love as by a limitless potential for rivalry and aggressive conflict.

Imitation: The process of copying actions of another in both behaviour and intention.

Impression management: The tactics and strategies individuals adopt to achieve positive self-presentation (e.g. dressing appropriately for a job interview).

Inferential model: A model of communication that assumes that pragmatics and some or all of semantics arise from non-automatic, inferential processes, which depend on context for their operation.

Informational influence: Influence that is brought about by means of new information. Informational influence is contrasted with normative influence.

Innovation: In studies of social influence, innovation refers to a novel belief, opinion, attitude, or behaviour that has been introduced within a social system where it did not previously exist.

Internalisation: The psychological reconstruction of an external action or operation. Once this cognitive operation has occurred, internal processes can be externalised in action.

Intersubjectivity: The relational space between persons.

Invention: One of the five faculties of classical rhetoric, invention or creativity is crucial in finding the best possible means of persuasion in any given situation. Classically, invention includes the three basic proofs of logos, ethos, and pathos.

Journalism, networked: The construction of news stories through the collaboration of professional journalists and laypeople – made possible primarily through digital technology such as online opinion forums, blogs, and video-sharing websites.

Journalism of conversation: A journalistic style that conceives of reporting as the development of socially constructed interpretations of complex and multifaceted situations. Ideally, such constructions result from dialogue and collaboration among journalists and a wide range of concerned parties, including not only health professionals, leaders, and policymakers, but also the voices of marginalised groups traditionally excluded from the dominant public sphere in particular social settings. This approach is often associated with an emphasis on the social and political determinants of health.

Journalism of information: A journalistic style that conceives of reporting as the neutral and value-free presentation of objective facts. Health issues tend to be framed primarily as individual concerns, often within the context of biomedical understandings of health and disease.

Judicial argumentation: One of the three genres of classical rhetoric, judicial statements are concerned with past events; judicial rhetoric accuses and/or defends before a judge or a jury in the quest for justice.

KAB (Knowledge + Attitudes = Behaviour) approach: The implicit model of health behaviour that underpins many information-based health campaigns: it is the assumption that if a person has information about a health risk and a negative attitude to it, s/he will form an intention to behave in a way that reduces that risk, with behaviour change often following from behaviour-change intentions.

Knowledge gap effect: The tendency for information from the media to be more easily acquired by segments of the population with higher socioeconomic status and more education.

Language games: The set of informal, everyday rules embedded in the ordinary language used by speakers of any given community. The notion was introduced by Wittgenstein to address the problem of meaning in ordinary language. The meaning of words or propositions can only be understood in relation to the language games that guide the real-life contexts in which words are used.

Leadership: In studies of social influence, leadership refers to the exercise of authority and direction by an individual or a group over a larger social group.

Lifeworld: The reservoir of taken-for-granted convictions, collective assumptions, and behaviours that constitute the shared background horizon which enables communication to take place.

Locution: The act of saying something (i.e. making an utterance). In Speech Act Theory, the locution refers to the constative dimension of a speech act, that is the content of a given speech act which describes a state of affairs in the world.

Logos: One of the classical means of rhetoric, logos concerns the strength of an argument as developed either in the form of deduction from plausible premises or in the form of induction from an example of either a historical or fictional sort. The focus on logos stems from the idea of a scientific rhetoric.

Majority: The numerically larger or otherwise dominant social group in a social system.

Méconnaissance: The systematic distortions whereby the ego hears on the basis of what is already 'known' by, or reflective of, its own interests. *Méconnaissance* entails the imaginary function of *immediate comprehension*, the attribution of ego-centred meanings as a primary means of understanding.

Mediation: A key term in Vygotsky's theory of cognitive development, mediation refers to a structured activity that aids in the transformation of elementary cognitive functions into higher cognitive functions. It is through mediation that one is able to appropriate psychological tools, such as scientific or 'schooled' concepts, that one would be unable to develop on one's own. For Cole, mediation refers to 'the dual process of shaping and being shaped through culture' (1996, p. 103).

Memory: A cognitive capacity which forms a basis of human identity on the personal and collective level. Some cultural theories make a distinction between 'communicative memory' and 'cultural memory'. Whereas the former is close to everyday life and is established by reciprocal communication, the latter refers to the essential events and experiences of the collective past of a community or society. Memory is activated, actualised, and performed in acts of remembrance.

Metacognition: The process of thinking about thinking. Flavell (1976) describes it as follows: 'Metacognition refers to one's knowledge concerning one's own cognitive processes or anything related to them, e.g., the learning-relevant properties of information or data. For example, I am engaging in metacognition if I notice that I am having more trouble learning A than B; if it strikes me that I should double check C before accepting it as fact' (p. 232). Flavell argued that metacognition explains why children of different ages deal with learning tasks in different ways; that is, they have developed new strategies for thinking.

Metaphor: Substituting one word (target) for another (source), whereby the connotations of the source are transferred onto the target. Example: 'She is an English rose'. She is no rose literally speaking, but I thereby suggest that she has features of a rose.

Metonymy: Using a word that stands in association with another; for example a part for the whole. Example: 'London decided today to resume diplomatic ties with a former enemy'. Here 'London' stands in for 'the British government'.

Minimal counter-intuitiveness: Representations that are largely intuitive or schema-based, but which incorporate the denial of a specific expectation associated with a category. Because they are only minimally counter-intuitive (i.e. not bizarre or maximally counter-intuitive), they generate high interpretive activity. The uncertainty in such representations may be resolved by relevant emotions. Boyer (2003) has suggested that such representations are the hallmark of religious beliefs; we suggest that similar patterns may also be at play in rumour.

Minority: The social group in a social system that is numerically smaller or otherwise perceived as secondary in status relative to the majority.

Miserly public: Reference to a public that rely on their pre-existing views and the information most readily available to them via the media and interpersonal sources to form opinions and make political decisions.

Narrative: The telling of stories is an important form of communication and action for individuals which enables an understanding of the past, and keeps their relevant histories and traditions. Individuals and communities develop and articulate a consciousness of identity, by which they imagine and anticipate their future. Bruner speaks of a 'narrative construction of reality'. Narrative analysis is used as a method in qualitative social research.

Nonverbal behaviour: A broad range of bodily behaviours that can be interpreted as communicative messages or acts; nonverbal behaviour includes the use of the face and eyes, the voice, and the whole body, as well as bodily use of space and time.

Nonverbal communication: The process through which one person simulates meaning in the mind of another person through nonverbal behaviour. As soon as another person interprets such behaviours as a message, and attributes meaning to it, then nonverbal behaviour becomes nonverbal communication.

Normalisation: The process of making a belief, attitude, opinion, or behaviour the expected standard. The emergence and fixation of norms constitutes a group with a frame of reference for future action.

Normative influence: Influence that is brought about by appealing to norms and by threatening sanctions within a certain group. Normative influence is contrasted with informational influence.

Norms: Standards of conduct including behaviours, opinions, beliefs, and attitudes that a group expects from its members. Such norms play an important role in the constitution and representation of a group. Norms are expectations of conduct that are relatively stable in the face of factual violation.

Obedience: An act that is carried out in accordance with the orders of a person of prestige and authority.

Optimal learning: For Vygotsky, the only learning that is truly productive learning happens in advance of development. That is, learning *leads* development. A child does not need to be cognitively already developed in order to learn; rather, learning itself leads to cognitive development. This type of learning happens in the zone of proximal development through mediation.

Other, the: The third-point in any dialogue, the extra-subjective point of reference which makes communication possible and which functions as a point of appeal and knowledge. The Other, in addition, operates as an amassed collection of social conventions and laws, as the embodiment of the authority of the 'rules of the game'.

Orator: The speaker, narrator, or performer addressing an audience by displaying certain characteristics and competences (virtues, persona). In many instances what are perceived as the speaker's characteristics are often effectively projections of the audience.

Pathos: One of the classical means of rhetoric, pathos concerns the psychology of the audience – their expectations, characteristics, and emotions – and how it may be successfully influenced. A focus on pathos defines the sophistic tradition of rhetoric: persuading by pandering to the emotions and weaknesses of the audience.

Perlocution: What is accomplished by saying something; in Speech Act Theory this refers to the result or consequence of the utterance on the beliefs, emotions, and actions of the hearers or the speaker (e.g. surprising, convincing, annoying, amusing someone).

Perspective-taking: Cognitive, psychological, and social process whereby interlocutors understand that others have minds and perspectives of their own that need to be recognised and taken into account. Perspective-taking is central in the development of the self, mind, and community.

Persuasion: The process of inducing an individual to adopt a certain belief, attitude, or opinion through any non-violent means. Rhetoric is classically called the art of persuasion.

Phatic communication: Seemingly redundant forms of communication in which no information is learned, no new knowledge gained, but that nonetheless function to maintain or extend a social bond, to keep communicative channels open and effective.

Polarisation: Occurs when members of a group, following discussion on some topic, move towards a more extreme point relative to the initial opinion taken up by the group. In politics, polarisation is problematic to the extent that it leads diverse social groups to adopt increasingly extreme and oppositional viewpoints, thereby interfering with the ability to agree upon solutions to collective problems.

Political trust: Belief that government officials and related institutions work towards a common good, that government services are reliable and responsive, and that if need be, government can step in effectively when problems are so great that they exceed the capacity of individuals or organisations to solve them on their own.

Popular science: The products of science communication; that is, of the communication of science to laypeople.

Public opinion: Sentiment, preferences, attitudes, and/or behaviour of a group of citizens, usually measured as the aggregate result of individual responses to representative surveys. Additional formal measurement techniques include focus groups and qualitative interviews. In political discourse, public opinion is also commonly referenced in terms of the outcome of elections; forms of social protest; depictions in news coverage; forms of online expression such as blogs; consumer behaviour and marketplace trends; and opinions expressed at public meetings or via letters, phone calls, and emails to elected officials.

Pragmatics: The significance attached to the use of language, derived via examining the intentions of the speakers and the context of utterance.

Praxis: Critical reflection and informed action, enacted upon the world to bring about change. For Freire, reflection without action leads to idle chatter or verbalism; action without reflection results in action for action's sake or uninformed activism. In Freire's view only human beings – who work, who possess a thought-language, who act and are capable of reflection on themselves and on their actions – are beings of praxis (1974/2005, p. 102).

Priming: By setting the agenda of issues the public considers most important, the news media shape the criteria that the public uses to evaluate candidates, leaders, and institutions.

Problematisation: A dialectic process of analysing concrete situations and the experiences of participating interlocutor-subjects, whereby subjects critically analyse the relations and structures of their world and in so doing jointly develop new knowledge with which to act on the world.

Problem-posing: An approach to education based on classic Socratic methods of posing questions and facilitating open-ended dialogue by way of response. Through problem-posing, people 'develop their power to perceive critically *the way they exist* in the world *with which* and *in which* they find themselves; they come to see the world not as a static reality, but as a reality in process, in transformation' (Freire, 1970, p. 56, emphasis in original).

Propaganda: The ideological manipulation of ideas to support and defend the political interests of a particular group (such as a political party).

Public engagement: A dialogic form of science communication in which experts and laypeople negotiate the values, promises, and applications of science.

Public sphere: The arena of modern societies where majority and minority positions are projected and mutual influence is exerted and protected under the constitutional 'freedom of expression'.

Question: The problematic for which answers are being proposed in rhetorical forms of speaking. The question concerns what is at stake in communication and it engages both speaker and audience. A given answer might be to a different, implicit question. For every statement we thus ask: What was the question? If the questions and answers come to match, persuasion is typically achieved.

Relevance theory: A pragmatic theory which proposes that interpretation is governed by a principle of relevance, which suggests that the hearer should balance the degree of cognitive effort required against the extent of cognitive effects or inferences. In most cases, less effort and more effects indicate greater relevance.

Religious-communicative practice: The notion that religion is better understood as a way of life rather than a world-view, and that religion takes place in a variety of forms of communication and action. By making use of linguistic and other forms of communication, religious action is performed in speech acts and other types of behaviour.

Resistance: The ways in which communicative exchange enables dominant representations to be challenged, rejected or transformed; for example, through the articulation of oppositional representations. A social psychological perspective examines the psychological processes that enable resistance (e.g. representation) and the communicative genres that also may facilitate resistance (e.g. particular community dialogues).

Rhetoric: See Persuasion.

Rhetorical situation: A context that consists of a pressing issue (exigency, question), a particular audience, a speaker with character and competences, and a window of opportunity (kairos) to exert influence.

Ritual: A highly formalised and strictly regulated communal activity which is performed on special occasions. Rituals are often part of celebrations and ceremonies, and can mark important points and passages in personal or social life.

Rumour: A chain of transmission of ideas attempting to interpret an ambiguous or anxiety-provoking object, event, or issue, which contains unverified and emotion-laden content, collectively generated via modes of informal communication.

Schema: A mental representation of default information regarding a type of person, object, situation, or event. Their use in thought is taken to involve a quick categorisation process to relate a specific instance of a person, object, or situation to its general type, and to result in inferences about that instance on the basis of the default properties of the type. Schematic processing supports a form of cognitive economy, but may generate errors and distortions.

Scientific (schooled) concepts: Abstract concepts one learns through instruction (as in the case of formal school environments), to be contrasted with the spontaneous concepts we derive from everyday experience. 'Scientific' here refers not to subject content, but rather to concepts (such as those of geometry or physics) that one needs to have been taught to acquire.

Self-presentation: The efforts individuals make to regulate their behaviour in order to create (usually) positive impressions on others. Self-presentation becomes important particularly during encounters with others whose opinions count.

Serial reproduction method: A method of investigating the rumour associated with Stern (1902) and Bartlett (1932), in which a chain of participants communicate a story from 'mouth to ear', so that the first participant tells the story to the second, the second then tells what they think they heard to the third, and so on. There are reliable kinds of distortion of the original story through the chain of transmission.

Social capital: Durable networks of socially advantageous intergroup relationships.

Social identity: Those aspects of a person's self-concept that arise from his or her membership of various social groups.

Social influence: An umbrella term for all modalities by which a person or a collective enables and constrains the beliefs, values, attitudes, opinions, or behaviours of others without the use of violence, external authority, or bribery. Social influence is often identified with 'soft power'.

Social representation: A system of common values, ideas, and practices that enable people to understand each other and communicate about similar issues. It also involves a degree of subjective interpretation that leads to differences in understanding, differences of opinion, and therefore the motivation to communicate.

There are different types of representations:

> **Dominant-hegemonic representations** support the dominant cultural order, defend the interests of the powerful, and saturate commonsense.

> **Negotiated representations** occur where the reader/viewer develops a complex reinterpretation that confirms, develops *and* resists dominant discourses in line with local conditions.

> **Oppositional representations** are in direct opposition to dominant representations and so critique mainstream beliefs and discourses.

Social trust: Belief that the world is a generally benign place and that other people are generally well motivated. Social trust helps alleviate concerns by individuals that others in society will simply pursue their own narrow interests instead of working towards a greater good, and therefore is necessary to collective behaviour and action.

Soft power: The exercise and influence of symbolic power that does not entail the use of force, coercion, and bribery. Soft power is often identified with modalities of social influence.

Speech acts: The acts performed through speech; in the work of Austin, Searle, and Habermas the notion of speech acts refers to the fact that our utterances are actions, i.e. when we say something we *do* something.

Speech act theory: A pragmatic theory that proposes that the use of language in itself generates or constitutes actions in the social world.

Strategic action: A concept developed by Habermas to refer to an instrumental mode of communication oriented at one party's gain. For him, strategic action is a deficient 'monological' form of social action in which the other is not recognised as a communication partner but is merely used as a tool in order to reach one's own goals. Strategic action can be understood in a broad sense as any linguistically mediated interaction where at least one participant is moved by egocentric calculations of success directed towards perlocutionary effects.

Style: One of the features of rhetorical composition and arrangement. Notions of styles regulate the use of tropes and figurative speech.

Symbolic, the: The symbolic denotes the effective operation of collective customs and institutions. It includes the functioning of language and related differential systems (the network of social roles, laws, and customs) which work not by reference to meaning, of symbols, but on the basis of how they locate subjects, by generating the symbolic coordinates that enable such subjects to take up positions in social reality.

Theory of mind (ToM): The capacity to interpret, predict, and explain the behaviour of others in terms of their underlying mental states; for example, goals, intentions, desires, and beliefs.

The 'three musketeers of rhetoric': A reference to a French Romantic novel, where the three main characters represent the means of rhetorical persuasion of logos, ethos, and pathos working in conjunction under the motto: 'one of all, and all for one'. The search for the best balance between all three means of persuasion defines an Aristotelian definition of rhetorical rationality.

Transcendent reality: Religious people believe that there is a reality beyond our empirical world. Religions either conceive of this world-transcending reality as a personal God who can be addressed by the believers or as impersonal powers beyond the reach of human beings.

Transformative social spaces: Supportive social settings in which people are able to engage in critical dialogue with trusted peers – that ideally leads to the development of actionable understandings of obstacles to their health and well-being, and strategies for tackling these at the individual, community, or macrosocial levels.

Tropes: Figures of speech such as metaphors or metonymy. Tropes expand the capacity of linguistic expression through the non-literal use of words and expressions.

Validity claims: For Habermas, every speech act with a propositional content requires validation in an intersubjective context. Speech acts raise claims to validity that need to be redeemed argumentatively and accepted in mutual understanding. These claims refer to three dimensions: the truth of propositions, the normative rightness of interactions, and the sincerity and authenticity of individual speakers.

Zone of proximal development (ZPD): When trying to solve a problem with the help of a more competent 'other', this is the space that opens up between you and the person who is helping you. It is the space in which mediation can happen. It is not a literal space, but rather a figurative space in which optimal learning happens. As Kozulin (1990) puts it, ZPD 'taps those psychological functions which are in the process of development and which are likely to be overlooked if the focus is exclusively on the unassisted child's performance' (p. 170).

References

Abelson, R. P. (1981). 'The Psychological Status of the Script Concept'. *American Psychologist*, 36: 715–29.

Achebe, C. (1966). *A Man of the People*. Essex: Heineman.

Abric, J. C. (1993). 'Central System, Peripheral System: Their Function and Roles in the Dynamic of Social Representations'. *Papers in Social Representations*, 2(2): 75–8.

Adonis, A. and Mulgan, G. (1994). 'Back to Greece: The Scope for Direct Democracy'. *Demos Quarterly*, 3:1–28.

Ahmad, W. I. U. (1993). *'Race' and Health in Contemporary Britain*. Buckingham: Open University Press.

Alexander, C. (1996). *The Art of Being Black: The Creation of Black British Youth Identities*. Oxford: Oxford University Press.

Alexander, C. (2000). *The Asian Gang: Ethnicity, Identity, Masculinity*. Oxford: Berg.

Allan, S. (2002). *Media, Risk and Science*. Buckingham and Philadelphia: Open University Press.

Allan, S. (2009). 'Making Science Newsworthy: Exploring the Conventions of Science Journalism'. In R. Holliman, J. Thomas, S. Smidt, E. Scanlon and E. Whitelegg (Eds), *Investigating Science Communication in the Information Age: Implications for Public Engagement and Popular Media*. Oxford: Oxford University Press.

Allport, G. and Postman, J. (1947a). 'An Analysis of Rumor'. *Public Opinion Quarterly*, 10: 501–17.

Allport, G. and Postman, J. (1947b). *The Psychology of Rumor*. New York: Henry Holt.

Altarriba, J., Basnight, D. M. and Canary, T. M. (2003). 'Emotion Representation and Perception across Cultures'. In W. J. Lonner, D. L. Dinnel, S. A. Hayes and D. N. Sattler (Eds), *Online Readings in Psychology and Culture* (Unit 4, Chapter 5), (http://www.wwu.edu/~culture), Center for Cross-Cultural Research, Western Washington University, Bellingham, Washington USA.

Amnesty International USA (AIUSA) (2002). *Threat and Humiliation: Racial Profiling, National Security and Human Rights in the United States*. AIUSA.

Anderson, C. A. and Bushman, B. J. (2002). 'The Effects of Media Violence on Society'. *Science*, 295 (5564): 2377–9.

Apperly, I. A., Riggs, K. J., Simpson, A., Samson, D. and Chiavarino, C. (2006). 'Is Belief Reasoning Automatic?' *Psychological Science*, 17 (10): 841–4.

Appiah, K. A. (2006). *Cosmopolitanism: Ethics in a World of Strangers*. Princeton: Princeton University Press.

Arendt, H. (1963). *Eichmann in Jerusalem: A Report on the Banality of Evil*. New York: Viking.

Arens, E. (1994). *The Logic of Pragmatic Thinking: From Peirce to Habermas*. Atlantic Highlands, NJ: Humanities Press.

Arens, E. (1995). *Christopraxis: A Theology of Action*. Minneapolis, MN: Fortress Press.

Arens, E. (2007). *Gottesverständigung: Eine kommunikative Religionstheologie*. Freiburg: Verlag Herder.

Argyle, M. (1975). *Bodily Communication*. New York: International Universities Press.

Aristotle (1991). *The Art of Rhetoric*. Harmondsworth: Penguin.

Aristotle (2007). *On Rhetoric – a Theory of Civic Discourse* (with introduction by G. A. Kennedy). Oxford: Oxford University Press.

Aronson, E., Wilson, T. D. and Akert, R. M. (1999). *Social Psychology* (3rd edn). New York: Longman.

Arpan, L. M. and Raney, A. A. (2003). 'An Experimental Investigation of News Source and the Hostile Media Effect'. *Journalism and Mass Communication Quarterly*, 80: 265–81.

Asch, S. E. (1952/1987). *Social Psychology*. Oxford: Oxford University Press.

Askari, H. (1991). *Spiritual Quest: An Inter-Religious Dimension*. Pudsey: Seven Mirrors.

Assmann, J. (2006). *Religion and Cultural Memory*. Stanford, CA: Stanford University Press.

Atran, S. (1990). *Cognitive Foundations of Natural History: Towards an Anthropology of Science*. Cambridge: Cambridge University Press.

Atran, S. (2002). *In Gods we Trust: The Evolutionary Landscape of Religion*. Oxford: Oxford University Press.

Atran, S. and Norenzayan, A. (2004). 'Religion's Evolutionary Landscape: Counterintuition, Commitment, Compassion, Communion'. *Behavioral and Brain Sciences*, 27: 713–70.

Atran, S. (1999). 'Itzaj Maya Folk Biology'. In D. Medin and S. Atran (Eds), *Folk Biology*. Cambridge, MA: MIT Press.

Attia, S. (2010). Unpublished PhD thesis. London: London School of Economics.

Auerbach, J., Parkhurst, J., Caceres, C. and Keller, K. (2009). *Addressing Social Drivers of HIV/AIDS: Some Conceptual, Methodological and Evidentiary Considerations*. Boston: AIDS2031 Social Drivers Working Group.

Augoustinos, M. and Riggs, D. (2007). 'Representing 'Us' and 'Them': Constructing White Identities in Everyday Talk'. In G. Moloney and I. Walker (Eds), *Social Representations and Identity: Content, Process and Power*. Basingstoke: Palgrave Macmillan.

Aunger, R. A. (Ed.) (2000). *Darwinizing Culture: The Status of Memetics as a Science*. Oxford University Press.

Austin, J. L. (1962) *How to Do Things with Words*. Oxford: Oxford University Press.

Austin, J. L. (1979). *Philosophical Papers*. Oxford: Clarendon Press.

Avis, M. and Harris, P. (1992). 'Belief-Desire Reasoning among Baka Children: Evidence for a Universal Conception of Mind'. *Child Development*, 62: 460–7.

Bach, K. (1994). *Thought and Reference*. London: Oxford University Press.

Bailey, W., Nowicki, S. and Cole, S. P. (1998). 'The Ability to Decode Nonverbal Information in African American, African and Afro-Caribbean, and European American Adults'. *Journal of Black Psychology*, 24 (4): 418–31.

Bakhtin, M. M. (1981). *The Dialogic Imagination: Four Essays*. Austin: University of Texas Press.

Barber, B. (1984). *Strong Democracy: Participatory Politics for a New Age*. Berkeley: University of California Press.

Bargh, J. A., Chen, M. and Burrows, L. (1996). 'Automaticity of Social Behavior: Direct Effects of Trait Construct and Stereotype Activation on Action'. *Journal of Personality and Social Psychology*, 71: 230–44.

Barkow, J.H. (1992). 'Beneath New Culture is Old Psychology: Gossip and Social Stratification'. In Barkow, J. H., Cosmides, L. and Tooby, J. (Eds), *The Adapted Mind: Evolutionary Psychology and the Generation of Culture*. Oxford: Oxford University Press.

Barkow, J. H. (1975). 'Prestige and Culture: A Biosocial Interpretation (and Replies)'. *Current Anthropology*, 16: 553–76.

Barley, S. and Kunda, G. (1992). 'Design and Devotion: Surges of Rational and Normative Ideologies of Control in Managerial Discourse'. *Administrative Science Quarterly*, 37 (3): 363–99.

Barnett, A. and Hodgetts, D. (2007). 'Child Poverty and Government Policy'. *Journal of Community & Applied Social Psychology*, 17 (4): 296–312.

Barnlund, D. C. (1975). 'Communicative Styles of Two Cultures: Public and Private Self in Japan and the United States'. In A. Kendon, R. M. Harris and M. R. Key (Eds), *Organization of Behaviour in Face-to-Face Interaction*. The Hague: Mouton.

Baron, R. A. and Byrne, D (1994). *Social Psychology: Understanding Human Interaction* (7th edn). Boston: Allyn and Bacon.

Barrett, J. L. (2008). 'Coding and Quantifying Counterintuitiveness in Religious Concepts: Theoretical and Methodological Reflections'. *Method & Theory in the Study of Religion*, 20 (4): 308–38.

Barrett, H. C. and Kurzban, R. (2006). 'Modularity in Cognition: Framing the Debate'. *Psychological Review*, 113: 628–47.

Barrick, M. R., Day, D. V., Lord, R. G. and Alexander, R. A. (1991). 'Assessing the Utility of Executive Leadership'. *The Leadership Quarterly*, 2: 9–22.

Barsalou, L. W. (2008). 'Grounded Cognition'. *Annual Review of Psychology*, 59: 617–45.

Barsalou, L. W. (1983). 'Ad hoc Categories'. *Memory & Cognition*, 11: 211–27.

Barthes, R. (1968). *Elements of Semiology*. New York: Hill and Wang.

Barthes, R. (1964). 'L' ancienne rhetorique – aide memoire'. *Communication*, 16: 254–337.

Bartlett, F. C. (1923). *Psychology and Primitive Culture*. London: Cambridge University Press.

Bartlett, F. C. (1928). 'An Experimental Repeated Reproduction'. *Journal of General Psychology*, 1: 54–63.

Bartlett, F. C. (1932). *Remembering: A Study in Experimental and Social Psychology*. London: Cambridge University Press.

Batel, S. and Castro, P. (2009). 'A Social Representations Approach to the Communication between Different Spheres: An Analysis of the Impacts of Two Discursive Formats'. *Journal for the Theory of Social Behaviour*, Vol. 39, No. 4, Pg. 415–433.

Bateson, G. (1972). *Steps to an Ecology of Mind*. New York: Ballantine Books.

Bateson, G. and Hinde, R. A. (Eds) (1976). *Growing Points in Ethology*. Cambridge: Cambridge University Press.

Bauer, M. W. (1991). 'Resistance to Change – a Monitor of New Technology'. *Systems Practice*, 4 (3): 181–96.

Bauer, M. W. (1997). 'Towards a Functional Analysis of Resistance'. In M. W. Bauer (Ed.), *Resistance to New Technology – Nuclear Power, Information Technology, Biotechnology*. Cambridge, Cambridge University Press, pp. 393–418.

Bauer, M. W. (2008). 'Social Influence by Artefacts'. *Diogenes*, 55: 68–83.

Bauer M. W. and Bonfadelli, H. (2002). 'Controversy, Media Coverage and Public Knowledge'. In M. W. Bauer and G. Gaskell (Eds), *Biotechnology: The Making of a Global Controversy*. Cambridge: Cambridge University Press.

Bauer, M., Durant, J., Ragnarsdottir, A. and Rudolphsdottir, A. (1995). 'Science and Technology in the British Press, 1946–1990'. *London Science Museum Technological Reports*, 1: 3–40.

Bauer, M. W. (1998). 'The Medicalisation of Science News: From the 'Rocket-Scalpel' to the 'Gene-Meteorite' Complex'. *Social Science Information*, 37 (4): 731–51.

Bauer, M. W. (2008). 'Survey Research and the Public Understanding of Science'. In B. Trench and M. Bucchi (Eds), *Handbook of Public Communication of Science and Technology*. New York: Routledge, pp. 111–30.

Bauer, M. W. and Gaskell, G. (2002). *Biotechnology: The Making of a Global Controversy*. Cambridge: Cambridge University Press.

Bauer, M. W. and Gregory, J. (2007). 'From Journalism to Corporate Communication in Post-War Britain'. In M. W. Bauer and M. Bucchi (Eds), *Journalism, Science, and Society: Science Communication between News and Public Relations*. London: Routledge.

Bauer, R. A. (1964). 'The Obstinate Audience: The Influence Process from the Point of View of Social Communication'. *American Psychologist*, 19: 319–28.

Baum, M. A. and Gussin, P. (2007). 'In the Eye of the Beholder: How Information Shortcuts Shape Individual Perceptions of Bias in the Media'. *Quarterly Journal of Political Science*, 3: 1–31.

Baumann, G. (1996). *Contesting Culture: Discourses of Identity in Multi-Ethnic London*. Cambridge: Cambridge University Press.

Baumeister, R. F., Zhang, L. and Vohs, K. D. (2004). 'Gossip as Cultural Learning'. *Review of General Psychology*, 8: 111–21.

Bechtel, W. (Ed.) (1986). *Integrating Scientific Disciplines*. Dordrecht: Martinus Nijhoff.

Bechtel, W. (1988). *Philosophy of Science: An Overview for Cognitive Science*. Hillsdale, NJ: Erlbaum.

Bechtel, W. and Hamilton, A. (2007). 'Reductionism, Integration, and the Unity of the Sciences'. In T. Kuipers (Ed.), *Philosophy of Science: Focal Issues* (Volume 1 of the *Handbook of the Philosophy of Science*). New York: Elsevier.

Beckett, C. (2008). *Supermedia: Saving Journalism so it can Save the World*. Chichester: Blackwell.

Beder, S. (1999). 'Public Participation or Public Relations?' With commentaries by G. McDonell and B. Selinger. In B. Martin (Ed.), *Technology and Public Participation*. Australia: Science and Technology Studies, University of Wollongong, pp. 169–92.

Belch, G. E. and Belch, M. A. (2004). *Advertising and Promotion: An Integrated Marketing Communications Perspective* (6th edn). New York: McGraw-Hill/Irwin.

Bell, C. (1992). *Ritual Theory, Ritual Practice*. Oxford: Oxford University Press.

Bell, C. (1997). *Ritual: Perspectives and Dimensions*. Oxford: Oxford University Press.

Benedictus, L. (2005). 'Every Race, Colour, Nation and Religion on Earth'. *The Guardian*, 14 August 2009, Retrieved from http://www.guardian.co.uk/uk/2005/jan/21/britishidentity1.

Benhabib, S. (2002). *The Claims of Culture: Equality and Diversity in the Global Era*. Princeton: Princeton University Press.

Benjamin Jr., L. T. and Simpson, J. A. (2009). 'The Power of the Situation: The Impact of Milgram's Obedience Studies on Personality and Social Psychology'. *American Psychologist*, 64: 12–19.

Benjamin, W. (2005). 'Theses on the Philosophy of History'. In E. Mendieta (Ed.), *The Frankfurt School on Religion: Key Writings by the Major Thinkers*. Milton Park: Routledge, pp. 265–73.

Bennett, J. M. (1993). 'Cultural Marginality: Identity and Issues in Intercultural Training'. In R. M. Paige (Ed.), *Education for the Intercultural Experience*. Yarmouth, ME: Intercultural Press, pp. 109–36.

Bennett, L. (2007). 'Relief in Hard Times: A Defense of Jon Stewart's Comedy in an Age of Cynicism'. *Critical Studies in Mass Communication*, 24 (3): 278–83.

Bennett, W. L. and Iyengar, S. (2008). 'A New Era of Minimal Effects? The Changing Foundations of Political Communication'. *Journal of Communication*, 58: 707–31.

Berger, P. (1974). *Pyramids of Sacrifice: Political Ethics and Social Change*. London: Penguin.

Berger, P. and Luckmann, T. (1966). *The Social Construction of Reality: A Treatise in the Sociology of Knowledge*. New York: Anchor Books.

Berger, P. and Luckman, T. (1966). *The Social Construction of Reality*. London: Penguin Books.

Bergmann, J. R. (1993). *Discreet Indiscretions: The Social Organization of Gossip*. New York: Aldine.

Berkman, L. (1984). 'Assessing the Physical Health Effects of Social Networks and Social Support'. *Annual Review of Public Health*, 5: 413–32.

Bermudez, J. L. (2002). 'The Domain of Folk Psychology'. In A. O'Hear (Ed.), *Minds and Persons*. Cambridge: Cambridge University Press.

Bicknell, S. and Farmelo, G. (1993). *Museum Visitor Studies in the 90s*. London: Science Museum.

Billig, M. (1996). *Arguing and Thinking*. Cambridge: Cambridge University Press.

Bird, S. R. (2009). *Light, Bright and Damned Near White*. Westport: Praeger.

Bitzer, L. (1968). 'The Rhetorical Situation'. *Philosophy and Rhetoric*, 1, 1–14. (republished in J. L. Lucaites, C. M. Condit and S. Caudill (Eds) (1999) *Contemporary Rhetorical Theory*, pp. 217–25. New York: Guildford Press).

Blackburn, J. (2000). 'Understanding Paulo Freire: Reflections on the Origins, Concepts, and Possible Pitfalls of his Educational Approach'. *Community Development Journal*, 35: 3–15.

Blass, T. (2009). 'From New Haven to Santa Clara: A Historical Perspective on the Milgram Obedience Experiments'. *American Psychologist*, 64: 37–45.

Blass, T. (2004). *The Man who Shocked the World: The Life and Legacy of Stanley Milgram*. New York: Basic Books.

Blum-Kulka, S., Danet, B. and Gerson, R. (1985). 'The Language of Requesting in Israeli Society'. In J. Forgas (Ed.), *Language and Social Situation*. New York: Springer.

Bochner, S. (1982). 'The Social Psychology of Cross-Cultural Relations'. In S. Bochner (Ed.), *Cultures in Contact: Studies in Cross-Cultural Interaction*. Oxford: Pergamon.

Bodenhausen, G. V., Sheppard, L. A. and Kramer, G. P. (1994). 'Negative Affect and Social Judgment: The Differential Impact of Anger and Sadness'. *European Journal of Social Psychology*, 24: 45–62.

Boehm, C. (1993). 'Egalitarian Behaviour and Reverse Dominance Hierarchy (and Replies)'. *Current Anthropology*, 34: 227–54.

Boone, J. L. (2000). 'Status Signaling, Social Power, and Lineage Survival'. In M. W. Diehl (Ed.), *Hierarchies in Action: Cui Bono?* Carbondale Ill.: Southern Illinois University, pp. 84–110.

Bordia, P. (1996). 'Studying Verbal Interaction on the Internet: The Case of Rumor Transmission Research'. *Behavior Research Methods, Instruments, & Computers*, 28: 148–51.

Bordia, P., DiFonzo, N. and Chang, A. (1999). 'Rumor as Group Problem-Solving: Development Patterns in Informal Computer-Mediated Groups'. *Small Group Research*, 30: 8–28.

Bordia, P. and DiFonzo, N. (2004). 'Problem Solving in Social Interactions on the Internet: Rumor As Social Cognition'. *Social Psychology Quarterly*, 67 (1): 33–49.

Bourdieu, P. (1994). *Language and Symbolic Power*. Cambridge: Polity Press.

Bourdieu, P. (1986). 'The Forms of Capital'. In J. Richardson (Ed.), *Handbook of Theory and Research for the Sociology of Education*. New York: Greenwood, pp. 241–8.

Bower, G. H. (1981). 'Mood and Memory'. *American Psychologist*, 36: 129–48.

Boyd, R. and Richerson, P. J. (1985). *Culture and the Evolutionary Process*. Chicago, IL: University of Chicago Press.

Boyer, P. (1993). *Cognitive Aspects of Religious Symbolism*. Cambridge: Cambridge University Press.

Boyer, P. (1994a). *The Naturalness of Religious Ideas*. London: University of California Press.

Boyer, P. (1994b). 'Cognitive Constraints on Cultural Representations: Natural Ontologies and Religious Ideas'. In L. A. Hirschfeld and S. Gelman (Eds), *Mapping the Mind: Domain Specificity in Cognition*. Cambridge: Cambridge University Press.

Boyer, P. (2000). 'Natural Epistemology or Evolved Metaphysics? Developmental Evidence for Early-Developed, Intuitive, Category-Specific, Incomplete, and Stubborn Metaphysical Presumptions'. *Philosophical Psychology*, 13: 277–97.

Boyer, P. (2001). *Religion Explained: The Human Instincts that Fashion Gods, Spirits and Ancestors*. London: Vintage.

Boyer, P. (2001). *Religion Explained: The Evolutionary Origins of Religious Thought*. New York: Basic Books.

Braet, A. C. (1992). 'Ethos, Pathos and Logos in Aristotle's Rhetoric: A Re-Examination'. *Argumentation*, 6, 307–20.

Braithwaite, C. A. (1999). 'Cultural Uses and Interpretations of Silence'. In L. K. Guerrero, J. A. DeVito and M. L. Hecht (Eds), *The Nonverbal Communication Reader: Classic and Contemporary Readings*. Prospect Heights, IL: Waveland Press, pp. 163–72.

Brewer, M. B. (1988). 'A Dual Process Model of Impression Formation'. In R. Wyer and T. Scrull (Eds), *Advances in Social Cognition*, volume 1. New York: Erlbaum.

Brown, P. and Levinson, S. (1986). *Politeness*. Cambridge: Cambridge University Press.

Brown, P. and Levinson, S. (1987). *Politeness: Some Universals in Language Usage*. Cambridge: Cambridge University Press.

Bruner, J. S. (1991). 'The Narrative Construction of Reality'. *Critical Inquiry*, 18(1): 1–21.

Bruner, J. S. (2002). *Making Stories: Law, Literature, Life*. New York: Farrer, Strauss and Giroux.

Bucchi, M. (2004). *Science in Society: An Introduction to Social Studies of Science*. London: Routledge.

Buehler, K. (1990/1934). *Theory of Language: The Representational Function of Language*. Translated by Donald F. Goodwin, with an Introduction by Achim Eschbach. Amsterdam and Philadelphia: John Benjamins.

Buller, D. J. (2005). *Adapting Minds*. Cambridge, MA: MIT Press.

Burger, J. M. (2009). 'Replicating Milgram: Would People still Obey Today?' *American Psychologist*, 64: 1–11.

Buss, D. (1999). *Evolutionary Psychology: The New Science of the Mind*. Boston, MA: Allyn & Bacon.

Calhoun, C. (Ed.) (1992). *Habermas and the Public Sphere*. Cambridge, MA: MIT Press.

Campbell, C. (2003). *Letting them Die: Why HIV Prevention Programmes Fail*. Oxford: James Currey.

Campbell, C. (2004). 'Health Psychology and Community Action'. In M. Murray (Ed.), *Critical Health Psychology*. Basingstoke: Palgrave Macmillan.

Campbell, C. and Jovchelovitch, S. (2000). 'Health, Community and Development: Towards a Social Psychology of Participation'. *Journal of Community and Applied Social Psychology*, 10: 255–70.

Campbell, C., Nair, Y. and Maimane, S. (2007). 'Building Contexts that Support Effective Community Responses to HIV/AIDS: A South African Case Study'. *American Journal of Community Psychology*, 39: 347–63.

Campbell, C. and Murray, M. (2004). 'Community Health Psychology: Promoting Analysis and Action for Social Change'. *Journal of Health Psychology*, 9 (2): 187–96.

Cappella, J. N. and Jamieson, K. H. (1997). *Spiral of Cynicism: The Press and the Public Good*. New York: Oxford University Press.

Caprariello, P. A., Cuddy, J. C. and Fiske, S. T. (2009). 'Social Structure Shapes Cultural Stereotypes and Emotions: A Causal Test of the Stereotype Content Model'. *Group Processes and Intergroup Behavior*, 12: 147–55.

Carassa, A. and Colombetti, M. (2009). 'Joint Meaning'. *Journal of Pragmatics*, 41 (9): 1837–54.

Carlson, W. S .(1991). 'Questioning in Classrooms: A Sociolinguistic Perspective'. *Review of Educational Research*, 61: 157–78.

Carruthers, P. (2006). *The Architecture of the Mind: Massive Modularity and the Flexibility of Thought*. Oxford: Oxford University Press.

Caro, P. (1993). *La roue des science*. France: Albin Michel.

Cassidy, A. (2005). 'Popular Evolutionary Psychology in the UK: An Unusual Case of Science in the Media?' *Public Understanding of Science*, 14: 115–41.

Cassidy, A. (2006) 'Evolutionary Psychology as Public Science and Boundary Work'. *Public Understanding of Science*, 15: 175–205.

Castells, M. (2000). *The Rise of the Network Society*. New York: Wiley, Blackwell.

Cazden, C. B. (1986). 'Classroom Discourse'. In M. C. Wittrock (Ed.), *Handbook of Research on Teaching: A Project of the American Educational Research Association*. New York: Macmillan, pp. 432–63.

Chaiken, S., Wood, W. and Eagly, A. H. (1996). 'Principles of Persuasion'. In E. T. Higgins and A. W. Kruglanski (Eds), *Social Psychology: Handbook of Basic Principles*. New York: Guilford Press.

Chemers, M. M. (2001). 'Leadership Effectiveness: An Integrative Review'. In M. A. Hogg and R. S. Tindale (Eds), *Blackwell Handbook of Social Psychology: Group Processes*. Oxford: Blackwell, pp. 283–310.

Cheney, D. and Seyfarth, R. (1990). *How Monkeys See the World: Inside the Mind of Another Species*. Chicago, IL: University of Chicago Press.

Christians, C. and Traber, M. (Eds) (1997). *Communication Ethics and Universal Values*. Thousands Oaks, CA: Sage Publications.

Cialdini, R. B., Borden, R. J., Thorne, A., Walker, M., Freeman, S., and Sloan, L. (1976). 'Basking in Reflected Glory: Three (Football) Field Studies'. *Journal of Personality and Social Psychology*, 34, 366–75.

Cieslik, A. and Verkuyten, M. (2006). 'National, Ethnic and Religious Identities: Hybridity and the case of the Polish Tatars'. *National Identities*, 8 (2): 77–93.

Clark, A. (1997). *Being There*. Cambridge: MIT Press.

Clark, A. (1999). 'An Embodied Cognitive Science?' *Trends in Cognitive Science*, 9: 345–51.

Clark, H. H. (1996). *Using Language*. Cambridge: Cambridge University Press.

Clore, G. L. and Huntsinger, J. R. (2007). 'How Emotions Inform Judgment and Regulate Thought'. *Trends in Cognitive Science*, 11: 393–9.

Clore, G. L. and Storbeck, J. (2006). 'Affect as Information about Liking, Efficacy, and Importance'. In J. Forgas (Ed.), *Affect in Social Thinking and Behavior*. New York: Psychology Press.

Coch, L. and French, L. R. P. (1948). 'Overcoming Resistance to Change'. *Human Relations*, 1: 512–32.

Cohen, B. (1963). *The Press and Foreign Policy*. Princeton, NJ: Princeton University Press.

Collins, H. M. (1981). 'The Role of the Core-Set in Modern Science: Social Contingency with Methodological Propriety in Science'. *History of Science*, 19: 6–19.

Collins, H. M. and Evans, R. J. (2007). *Rethinking Expertise*. Chicago, IL: The University of Chicago Press.

Collins, H. and Pinch, T. (1979). 'The Construction of the Paranormal: Nothing Unscientific is Happening'. In R. Wallis (Ed.), *On the Margins of Science: The Social Construction of Rejected Knowledge*. *Sociological Review* Monograph No. 27 Keele, UK: University of Keele Press.

Comblin, J. (1990). *Retrieving the Human: A Christian Anthropology*. Maryknoll, NY: Orbis Books.

Commission for Racial Equality/Ethnos (2005). *Citizenship and Belonging: What is Britishness?* London: Commission for Racial Equality.

Converse, B. A., Lin, S., Keysar, B. and Epley, N. (2008). 'In the Mood to Get Over Yourself: Mood Affects Theory-of-Mind Use'. *Emotion*, 8: 725–30.

Corbett, E. P. J. (1999). *Classical Rhetoric for the Modern Student*. Oxford: Oxford University Press.

Cornish, F. (2004a). *Constructing an Actionable Environment: Collective Action for HIV Prevention among Kolkata Sex Workers*. Unpublished PhD Thesis. London: London School of Economics.

Cornish, F. (2004b). 'Making "Context" Concrete: A Dialogical Approach to the Society-Health Relation'. *Journal of Health Psychology*, 9: 281–94.

Corno, Lyn, and Snow, Richard E. (1986). 'Adapting Teaching to Individual Differences among Learners'. In Merlin C. Wittrock (Ed.), *Handbook of Research on Teaching*. 3rd edn. New York: Macmillan.

Counselman, E. (1991). 'Leadership in a Long-Term Leaderless Women's Group'. *Small group Research*, 22: 240–57.

Cranach, M. v (1986). 'Leadership as a Function of Group Action'. In C. F. Graumann and S. Moscovici (Eds), *Changing Conceptions of Leadership*. New York: Springer, pp. 115–34.

Cranach, M. v (1996). 'Towards a Theory of the Acting Group'. In E. Witte and J. Davis (Eds), *Understanding Group Behaviour. Vol. 2: Small Group Processes and Personal Relations*. New Jersey: Lawrence Erlbaum.

Crocker, J. (1999). 'Social Stigma and Self-Esteem: Situational Construction of Self-Worth'. *Journal of Experimental Social Psychology*, 35: 89–107.

Crossley, M. (2000). *Rethinking Health Psychology*. Buckingham: Open University Press.

Crowther, J. G. (1967). *Science in Modern Society*. London: Cresset.

Connolly, P (1998). *Racism, Gender Identities and Young Children: Social Relations in a Multi-Ethnic, Inner-City Primary School*. London: Routledge.

Cowen, T. (2002). *Creative Destruction: How Globalization is Changing the World's Cultures*. Princeton, NJ: Princeton University Press.

Curran, J., Iyengar, S., Lund, A. B. and Salovaara-Moring, I. (2009). 'Media System, Public Knowledge and Democracy'. *European Journal of Communication*, 24: 5–26.

Curtin, P. (Ed.) (1972). *Africa and the West: Intellectual Responses to European Culture*. Wisconsin: University of Wisconsin Press.

D'Alessio, D. and Allen, M. (2000). 'Media Bias in Presidential Elections: A Meta-Analysis'. *Journal of Communication*, 50(4): 133–56.

D'Andrade, R. (1995). *The Development of Cognitive Anthropology*. Cambridge: Cambridge University Press.

D'Andrade, R. G. (1992). 'Schemas and Motivation'. In R. G. D'Andrade and C. Strauss (Eds), *Human Motives and Cultural Models*. Cambridge: Cambridge University Press.

Daniels, H. (2001). *Vygotsky and Pedagogy*. New York: Routledge.

Darcy De Oliveira, R. and Dominice, P. (1974). *Freire, Illich: The Pedagogy of the Oppressed. The Oppression of Pedagogy*. Geneva: Institute of Cultural Action.

Darden, L. and Maull, N. (1977). 'Interfield Theories'. *Philosophy of Science*, 44: 43–64.

Damasio, A. (1995). *Descartes' Error*. Oxford: Oxford University Press.

Davies, B. (2007). 'Grice's Cooperative Principle: Meaning and Rationality'. *Journal of Pragmatics*, 39: 2308–31.

Davydov, V. V. (1975). 'Logical and Psychological Problems of Elementary Mathematics as an Academic Subject'. *Soviet Studies in the Psychology of Learning and Teaching Mathematics*, 7: 55–108.

Davydov, V. V. (1982). 'The Psychological Structure and Contents of the Learning Activity in School Children'. In R. Glaser and J. Lompscher (Eds), *Cognitive and Motivational Aspects of Instruction*. Berlin: Deutscher Verlag der Wissenschaften.

Dawkins, R. (1976). *The Selfish Gene*. Oxford: Oxford University Press.

Dawkins, R. (2006). *The God Delusion*. London: Bantam Press.

Deaux, K. and Wiley, S. (2007). 'Moving People and Shifting Representations: Making Immigrant Identities'. In G. Moloney and I. Walker (Eds), *Social Representations and Identity: Content, Process and Power*. Basingstoke: Palgrave Macmillan.

De Backer, C., Nelissen, M., Vyncke, P., Braeckman, J. and McAndrew, F. (2007). 'Celebrities: From Teachers to Friends: A Test of Two Hypotheses on the Adaptiveness of Celebrity Gossip'. *Human Nature*, 18 (4): 334–54.

Delli Carpini, M. X. and Keeter, S. (1996). *What Americans Know About Politics and Why it Matters*. New Haven, CT: Yale University Press.

Delli Carpini, M. X., Cook, F. L. and Jacobs, L. (2004). 'Public Deliberation, Discursive Participation and Citizen Engagement: A Review of the Empirical Literature'. *Annual Review of Political Science*, 7: 315–44.

Dennett, D. C. (2000). 'Making Tools for Thinking'. In D. Sperber (Ed.), *Metarepresentations*. Oxford: Oxford University Press.

Deutsch, M. and Gerrard, H. B. (1955). 'A Study of Normative and Informational Social Influences upon Individual Judgment'. *Journal of Abnormal and Social Psychology*, 51: 629–36.

De Waal, F. (1998). *Chimpanzee Politics*. Baltimore, MD: John Hopkins University.

Dhesi, J. (2009). 'Made to Stick? Exploring the Potentials of a Cognition and Culture Account of Social Group Stereotypes'. Unpublished PhD Thesis. London: London School of Economics.

Diaz. R. M., Neal, C. J. and Amaya-Williams. (1993). 'The Social Origins of Self-Regulation'. In L. Moll (Ed.), *Vygotsky and Education: Instructional Implications and Applications of Sociohistorical Psychology*. Cambridge: Cambridge University Press, pp. 127–52.

DiFonzo, N. and Bordia, P. (1998). *How Top PR Professionals Handle Hot Air: Types of Corporate Rumors, their Effects, and Strategies to Manage them*. Gainesville, FL: Institute for Public Relations.

DiFonzo, N. and Bordia, P. (2000). 'How Top PR Professionals Handle Hearsay: Corporate Rumors, their Effects, and Strategies to Manage them'. *Public Relations Review*, 26: 173–90.

DiFonzo, N., Bordia, P. and Rosnow, R. L. (1994). 'Reining in Rumors'. *Organizational Dynamics*, 23: 47–62.

Dijksterhuis, A. and Bargh, J. A. (2001). 'The Perception-Behavior Expressway: Automatic Effects of Social Perception on Social Behavior'. In M. P. Zanna (Ed.), *Advances in Experimental Social Psychology*. San Diego: Academic Press, pp. 1–40.

Dillon, J. T. (1986). 'Student Questioning and Individual Learning'. *Educational Theory*, 36(4): 333–41.

Dillon, J. T. (1988). *Questioning and Teaching: A Manual of Practice*. London: Croom Helm.

DiMaggio, P., Hargittai, E., Celeste, C. and Shafer, S. (2004). 'Digital Inequality: From Unequal Access to Differentiated Use'. In K. M. Neckerman (Ed.), *Social Inequality*. New York: Russell Sage Foundation, pp. 355–400.

Djurodie, B. (2003). 'Limitations of Public Dialogue about Science and the Rise of the New "Experts"'. *Critical Review of International Social and Political Philosophy*, 6(4): 82–92.

Doi, T. (1971). *The Anatomy of Dependency – the Key Analysis of Japanese Behavior*. Tokyo: Kodansha International Ltd.

Doise, W. and Palmonari, A. (1984). *Social Interaction and Individual Development*. Cambridge and Paris: Cambridge University Press and Editions de la Maison des Sciences de l'Homme.

Dornan, C. (1990). 'Some Problems in Conceptualizing the Issue of "Science and the Media"'. *Critical Studies in Mass Communication*, 7: 48–71.

Driver, T. F. (1991). *The Magic of Ritual: Our Need for Liberating Rites that Transform Our Lives and Our Communities*. San Francisco, CA: Harper.

Dunbar, R. (1998). *Grooming, Gossip, and the Evolution of Language*. Cambridge, MA: Harvard University Press.

Durkheim, E. (1898). 'Representations indivuelles et representations collectives'. *Revue de Metaphysique et de Morale*, 6: 273–302.

Duveen, G. (1994). 'Children as Social Actors: A Developmental Perspective on Social Representations'. In P. Guareschi and S. Jovchelovitch (Eds), *Testos sobre representaces sociais*.

Duveen, G. (2000). 'The Power of Ideas'. In S. Moscovici *Social Representations: Explorations in Social Psychology*. Cambridge: Polity Press.

Duveen, G. (2008). 'Social Actors and Social Groups: A Return to Heterogeneity in Social Psychology'. *Journal for the Theory of Social Behaviour*, 34 (4): pp. 369–74.

Duveen, G. and Lloyd, B. (1986). 'The Significance of Social Identities'. *British Journal of Social Psychology*, 25: 219–30.

Duveen, G. and Lloyd, B. (1990). *Social Representations and the Development of Knowledge*. Cambridge: Cambridge University Press.

Eagly, A. H. and Chaiken, S. (1984). 'Cognitive Theories of Persuasion'. In L. Berkowitz (Ed.), *Advances in Experimental Social Psychology*. New York: Academic Press, pp. 268–59.

Eagly, A. H. and Chaiken, S. (1993). *The Psychology of Attitudes*. San Diego, CA: Harcourt Brace Jovanovich.

Eco, U. (1976). *A theory of Semiotics*. Bloomington: Indiana University Press.

Edelman, M. S. and Omark, D. R. (1973). 'Dominance Hierarchies in Young Children'. *Social Science Information*, 12: 103–10.

Eggins, S. and Martin, J. R. (1997). 'Genres and Registers of Discourse'. In T. A. van Dijk (Ed.), *Discourse as Structure and Process*. London: Sage.

Eggins, S. and Slade, D. (1997). *Analyzing Casual Conversation*. London: Cassell.

Eibl-Eibesfeldt, I. (1970). *Ethology: The Biology of Behaviour*. New York: Holt, Rinehart & Winston.

Einsiedel, E. (2008). 'Public Engagement and Dialogue: A Research Review'. In M. Bucchi and B. Smart (Eds), *Handbook of Public Communication on Science and Technology*. London: Routledge, pp. 173–84.

Eisenberger, N. I., Liebermann, M. D. and Williams, K. D. (2003). 'Does Rejection Hurt? An fMRI Study of Social Exclusion'. *Science*, 302: 290–2.

Ekman, P. (2003). *Emotions Revealed: Recognizing Faces and Feelings to Improve Communication and Emotional Life.* New York: Henry Holt and Company.

Ekman, P. and Friesen, W. V. (1986). 'A New Pan Cultural Expression of Emotion'. *Motivation and Emotion*, 10: 159–68.

Elam, M. and Bertilsson, M. (2003). 'Consuming, Engaging and Confronting Science: The Emerging Dimensions of Scientific Citizenship'. *European Journal of Social Theory*, 6(2): 233–51.

Eliade, M. (1985). *A History of Religious Ideas.* 3 Volumes. Chicago, IL: University of Chicago Press.

Elias, J. and Merriam, S. (1980). *Philosophical Foundations of Adult Education.* Huntington, NY: Krieger Publishing.

Ellsworth, E. (1989). 'Why Doesn't this Feel Empowering? Working through the Repressive Myths of Critical Pedagogy'. *Harvard Educational Review*, 59: 297–324.

Emler, N. (1994). 'Gossip, Reputation and Social Adaptation'. In R. Goodman and A. Ben Ze'ev (Eds), *Good Gossip.* Kansas: Kansas University Press.

Engeström, Y. (1987). *Learning by Expanding: An Activity-Theoretic Approach to Developmental Research.* Helsinki: Orienta-Konsultit Oy.

Engeström, Y. (1989). 'The Cultural-Historical Theory of Activity and the Study of Political Repression'. *International Journal of Mental Health*, 17 (4): 29–41.

Engeström, Y. (1990). *Learning, Working and Imagining Twelve Studies in Activity Theory.* Helsinki: Orienta-Konsultit Oy.

Engeström, Y. (1991). 'Non scolae sed vitae discimus: Toward Overcoming the Encapsulation of School Learning'. *Learning and Instruction*, 1: 243–59.

Entman, R. M. (1993). ,Framing: Toward Clarification of a Fractured Paradigm'. *Journal of Communication*, 43 (4): 51–8.

Epley, N., Morewedge, C. K. and Keysar, B. (2004) 'Perspective Taking in Children and Adults: Equivalent Egocentrism but Differential Correction'. *Journal of Experimental Social Psychology*, 40 (6): 760–8.

Epstein, S. (1996). *Impure Science; AIDS, Activism, and the Politics of Knowledge.* Berkeley, CA: University of California Press.

Eshun, E. (2005). *Black Gold of the Sun: Searching for Home in England and Africa.* London: Penguin Books.

Evans, D. (1996). *An Introductory Dictionary of Lacanian Psychoanalysis.* London and New York: Routledge.

Eveland, W. P., Jr. and Scheufele, D. A. (2000). ,Connecting News Media Use with Gaps in Knowledge and Participation'. *Political Communication*, 17 (3): 215–37.

Eveland, W. P., Jr. (2003). 'A Mix of Attributes Approach to the Study of Media Effects and New Communication Technologies'. *Journal of Communication*, 53 (3): 395–410.

Eveland, W. P., Jr. and Shah, D. V. (2003). 'The Impact of Individual and Interpersonal Factors on Perceived News Media Bias'. *Political Psychology*, 24: 101–17.

Facundo, B. (1984). *Freire Inspired Programs in the United States and Puerto Rico: A Critical Evaluation.* Washington, DC: Latino Institute.

Fahnestock, J. (1993). 'Accommodating Science: The Rhetorical Life of Scientific Facts'. In W. McRae (Ed.), *The Literature of Science – Perspectives on Popular Scientific Writing.* Athens, GA: University of Georgia Press.

Farmer, P. (2003). *Pathologies of Power: Health, Human Rights and the New War on the Poor.* Berkeley: University of California Press.

Faubert, M., Locke, D., Sprinthall, N. and Howland, W. (1996). 'Promoting Cognitive and Ego Development of African-American Rural Youth: A Program of Deliberate Psychological Education'. *Journal of Adolescence*, 19: 533–43.

Faucheux, C. and Moscovici, S. (1967). 'Le style de comportement d'une minorité et son influence sur les réponses d'une majorité'. *Bulletin du C.E.R.P.*, 16: 337–60.

Faulstich, W. (1997). *Das Medium als Kult. Von den Anfängen bis zur Spätantike (8. Jahrhundert)*. Göttingen: Vandenhoek & Ruprecht.

Feldman, M. W. and Cavalli-Sforza, L. L. (1976). 'Cultural and Biological Evolutionary Processes, Selection for a Trait under Complex Transmission'. *Theoretical Population Biology*, 9: 238–59.

Figueroa, E. and Patrick, P. L. (2002). 'Kiss-Teeth'. *American Speech*, 77 (4): 383–97.

Fishbein, M., Middlestadt, S. and Hitchcock, P. (1994). 'Using Information to Change Sexually Transmitted Disease-Related Behaviors: An Analysis Based on the Theory on the Theory of Reasoned Action'. In R. Diclemente and J. Peterson (Eds), *Preventing AIDS: Theories and Methods of Behavioural Interventions*. New York: Plenum Press.

Fishkin, J. S. (1995). *The Voice of the People: Public Opinion and Democracy*. New Haven, CT: Yale University Press.

Fishkin, J. and Luskin, R. (1999). 'Bringing Deliberation to the Democratic Dialogue'. In M. McCombs and A. Reynolds (Eds), *A Poll with a Human Face: The National Issues Convention Experiment in Political Communication*. Mahwah, NJ: Lawrence Erlbaum, pp. 3–38.

Fiske, S. T. (1998). 'Stereotyping, Prejudice, and Discrimination'. In D. T. Gilbert, S. T. Fiske and G. Lindzey (Eds), *The Handbook of Social Psychology*. New York: McGraw-Hill.

Fiske, S. T. and Taylor, S. E. (1991). *Social Cognition*. New York: McGraw-Hill.

Fitch, K. L. (1998). *Speaking Relationally: Culture, Communication and Interpersonal Connection*. New York: Guilford Press.

Flick, U. (1998). 'Everyday Knowledge in Social Psychology'. In U. Flick (Ed.), *The Psychology of the Social*. Cambridge: Cambridge University Press, pp. 41–59.

Flicker, E. (2003). 'Between Brains and Breasts – Women Scientists in Fiction Film: On the Marginalization and Sexualization of Scientific Competence'. *Public Understanding of Science*, 12: 307.

Fodor, J. A. (2000). *The Modularity of the Mind*. Cambridge, MA: MIT Press.

Fodor, J. A. (2001). *The Mind Doesn't Work That Way*. Cambridge, MA: MIT Press.

Foucault, M. (1973). *The Birth of the Clinic: An Archaelogy of Medical Perception*. New York: Pantheon Books.

Foucault, M. (1975). *Discipline and Punish: The Birth of the Prison*. New York: Random House.

Foucault, M. (1980). *Power/Knowledge*. New York: Pantheon Books.

Foucault, M. (1981). *Power/Knowledge: Selected Interviews and Other Writings 1972–1977*. New York: Pantheon Books.

Frameworks Institute (2009). *Strategic Frame Analysis*. Retrieved 12 October from http://people-press.org/news-interest/.

Frank, A. W. (2005). 'What is Dialogical Research, and why Should we do it?' *Qualitative Health Research*, 15: 964–74.

Frankfurt, H. G. (2005). *On Bullshit*. Princeton, NJ: Princeton University Press.

Franks, B. and Braisby, N. R. (1990). 'Sense Generation or how to Make a Mental Lexicon Flexible'. In *Proceedings of the 12th Annual Conference of the Cognitive Science Society*. Cambridge, MA: MIT Press.

Franks, B. (2003). 'Negation and Doubt in Religious Representations: Context-Dependence, Emotion and Action'. Paper to New England Institute Conference on Cognitive Science and Religious Beliefs.

Franks, B. and Braisby, N. (1997). 'Concepts in Action: The Evolutionary Role of Concepts and Similarity'. In M. Ramscar, U. Hahn, E. Cambouropolos and H. Pain (Eds), *Proceedings of SimCat 97: Interdisciplinary Workshop on Similarity and Categorisation*, Department of Artificial Intelligence: Edinburgh University.

Fraser, N. (1990). 'Rethinking the Public Sphere: A Contribution to the Critique of Actually Existing Democracy'. *Social Text*, 25 (26): 56–80.

Freire, P. (1970). *Pedagogy of the Oppressed*. Middlesex: Penguin Education.

Freire, P. (1978). *Pedagogy in Progress: The Letters to Guinea Bissau*. New York: The Seabury Press.

Freire, P. (1985). *The Politics of Education*. New York: Bergin and Garvey.

Freire, P. (1998). *Pedagogy of Freedom: Ethics, Democracy and Civic Courage*. Oxford: Rowman & Littlefield Publishers Inc.

Freire, P (2005). *Education for Critical Consciousness*. New York: Seabury Press.

Fridlund, A. J. (1994). *Human Facial Expression: An Evolutionary View*. San Diego, CA: Academic Press.

Frost, D. and Zelnick, B. (2007). *Frost/Nixon*. London: Pan-Macmillan.

Galison, P. (1998). *Image and Logic*. Chicago: University of Chicago Press.

Gallacher, S. (2001). 'The Practice of Mind: Theory, Simulation or Interaction?' *Journal of Consciousness Studies*, 8: 83–107.

Gallese, V. and Goldman, A. (1999). 'Mirror Neurons and the Simulation Theory of Mind-Reading'. *Trends in Cognitive Sciences*, 12: 493–501.

Gallimore, R. and Tharp, R. (1993). 'Teaching Mind in Society: Teaching, Schooling and Literate Discourse'. In L. Moll (Ed.), *Vygotsky and Education: Instructional Implications and Applications of Sociohistorical Psychology* (pp. 175–205). Cambridge: Cambridge University Press.

Gamble, T. K. and Gamble, M. W. (2003). *The Gender Communication Connection*. Boston: Houghton Mifflin.

Gamson, W. A. and Modigliani, A. (1989). 'Media Discourse and Public Opinion on Nuclear Power: A Constructionist Approach'. *American Journal of Sociology*, 95: 1–37.

Gamson, W. A. (1992). *Talking Politics*. New York: Cambridge University Press.

Gärdenfors, P. (2008). 'Evolutionary and Developmental Aspect of Intersubjectivity'. In H. Liljenström and P. Århem (Eds), *Consciousness Transitions – Phylogenetic, Ontogenetic and Physiological Aspects*. Amsterdam: Elsevier.

Gaskell, G. (2001). 'Attitudes, Social Representations and Beyond'. In K. Deaux and G. Philogene (Eds), *Social Representations: Introductions and Explorations*. Oxford: Blackwell.

Gaventa, J. and Cornwall, A. (2001). 'Power and Knowledge'. In: P. Reason and H. Bradbury, H. (Eds), *Handbook of Action Research*. London: Sage.

Gelman, S. A. and Hirschfeld, L.A. (1999). 'How Biological is Essentialism?' In D. L. Medin and S. Atran (Eds), *Folkbiology*. Cambridge, MA: MIT Press.

Giddens, A. (1998). *The Third Way: The Renewal of Social Democracy*. Cambridge: Polity Press.

Gieryn, T. (1995). 'Boundaries of Science'. In S. Jasanoff, G. E. Markle, J. C. Petersen and T. Pinch (Eds), *Handbook of Science and Technology Studies*. Thousand Oaks, CA: Sage.

Gieryn, T. (1999). *Cultural Boundaries of Science: Credibility on the Line.* Chicago, IL: Chicago University Press.

Gigerenzer, G. (2007). *Gut Feelings.* New York: Viking.

Gilbert, M. (1989). *On Social Facts.* Princeton, NJ: Princeton University Press.

Gilbert, D. T., Fiske, S. T. and Lindzey, G. (Eds) (1998). *Handbook of Social Psychology* (4th edn). New York: McGraw-Hill, Vol. 2, pp. 357–411.

Gilroy, P. (2004). *After Empire: Multiculture or Postcolonial Melancholia.* London: Routledge.

Gil-White, F. J. (2001). 'Are Ethnic Groups "species" to the Human Brain? Essentialism in our Cognition of some Social Categories'. *Current Anthropology,* 42 (4): 515–54.

Ginneken van, J. (1992). *Crowds, Psychology and Politics, 1871–1899.* Cambridge: Cambridge University Press.

Gladwell, M. (2000). *The Tipping Point: How Little Things can make a Big Difference.* Boston: Little Brown.

The Global Deception Team. (2006). 'A World of Lies'. *Journal of Cross-Cultural Psychology,* 37 (1): 60–74.

Goffman, E. (1956). 'Embarrassment and Social Organization'. *American Journal of Sociology,* 62: 264–71.

Goffman, E. (1959). *The Presentation of Self in Everyday Life.* New York: Doubleday.

Goffman, E. (1967). 'On Face-Work: An Analysis of Ritual Elements in Social Interaction'. In *Interaction Ritual: Essays on Face-to-Face Behaviour.* New York: Random House.

Goodell, R. (1977). *The Visible Scientists.* Boston: Little, Brown.

Goody, E. (1998). 'Social Intelligence and the Emergence of Roles and Rules'. *Proceedings of the British Academy,* 97: 114–47.

Göpfert, W. (1996). 'Scheduled Science: TV Coverage of Science, Technology, Medicine and Social Science and Programming Policies in Britain and Germany'. *Public Understanding of Science,* 5 (4): 361–74.

Göpfert, W. (2007). 'The Strength of PR and the Weakness of Science Journalism'. In M. Bauer and M. Bucchi (Eds), *Science Communication in the 21st Century: Between Journalism and Public Relations.* London: Routledge, pp. 215–26.

Graebner, W. (1986). 'The Small Group and Democratic Social Engineering, 1900–1950'. *Journal of Social Issues,* 42: 137–54.

Grantham, T. (2004). 'Conceptualizing the (Dis)Unity of Science'. *Philosophy of Science,* 71: 133–55.

Greene, J. (1990). 'Topics in Language and Communication'. In I. Roth (Ed.), *Introduction to Psychology, Vol 2.* Hove: The Open University.

Greenhalgh, T., Robb, N. and Scambler, G. (2006). 'Communicative and Strategic Action in Interpreted Consultations in Primary Health Care: A Habermasian Perspective'. *Social Science and Medicine,* 63: 1170–87.

Gregory, J. and Miller, S. (1998). *Science in Public: Communication, Culture and Credibility.* New York: Plenum.

Gregory, J. (2003a). 'Popularisation and Excommunication of Fred Hoyle's "life-from-space" Theory'. *Public Understanding of Science,* 12: 25–46.

Gregory, J. (2003b). 'Understanding "Science and the Public"'. *Journal of Commercial Biotechnology,* 10 (2): 131–9.

Gregory, J. (2005). *Fred Hoyle's Universe.* Oxford: Oxford University Press.

Gregory, J. and Lock, S. J. (2008). 'The Evolution of "Public Understanding of Science" in the UK'. *Sociology Compass,* 2 (4): 1252–65.

Gregory, J., Agar, J., Lock, S. J. and Harries, S. (2008). 'Public Engagement in the Private Sector: A New Form of Public Relations?' In M. Bauer and M. Bucchi (Eds),

Science Communication in the 21st Century: Between Journalism and Public Relations. London: Routledge, pp. 203–14.

Grice, H. P. (1975). 'Logic and Conversation'. In P. Cole and J. L. Morgan (Eds), *Syntax and Semantics: Speech Acts*. Volume 3. New York: Academic.

Grice, H. P. (1989). *Studies in the Way of Words*. Cambridge, MA: Harvard University Press.

Guareschi, P. A. and Jovchelovitch, S. (2004). 'Participation, Health and the Development of Community Resources in Southern Brazil'. *Journal of Health Psychology*, 9: 311–22.

Gudykunst, W. B. (1988). 'Culture and Intergroup Processes'. In M. H. Bond (Ed.), *The Cross-Cultural Challenge to Social Psychology*. Newbury Park, CA: Sage.

Gudykunst, W. B., Gao, G., Schmidt, K. L., Nishida, T., Bond, M. H., Wang, G., & Barraclough,. R. A. (1992). 'The Influence of Individualism-Collectivism, Self-Monitoring and Predicted Outcome Value on Communication in Ingroup and Outgroup Relationships'. *Journal of Cross-Cultural Psychology*, 23: 196–213.

Gudykunst, W. B., Ting-Toomey, S. and Nishida, T. (1996). *Communication in Personal Relationships across Cultures*. Thousand Oaks, CA: Sage Publications.

Guenthner, S. and Knoblauch, H. (1995). 'Culturally Patterned Speaking Practices: The Analysis of Communicative Genres. *Pragmatics*, 5: 1–32.

Gunther, A. C., Christen, C. T., Liebhart, J. and Chia, S. (2001). 'Congenial Public, Contrary Press, and Biased Estimates of the Climate of Opinion'. *Public Opinion Quarterly*, 65: 295–320.

Gunther, A. C. and Schmitt, K. (2004). 'Mapping Boundaries of the Hostile Media Effect'. *Journal of Communication*, 54: 55–70.

Habermas, J. (1982). *Theorie des kommunikativen Handelns (2 Bände)*. Frankfurt: Suhrkamp.

Habermas, J. (1984a). *Theory of Communicative Action Vol. I: Reason and Rationalization of Society*. Cambridge: Polity Press.

Habermas, J. (1984b). *Communication and the Evolution of Society*. Cambridge: Polity Press.

Habermas, J. (1987). *Theory of Communicative Action Vol. II: The Critique of Functionalistic Reason*. Cambridge: Polity Press.

Habermas, J. (1989a). *The Structural Transformation of the Public Sphere: An Inquiry into a Category of Bourgeois Society*. Cambridge: Polity Press.

Habermas, J. (1989b) *The Theory of Communicative Action: Life World and System, A Critique of Functionalist Reason*. Cambridge: Polity Press.

Habermas, J. (1990). *The Theory of Communicative Action: Reason and the Rationalisation of Society*. Cambridge: Polity Press.

Habermas, J. (1995/1976). 'Moral Development and Ego Identity'. In *Communication and the Evolution of Society*. Cambridge: Polity Press, pp. 69–94.

Habermas, J. (1998/1976). 'What is Universal Pragmatics?' In *On the Pragmatics of Communication*. Cambridge: Polity Press, pp. 21–103.

Habermas, J. (1998/1981). 'Social Action, Purposive Activity, and Communication'. In *On the Pragmatics of Communication*. Cambridge: Polity Press, pp. 105–82.

Habermas, J. (1998/1988). 'Actions, Speech Acts, Linguistically Mediated Interactions, and the Lifeworld'. In *On the Pragmatics of Communication*. Cambridge: Polity Press, pp. 215–55.

Habermas, J. (2003). *The Future of Human Nature*. Cambridge: Polity Press.

Habermas, J. (2004). 'Public Space and the Political Public Sphere – the Biographical Roots of Two Motives in my Thought'. *The Kyoto Lecture*. Retrievable at http://www.johnkeane.net/pdf_docs/teaching_sources/habermas_Kyoto_lecture_Nov_2004.pdf.

Habermas, J. (2005). 'Faith and Knowledge'. In E. Mendieta (Ed.), *The Frankfurt School on Religion: Key Writings by the Major Thinkers*. Milton Park: Routledge, pp. 327–37.

Habermas, J. (2008). *Between Naturalism and Religion*. Cambridge: Polity Press.

Hall, S. (1980). 'Encoding/Decoding'. In Centre for Contemporary Cultural Studies (Ed.), *Culture, Media, Language: Working Papers in Cultural Studies, 1972–79*. London: Hutchinson, pp. 128–38.

Hall, S. (1981). 'The Determinations of News Photographs'. In S. Cohen and J. Young (Eds), *The Manufacture of News: Social Problems, Deviance and the Mass Media*. London: Constable.

Hall, S. (1988). 'New Ethnicities'. In K. Mercer (Ed.), *Black Film, British Cinema*. London: Institute for Contemporary Arts, pp. 27–31.

Hall, S. (1991). 'Old and New Identities; Old and New Ethnicities'. In A. D. King (Ed.), *Culture, Globalisation and the World-System: Contemporary Conditions for the Representation of Identity*. Basingstoke: Macmillan.

Hall, S. (1993). 'Encoding, Decoding'. In S. During (Ed.), *The Cultural Studies Reader*. London and New York: Routledge.

Hall, S. (1997). *Representation: Cultural Representations and Signifying Practices*. London: Sage.

Halliday, M. A. K. (1993). 'On the Language of Physical Science', in M. A. K. Halliday and J. R. Martin (Eds), *Writing Science*. Briston: The Falmer Press.

Hansen, A. and Dickinson, R. (1992). 'Science Coverage in the British Mass Media: Media Output and Source Input'. *Communications*, 17 (3): 365–78.

Hansen, A. (1994). 'Journalistic Practices and Science Reporting in the British Press'. *Public Understanding of Science*, 3 (2): 111–34.

Hardman, J. (2000). 'The Epistemology of Questioning'. Unpublished masters thesis. University of Natal, Durban.

Hardman, J. (2004). *How do Teachers Use Computers to Teach Mathematics?* Khanya project report, pp. 1–26.

Hardman, J. (2005b). 'An Exploratory Case Study of Computer Use in a Primary School Mathematics Classroom: New Technology New Pedagogy?' *Perspectives in Education*, 23 (4): 1–13.

Hardman, J. (2005c). 'Activity Theory as a Framework for Understanding Teachers' Perceptions of Computer Usage at a Primary School Level in South Africa'. *South African Journal of Education*, 25 (4): 258–65.

Hardman, J. (2007a). 'Towards a Methodology for Using Activity Theory to Explicate the Pedagogical Object in a Primary School Mathematics Classroom'. *Outlines*, 1: 53–69.

Hardman, J. (2008). *New Technology, New Pedagogy: An Activity Theory Analysis of Pedagogy with Computers*. Unpublished PhD Thesis. Cape Town: University of Cape Town.

Harris, R. (2006). 'New Ethnicities and Diaspora Identities'. Paper presented at The State and Ethnic Definition Conference, Oxford.

Hasan, R. (1992). 'Speech Genre, Semiotic Mediation and the Development of Higher Mental Functions'. *Language Sciences*, 14 (4): 489–528.

Haselton, M. G. and Nettle, D. (2006). 'The Paranoid Optimist: An Integrative Evolutionary Model of Cognitive Biases'. *Personality and Social Psychology Review*, 10 (1): 47–66.

Hauser, M. D. (1997). *The Evolution of Communication*. Cambridge, MA: MIT Press.

Hauser, M. D., Chomsky, N. and Fitch, W. T. (2002). 'The Faculty of Language: What Is It, Who Has It, and How Did It Evolve?' *Science*, 298: 1569–79.

Hauser, M. D. (2005). 'Moral Ingredients: How we Evolved the Capacity to do the Right Thing'. In S. C. Levinson and P. Jaisson (Eds), *Evolution and Culture*. Cambridge, MA: MIT Press.

Hayakawa, S. I. (1978). *Through the Communication Barrier*. New York: Harper and Row.

Haynes, R. D. (1994). *From Faust to Strangelove: Representations of the Scientist in Western Literature*. Baltimore, MD: The Johns Hopkins University Press.

Hedegaard, M. (1998). 'Situated Learning and Cognition: Theoretical Learning and Cognition'. *Mind, Culture and Activity*, 5 (2): 114–26.

Heidegger, M. (1927). *Being and Time*. Trans. J. Macquarrie and E. Robinson. London: SCM Press.

Hervieu-Léger, D. (2000). *Religion as a Chain of Memory*. New Brunswick, NJ: Rutgers University Press.

Hibbing, J. R. and Theiss-Morse, E. (2002). *Stealth Democracy: Americans Beliefs about how Government should Work*. New York: Cambridge University Press.

Hickson, M. L. III, Stacks, D. W. and Moore, N-J. (2004). *Nonverbal Communication: Studies and Applications*. Los Angeles, CA: Roxbury.

Hilgartner, S. (1990). 'The Dominant View of Popularization: Conceptual Problems, Political Uses'. *Social Studies of Science*, 20: 519–39.

Hirschfeld, L. A. and Gelman, S. A. (Eds) (1994). *Mapping The Mind: Domain-Specificity in Culture and Cognition*. New York: Cambridge University Press.

Hirschfeld, L. A. (1996). *Race in the Making: Cognition, Culture, and the Child's Construction of Human Kinds*. Cambridge, MA: MIT Press.

Hirschfeld, L. A. (2001). 'On a Folk Theory of Society: Children, Evolution and Mental Representations of Social Groups'. *Personality and Social Psychology Review*, 5 (2): 106–16.

Hochschild, A. R. (2003). *The Managed Heart: The Commercialization of Human Feeling*. Berkeley, CA: University of California Press.

Hodgetts, D. and Chamberlain, K. (2006). 'Developing a Critical Media Research Agenda for Health Psychology'. *Journal of Health Psychology*, 11: 317–27.

Hodgetts, D. and Chamberlain, K. (2007) 'Constructing Health News: Possibilities for a Civic-Oriented Journalism'. *Health*, 12 (1): 43–66.

Hoffe, O. (2003). *Aristotle*. Albany, NY: State University of New York Press.

Hogg, M. A. (2007). 'Social Psychology of Leadership'. In A. W. Kruglanski and E. T. Higgins (Eds), *Social Psychology: A Handbook of Basic Principles* (2nd edn). New York: Guilfoed.

Holdcroft, D. (1979). 'Speech Acts and Conversation'. *The Philosophical Quarterly*, 29: 125–41.

Holland, D. and N. Quinn (Eds) (1987). *Cultural Models in Language and Thought*. Cambridge: Cambridge University Press.

Holliday, A., Hyde, M. and Kullman, J. (2004). *Inter-Cultural Communication: An Advanced Resource Book*. New York: Routledge.

Honneth, A. and Joas, H. (Eds) (1991). *Communicative Action: Essays on Jürgen Habermas' The Theory of Communication Action*. Cambridge: Polity.

Hook, D. (2007). *Foucault, Psychology and the Analytics of Power*. London and New York: Palgrave Macmillan.

Hooks, B. (1993). 'Speaking about Paulo Freire – The Man, His Work'. In P. Mclaren and P. Leonard (Eds), *Paulo Freire: A Critical Encounter*. New York: Routledge.

Hornig, S. (1993). 'Reading Risk: Public Response to Print Media Accounts of Technological Risk'. *Public Understanding of Science*, 2 (2): 95–109.

Horton, R. (1993). *Patterns of Thought in Africa and the West: Essays on Magic, Religion and Science*. Cambridge: Cambridge University Press.

House of Lords Select Committee on Science and Technology. (2000). *Science and Society*. London: HMSO.

Hovland, C. I. and Weiss, W. (1951). 'The Influence of Source Credibility on Communication Effectiveness'. *Public Opinion Quarterly*, 15 (4): 635–50.

Hovland, C. I., Janis, I. L. and Kelley, H. H. (1953). *Communication and Persuasion: Psychological Studies of Opinion Change*. New Haven: Yale University Press.

Hovland, C. I. (1959). 'Reconciling Conflicting Results Derived from Experimental and Survey Studies of Attitude Change'. *The American Psychologist*, 14: 8–17.

Howarth, C. (2002). '"So, you're from Brixton?" The Struggle for Recognition and Esteem in a Multicultural Community'. *Ethnicities*, 2 (2): 237–60.

Howarth, C. (2002b) 'Identity in Whose Eyes? The Role of Representations in Identity Construction'. *Journal of the Theory of Social Behaviour*, 32: 2.

Howarth, C. (2004) 'Representation and Resistance in the Context of School Exclusion: Reasons to be Critical'. *Journal of Community and Applied Social Psychology*, 14: 356–77.

Howarth, C. (2006a). 'A Social Representation is not a Quiet Thing: Exploring the Critical Potential of Social Representations Theory'. *British Journal of Social Psychology*, 45: 65–86.

Howarth, C. (2006b). 'Race as Stigma: Positioning the Stigmatized as Agents, Not Objects'. *Journal of Community & Applied Social Psychology*, 16: 442–51.

Howarth, C. (2007). '"It's not their fault they have that skin colour, is it?" Young British Children and the Possibility for Contesting Racialising Representations'. In G. Moloney and I. Walker (Eds), *Social Representations and Identity: Content, Process and Power*. London: Palgrave Macmillan.

Howarth, C. (2009a). '"I hope we won't have to understand racism one day": Researching or Reproducing "race" in Social Psychological Research?' *British Journal of Social Psychology*, 45: 65–86.

Howarth, C. (2009b). 'Towards a Visual Social Psychology of Identity and Representation: Photographing the Self, Weaving the Family in a Multicultural British Community'. In P. Reavey (Ed.), *Visual Psychologies: Using and Interpreting Images in Qualitative Research*. London: Routledge.

Humphrey, N. K. (1976). 'The Social Function of the Intellect'. In P. P. G. Bateson and R. A. Hinde (Eds), *Growing Points in Ethology*. Cambridge: Cambridge University Press, pp. 303–17.

Humphreys, P. and Brezillon, P. (2002). 'Combining Rich and Restricted Languages in Multimedia: Enrichment of Context for Innovative Decisions'. In F. Adam, P. Brezillon, P. Humphreys and J. C. Pomerol (Eds), *Decision Making and Decision Support in the Internet Age*. Cork: Oaktree Press.

Hurley, S. (2006). 'Bypassing Conscious Control: Media Violence, Unconscious Imitation, and Freedom of Speech'. In S. Pockett, W. Banks and S. Gallagher (Eds), *Does Consciousness Cause Behavior? An Investigation of the Nature of Volition*. Cambridge, MA: MIT Press.

Husserl, E. (1970). *The Crisis of the European Sciences and Transcendental Phenomenology*. Evanston: Northwestern University Press.

Hutchins, E. (1995). *Cognition in the Wild*. Cambridge, MA: The MIT Press.

Hutto, D. D. (2004). 'The Limits of Spectatorial Folk Psychology'. *Mind & Language*, 19: 548–73.

Ichheiser, G. (1949). 'Misunderstandings in Human Relations: A Study in False Social Perception'. *American Journal of Sociology*, 55 (Supplement): 1–72.

Igou, E. R. and Bless, H. (2005). 'The Conversational Basis for the Dilution Effect'. *Journal of Language and Social Psychology*, 24: 25–35.

Internet World Stats (2009). *Usage and Population Statistics*. http://www.internetworld stats.com/stats.htm, accessed 9 September 2009.

Irving, P., Rampton, D. and Shanahan, F. (2006). *Clinical Dilemmas in Inflammatory Bowel Disease*. Oxford: Blackwell.

Irwin, A. and Wynne, B. (1996). *Misunderstanding Science?: The Public Reconstruction of Science and Technology*. Cambridge: Cambridge University Press.

Iyengar, S. and Kinder, D. (1987). *News that Matters: Television and American Public Opinion*. Chicago: University of Chicago Press.

Iyengar, S., Hahn, K., Bonfadelli, H. and Marr, M. (2009). '"Dark areas of ignorance" Revisited: Knowledge in Switzerland and the United States'. *Communication Research*, 36: 341–58.

Jakobson, R. (1960). 'Linguistics and Poetics'. In T. Sebeok (Ed.), *Style in Language*. Cambridge, MA: MIT Press, pp. 350–77.

James, W. (1890). *The Principles of Psychology*. New York: Holt.

Janis, I. L. and Hovland, C. I. (1959). 'An Overview of Persuasibility Research'. In C. I. Hovland and I. L. Janis (Eds), *Personality and Persuasibility*. New Haven, CT: Yale University Press, pp. 1–26.

Janis, I. L. (1972). *Victims of Groupthink: A Psychological Study of Foreign Policy Decisions and Fiascoes*. Boston, MA: Houghton Mifflin.

Janis, I. L. and Mann, L. (1977). *Decision Making*. New York: Free Press.

Jolly, A. (1966). 'Lemur Social Behaviour and Primate Intelligence'. *Science*, 153: 501–6.

Jenkins, He. (2006). *Convergence Culture: Where Old and New Media Collide*. New York: New York University Press.

Jodelet, D. (1991). *Madness and Social Representations*. Hemel Hempstead: Harvester Wheatsheaf.

Jones, R. A. (1998). 'The Scientist as Artist: A Study of The Man in the White Suit and Some Related British Film Comedies of the Postwar Period (1945–1970)'. *Public Understanding of Science*, 7: 135–47.

Jones, R. A. (2001). '"Why can't you scientists leave things alone?" Science Questioned in British Films of the Post-War Period (1945–1970)'. *Public Understanding of Science*, 10: 365–82.

Jones, T. (2009). 'I Delve into a Character's Physicality'. *The Guardian and Observer Guides to Performing*. Part 1, 34.

Josephs, R. A., Newman, M. L., Brown, R. P. and Beer, J. M. (2003). 'Status, Testosterone, and Human Intellectual Performance: Stereotype Threat as Status Concern'. *Psychological Science*, 14: 158–63.

Jovchevolitch, S. and Bauer, M. W. (2000). 'Narrative Interviewing'. In M. W. Bauer and G. D. Gaskell (Eds), *Qualitative Researching with Text, Image, and Sound: A Practical Handbook for Social Research*. London: Sage, pp. 57–74.

Jovchelovitch, S. (2007). *Knowledge in Context: Representations, Community and Culture*. London: Routledge.

Jurdant, B. (1969). 'Vulgarisation scientifique et ideologie', *Communications*, 14: 150–61.

Jurdant, B. (1993). 'Popularisation as the Autobiography of Science'. *Public Understanding of Science*, 2: 365–73.

Kapferer, J. N. (1990). *Rumors: Uses, Interpretations, and Images*. New Brunswick, NJ: Transaction.

Karpov, Y. (2003). 'Vygotsky's Doctrine of Scientific Concepts; its Role for Contemporary Education'. In A. Kozulin, B. Gindis, V. S. Ageyev and S. M. Miller (Eds), *Vygotsky's*

Educational Theory in Cultural Context. Cambridge: Cambridge University Press, pp. 65–82.

Kashima, Y. (2000). 'Recovering Bartlett's Social Psychology of Cultural Dynamics'. *European Journal of Social Psychology*, 30(3): 383–403.

Kellerman, B. (2004). *Bad Leadership: What it is, how it Happens, why it Matters*. Cambridge, MA: Harvard Business School Press.

Keltner, D. and Haidt, J. (2000). 'Social Functions of Emotions at Four Levels of Analysis'. In W. G Parrot (Ed.), *Emotions in Social Psychology: Essential Readings*. Hove: Psychology Press, pp. 175–84.

Keltner, D., Haidt, J. and Shiota, M. N. (2006). 'Social Functionalism and the Evolution of Emotion'. In M. Schaller, J. A. Simpson and D. T. Kenrick (Eds), *Evolution and Social Psychology*. New York, NY: Psychology Press, pp. 115–42.

Kepel, G. (1994). *The Revenge of God: The Resurgence of Islam, Christianity and Judaism in the Modern World*. Cambridge: Polity Press.

Keysar, B. (2007). 'Communication and Miscommunication: The Role of Egocentric Processes'. *Intercultural Pragmatics*, 4: 71–84.

Keysar, B. and Barr, D. J. (2002). 'Self Anchoring in Conversation: Why Language Users do not do what they "should"'. In T. Gilovich, D. W. Griffin and D. Kahneman (Eds), *Heuristics and Biases: The Psychology of Intuitive Judgment*. Cambridge: Cambridge University Press.

Kennedy, G. A. (1980). *Classical Rhetoric and its Christian and Secular Tradition from Ancient to Modern Times*. Chapel Hill: University of Southern Carolina Press.

Kennedy, G. A. (1998). *Comparative Rhetoric: An Historical and Cross-Cultural Introduction*. New York, NY: Oxford University Press.

Keysar, B. and Henley, A. S. (2002). 'Speaker's Overestimation of their Effectiveness'. *Psychological Science*, 13: 207–12.

Keysar, B., Lin, S. and Barr, D. J. (2003). 'Limits on Theory of Mind Use in Adults'. *Cognition*, 89: 25–41.

Keysar, B. (2008). 'Egocentric Processes in Communication and Miscommunication'. In I. Kecskes and J. Mey (Eds), *Intention, Common Ground and the Egocentric Speaker-Hearer*. Berlin: Mouton de Gruyter.

Kiernan, V. (2006). *Embargoed Science*. Champaign, IL: University of Illinois Press.

Kilham, W. and Mann, L. (1974). 'Level of Destructive Obedience as a Function of Transmitter and Executant Roles in the Milgram Obedience Paradigm'. *Journal of Personality and Social Psychology*, 29: 696–702.

Kim, S., Scheufele, D. A. and Shanahan, J. E. (2002). 'Agenda-Setting, Priming, Framing and Second-Levels in Local Politics'. *Journalism & Mass Communication Quarterly*, 79: 7–25.

Kimmel, A. J. and Keefer, R. (1991). 'Psychology Correlates of the Acceptance and Transmission of Rumors about AIDS'. *Journal of Applied Social Psychology*, 21: 1608–28.

Kirby, D. A. (2008). 'Cinematic Science: The Public Communication of Science and Technology in Popular Film'. In B. Trench and M. Bucchi (Eds), *Handbook of Public Communication of Science and Technology*. New York: Routledge, pp. 67–94.

Kitcher, P. (2003). 'Infectious Ideas: Some Preliminary Explorations'. In *Mendel's Mirror – Philosophical Reflections on Biology*. Oxford: Oxford University Press, pp. 212–32.

Knapp, R. H. (1944). 'A Psychology of Rumor'. *Public Opinion Quarterly*, 8: 22–37.

Knight Commission on the Information Needs of Communities. (2009). *Informing Communities: Sustaining Democracy in the Digital Age*. Available at http://www.report. knightcomm.org.

Knowles, E. S. and Riner, D. D. (2007). 'Omega Approaches to Persuasion: Overcoming Resistance'. In A. R. Pratkanis (Ed.), *The Science of Social Influence*. New York: Psychology Press, pp. 83–114.

Kondo, D. K. (1990). *Crafting Selves: Power, Gender and Discourses of Identity in a Japanese Workplace*. Chicago: University of Chicago Press.

Krausz, E. (1971). *Ethnic Minorities in Britain*. London: Granada Publishing Limited.

Kronberger, N. and Wagner, W. (2007). 'Inviolable versus Alterable Identities: Culture, Biotechnology and Resistance'. In G. Moloney and I. Walker (Eds), *Social Representations and Identity: Content, Process and Power*. London: Palgrave Macmillan.

Kwak, N. (1999). 'Revisting the Knowledge Gap Hypothesis: Education, Motivation, and Media Use'. *Communication Research*, 26: 385–413.

Lacan, J. (2006). *Écrits the First Complete Edition in English*. Translated by Bruce Fink. New York and London: W.W Norton & Company.

LaFollette, M. C. (1990). *The One Culture Making Science Our Own: Public Images of Science 1910–1955*. Chicago: University of Chicago Press.

Lakoff, R. (1973). 'Logic of Politeness or Minding your P's and Q's'. In C. Colum (Ed.), *Papers from the Ninth Regional Meeting of Chicago Linguistic Society*. Chicago: Chicago Linguistic Society.

Lakoff, R. (1975). *Language and Women's Place*. New York: Harper and Row.

Lakoff, G. and Johnson, M. (1980). *Metaphors we Live by*. Chicago: University of Chicago Press.

Lakoff, G. and Johnson, M. (1999). *Philosophy in the Flesh: The Embodied Mind and its Challenge to Western Thought*. New York: Basic Books.

Laland, K. N., Odling-Smee, F. J. and Feldman, M. W. (2001). 'Cultural Niche Construction and Human Evolution'. *Journal of Evolutionary Biology*, 14: 22–33.

Langmead, L. and Irving, P. (2008). *The Facts: Inflammatory Bowel Disease*. Oxford: Oxford University Press.

Laszlo, P. (1993). *La vulgarisation scientifique*. Paris: Flammarion.

Latané, B. and Wolfe, S. (1981). 'The Social Impact of Majorities and Minorities'. *Psychological Review*, 88: 438–53.

Latour, B. (1987). *Science in Action: How to Follow Scientists and Engineers through Society*. Cambridge, MA: Harvard University Press.

Lave, J. (1988). *Cognition in Practice*. Cambridge: Cambridge University Press.

Lazzarato, M. (1996). 'Immaterial Labor'. In P. Virno and M. Hardt (Eds), *Radical Thought in Italy*. Minneapolis, MN: Minnesota University Press, pp. 132–46.

LeBaron, M. (2003a). 'Cross-Cultural Communication'. In G. Burgess and H. Burgess (Eds), *Beyond Intractability*. University of Colorado, Boulder: Conflict Research Consortium, Posted July 2003, http://www.beyondintractability.org/essay/cross-cultural_communication.

LeBaron, M. (2003b). *Bridging Cultural Conflicts: A New Approach for a Changing World*. San Francisco: Jossey Bass.

Le Bon, G. (1896/2006). *The Crowd: A Study of the Popular Mind*. West Valley City, UT: Waking Lion Press.

Leech, G. N. (1966). *English in Advertising: A Linguistic Study of Advertising in Great Britain*. London: Longman.

Leech, G. N. (1983). *Principles of Pragmatics*. London: Longman.

Leffler, A., Gillespie, D. L. and Conaty, J. C. (1982). 'The Effects of Status Differentiation on Nonverbal Behaviour'. *Social Psychology Quarterly*, 45(3): 153–61.

Leigh, T. W. and Rethans, A. J. (1983). *Experiences with Script Elicitation within Consumer Decision-Making Contexts: Advances in Consumer Research*. Thirteenth Annual Conference. San Francisco: Association for Consumer Research, pp. 667–72.

Lektorsky, V. A. (1990). *Activity Theory: Theories, Methodology and Problems*. Orlando, FL: Paul M. Deutsch.

León, B. (2007). *Science on Television: The Narrative of Scientific Documentary*. London: Pantaneto Press.

Leontiev, A. N. (1981). 'The Problem of Activity in Psychology'. In J. V. Wertsch (Ed.), *The Concept of Activity in Soviet Psychology*. Armonk, NY: M.E. Sharpe.

Leslie, A. M., Friedman, O. and German, T. P. (2004). 'Core Mechanisms in 'Theory of Mind'. *Trends in Cognitive Sciences*, 8: 528–33.

Leslie, A. M., German, T. P. and Pollizi, P. (2005). 'Belief-Desire Reasoning as a Process of Selection'. *Cognitive Psychology*, 50: 45–85.

Levenson, R. W., Ekman, P., Heider, K. and Friesen, W. V. (1992). 'Emotion and Autonomic Nervous System Activity in the Minangkabau of West Sumatra'. *Journal of Personality and Social Psychology*, 62: 972–88.

Levidow, L. (2007). *Democratising Technology Choices? European Public Participation in Agbiotech Assessments*. IIED Gatekeeper Series No. 135, December 2007, International Institute for Environment and Development. Available at http://www.iied.org/NR/agbioliv/gatekeepers.

Levinson, S. C. (1983). *Pragmatics*. Cambridge: Cambridge University Press.

Levinson, S. C. (2005). 'Introduction: The Evolution of Culture in Microcosm'. In S. C. Levinson and P. Jaisson (Eds), *Evolution and Culture*. Cambridge, MA: MIT Press.

Lévi-Strauss, C. (1976). *Tristes Tropiques*. London: Penguin.

Levitt, B. and March, M. G. (1988). 'Organisational Learning'. *Annual Review of Sociology*, 14: 319–40.

Lewenstein, B. V. (1992). 'Public Understanding of Science in the United States after WWII'. *Public Understanding of Science*, 1: 45–68.

Lewenstein, B. V. (1995). 'From Fax to Facts: Communication in the Cold Fusion Saga'. *Social Studies of Science*, 25: 403–36.

Lewenstein, B. V. (2009). 'Science Books Since 1945'. In D. P. Nord, J. S. Rubin and M. Schudson (Eds), *The Enduring Book: Print Culture in Postwar America*. Chapel Hill: University of North Carolina Press, pp. 347–60.

Lewin, K. (1947). 'Frontiers in Group Dynamics'. *Human Relations*, 1: 5–42.

Lewis, J. (1994). 'The Meaning of Things: Audiences, Ambiguity, and Power'. In J. Cruz and J. Lewis (Eds), *Viewing, Reading, Listening: Audiences and Cultural Reception*. Boulder: Westview Press.

Lezuan, J. and Soneryd, L. (2007). 'Consulting Citizens: Technologies of Elicitation and the Mobility of Publics'. *Public Understanding of Science*, 16: 279–97.

Liakopoulos, M. (2000). 'Argumentation Analysis'. In M. W. Bauer and G. Gaskell (Eds) *Qualitative Researching with Text, Image and Sound – A Practical Handbook* (pp. 152–71). London: Sage.

Lock, S. J. (2009). 'Lost in Translations: Discourses, Boundaries and Legitimacy in the Public Understanding of Science in the UK'. Unpublished PhD Thesis. London: University of London.

Locke, S. (2005). 'Fantastically Reasonable: Ambivalence in the Representation of Science and Technology in Super-Hero Comics'. *Public Understanding of Science*, 14: 25–46.

Lord, R. and Hall, R. (2003). 'Identity, Leadership Categorization, and Leadership Schema'. In D. van Knippenberg and M. A. Hogg (Eds), *Leadership and Power: Identity Processes in Groups and Organizations*. London: Sage, pp. 48–64.

Lord, R. G., Brown, D. J. and Harvey, J. L. (2001). 'System Constraints on Leadership Perceptions, Behavior and Influence: An Example of Connectionist Level Processes'. In M. A. Hogg and R. S. Tindale (Eds), *Blackwell Handbook of Social Psychology: Group Processes*. Oxford: Blackwell, pp. 283–310.

Lowery, S. A. and DeFleur, M. L. (1995). *Milestones in Mass Communication Research – Media Effects* 3rd edn. London: Longman Publishers.

Lucaites, J. L., Condit, C. M. and Caudill, S. (Eds) (1999). *Contemporary Rhetorical Theory: A Reader*. New York: The Guilford Press.

Luckhurst, R. (2005). *Science Fiction*. London: Polity.

Luckmann, T. (1992). 'On the Communicative Adjustment of Perspectives, Dialogue and Communicative Genres'. In A. Wold (Ed.), *The Dialogical Alternative: Towards a Theory of Language and Mind*. Oslo: Scandinavian University Press.

Luhmann, N. (1990). 'The Improbability of Communication'. In *Essays on Self-Reference*. New York: Columbia University Press.

Luhmann, N. (1995). *Social Systems*. Stanford, CA: Stanford University Press.

Luria, A. R. (1976). *Cognitive Development: Its Cultural and Social Foundations*. Translated by M. Cole. Cambridge, MA: Harvard University Press.

Maibach, E.W., Nisbet, M.C., Baldwin, P., Akerlof, K., & Diao, G. (2010). 'Reframing climate change as a public health issue: An exploratory study of public reactions'. *BMC Public Health*, 10 (299).

Malle, B. F. and Hodges, S. D. (Eds) (2005). *Other Minds: How Humans Bridge the Divide between Self and Other*. The Guilford Press: New York.

Mantell, D. M. (1971). 'The Potential for Violence in Germany'. *Journal of Social Issues*, 27: 101–12.

Marková, I. (2000). 'Amédée or How to Get Rid of it: Social Representations from a Dialogical Perspective'. *Culture and Psychology*, 6 (94): 419–60.

Marková, I. (2003). *Dialogicality and Social Representations: The Dynamics of Mind*. Cambridge: Cambridge University Press.

Marková, I. (2007). 'Social Identities and Social Representations: How are they related?' In G. Moloney and I. Walker (Eds), *Social Representations and Identity: Content, Process and Power*. London: Palgrave Macmillan.

Markus, H. and Kitayama, S. (1991). 'Culture and the Self: Implications for Cognition, Emotion and Motivation'. *Psychological Review*, 98: 224–53.

Markus, H. and Kitayama, S. (2000). 'The Cultural Construction of Self and Emotion: Implications for Social Behaviour'. In W. G. Parrot (Ed.), *Emotions in Social Psychology: Essential Readings*. Hove: Psychology.

Marrou, H. I. (1984). 'Education and Rhetoric'. In M. I. Finley (Ed.) *The Legacy of Greece* (pp. 185–201). Oxford: Oxford University Press.

Marsden, P. S. (1998). *Operationalising Memetics – Suicide, the Werther Effect, and the Work of David P. Phillips*. Proceedings of the 15th International Congress on Cybernetics, Namur: Belgium.

Marsden, P. S. and Attia, S. (2005). 'A Deadly Contagion?' *The Psychologist*, 18: 152–5.

Martin, J. N. and Nakayama, T. K. (2005). *Intercultural Communication in Contexts*. London: McGraw-Hill.

Marx, K. (1968). 'The Eighteenth Brumaire of Louis Napoleon'. In K. Marx and F. Engels (Eds), *Selected Works*. London: Lawrence and Wishart.

Matsumoto, D., Consolacion, T., Yamada, H., Suzuki, R., Franklin, B., Paul, S., Ray, R. and Uchida, H. (2002). 'American-Japanese Cultural Differences in Judgments of Emotional Expressions of Different Intensities'. *Cognition and Emotion*, 16: 721–47.

Matthews, D. (1994). *Politics for the People: Finding a Responsible Public Voice*. Chicago: University of Chicago Press.

Maynard Smith, J. and Harper, D. (2003). *Animal Signals*. Oxford: Oxford University Press.

Mayo, P. (1999). *Gramsci, Freire and Adult Education*. New York: Palgrave Macmillan.

Mccaffery, J. (2005). 'Using Transformative Models of Adult Literacy in Conflict Resolution and Peacebuilding Processes at Community Level: Examples from Guinea, Sierra Leone and Sudan'. *Compare*, 35: 443–62.

McCauley, R. N. (2000). 'The Naturalness of Religion and the Unnaturalness of Science'. In F. Keil and R. Wilson (Eds), *Explanation and Cognition*. Cambridge: MIT Press.

McComas, K. A. (2001). 'Theory and Practice of Public Meetings'. *Communication Theory*, 11: 36–55.

McCombs, M. E. and Shaw, D. (1972). 'The Agenda-Setting Function of the Mass Media'. *Public Opinion Quarterly*, 36: 176–85.

McCombs, M. E. (2005). 'The Agenda-Setting Function of the Press'. In G. Overholser and K. H. Jamieson (Eds), *The Press*. New York: Oxford University Press, pp. 156–68.

McDevitt, M. and Chaffee, S. (2000). 'Closing Gaps in Political Communication and Knowledge'. *Communication Research*, 27: 259–92.

McGuire, W. J. and Papageorgis, D. (1962). 'The Effects of Forewarning in Developing Resistance to Persuasion'. *Public Opinion Quarterly*, 26: 24–34.

McGuire, W. J. (1986). 'The Vissicitudes of Attitudes and Similar Representational Constructs in 20th Century Psychology'. *European Journal of Social Psychology*, 16: 89–130.

McLeod, D. M., Kosicki, G. M. and McLeod, J. M. (2002). 'Resurveying the Boundaries of Political Communications Effects'. In J. Bryant and D. Zillmann (Eds), *Media Effects: Advances in Theory and Research* 2nd edn. Hillsdale, NJ: Erlbaum, pp. 215–67.

McLeod, J. M., Guo, Z., Daily, K., Steele, C. A., Huang, H., Horowitz, E. and Chen, H. (1996). 'The Impact of Traditional and Nontraditional Media Forms in the 1992 Presidential Election'. *Journalism & Mass Communication Quarterly*, 73: 401–16.

McQuail, D. (1987). *Mass Communication Theory: An Introduction*. London: Sage.

Mead, G. H. (1962). *Mind, Self and Society*. Chicago: University of Chicago Press.

Meeus, W. and Raaijmakers, Q. (1986). 'Administrative Obedience as a Social Phenomenon'. In W. Doise and S. Moscovici (Eds), *Current Issues in European Social Psychology*. Cambridge: Cambridge University Press, Vol. 2, pp. 183–230.

Mellor, F. (2009). 'Image-Music-Text of Popular Science'. In R. Holliman, J. Thomas, S. Smidt, E. Scanlon and E. Whitelegg (Eds), *Investigating Science Communication in the Information Age: Implications for Public Engagement and Popular Media*. Oxford: Oxford University Press.

Mercer, N. and Fisher, E. (1997a). 'Scaffolding through Talk'. In R. Wegerif and P. Scrimshaw (Eds), *Computers and Talk in the Primary Classroom*. Clevedon: Multilingual Matters, pp. 196–211.

Mercer, N. (2005). 'Sociocultural Discourse Analysis: Analysing Classroom Talk as a Social Mode of Thinking'. *Journal of Applied Linguistics*, 1(2): 137–68.

Merleau-Ponty, M. (1962). *Phenomenology of Perception*. London: Routledge Kegan.

Merton, R. (1968). *Social Theory and Social Structure*. New York: Free Press.

Meteyard, L. and Vigliocco, G. (2008). 'The role of Sensory and Motor Information in Semantic Representation'. In P. Calvo and A. Gomilla (Eds), *Elsevier Handbook of Embodied Cognition*. Amsterdam: Elsevier.

Mette, N. (1994). '(Religions-)Pädagogisches Handeln'. In E. Arens (Ed.), *Gottesrede – Glaubenspraxis: Perspektiven theologischer Handlungstheorie*. Darmstadt: Wissenschaftliche Buchgesellschaft, pp. 164–84.

Metz, J. B. (2005). *Faith in History and Society: Toward a Practical Fundamental Theology*. New York: Herder & Herder.

Meyer, M. (1994). *Rhetoric, Language and Reason*. New York, NY: Pennsylvania State University Press.

Meyer, M. (2004a). *Rhetoric. "Que sais-je?"* Paris: PUF.

Meyer, M. (2004b). *Perelman – Le renouveau de la rhetorique*. Paris: PUF.

Meyer, M. (2008). *Principia Rhetorica – une theorie generale de l'argumentation*. Paris: Fayard.

Meyer M. (2010). The Brussels School of Rhetoric: from the New Rhetoric to Problematology, *Philosophy and Rhetoric*, 43, 4, 403–429.

Miike, Y. (2004). 'Rethinking Humanity, Culture and Communication: Asiacentric Critiques and Contributions'. *Human Communication*, 7: 69–82.

Miller, D. (1995). 'Introducing the "Gay Gene": Media and Scientific Representations'. *Public Understanding of Science*, 4(3): 269–84.

Milgram, S. (1974). *Obedience to Authority*. London: Tavistock.

Miller, G. (2002). *The Mating Mind*. New York: Heineman.

Millikan, R. G. (1993). *White Queen Psychology and Other Essays for Alice*. Cambridge, MA: MIT Press.

Millikan, R. G. (1996). 'Pushmi-Pullyu Representations'. In J. Tomberlin (Ed.), *Philosophical Perspectives* vol. IX. Atascadero, CA: Ridgeview Publishing. Reprinted in L. May and M. Friedman (Eds), *Mind and Morals*. Cambridge, MA: MIT Press.

Millikan, R. G. (2004). 'On Reading Signs: Some Differences between Us and the Others'. In D. Kimbrough Oller and U. Griebel (Eds), *Evolution of Communication Systems: A Comparative Approach*. Cambridge, MA: MIT Press.

Modood, T. (2004). 'Defined by Some Distinctly Hyphenated Britishness'. *Times*, 3 September.

Moll, L. C. and Greenberg, J. B. (1993). 'Creating Zones of Possibilities: Combining Social Contexts for Instruction'. In L. Moll (Ed.), *Vygotsky and Education: Instructional Implications and Applications of Sociohistorical Psychology*. Cambridge: Cambridge University Press, pp. 319–48.

Moloney, G. (2007). 'Social Representations and the Politically Satirical Cartoon: The Construction and Reproduction of the Refugee and Asylum-Seeker Identity'. In G. Moloney and I. Walker (Eds), *Social Representations and Identity: Content, Process and Power*. London: Palgrave Macmillan.

Morgan, M., Shanahan, J. and Signorelli, N. (2009). 'Growing up with Television: Cultivation Processes'. In J. Bryant and M. B. Oliver (Eds), *Media Effects: Advances in Theory and Research* (3rd edn) Hillsdale, NJ: Erlbaum, pp. 17–33.

Morrison, T., Conaway, W. A. and Borden, G. A. (1994). *Kiss, Bow or Shake Hands: How to do Business on 60 Countries*. Holbrook, MA: Adams Media Corporation.

Moscovici, S. (1961/2008). *Psychoanalysis: Its Image and its Public*. Cambridge: Polity Press. (First published as *La psychanalyse, son image et son public*. Paris: Presses universitaires de France.)

Moscovici, S. (1973). 'Foreword'. In C. Herzlich (Ed.), *Health and Illness: A Social Psychological Analysis*. London: Academic Press.

Moscovici, S. (1976). *Social Influence and Social Change*. London: Academic Press.

Moscovici, S. (1984). 'The Phenomenon of Social Representations'. In R. Farr and S. Moscovici (Eds), *Social Representations*. Cambridge: Cambridge University Press, pp. 3–69.

Moscovici, S. (1985a). 'Social Influence and Conformity'. In G. Lindzey and E. Aronson (Eds), *Handbook of Social Psychology* (3rd edn) New York: Random House, Vol. 2 pp. 347–412.

Moscovici, S. (1985b). *The Age of the Crowd*. Cambridge: Cambridge University Press.

Moscovici, S. (1998). 'Social Consciousness and its History'. *Culture and Psychology*, 4(3): 411–29.

Moscovici, S and Duveen, G (2000). *Social Representations: Explorations in Social Psychology*. New York: New York University Press.

Moscovici, S. (2000). *Social Representations: Explorations in Social Psychology*. Cambridge: Polity Press.

Moscovici, S. and Marková, I. (2000). 'Ideas and their Development: A Dialogue between Serge Moscovici and Ivana Marková'. In S. Moscovici (Ed.) *Social Representations*. Cambridge: Polity.

Moscovici, S. (2001). 'Why a Theory of Social Representations?' In K. Deaux and G. Philogene (Eds), *Social Representations: Introductions and Explorations*. Oxford: Blackwell.

Moy, P. and Pfau, M. (2000). *With Malice towards All? The Media and Public Confidence in Democratic Institutions*. Westport, CT: Praeger.

Mugny, G. (1982). *The Power of Minorities*. London: Academic Press.

Murphy, G. L. (2002). *The Big Book of Concepts*. Cambridge, MA: MIT Press.

Mutz, D. C. (2006). *Hearing the Other Side: Deliberative versus Participatory Democracy*. New York: Cambridge University Press.

Nazroo, J. Y. (1997). *The Health of Britain's Ethnic Minorities*. London: Policy Studies Institute.

Nee, V. and Ingram, P. (1998). 'Embeddedness and Beyond: Institutions, Exchange, and Social Structure'. In M. Brinton and V. Nee (Eds), *The New Institutionalism in Sociology*. Stanford, CA: Stanford University Press, pp. 19–45.

Nelkin, D. (1995). *Selling Science*. New York: Freeman.

Newman, F. and Holzman, L. (1993). *Lev Vygotsky: Revolutionary Scientist*. New York: Routledge.

Nieman, A. (2000). *The Popularisation of Physics: Boundaries of Authority and the Visual Culture of Science*. Unpublished PhD Thesis. Bristol: University of the West of England.

Nisbett, R. E. and Norenzayan, A. (2002). 'Culture and Cognition'. In D. Medin and H. Pashler (Eds), *Stevens' Handbook of Experimental Psychology* (3rd edn), Vol. II. New York: John Wiley & Sons.

Nisbet, M. C. and Scheufele, D. A. (2004). 'Political Talk as a Catalyst for Online Citizenship'. *Journalism & Mass Communication Quarterly*, 81 (4): 877–96.

Nisbet, M. C. (2005). 'The Competition for Worldviews: Values, Information, and Public Support for Stem Cell Research'. *International Journal of Public Opinion Research*, 17 (1): 90–112.

Nisbet, M. C. (2009). 'Communicating Climate Change: Why Frames Matter to Public Engagement'. *Environment*, 51 (2): 12–23.

Nisbet, M. C. (2009b). 'Knowledge into Action: Framing the Debates Over Climate Change and Poverty'. In P. D'Angelo and J. Kuypers (Eds), *Doing News Framing Analysis: Empirical, Theoretical, and Normative Perspectives*. New York: Routledge, pp. 46–83.

Norris, P. (2001). *A Digital Divide: Civic Engagement, Information Poverty, and the Internet in Democratic Societies*. New York: Cambridge University Press.

Novinger, T. (2001). *Intercultural Communication*. Austin, TX: University of Texas Press.

Noelle-Neumann, E. (1990). 'The Theory of Public Opinion: The Concept of the Spiral of Silence'. *Communication Yearbook*, 14: 256–87.

Nutbeam, D. and Harris, E. (1998). *Theory in a Nutshell: A Practitioner's Guide to Commonly used Theories and Models in Health Promotion*. Sydney: University of Sydney.

Nye, J. S. (1990). *Bound to Lead: The Changing Nature of American Power*. New York: Basic Books.

Nye, J. S. (2004). *Soft Power: The Means to Success in World Politics*. New York: Public Affairs.

Nystrand, M., Wu, L., Gamoran, A., Zeiser, S. and Long, D. (2003). 'Questions in Time: Investigating the Structure and Dynamics of Unfolding Classroom Discourse'. *Discourse Processes*, 35 (2): 135–98.

Oaksford, M., Morris, F., Grainger, B. and Williams, J. M. G. (1996). 'Mood, Reasoning, and Central Executive Processes'. *Journal of Experimental Psychology: Learning, Memory, and Cognition*, 22 (2): 476–92.

Odling-Smee F. J., Laland, K. N. and Feldman, M. W. (2003). *Niche Construction: The Neglected Process in Evolution*. Monographs in Population Biology. 37. Princeton, NJ: Princeton University Press.

Ogden, J. (2007) *Health Psychology: A Textbook*. Buckingham: Open University Press.

Okun, B. F., Fried, J. and Okun, M. L. (1999). *Understanding Diversity. A Learning as Practice Primer*. Pacific Grove, CA: Brooks/Cole Publishing.

Olson, D. R., Astington, J. W. and Harris, P. (1998). (Eds) *Developing Theories of Mind*. Cambridge: Cambridge University Press.

Orbe, M. (1998). *Constructing Co-Cultural Theory: An Explication of Culture, Power and Communication*. Thousand Oaks, CA: Sage.

Orgad, S. (2006). *Patient Users and Medical Websites*. LSE Research Online. http://eprints.lse.ac.uk/2518, accessed 9 September 2009.

Origgi, G. and Sperber, D. (2000). 'Evolution, Communication and the Proper Function of Language'. In P. Carruthers and A. Chamberlain (Eds), *Evolution and the Human Mind: Language, Modularity and Social Cognition*. Cambridge: Cambridge University Press.

Orwell, G. (1946). 'Politics and the English Language'. *Horizon*, 13 (76), 252–65.

Paicheler, G. (1988). *The Psychology of Social Influence*. Cambridge: Cambridge University Press.

Painter, D. (2008). 'The Voice Devoid of any Accent: Language, Subjectivity and Social Psychology'. *Subjectivity*, 23: 174–87.

Palincsar, A. S. (1986). 'The Role of Dialogue in Providing Scaffolded Instruction'. *Educational Psychologist*, 26: 73–98.

Paltridge, B. (1997). *Genre, Frames and Writing in Research Settings*. Amsterdam: Benjamins.

Parfitt, T. (2004). 'The Ambiguity of Participation: A Qualified Defence of Participatory Development'. *Third World Quarterly*, 25: 537–56.

Parsons, T. (1963). 'On the Concept of Social Influence'. *The Public Opinion Quarterly*, 27: 37–62.

Patterson, M. L. (2001). 'Toward a Comprehensive Model of Non-Verbal Communication'. In W. P. Robinson and H. Giles (Eds), *The New Handbook of Language and Social Psychology*. London: John Wiley & Sons Ltd.

Pavlidou, T. S. (2000). 'Telephone Conversations in Greek and German: Attending to the Relationship Aspects of Communication'. In H. Spencer-Oatley (Ed.), *Culturally Speaking: Managing Rapport through Talk across Cultures*. London: Continuum, pp. 121–40.

Pecher, D., Zeelenberg, R. and Barsalou, L. W. (2003). 'Verifying Properties from Different Modalities for Concepts Produces Switching Costs'. *Psychological Science*, 14: 119–24.

Pendleton, S. C. (1998). 'Rumor Research Revisited and Expanded'. *Language & Communication*, 1 (18): 69–86.

Perelman, C. and Olbrechts, L. (1958/1988). *A Treatise of Argumentation: The New Rhetoric*, 5th edn. Bruxelles: Editions de l'Université de Bruxelles.

Perelman, C. (1989). *Rhetorics*. Bruxelles: Edition de l'Université de Bruxelles.

Perret-Clermont, A-N. (1980) *Social Interaction and Cognitive Development in Children*. European Monographs in Social Psychology. London: Academic Press.

Pestre, D. (2008). 'Challenges for the Democratic Management of Technoscience: Governance, Participation and the Political Today'. *Science as Culture*, 17 (2): 101–19.

Petty, R. E. and Cacioppo, J. T. (1981). *Attitudes and Persuasion: Classic and Contemporary Approaches*. Dubuque, IA: Brown.

Petty, R. E. and Cacioppo, J. T. (1986a). *Communication and Persuasion: Central and Peripheral Routes to Attitude Change*. New York: Springer.

Petty, R. E. and Cacioppo, J. T. (1986b). 'The Elaboration Likelihood Model of Persuasion'. In L. Berkowitz (Ed.), *Advances in Experimental Social Psychology*. New York: Academic Press, pp. 123–205.

Peukert, H. (1984). *Science, Action and Fundamental Theology: Toward a Theology of Communicative Action*. Cambridge, MA: MIT Press.

Pew News Index (2009). Retrieved 12 Oct, 2009 from http://people-press.org/news-interest/.

Pew Research Center. (17 August 2008). *Key News Audiences Now Blend Online and Traditional Sources*. Retrieved 3 June 2009, from http://people-press.org/report/444/news-media.

Philogène, G. (2001). 'From Race to Culture: The Emergence of African American'. In K. Deaux and G. Philogene (Eds), *Social Representations: Introductions and Explorations*. Oxford: Blackwell.

Pinch, T. (2001). 'It's a Conversation!' In J. Labinger and H. M. Collins (Eds), *The One Culture? A Conversation about Science*. Chicago: University of Chicago Press.

Pinker, S. (1997). *How the Mind Works*. New York: Norton.

Pinker, S. (2007). *The Stuff of Thought*. London and New York: Allen Lane.

Plato (1994). *Gorgias*. Oxford: Oxford University Press.

Polanyi, M. (1962) 'The Republic of Science: Its Political and Economic Theory'. *Minerva*, 1: 54–74.

Popkin, S. (1991). *The Reasoning Voter: Communication and Persuasion in Presidential Campaigns*. Chicago: University of Chicago Press.

Porter, R. E. and Samovar, L. A. (Eds) (1988). *Intercultural Communication: A Reader* 5th edn. Belmong: Wadsworth Publishing Company.

Poulakos, J. (1999). 'Toward a Sophistic Definition of Rhetoric'. In J. L. Lucaites, C. M. Condit and S. Caudill (Eds) *Contemporary Rhetorical Theory* (pp. 25–34). New York: Guildford Press.

Povinelli, D. J. and Vonk, J. (2003). 'Chimpanzee Minds: Suspiciously Human?' *Trends in Cognitive Science*, 7: 157–60.

Price, V. and Zaller, J. (1993). 'Who Gets the News? Alternative Measures of News Reception and their Implications for Research'. *Public Opinion Quarterly*, 57: 133–64.

Price, V. and Tewksbury, D. (1997). 'News Values and Public Opinion: A Theoretical Account of Media Priming and Framing'. In G. A. Barett and F. J. Boster (Eds),

Progress in Communication Sciences: Advances in Persuasion. Greenwich, CT: Ablex, Vol. 13, pp. 173–212.

Price, V. and Cappella, J. N. (2002). 'Online Deliberation and its Influence: The Electronic Dialogue Project in Campaign 2000'. *IT and Society*, 1: 303–28.

Price, V., Nir, L. and Capella, J. N. (2005). 'Framing Public Discussion of Gay Civil Unions'. *Public Opinion Quarterly*, 69 (2): 179–212.

Putnam, R. D. (2000). *Bowling Alone: The Collapse and Revival of American Community*. New York: Simon & Schuster.

Queneau, R. (2009). *Exercises in Style* (translation by Barbara Wright, in original 1947). Richmond: London House.

Ramella, M. and De La Cruz, R. B. (2000). 'Taking Part in Adolescent Sexual Health Promotion in Peru: Community Participation from a Social Psychological Perspective'. *Journal of Community and Applied Social Psychology*, 10: 271–84.

Rampton, S. and Stauber, J. (2003). *Weapons of Mass Deception: The Uses of Propaganda in Bush's War on Iraq*. London: Robinson.

Rappaport, J. (1995). 'Empowerment Meets Narrative: Listening to Stories and Creating Settings'. *American Journal of Community Psychology*, 23: 795–807.

Rappaport, R. A. (1999). *Ritual and Religion in the Making of Humanity*. Cambridge: Cambridge University Press.

Richmond, V. P. and McCroskey, J. C. (1998). *Communication: Apprehension, Avoidance and Effectiveness* (5th edn). Scottsdale, AZ: Gorsuch Scarisbrick.

Richmond, V. P., McCroskey, J. C. and Hickson, M. L. (2008). *Nonverbal Behaviour in Interpersonal Relations*. Boston: Allyn and Bacon.

Ricoeur, P. (1978). *The Rule of Metaphor*. London: Routledge.

Ricoeur, P. (2004). *Memory, History, Forgetting*. Chicago, IL: University of Chicago Press.

Roberts, A. (2005). *The History of Science Fiction*. London: Palgrave Macmillan.

Roberts, P. (1996). 'Rethinking Conscientisation'. *Journal of Philosophy of Education*, 30: 179–96.

Robinson, R., Keltner, D., Ward, A. and Ross, L. (1995). 'Actual versus Assumed Differences in Construal: "Naïve realism" in Intergroup Perception and Conflict'. *Journal of Personality and Social Psychology*, 68: 404–17.

Rodriguez, C. (2003). 'The Bishop and His Star: Citizens' Communication in Southern Chile'. In N. Couldry and J. Curran (Eds), *Contesting Media Power: Alternative Media in a Networked World*. London: Rowman and Littlefield.

Rosnow, R. L. (1991). 'Inside Rumor: A Personal Journey'. *American Psychologist*, 46: 484–96.

Rosnow, R. L. (1980). 'Psychology of Rumors Reconsidered'. *Psychological Bulletin*, 87: 578–91.

Rosnow, R. L., Yost, J. H. and Esposito, J. L. (1986). 'Belief in Rumor and Likelihood of Rumor Transmission'. *Language and Communication*, 6: 189–94.

Ross, L. (1990). 'Recognizing the Role of Construal Processes'. In I. Rock (Ed.), *The Legacy of Solomon Asch: Essays in Cognition and Social Psychology*. New Jersey: Lawrence Erlbaum.

Royal Society (1985) *The Public Understanding of Science*. London: Royal Society.

Russell, J. A. (1991). 'Culture and the Categorization of Emotions'. *Psychological Bulletin*, 110: 426–50.

Sagarin, B. J. and Wood, S. E. (2007). 'Resistance to Influence'. In A. R. Pratkanis (Ed.), *The Science of Social Influence*. New York: Psychology Press, pp. 321–40.

Sandbothe, M. (2001). *Pragmatische Medienphilosophie: Grundlegung einer neuen Disziplin im Zeitalter des Internet*. Weilerswist: Velbrück Wissenschaft.

De Saussure, F. (1959). *Course in General Linguistics*. New York: McGraw Hill.

Schachter, S. and Burdick, H. (1955). 'A Field Experiment on Rumor Transmission'. *Journal of Abnormal and Social Psychology*, 50: 363–71.

Scheufele, D. A. (1999). 'Framing as a Theory of Media Effects'. *Journal of Communication*, 29: 103–23.

Scheufele, D. A. (2000). 'Talk or Conversation? Dimensions of Interpersonal Discussion and their Implications for Participatory Democracy'. *Journalism & Mass Communication Quarterly*, 77: 727–43.

Scheufele, D. A., Nisbet, M. C. and Brossard, D. (2003). 'Pathways to Participation? Religion, Communication Contexts, and Mass Media'. *International Journal of Public Opinion Research*, 15 (3): 300–24.

Scheufele, D. A. and Tewksbury, D. (2007). ,Framing, Agenda Setting, and Priming: The Evolution of Three Media Effects Models'. *Journal of Communication*, 57 (1): 9–20.

Schiele, B. (2008). 'Science Museums and Science Centres'. In B. Trench and M. Bucchi (Eds), *Handbook of Public Communication of Science and Technology*. New York: Routledge, pp. 27–40.

Schmidt Kjaergaard, R. (2009). 'Electric Adventures and Natural Wonders: Exhibitions, Museums and Gardens in Nineteenth-Century Denmark'. In F. Papanelopoulou, A. Nieto-Galan and E. Perdriguero (Eds), *Popularizing Science and Technology in the European Periphery 1800–2000*. London: Ashgate.

Schmitt, K. M., Gunther, A. C. and Liebhart, J. L. (2004). 'Why Partisans See Mass Media as Biased'. *Communication Research*, 31: 623–41.

Schopenhauer, A. (2009/1830). *The Art of Always being Right*. London: Gibson Square.

Schugurensky, D. (2002). 'Transformative Learning and Transformative Politics: The Pedagogical Dimension of Participatory Democracy and Social Action'. In E. O'Sullivan, A. Morrell and M. O'Connor (Eds), *Expanding the Boundaries of Transformative Learning: Essays on Theory and Praxis*. New York: Palgrave Macmillan.

Schurr, P. H. (1986). *Four Script Studies: What we have Learnt. Advances in Consumer Research: 498–503*. Sixteenth Annual Conference: Association for Consumer Research.

Schutz, A. (1970). *On Phenomenology and Social Relations*. In H. R. Wagner (Ed.) Chicago: The University of Chicago Press.

Searle, J. R. (1969). *Speech Acts: An Essay on the Philosophy of Language*. New York: Cambridge University Press.

Searle, J. R. (1979). 'A Taxonomy of Illocutionary Acts'. In J. R. Searle (Ed.), *Expression and Meaning*. Cambridge: Cambridge University Press.

Searle, J. R. (1979) *Expression and Meaning: Studies in the Theory of Speech Acts*. Cambridge: Cambridge University Press.

Searle, J. R. (1990). 'Collective Intentions and Actions'. In P. R. Cohen, J. Morgan, and M. E. Pollack (Eds), *Intentions in Communication*. Cambridge, MA: MIT Press.

Searle, J. R. (1996). *The Construction of Social Reality*. London: Penguin.

Searle, J. R. (2001). *Rationality in Action*. Cambridge, MA: MIT Press.

Sedikides, C. and Brewer, M. B. (Eds) (2003). *Individual Self, Relational Self, Collective Self*. Hove: Psychology Press.

Semic, B. (1999). 'Vocal Attractiveness: What Sounds Beautiful is Good'. In L. K. Guerrero, J. A. DeVito, and M. L. Hecht (Eds), *The Nonverbal Communication*

Reader: Classic and Contemporary Readings. Prospect Heights, IL: Waveland Press. pp. 149–55.

Sewell, T. (1997). *Black Masculinities and Schooling: How Black Boys Survive Modern Schooling*. Stoke on Trent: Trentham Books Ltd.

Shack, W. A and Skinner, E. P. (Eds) (1979). *Strangers in African Societies*. Los Angeles: University of California Press.

Shah, D., Kwak, N. and Holbert, L. R. (2001). '"Connecting" and "Disconnecting" With Civic Life: Patterns of Internet Use and the Production of Social Capital'. *Political Communication*, 18 (2): 41–162.

Shah, D. V., McLeod, J. M. and Yoon, S. (2001). 'Communication, Context, and Community: An Exploration of Print, Broadcast, and Internet Influences'. *Communication Research*, 28: 464–506.

Sherif, M. (1935). 'A Study of Some Social Factors in Perception'. *Archives of Psychology*, 27: 1–60.

Shibutani, T. (1966). *Improvised News*. Indianapolis, IN: Bobbs Merrill.

Shinn, T. and Whitley, R. (1985). *Expository Science: Forms and Functions of Popularisation*. Dordrecht: Reidel.

Shore, B. (1996). *Culture in Mind: Cognition, Culture and the Problem of Meaning*. New York and Oxford: Oxford University Press.

Shortland, M. and Gregory, J. (1991). *Communicating Science: A Handbook*. London: Longman.

Shotter, J. and Gergen, K. (Eds) (1992). *Texts of Identity*. London: Sage Publications.

Shuter, R. (1976). 'Proxemics and Tactility in Latin America'. *Journal of Communication*, 26: 46–52.

Shweder, R. A. (2003). *Why do Men Barbecue? Recipes for Cultural Psychology*. Cambridge: Harvard University Press.

Shweder, R. A and Haidt, J. (2003). 'Cultural Psychology of Emotions: Ancient and New'. In R. A. Shweder (Ed), *Why do Men Barbecue? Recipes for Cultural Psychology*. Cambridge: Harvard University Press, pp. 134–67.

Simmel, G. (1950). 'The Stranger'. In K. Wolff (Ed. and trans.), *The Sociology of George Simmel*. New York: Free Press.

Singhal, A. and Rogers, E. (2002). 'A Theoretical Agenda for Education-Edutainment'. *Communication Theory*, 12 (2): 117–35.

Skeggs, B. (1997). *Formations of Class and Gender: Becoming Respectable*. London: Sage.

Sloane, T. O. (Ed.) (2001). *Encyclopaedia of Rhetoric*. Oxford: Oxford University Press.

Smart, N. (1996). *Dimensions of the Sacred: An Anatomy of the World's Beliefs*. Berkeley, CA: University of California Press.

Smith, P. B. and Bond, M. H. (1994). *Social Psychology across Cultures: Analysis and Perspectives*. Massachusetts: Allyn and Bacon. (2nd edn 1998, Prentice Hall).

Smith, P. K. (1988). 'The Cognitive Demands of Children's Social Interaction with Peers'. In R. Byrne and A. Whiten (Eds), *Machiavellian Intelligence: Social Expertise and the Evolution of Intellect in Monkeys, Apes, and Humans*. Oxford: Clarendon Press.

Spears, R. and Leach, C. W. (2004). 'Intergroup Schadenfreude: Conditions and Consequences'. In L. Z. Tiedens and C. W. Leach (Eds), *The Social Life of Emotions*. Cambridge: Cambridge University Press, pp. 336–55.

Sperber, D. (1990). 'The Epidemiology of Beliefs'. In C. Fraser and G. Gaskell (Eds), *The Social Psychology of Widespread Beliefs*. Oxford: Clarendon Press, pp. 25–44.

Sperber, D. (1994). 'The Modularity of Thought and the Epidemiology of Representations'. In L. A. Hirschfeld and S. A. Gelman (Eds), *Mapping the*

Mind: Domain Specificity in Cognition and Culture. New York: Cambridge University Press, pp. 39–67.

Sperber, D. and Wilson, D. (1995). *Relevance: Communication and Cognition.* 2nd Edn. Oxford: Blackwell.

Sperber, D., Premack, D. and Premack, A. (Eds) (1995). *Causal Cognition.* Oxford: Oxford University Press.

Sperber, D. (1996). *Explaining Culture: A Naturalistic Approach.* Oxford: Blackwell.

Sperber, D. and Wilson, D. (1996). 'Fodor's Frame Problem and Relevance Theory'. *Behavioral and Brain Sciences,* 19 (3): 530–2.

Sperber, D. (2000). 'Metarepresentations in an Evolutionary Perspective'. In D. Sperber (Ed.), *Metarepresentations: A Multidisciplinary Perspective.* New York: Oxford University Press.

Sperber, D. and Wilson, D. (2002). 'Pragmatics, Modularity and Mind-Reading'. *Mind and Language,* 17: 3–23.

Sperber, D. and Hirschfeld, L. A (2004). 'The Cognitive Foundations of Cultural Stability and Diversity'. *Trends in Cognitive Sciences,* 8: 40–6.

Spitz, R. A. (1945). 'Hospitalism: An Inquiry into the Genesis of Psychiatric Conditions in Early Childhood', *Psychoanalytic Study of the Child,* 1: 68.

Stamm, K., Emig, A. and Hesse, M. (1997). ,The Contribution of Local Media to Community Involvement'. *Journalism and Mass Communication Quarterly,* 76 (1): 97–107.

Stanley, M. (1972). 'Literacy: The Crisis of a Conventional Wisdom'. *The School Review,* 80: 373–408.

Stephens, C. (2008). *Health Promotion: A Psycho-Social Approach.* Milton Keynes: Open University Press.

Stern, D. (1985). *The Interpersonal World of the Infant: A View from Psychoanalysis and Developmental Psychology.* New York: Basic Books.

Stern, L. W. (1902). 'Zur Psychologie der Aussage: Experimentelle Untersuchungen über Erinnerungstreue'. *Zeitschrift für die gesamte Strafechtswissenschaft.* Vol. XXII, cahier 2/3.

Stilgoe, J. (2007). *Nanodialogues: Experiments in Public Engagement with Science.* London: Demos.

Stocking, S. H. (1998). 'On Drawing Attention to Ignorance'. *Science Communication,* 20: 165–78.

Struck, F and Mussweiler, T. (2001). 'Resisting Influence'. In J. P. Forgas and K. D. Williams (Eds), *Social Influence: Direct and Indirect Processes.* Philadelphia, PA: Psychology Press.

Sunstein, C. (2001). *Republic.com.* Princeton, NJ: Princeton University Press.

Swales, J. M. (1990). *Genre Analysis: English in Academic and Research Settings.* Cambridge: Cambridge University Press.

Taillard, M.-O. (2000). 'Persuasive Communication: The Case of Marketing'. *UCL Working Papers in Linguistics,* 12: 145–72.

Tajfel, H. (1978). 'Social Categorization, Social Identity and Social Comparison'. In H. Tajfel (Ed.), *Differentiation between Social Groups.* London: Academic Press, pp. 61–76.

Tam, C. (2006). 'Harmony Hurts: Participation and Silent Conflict at an Indonesian Fish Pond'. *Environmental Management,* 38: 1–15.

Tanaka, K. (1994). *Advertising Language: A Pragmatic Approach to Advertisements in Britain and Japan.* London: Routledge.

Tarde, G. (1962). *The Laws of Imitation* (trans. from the 2nd French edn by E. C. Parsons). Gloucester, MA: Peter Smith.

Tarde, G. (2006) *L'opinion et la foule*. Paris: Edition du Sandre.

Taylor, C. (2007). *A Secular Age*. Cambridge, MA: Belknap Press.

Taylor, S. A., Cronn, J. J. jr. and Hansen, R. S. (1991). 'Schema and Script Theory in Channels Research: Marketing Theory and Applications'. *American Marketing Association Winter's Conference*, 2: 15–24.

Teitelbaum, S. and Geiselman, R. E. (1997). 'Observer Mood and Cross-Racial Recognition of Faces'. *Journal of Cross-Cultural Psychology*, 28: 93–106.

Tharp, R. G. and Gallimore, R. (1988). *Rousing Minds to Life: Schooling in Social Context*. New York: Cambridge University Press.

Theissen, G. and Merz, A. (1998). *The Historical Jesus*. London: SCM Press.

Thorpe, C. and Gregory, J. (2010). 'Producing the Post-Fordist Public: The Political Economy of Public Engagement with Science'. *Science as Culture*, Volume 19, Issue 3: 273–301.

Tichenor, P. J., Donohue, G. A. and Olien, C. N. (1970). 'Mass Media Flow and Differential Growth in Knowledge'. *Public Opinion Quarterly*, 34: 159–70.

Tomasello, M., Kruger, A. C. and Ratner, H. H. (1993). 'Cultural Learning'. *Behavioral and Brain Sciences*, 16: 495–552.

Tomasello, M. (1999). *The Cultural Origins of Human Cognition*. Cambridge, MA: MIT Press.

Tomasello, M. (2003). *Constructing a Language: A Usage-Based Theory of Language Acquisition*. Cambridge, MA: Harvard University Press.

Tomasello, M. and Racoczy, H. (2003). 'What Makes Human Cognition Unique? From Individual to Shared to Collective Intentionality'. *Mind and Language*, 23: 157–75.

Tomasello, M., Call, J. and Hare, B. (2003). 'Chimpanzees Understand Psychological States: The Question is which Ones and to what Extent'. *Trends in Cognitive Science*, 7: 153–6.

Tomasello, M., Carpenter, M., Call, J., Behne, T. and Moll, H. (2005). 'Understanding and Sharing Intentions: The Origins of Cultural Cognition'. *Behavioural and Brain Sciences*, 28 (5): 675–735.

Tomasello. M. (2008) *Origins of Human Communication*. Cambridge, MA, London: MIT Press.

Tooby, J., and Cosmides, L. (1992). 'The Psychological Foundations of Culture'. In J. H. Barkow, J. Tooby and L. Cosmides (Eds), *The Adapted Mind: Evolutionary Psychology and the Generation of Culture*. New York: Oxford University Press.

Tooby, J., Cosmides, L. and Barrett, H. C. (2005). 'Resolving the Debate on Innate Ideas: Learnability Constraints and the Evolved Interpenetration of Motivational and Conceptual Functions'. In P. Carruthers, S. Laurence and S. Stich (Eds), *The Innate Mind: Structure and Content*. New York: Oxford University Press.

Toulmin, S. (1958). *The Uses of Argumentation*. Cambridge: Cambridge University Press.

Tracy, K. (2002). *Everyday Talk: Building and Reflecting Identities*. New York: The Guildford Press.

Trench, B. (2009). 'Science Reporting in the Electronic Embrace of the Internet'. In R. Holliman, J. Thomas, S. Smidt, E. Scanlon and E. Whitelegg (Eds), *Investigating Science Communication in the Information Age: Implications for Public Engagement and Popular Media*. Oxford: Oxford University Press.

Trevarthen, C. (1979). 'Instincts for Human Understanding and for Cultural Cooperation: Their Development in Infancy'. In M. von Cranach, K. Foppa, W. Lepenies, and D. Ploog (Eds), *Human Ethology: Claims and Limits of a New Discipline*. Cambridge: Cambridge University Press, pp. 530–71.

Trivers, R. (2000). 'The Elements of a Scientific Theory of Self-Deception'. *Annals of the New York Academy of Sciences*, 907: 114–31.

Tsfati, Y. and Cohen, J. (2005). 'Democratic Consequences of Hostile Media Perceptions: The Case of Gaza Settlers'. *Press/Politics*, 11: 28–51.

Tuckman, B. W. (1965). 'Developmental Sequences in Small Groups'. *Psychological Bulletin*, 63: 384–99.

Tuomela, R. (2003). 'The We-Mode and the I-Mode'. In F. Schmitt (Ed.), *Socializing Metaphysics*. New York: Rowman & Littlefield.

Turner, V. (1969). *The Ritual Process: Structure and Anti-Structure*. Chicago, IL: Aldine Publishing Co.

Turner, V. (Ed.) (1982). *Celebration: Studies in Festivity and Ritual*. Washington, DC: Smithsonian Books.

Turney, J. (2007). 'The Latest Boom in Popular Science Books'. In M. W. Bauer and M. Bucchi (Eds), *Journalism, Science and Society – Science Communication between News and Public Relations*. London: Routledge.

Twenge, J. M. (2009). 'Change Over Time in Obedience: The Jury's Still Out, but it Might be Decreasing'. *American Psychologist*, 64: 28–31.

Unger, C. (2006). *Genre, Relevance and Global Coherence*. Basingstoke: Palgrave Macmillan.

Upal, M. A., Gonce, L., Tweney, R. and Slone, D. J. (2007). 'Contextualizing Counterintuitiveness: How Context Affects Comprehension and Memorability of Counterintuitive Concepts'. *Cognitive Science*, 31 (3): 415–39.

Usdin, S., Singhal, A. and Shongwe, T. (2002). *No Short-Cuts in Entertainment-Education: Designing Soul City Step-by-Step*. www.soulcity.org.za, accessed 10 December 2008.

Uslaner, E. C. (2000). 'Producing and Consuming Trust'. *Political Science Quarterly*, 115: 569–90.

Valente, T. W. and Rogers, E. M. (1995). 'The Origins and Development of the Diffusion of Innovation Paradigm as an Example of Scientific Growth'. *Science Communication*, 16 (3): 242–73.

Vallone, R. P., Ross, L. and Lepper, M. R. (1985). 'The Hostile Media Phenomenon: Biased Perception and Perceptions of Media Bias in Coverage of the Beirut Massacre'. *Journal of Personality and Social Psychology*, 40: 577–85.

Vigliocco, G., Vinson, D. P., Woolfe, T., Dye, M. W. and Woll, B. (2005). 'Words, Signs and Imagery: When the Language Makes the Difference'. *Proceedings of the Royal Society B*, 272: 1859–63.

Vygotsky, L. S. (1978). *Mind in Society: The Development of Higher Psychological Processes*. Cambridge, MA: Harvard University Press.

Vygotsky, L. S. (1986). *Thought and Language*. Cambridge, MA: MIT Press.

Vygotsky, L. S.(1987). 'The Collected Works of L. S. Vygotsky, Vol. 1: Problems of General Psychology'. In R. W. Rieber and A. S. Carton (Eds), (N. Minick, Trans). New York: Plenum Press.

Vygotsky, L. S. (1994). 'Tool and Symbol in Child Development'. In R. Van der Veer and J. Valsiner (Eds), *The Vygotsky Reader*. Oxford, UK; Cambridge, US: Blackwell.

Wagner, W. and Kronberger, N. (2001). 'Killer Tomatoes! Collective Symbolic Coping with Biotechnology'. In K. Deaux and G. Philogene (Eds), *Social Representations: Introductions and Explorations*. Oxford: Blackwell.

Wagner, C. S. (2009). *The New Invisible College: Science for Development*. Washington DC: Brookings Institution Press.

Wallack, L. (2003). 'Role of Mass Media in Creating Social Capital'. In R. Hofrichter (Ed.), *Health and Social Justice*. San Francisco: Jossey-Bass.

Wallack, L. (1994). 'Media Advocacy: A Strategy for Empowering People and Communities'. *Journal of Public Health Policy*, 15 (4): 420–36.

Wallerstein, N. and Sanchez-Merki, V. (1994). 'Freirian Praxis in Health Education: Research Results from an Adolescent Prevention Program'. *Health Education Research*, 9: 105–18.

Walzer, M. (1990). *Interpretation and Social Criticism*. Cambridge, MA: Harvard University Press.

Wang, C. and Burris, M. A. (1997). 'Photovoice: Concept, Methodology, and Use for Participatory Needs Assessment'. *Health Education and Behavior*, 24: 369–87.

Watts, M. D., Domke, D., Shah, D. V. and Fan, D. P. (1999). 'Elite Cues and Media Bias in Presidential Campaigns: Explaining Public Perceptions of a Liberal Press'. *Communication Research*, 26: 144–75.

Weathers, M. D., Frank, E. M. and Spell, L. A. (2002). 'Differences in the Communication of Affect: Members of the Same Race Versus Members of a Different Race'. *Journal of Black Psychology*, 28 (1): 66–77.

Weaver, W. and Shannon, C. E. (1963). *The Mathematical Theory of Communication*. Illinois: University of Illinois Press.

Weiler, K. (1994). 'Freire and a Feminist Pedagogy of Difference'. In P. Mclaren and C. Lankshear (Eds), *Politics of Liberation*. New York: Routledge.

Weldon, E. and Weingart, L. (1993). 'Group Goals and Group Performance'. *British Journal of Social Psychology*, 32: 307–34.

Wellman, H. M., Cross, D. and Watson, J. (2001). 'Meta-Analysis of Theory of Mind Development: The Truth about False Belief'. *Child Development*, 72: 655–84.

Wells, G. (1999). *Dialogic Inquiry: Towards a Socio-Cultural Practice and Theory of Education*. Cambridge: Cambridge University Press.

Wells, G. L. and Petty, R. E. (1980). 'The Effects of Head Movement on Persuasion: Compatibility and Incompatibility of Responses'. *Basic and Applied Social Psychology*, 1: 219–30.

Wert, S. R. and Salovey, P. (2004). 'A Social Comparison Account of Gossip'. *Review of General Psychology*, 8: 122–37.

Wertsch, J. V. (1991). *Voices of the Mind: A Socio-Cultural Approach to Mediated Action*. Cambridge, MA: Harvard University Press.

Wertsch, J. V. (1998). *Mind as Action*. New York: Oxford University Press.

Westhues, A., Ochocka, J., Jacobson, N., Simich, L., Maiter, S., Janzen, R. and Fleras, A. (2008). 'Developing Theory from Complexity: Reflections on a Collaborative Mixed Method Participatory Action Research Study'. *Qualitative Health Research*, 18: 701–17.

Wheeler, M. and Clark, A. (2008). 'Culture, Embodiment and Genes: Unravelling the Triple Helix'. *Philosophical Transactions of the Royal Society B: Biological Sciences*, 363 (1509): 3563–75.

Whitehouse, H. (2000). *Arguments and Icons*. Oxford: Oxford University Press.

Whitehouse, H. (2002). 'Modes of Religiosity: Towards a Cognitive Explanation of the Sociopolitical Dynamics of Religion'. *Method and Theory in the Study of Religion*, 14: 293–315.

Whitney, J. C. and John, G. (1983). *An Empirical Investigation of the Serial Nature of Scripts: Advances in Consumer Research: 75–79*. Twelfth Annual Conference: Association for Consumer Research.

WHO. (2008). *Closing the Gap in a Generation: Health Equity through Action on the Social Determinants of Health*. Commission on Social Determinants of Health.

Wilsdon, J. and Willis, R. (2004). *See-Through Science: Why Public Engagement Needs to Move Upstream*. London: Demos.

Wilson, D. and Sperber, D. (1981). 'On Grice's Theory of Conversation'. In P. Werth (Ed.), *Conversation and Discourse*. London: Croom Helm, pp. 155–78.

Wilson, M. (2002). 'Six Views of Embodied Cognition'. *Psychological Bulletin and Review*, 9 (4), 625–36.

Winnicott, D. (1988). *Human Nature*. London: Free Association Books.

Winnicott, D. (1965). *The Maturational Process and the Facilitating Environment*. London: The Hogarth Press.

Winograd, T. and Flores, F. (1986). *Understanding Computers and Cognition: A New Foundation for Design*. Norwood: Ablex.

Wittgenstein, L. (1953). *Philosophical Investigations*. Oxford: Basil Blackwell.

Wittgenstein, L. (1969). *On Certainty*. Oxford: Basil Blackwell.

Woock, R. (1972). 'Paulo Freire'. *American Educational Studies Association Conference*. Chicago.

Wood, D., Bruner, J. S., and Ross, G. (1976). 'The Role of Tutoring in Problem Solving'. *Journal of Child Psychology and Psychiatry*, 17, 89–100.

Wu, S. and Keysar, B. (2007). 'Cultural Effects on Perspective Taking'. *Psychological Science*, 18: 600–6.

Wynne, B. (1992). 'Public Understanding of Science Research: New Horizons or Hall of Mirrors?' *Public Understanding of Science*, 1: 37–43.

Wynne, B. (1996). 'Misunderstood Misunderstandings: Social Identities and Public Uptake of Science'. In A. Irwin and B. Wynne (Eds), *Misunderstanding Science? The Public Reconstruction of Science and Technology*. Cambridge: Cambridge University Press, pp. 19–46.

Yankelovich, D. (1991). *Coming to Public Judgment: Making Democracy Work in a Complex World*. Syracuse, NY: Syracuse University Press.

Yates, F. (1966). *The Art of Memory*. London: Pimlico Press.

Zahavi, A. and Zahavi, A. (1997). *The Handicap Principle*. Oxford: Oxford University Press.

Zerubavel, E. (1997). *Social Mindscape: An Invitation to Cognitive Sociology*. Cambridge, MA: Harvard University Press.

Zhong, C. B. and Leonardelli, G. (2008). 'Cold and Lonely – does Social Exclusion Literally Feel Cold?' *Psychological Science* 19: 838–42.

Ziman, J. (1984). *An Introduction to Science Studies: The Philosophical and Social Aspects of Science and Technology*. Cambridge: Cambridge University Press.

Ziman, J. (2002) *Real Science: What it Is, and What it Means*. Cambridge: Cambridge University Press.

Index